Macintosh® Revealed

Volume Four: Expanding the Toolbox

RELATED TITLES

Macintosh® Revealed Volume 1: Unlocking the Toolbox,
Second Edition
Stephen Chernicoff

Macintosh® Revealed Volume 2: Programming with the Toolbox,
Second Edition
Stephen Chernicoff

Macintosh® Revealed Volume 3: Mastering the Toolbox
Stephen Chernicoff

The Macintosh® Advisor (Updated for MultiFinder™)
Cynthia Harriman and Bencion Calica

How to Write Macintosh® Software, Second Edition
Scott Knaster

Macintosh® Hard Disk Management, Second Edition
Charles Rubin and Bencion Calica

Object-Oriented Programming for the Macintosh®, Second Edition
Kurt J. Schmucker and Carl Nelson
(forthcoming)

HyperTalk® Programming (Version 1.2), Revised Edition
Dan Shafer

Understanding HyperTalk™
Dan Shafer

Using ORACLE® with HyperCard®
Dan Shafer

Personal Publishing with the Macintosh®
(Featuring PageMaker® Version 2.0), Second Edition
Terry M. Ulick

The Waite Group's HyperTalk® Bible
The Waite Group

The Waite Group's Tricks of the HyperTalk® Masters
The Waite Group

*For the retailer nearest you, or to order directly from the publisher, call
800-257-5755. International orders telephone 609-461-6500.*

Macintosh® Revealed

Volume Four: Expanding the Toolbox

Stephen Chernicoff

HAYDEN BOOKS

A Division of Howard W. Sams & Company
11711 North College, Suite 141, Carmel, IN 46032 USA

For

Helen,

who is always there.

International Standard Book Number: 0-672-48413-7
Library of Congress Catalog Card Number: 85-8611

Acquisitions Editor: *Greg Michael*
Development Editor: *C. Herbert Feltner*
Editor: *Albright Communications, Inc.*
Cover Design: *Celeste Design*
Indexer: *Sharon Hilgenberg*
Production Coordinator: *Becky Imel*
Production: *William Hartman, Marj Hopper, Jodi Jensen, David Kline,*
 Lori Lyons, Jennifer Matthews, Dennis Sheehan,
 Bruce D. Steed, Nora Westlake
Composition: *Hartman Publishing*

Printed in the United States of America

Trademark Acknowledgments

All terms mentioned in this book that are known to be trademarks or service marks are listed below. In addition, terms suspected of being trademarks or service marks have been appropriately capitalized. Howard W. Sams & Company cannot attest to the accuracy of this information. Use of a term in this book should not be regarded as affecting the validity of any trademark or service mark.

Apple, the Apple logo, Macintosh, ImageWriter, LaserWriter, AppleTalk, A/UX, and Lisa are registered trademarks of Apple Computer Inc.

Crayola is a registered trademark of Binney & Smith, Inc., and is used with permission.

Finder, MultiFinder, Switcher, Apple Desktop Bus, HyperTalk, HyperCard, APDA, and MPW are trademarks of Apple Computer Inc.

MacPaint is a registered trademark of Claris Corp.

Motorola, MC68000, MC68010, MC68020, MC68030, MC68881, MC68882, and MC68851 are trademarks of Motorola, Inc.

NuBus is a trademark of Texas Instruments.

PostScript is a trademark of Adobe Systems, Inc.

Sony is a trademark of Sony Corporation.

UNIX is a registered trademark of AT&T Information Systems.

SY6522 is a trademark of Synertek, Inc.

Z8530 is a trademark of Zilog, Inc.

Contents

v

Preface

Pity the poor technical writer. Trying to keep up with a beast as nimble as the Macintosh is an exercise in futility. Not only does the target never stop moving, but even if you manage to score a direct hit, it just springs to its feet and keeps right on running. You can't keep a good computer down.

So it's been with *Macintosh Revealed.* No sooner were the original two volumes written than I was already thinking about a third, tentatively titled "Everything I Wanted to Put in Volumes One and Two If I'd Only Had the Time and Space." But before I could get around to writing that third book, Apple introduced the Macintosh Plus, with its expanded version of the Toolbox ROM, and it was time for a revised edition of the first two volumes. By the time Volume Three was done, along came the Macintosh II and it was back to the keyboard one more time. The result is the book you're now holding, the latest installment in what has become the longest-running saga since *The Ring of the Nibelung.*

Even as I was writing, of course, the Macintosh has continued to evolve. By the time you read these words, this book will already have begun to go out of date—the moving target just refuses to lie still. Also, predictably, there are again topics I had to leave out that I wish I could have included: hierarchical and popup menus,

Control Panel devices (CDEVs), the new sound facilities, and more. There's probably enough material left over to add yet another volume to this epic series, but the line has to be drawn somewhere. Even Richard Wagner had the sense to wrap up the *Ring* after four interminable operas. Besides, there comes a time to move on to other things. I already have a new project in mind. I'm thinking of calling it *The Decline and Fall of the Roman Empire.*

Acknowledgments

As always, it takes more to make a book than one person sitting at a keyboard. These people helped me make this one:

My wife and companion, **Helen,** after years of unfaltering dedication, has finally received a dedication of her own. I only regret that it cannot adequately express my love and appreciation. My children, **Ann** and **David,** are an unending source of astonishment and wonder.

Scott Knaster of Apple Computer and **Brian Hamlin** of Farallon Computing helped with technical information.

Nancy Albright of Albright Communications did her usual superlative job of editing the manuscript.

Scott Arant, Herb Feltner, Wendy Ford, and their colleagues at Howard W. Sams & Company helped pull it all together and make a book out of it.

Bill Gladstone of Waterside Productions looked after the numbers so I could concentrate on the words.

Mac by Popular Demand

The Macintosh has come a long way since its introduction in 1984. As revolutionary as the original Mac was, with its high-resolution bit-mapped display, mouse pointing device, overlapping windows, pulldown menus, and iconic user interface, it suffered significant shortcomings as well. Its meager 128K memory, 9-inch monochrome screen, and 400K, single-sided disk drive seriously limited its usefulness for practical computing tasks; its closed architecture made it difficult to add specialized options and peripheral devices; its lack of a color display compared unfavorably, not only with the competition, but even with Apple's own lower-end product line, the Apple II; and its ability to execute only one application program at a time represented a step backward from the multitasking features of its predecessor, the Lisa. Almost from the day the first Macintosh appeared, speculation began about coming models with more power and enhanced capabilities.

The first improvement was the "Fat Mac," which expanded the machine's memory capacity from the original 128K to 512K. Next came the Macintosh Plus, boasting a full megabyte of memory, a double-sided 800K disk drive, and a high-speed SCSI (Small Computer Standard Interface) parallel port. At about the same time, hard disks of 20 megabytes and more began appearing, first from independent manufacturers and then from Apple itself. Among the new features in the Mac Plus's expanded 128K Toolbox ROM (up from 64K in the original models) was a Hierarchical File System to put the new disk capacity to efficient use.

Another significant advance was the advent of software concurrency—first through the ingenious Switcher program, developed by independent programmer Andy Hertzfeld, and later through Apple's own official version, MultiFinder. These new operating environments allowed the user to keep two or more programs active in memory at once, moving quickly and easily from one to another as the occasion demanded. They thus offered a reasonable approximation to the convenience of full multitasking that pioneering users had enjoyed in the bygone Lisa days. The pieces were finally coming together and the Macintosh was well on its way.

But the real breakthrough came with the introduction of the Macintosh II, the most powerful model yet in the continuing evolution of the Macintosh family. Here at last was the Macintosh we'd all been waiting for, packed with goodies galore: memory configurations up to 8 megabytes, a new high-density disk technology capable of storing 1.44 megabytes on a 3.5-inch floppy, hard disk options as large as 160 megabytes, screen sizes ranging up to 19 inches and nearly a million pixels, a 68020 processor effectively five times faster than the original 68000, a floating-point coprocessor and optional paged memory management unit. As if all this weren't enough, the new model also offered two features that users had been clamoring for from the start: an open architecture, with six expansion slots based on the NuBus interface standard developed by Texas Instruments, and best of all, a full-color display capability with built-in software support. It was truly a Mac by popular demand.

For those with more modest needs (and budgets!), Apple simultaneously announced a new midrange model, the Macintosh SE, with many of the same features as the II (minus the color display, unfortunately) packed in a case the size of the original Mac. Over time, the Mac II and SE lines have been upgraded to even faster 68030-based versions (the IIx and SE/30) and supplemented with newer variants (the IIcx, with only three expansion slots instead of six, and, most recently, the IIci and Macintosh Portable). Any future developments Apple may have in store can be expected to continue building on these same established designs.

Through it all, great care has been taken to keep each new version of the system compatible with what has gone before. New features have been designed to add power and capabilities without disturbing the operation of existing software. For the programmer, this means that correctly functioning programs (provided they obey all of Apple's guidelines and recommendations) needn't be constantly revised and updated just to keep working the way they always have. Our own MiniEdit program, first developed in Volume Two of this series, is a case in point. Originally written for the earliest of all Macintosh models, the 128K "Skinny Mac," it has survived without modification through the transition from the original Macintosh File System to the Hierarchical File System, from Finder to Switcher to MultiFinder, from Skinny Mac to Fat Mac to Mac Plus, and now feels comfortably at home on a 5-megabyte Macintosh IIx with a 19-inch two-page display.

Nevertheless, if you want to take full advantage of all the fancy new features, you'll naturally have some extra learning to do. That's where this book comes in. Building on what we already know about the Macintosh Toolbox from earlier volumes of this series, we'll learn how the most important of the new features fit in and how you can incorporate them into your own programs. (If you haven't already read the first three volumes, put this one down right now and don't pick it up again until you have. You have to learn to crawl before you can roller skate!) Here's a quick preview of what you'll find in the pages to come:

- Chapter 2, "Old Genies in New Bottles," presents some general utilities that have been added to recent versions of the Toolbox.

- Chapter 3, "Going for the Juggler," shows how to structure your programs to operate most efficiently in the new Multi-Finder environment.

- Chapter 4, "Chasing Rainbows," introduces the basic concepts and principles on which the Toolbox color facilities are built.

- Chapter 5, "Showing Your Colors," tells how to use the new facilities to draw things in color.

- Chapter 6, "Through Rose-Colored Windows," discusses the use of color in the Macintosh user interface itself.

- Chapter 7, "Editing with Style," describes the latest version of the TextEdit editing routines, which allows you to mix typefaces, sizes, and styles within a single passage of text.

Since you're already assumed to be familiar with the earlier volumes of the series, you should find the overall format and style old hat by now. You don't need to be told about the text and reference halves of each chapter, about bracketed section references, "by-the-way" boxes, hexadecimal numbering conventions, and the `computer-voice` typeface. So instead of wasting time explaining them all again, we can just get down to business. Proceed to the next page and let's let the genie out of the bottle.

CHAPTER

2

Old Genies in New Bottles

One of the most remarkable things about the Macintosh Toolbox, as it has evolved over time, is how little it has changed in its basic design and operation. New features and capabilities have been carefully designed to build on the existing system structures established in previous models. For us, this means that everything we've already learned in earlier volumes of this series is still true. The Toolbox genie may have grown in maturity and acquired some dazzling new magical powers, but he's still recognizably the same faithful servant we've known since his youth.

Still, a growing genie naturally needs a roomier bottle in which to dwell. Before learning about the fancier new tricks up the genie's sleeve—MultiFinder, Color QuickDraw, styled TextEdit—we'll have to spend a little time exploring some of the more mundane features of his new domicile. In this chapter, we'll deal with a few preliminaries like model-to-model compatibility, memory management, and access to system resources. Once those are out of the way, we'll be ready to uncork the bottle and let the genie show his stuff.

System Configuration

Once upon a time, all Macintoshes were the same. Anyone writing a program for the machine knew just what to expect: 128 kilobytes of RAM, 64K of ROM, an MC68000 processor, a 9-inch monochrome display measuring 512 pixels by 342, one or two single-sided, 400K floppy-disk drives, two serial ports, and that about covered it. No frills, no variations, one size fits all.

Not any more. Today's Macintosh programmer is confronted with an ever-growing variety of options and configurations. The original 68000 processor has been supplanted, at the high end of the product line, by the newer and more powerful 68020 and 68030, supplemented in some models with a 68881 or 68882 floating-point coprocessor. Memory sizes range up to 8 megabytes and higher, with the gigabyte horizon coming into view. To help cope with the memory explosion, some systems now come equipped with the 68851 paged memory management unit, or PMMU. Disk capacities have evolved from single-sided 400K floppies to double-sided 800K to the current high-density 1.44-megabyte standard, along with a profusion of internal and external hard disks at capacities up to 160 megabytes, 300 megabytes, and beyond.

With the increasing number of models in the Macintosh line, different versions of the Toolbox ROM have also proliferated, growing from the original 64K to 128K in the Macintosh Plus, 256K in the Macintosh SE and Macintosh II, and all the way to 512K in the current latest-and-greatest, the Macintosh IIci. The old, built-in 9-inch screen has given way to more spacious full-page and two-page outboard displays, in full color and gray-scale as well as plain black-and-white—and even to the possibility of multiple independent screens in the same system. Keyboard options range from the original 58-key arrangement to the 105-key, Brand-X-compatible Apple Extended Keyboard, a behemoth of such imposing dimensions that its internal code name while under development was "USS Saratoga." SCSI (Small Computer Standard Interface) parallel ports have been added alongside the old RS–232/RS–422 serial ports, supporting a varied array of printers, plotters, scanners, and other peripheral devices, mundane and exotic. The range of peripheral options has been further extended with NuBus expansion slots and remote-access network connections. It's a different world out there.

Faced with all this bewildering diversity, it's essential for a program to be able to learn the characteristics of the system it's running on. This problem was first addressed in a rudimentary way with the Environs procedure [I:3.1.3], added to the Toolbox in the expansion from the original 64K ROM to the 128K Macintosh Plus version. Now this simple facility has been replaced with a more elaborate version, SysEnvirons [2.1.1], providing a wider range of information about the system and its configuration.

SysEnvirons accepts a *system environment record* as a parameter and fills it with descriptive information about the current system configuration. The format of this record is designed for expandability as the Macintosh system environment evolves over time. The first field, environsVersion, identifies the version of the SysEnvirons routine that created the record, which in turn determines its overall size and structure. In each release of the Toolbox interface files, the constant CurSysEnvVers gives the current version number for SysEnvirons; the one described here is version 1. SysEnvirons accepts a parameter, whichVersion, identifying the desired format for the environment record; if this number is higher than the available version of SysEnvirons can provide, it will return the error code EnvVersTooBig [2.1.1], warning you that the record you receive is smaller than you're expecting and that some of the desired fields are missing.

The remaining fields of the environment record give specific information about the system you're running on. The machineType field contains an integer code number identifying an overall Macintosh model—512K enhanced, SE/30, IIcx, or whatever. If this field is positive, you can count on the availability of at least those Toolbox features included in the 128K Macintosh Plus version of the ROM, as described in the earlier volumes of this series. Negative values denote such antediluvian species as the Skinny Mac, Fat Mac, and Macintosh XL (née Lisa). The list of values given in [2.1.1] is sure to grow as new models appear, and will probably be out of date by the time this book goes to print.

The fields processor and keyboardType contain similar code numbers representing the type of processor and keyboard installed in the system. systemVersion gives the version number of the System file from which the system was started: for example, $0420 for System version 4.2. (The earliest valid system version is 4.1; all earlier versions return 0 in this field.) The sysVRefNum field holds the reference number of the startup volume or system folder in which the System file is located. hasFPU and hasColorQD are

Boolean flags telling whether the current system has a floating-point coprocessor installed and whether it includes the new color version of the QuickDraw graphics routines. Finally, `atDrvrVersNum` gives the version number of the currently installed AppleTalk network driver, if any. If AppleTalk is not present, this field will be 0.

Dispatch Table Access

Often, the information you really need is not what model of processor or version of the system you're running on, but whether a specific Toolbox feature or capability is available. The way to find this out is by looking directly in the system *dispatch table* for the particular Toolbox routine (procedure or function) you need. The dispatch table contains the addresses of all Toolbox routines that are built into the system in ROM, as well as those loaded into RAM from the `System` file at startup. If the routine you want is included in the table, you can go ahead and use it; if not, you can post a suitable alert message, disable some of your menu commands, or take whatever other measures are appropriate.

As we learned in Volume One, Toolbox calls are implemented at the machine level via the processor's *emulator trap* mechanism. Each call to a Toolbox routine is represented in machine language by a special *trap word* beginning with the hexadecimal digit $A (binary 1010), which doesn't correspond to any valid machine instruction. On encountering such an *unimplemented instruction*, the processor suspends what it's doing and executes a *trap handler* routine to deal with the abnormal condition. The trap handler for unimplemented instructions in the Macintosh system, called the *Trap Dispatcher*, analyzes the trap word to determine what Toolbox or system routine it represents, looks up the routine's address in the dispatch table, and executes the routine with a subroutine jump before resuming program execution from the point of the trap.

Trap words come in two slightly different formats, known as *Operating System* or *OS traps* and *Toolbox traps* (see Figure 2–1). The former typically denote low-level system management operations like memory allocation and input/output, while the latter deal with the higher-level elements of the Macintosh user interface, such as windows, menus, and dialog boxes. Also, in general, OS traps receive their parameters and return their results directly in the processor's registers and Toolbox traps pass them on the stack, though there are occasional exceptions both ways.

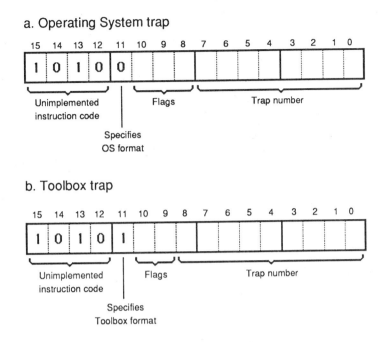

Figure 2–1 Trap word formats

Both types of trap word begin with the bit pattern 1010 (hexadecimal $A), which the M68000-series processors recognize as an unimplemented instruction to be handled via the emulator trap. The next bit (bit 11) is a flag distinguishing the two types of trap: 0 for OS, 1 for Toolbox. This is followed by a few more flag bits controlling things like register usage and synchronous or asynchronous execution. At the end of the word is a *trap number* identifying the specific OS or Toolbox operation the trap represents. An important point to note is that the trap numbers for the two types of trap are of different lengths: 8 bits for OS traps, 9 for Toolbox traps.

In the earliest models of Macintosh (those with the original 64K ROM), there was no overlap between the two types of trap. A given trap number could designate either an OS or a Toolbox trap, but not both: for example, trap number $40 referred to the OS trap ResrvMem [I:3.2.5] and $50 to the Toolbox trap InitCursor

[II:2.5.2]. Both types shared a single dispatch table giving the addresses of the corresponding routines in ROM; the table had room for 512 entries, with OS traps restricted to the first half of the table because of their 8-bit trap numbers. Beginning with the Macintosh Plus and its 128K ROM (version $75), each type of trap has its own dispatch table—one 256 entries long for OS traps and another of 512 entries for Toolbox traps. Thus the same trap number can now refer to two different traps, one in each table. For example, trap number $40 now designates both the OS trap ResrvMem [I:3.2.5] and the Toolbox trap Fix2Long [I:2.3.1]; $50 stands for RelString [I:2.1.2] in the OS dispatch table as well as InitCursor [II:2.5.2] in the Toolbox table.

To find the number for a given trap, look up its trap word alphabetically in Appendix F. The trap word will always begin with the hexadecimal digit $A. If the second digit is between $0 and $7 (usually $0 or $1), then the trap resides in the OS dispatch table under the number given by its last two digits: for example, the trap PostEvent [II:2.3.2], with a trap word of $A02F, is OS trap number $2F. If the second digit is between $8 and $F (usually $8 or $9), it's a Toolbox trap; the last two digits again give the trap number, but in this case it must be increased by $100 if the second digit is odd (that is, if bit 8 is 1). Thus FrameRect [I:5.3.2], whose trap word is $A8A1, is Toolbox trap number $A1, while GetNamedResource [I:6.3.1], with trap word $A9A1, is Toolbox trap $1A1.

Don't make the mistake of applying this same rule to OS traps. In an OS trap, bit 8 is not part of the trap number, but a flag governing register usage at the machine-language level. An OS trap such as NewHandle [I:3.2.1], whose trap word is $A122, still has trap number $22, *not* $122.

The original ROM provides a pair of utility routines, GetTrap-Address and SetTrapAddress [2.1.2], for manipulating the contents of the dispatch table. Both accept the desired trap number as a parameter. GetTrapAddress returns a long integer representing the numerical address of the corresponding OS or Toolbox routine, taken from the table; SetTrapAddress accepts the address as a parameter and stores it into the table, replacing the previous address for that trap number. On more recent models with separate OS and Toolbox dispatch tables, these two routines are replaced with newer versions, NGetTrapAddress and NSetTrapAddress [2.1.2]. The new routines work just the same as the old ones, except that they take an additional parameter of type TrapType [2.1.2]. The values of this enumerated type, OSTrap and ToolTrap, designate the type of trap to which the trap number parameter refers and thus which dispatch table it resides in.

At the assembly-language level, the new routines NGetTrap-Address and NSetTrapAddress are called via the same pair of traps as the older versions, GetTrapAddress and SetTrap-Address. The two forms are distinguished by bit 9 of the trap word, which is 0 for the old versions (combined dispatch table) or 1 for the new (dual dispatch tables). In the latter case, bit 10 selects one of the two tables (0 for OS, 1 for Toolbox). See [2.1.2, note 17] for further details.

On older machines that use a combined dispatch table, these flag bits in the trap word are ignored and the new routines simply revert to the same behavior as the old. Where two traps, one of each type, share the same trap number, the call will thus affect the older of the two, whichever was included in the original 64K ROM. This can get you in trouble if you're not careful: you may think you're asking for RelString (OS trap number $50) and get InitCursor (Toolbox trap $50) instead. To stay on the safe side, be sure to call SysEnvirons first and verify that you're running under ROM version $75 or later. The easiest way to check this is by looking at the machineType field of the environment record [2.1.1]: as long as this field is positive, you're on a system with dual dispatch tables and you can trust NGetTrapAddress and NSetTrapAddress to work the way you expect.

By convention, all OS and Toolbox traps that are not available in a given version of the system have their dispatch table entries set to the same standard ROM address. For reference, one special trap, number $9F in the Toolbox series, is set aside and guaranteed to remain forever unimplemented. (Some versions of the Toolbox interface files define its trap number as a constant named `UnimplTrapNum` [2.1.2]; in others, it's been inadvertently left out and you have to define it explicitly for yourself.) Thus you can test whether another trap is available by comparing its trap address with that of this standard unimplemented trap: if the addresses match, then the trap you're testing is not available in the system you're running on. As an example, if `thisTrapNum` is the number of a Toolbox trap that was not present in the original 64K ROM, the following code will test whether it's available in the current system:

```
result := SysEnvirons (CurSysEnvVers, theEnvirons);
if theEnvirons.machineType < 0 then
  {Trap is not available}
else
  begin
    unimplAddr   := NGetTrapAddress (UnimplTrapNum, ToolTrap);
    thisTrapAddr := NGetTrapAddress (thisTrapNum, ToolTrap);
    if thisTrapAddr = unimplAddr then
      {Trap is not available}
    else
      {Trap is available}
  end {else}
```

`NSetTrapAddress` is useful mainly for "patching" the dispatch table to substitute your own version of a Toolbox routine in place of the standard version. Many of the `INIT` utilities that are so popular nowadays operate this way, installing their own code in the dispatch table to capture calls to key routines and handle them in nonstandard ways. It's a tricky business, however, and not recommended for those with faint hearts or careless coding styles. One wrong move can easily turn the most useful gadgets in your Toolbox into lethal instruments of self-destruction. Don't try it unless you know what you're doing.

If you do attempt patching a trap in the dispatch table, it's much safer just to add a bit of extra code to the existing routine instead of replacing it wholesale. The way to do this is to fetch the existing trap address with `NGetTrapAddress` and save it in an accessible location before replacing it with `NSetTrapAddress`. Then you can call the original Toolbox routine from within your substitute version, merely adding some extra pre- or postprocessing of your own. This technique also gives you a better chance of staying compatible with other `INIT`s or similar pieces of code that may be patching the same trap. Finally, if you're patching the dispatch table from within an application program, don't forget to undo your patches and restore the table to its original state before exiting. Remember—only you can prevent system pollution.

Keep in mind that in today's Macintosh environment, your program may find itself sharing the system with one or more others under the control of MultiFinder. Any patches you install in the dispatch table may have unwanted and probably toxic effects on the operation of these other programs. Luckily, MultiFinder is smart enough to maintain a separate dispatch table for each program and swap it in only when that program assumes active control of the system. If you're careful to locate your patch routine in your own application heap, MultiFinder will see to it that it affects only your own program and no others. Conversely, patches that *are* intended to affect the global environment in which all programs operate (such as those installed by `INIT` routines) should reside in the system heap. (We'll be learning more about MultiFinder in the next chapter.)

Since MultiFinder automatically disposes of your private dispatch table when your program terminates, there would seem to be no need to remove your patches before exiting. Don't forget, though, that you may equally well be running in the single-Finder environment—so it's still important to clean up after yourself to avoid sabotaging the program that follows you.

Shutdown and Restart

A pair of new Toolbox routines, ShutDwnPower and ShutDwnStart [2.1.5], allow you to shut down or restart the system under program control. These correspond to the Shut Down and Restart commands on the Finder's Special menu. On the Macintosh II, which has a software-controlled main power switch, ShutDwnPower actually turns off the machine; on other models, it displays an alert message prompting the user to turn off the power manually (You may now switch off your Macintosh safely). ShutDwnStart replaces the earlier Toolbox routine Restart [I:7.1.3], restarting the system as if the user had pressed the reset button or toggled the power switch off and back on again. Both routines perform all necessary housekeeping chores to leave the system in an orderly and consistent state:

1. Issue a "good-bye kiss" [III:3.1.2] to each active driver or desk accessory that requires one, then close all active drivers and desk accessories.
2. Unload the contents of the desk scrap to a disk file [I:7.4.4].
3. Eject and unmount all mounted volumes [II:8.1.3].
4. If running under MultiFinder, send each active program the equivalent of a Quit command, allowing it to save files, if necessary, and exit in an orderly way.
5. Shut down or restart the system as requested.

If an application program has any last-minute housekeeping to do before system shutdown, it will get its chance in step 4; step 1 offers the same opportunity to drivers and desk accessories. Other types of program (INIT routines, for example) must explicitly schedule their own *shutdown procedure* for execution during the shutdown or restart sequence, using the Toolbox routine ShutDwn-Install [2.1.6]. The shutdown procedure accepts no parameters and returns no results, simply carries out its needed housekeeping tasks and exits. A parameter to ShutDwnInstall specifies when in the shutdown sequence the procedure is to be executed: before issuing good-bye kisses and closing drivers (step 1), before ejecting and unmounting volumes (step 3), before restarting the system (step 5), or before shutting off the power (step 5). If necessary, a procedure could be scheduled for execution at more than one of these times, though this would be an unusual thing to do. The Toolbox routine ShutDwnRemove cancels a previously installed shutdown procedure.

Memory Management

Although all memory addresses on the Macintosh are theoretically 32 bits long, the original models actually used only 24 of the 32. This is because the MC68000 processor used in those early models ignores the first 8 bits of the address and carries only the last 24 bits "off-chip" onto the *address bus* that supplies addresses to physical memory. Thus these early models were limited in practice to a maximum address space of 16 megabytes (2^{24}, or 16,777,216 bytes). Those 8 unused bits at the high end of each address provided a convenient place for the Toolbox to stash additional information, such as the lock and purge bits in a handle's master pointer [I:3.2.4] or the variation code in a window's or control's definition function handle [II:3.1.1, II:6.1.1].

The newer Macintoshes, with their more powerful 68020 and 68030 processors, now include a full 32-bit address bus, expanding the effective address space to 4 gigabytes (2^{32} = 4,294,967,296 bytes). For backward compatibility with existing software, these newer models can also operate in 24-bit mode, suppressing the first 8 bits of each address as before. All Toolbox and system software is limited to 24-bit addresses; the system starts up automatically in 24-bit mode, and application programs ordinarily run in this mode. At the time of writing, the only Macintosh software that uses full 32-bit addresses is Apple's version of the Unix operating system, A/UX, which also requires the optional paged memory management unit (PMMU) to maintain its virtual memory space.

The new Macintosh IIci, announced just before this book went to press, features a redesigned version of the Toolbox that's "32-bit-clean"—that is, with no extraneous information in the high-order byte of an address, allowing unimpeded operation for all software in 32-bit mode.

The choice between 24- and 32-bit address mode (also called *MMU mode*, for "Memory Management Unit") is determined by a flag bit in the control register of one of the VIA (Versatile Interface Adapter) chips. A pair of new Toolbox routines, `GetMMUMode` and

SwapMMUMode [2.1.3], allow you to read or change this setting. GetMMUMode simply returns an integer code (False32B or True32B [2.1.3]) representing the current address mode. SwapMMUMode accepts a similar constant giving the new mode to be set, and returns the previous mode via the same variable parameter. Thus you can use paired calls to this routine to save the address mode and later restore it to its previous state:

```
mmuMode := True32B;              {Set 32-bit mode}
SwapMMUMode (mmuMode);           {Swap and save old mode}
      . . . ;                    {Work in 32-bit mode}
SwapMMUMode (mmuMode)           {Restore previous mode}
```

Another utility routine, StripAddress [2.1.3], strips off the high-order byte of a 32-bit pointer, removing any private data the Toolbox may have stored there and converting the pointer to a "clean" 24-bit address. This operation is meaningful only in 24-bit mode; in 32-bit mode, it simply leaves the full 32-bit address unchanged.

Memory Layout

What we usually think of when we talk about a computer's memory is its *random access memory*, or RAM. (This is actually a misleading term, since other forms of memory can also be accessed in random fashion; a more descriptive term would be "read/write memory.") In practice, however, not all of the available address space is devoted to RAM. Read-only memory (ROM) occupies part of the space, and addresses are also reserved for *memory-mapped input/output*—that is, for communication with peripheral devices using the various interface controllers built into the system. Thus there are portions of the address space set aside for each of the two Versatile Interface Adapters (VIAs), for the Serial Communications Controller (SCC), the Small Computer Standard Interface (SCSI), the Integrated Wozniak Machine (IWM) disk controller, the Apple Sound Chip (ASC), and so on. In addition, on the Macintosh II, each of the six expansion slots is allotted a portion of address space for memory and control functions residing on an expansion card plugged into the slot.

Memory layouts for the Macintosh II in both 24- and 32-bit address mode are shown in [2.2.1]. In 24-bit mode, the available 16-megabyte address space is divided into 1-megabyte segments according to the first hexadecimal digit of the address. Addresses from $000000 to $7FFFFF are reserved for RAM, allowing a maximum configuration of 8 megabytes. If less than this maximum amount of RAM is actually installed, some of the high-order bits of each address are ignored, causing the existing memory locations to repeat cyclically throughout the logical address space. For example, on a machine with 1 megabyte ($100000 bytes) of physical RAM, addresses $012446, $112446, $212446, and so on, all refer to the same physical byte of memory.

The next megabyte of addresses, from $800000 to $8FFFFF, are assigned to ROM. The first 256 kilobytes of this space, from $800000 to $83FFFF, are actually used by the initial release of the Macintosh II ROM (version $78); the rest are reserved for future expansion. Following ROM are the spaces assigned to the six expansion slots. For convenient reference, the slots are numbered with hexadecimal digits from $9 to $E, rather than from 0 to 5 or 1 to 6; each slot's address space consists of the megabyte of addresses beginning with the corresponding digit ($B00000 to $BFFFFF for slot $B, for example). Finally, the last megabyte of address space, from $F00000 to $FFFFFF, is reserved for memory-mapped I/O. This space is further subdivided among the various interface chips mentioned earlier, such as the VIAs and SCC; if you need further details on these specific address assignments, you can find them in Apple's *Macintosh Family Hardware Reference* manual, published by Addison-Wesley.

In 32-bit mode, the address space is again divided into sixteen zones by the first hexadecimal digit of the address—but since the total space is 4 gigabytes, each zone is now 256 megabytes long instead of just 1 megabyte. Addresses $00000000 to $3FFFFFFF are allotted to RAM, occupying a quarter of the total space, or 1 gigabyte in all. (The machine can't physically accommodate this much memory, but it could be addressed as virtual memory under control of the PMMU.) The next zone, $40000000 to $4FFFFFFF, is assigned to ROM, with the actual 256K ROM running from $40000000 to $4003FFFF. Memory-mapped I/O resides in zone $5 (addresses $50000000 to $5FFFFFFF); zones 6 to 8 ($60000000 to $8FFFFFFF) are unused and reserved for future expansion.

Each of the six expansion slots has two separate areas of address space assigned to it in 32-bit mode: a 16-megabyte *regular slot space* in zone $F and an additional *super slot space* consisting of one whole 256-megabyte zone. For slot $B, for example, the regular slot space runs from $FB000000 to $FBFFFFFF and the super slot space from $B0000000 to $BFFFFFFF. The 1 megabyte allotted to the slot in 24-bit mode maps into the first megabyte of regular slot space in 32-bit mode (in this case, from $FB000000 to $FB0FFFFF). The remaining ten subzones of zone $F ($F0000000 to $F8FFFFFF and $FF000000 to $FFFFFFFF) are reserved for future use.

Memory Allocation

A set of new memory allocation routines have been added to the Toolbox [2.2.2], supplementing the original NewHandle and NewPtr [I:3.2.1] for allocating relocatable and nonrelocatable blocks, respectively. NewHandleSys and NewPtrSys allocate a block from the system heap instead of the normal application heap; New-HandleClear and NewPtrClear clear the new block to all zeros before returning it; NewHandleSysClear and NewPtrSysClear do both. (These facilities have always been available from assembly language via flag bits in the trap words for NewHandle and NewPtr; the new Toolbox calls make them available from the Pascal level as well.)

For programs running under MultiFinder, a new form of memory allocation is available in addition to the normal system and application heaps. The new routine MFTempNewHandle [2.2.3] allocates a relocatable block from the unused portion of memory not currently assigned to any running program. Such temporary memory blocks are intended for short-term use only, and should be released before the next pass of the program's event loop (that is, before retrieving the next event for processing). This makes the space available in case the user wishes to launch a new program, or for similar temporary memory requests by other programs with which you are already sharing the system.

Such temporary memory blocks allocated by MultiFinder are *not* interchangeable with those created by NewHandle [I:3.2.1] or related allocation calls [2.2.2]. You should never attempt to apply ordinary memory-management operations to them, such as GetHandleSize, SetHandleSize [I:3.2.3], HLock, HUnlock, HPurge, HNoPurge [I:3.2.4], MoveHHi [I:3.2.5], EmptyHandle, Re-allocHandle [I:3.2.1], or RecoverHandle [I:3.2.1]. In particular, always be sure to use the new routine MFTempDisposHandle [2.2.3] to release temporary blocks and the old DisposHandle [I:3.2.1] for ordinary blocks, never the other way around. If necessary, you can lock and unlock temporary blocks with the new routines MFTemp-HLock and MFTempHUnlock [2.2.3], but there are no equivalent routines for marking them purgeable or unpurgeable; temporary blocks can never be purged.

Depending on the number of programs running concurrently under MultiFinder and the amount of space used by each, there may not be enough space available to allocate a temporary block of the requested size. If the block cannot be allocated, MFTempNewHandle will return the error code MemFullErr [I:3.1.2] in its variable parameter resultCode. Your program should always have a backup plan for dealing with this contingency, so that it can function properly without failing, even if the requested temporary space is not available. For example, the Finder uses MFTempNewHandle to allocate a large temporary buffer when copying a file; if the space for the buffer isn't available, it uses a smaller buffer preallocated for the purpose within its own application heap. The MultiFinder routine MFFreeMem [2.2.4] returns the total amount of memory space available for temporary allocation; MFMaxMem [2.2.4] compacts the temporary heap and then returns the size of the largest available free block.

Small Fractions

A new numeric data type, SmallFract [2.4.1], represents a 16-bit fractional value between 0 and 1, with an implicit binary point preceding the first bit. The value of such a small fraction is equivalent to that of the corresponding *unsigned* integer divided by 65536 (2^{16}). It thus corresponds to the low-order (fractional) half of a 32-bit fixed-point number of type Fixed [I:2.3.1]. The largest possible small fraction, $FFFF, has a numerical value equal to 65535 divided by 65536, or 0.999984741; this value is defined as a Toolbox constant named `MaxSmallFract`. This constant is declared as a *long* integer, $0000FFFF, so that it can be used in combination with full-length fixed-point numbers. A pair of utility routines, `Fix2SmallFract` and `SmallFract2Fix` [2.4.1] convert between fixed-point numbers and small fractions. Small fractions are used mainly for expressing the components of color values for drawing with the new Color QuickDraw routines; we'll have more to say on this subject in Chapter 4.

REFERENCE

2.1 System Configuration

2.1.1 Operating Environment

 Definitions

```
function SysEnvirons
            (whichVersion    : INTEGER;        {Desired version of environment record}
            var theEnvirons : SysEnvRec)       {Description of operating environment}
            : OSErr;                           {Result code}

type
    SysEnvRec = record
                environsVersion : INTEGER; {Version number of environment record}
                machineType     : INTEGER; {Model of Macintosh hardware}
                systemVersion   : INTEGER; {Version number of System file}
                processor       : INTEGER; {CPU type}
                hasFPU          : BOOLEAN; {Floating-point coprocessor present?}
                hasColorQD      : BOOLEAN; {Color QuickDraw available?}
                keyboardType    : INTEGER; {Type of keyboard}
                atDrvrVersNum   : INTEGER; {Version number of AppleTalk driver}
                sysVRefNum      : INTEGER  {Volume or directory containing System file}
            end;

const
    CurSysEnvVers = 1;                         {Current version of SysEnvirons}
```

```
                                      {Machine codes: }
EnvMachUnknown =  0;                    {Unrecognized hardware model}
EnvXL          = -2;                    {Macintosh XL (Lisa)}
EnvMac         = -1;                    {Original Skinny or Fat Mac}
Env512Ke       =  1;                    {Macintosh 512K enhanced}
EnvMacPlus     =  2;                    {Macintosh Plus}
EnvSE          =  3;                    {Macintosh SE}
EnvMacII       =  4;                    {Macintosh II}
EnvMacIIx      =  5;                    {Macintosh IIx}
EnvMacIIcx     =  6;                    {Macintosh IIcx}
EnvSE30        =  7;                    {Macintosh SE/30}

                                      {CPU codes: }
EnvCPUUnknown  =  0;                    {Unrecognized processor}
Env68000       =  1;                    {MC68000 processor}
Env68010       =  2;                    {MC68010 processor}
Env68020       =  3;                    {MC68020 processor}
Env68030       =  4;                    {MC68030 processor}

                                      {Keyboard codes: }
EnvUnknownKbd  =  0;                    {Unrecognized keyboard type}
EnvMacKbd      =  1;                    {Original Macintosh keyboard}
EnvMacAndPad   =  2;                    {Original keyboard with optional keypad}
EnvMacPlusKbd  =  3;                    {Macintosh Plus keyboard}
EnvAExtendKbd  =  4;                    {Apple Extended Keyboard}
EnvStandADBKbd =  5;                    {Standard Apple Desktop Bus keyboard}

                                      {Result codes: }
EnvNotPresent  = -5500;                 {SysEnvirons  not implemented}
EnvBadVers     = -5501;                 {Invalid version number requested}
EnvVersTooBig  = -5502;                 {Requested version not available}
```

 Notes

1. SysEnvirons returns an *environment record* describing the hardware and system software on which a program is running. This allows the program to test for the availability of specific features and to adjust gracefully in case they are absent.

2. The contents of the environment record will be extended with additional fields as new features and capabilities are added to the Macintosh system. The record's `environsVersion` field identifies the version of `SysEnvirons` that created it, and hence its overall size and structure.

3. The program specifies the desired version of the environment record via the `whichVersion` parameter. If the requested version number is higher than the available version of `SysEnvirons` can provide, it will return the error code `EnvVersTooBig`. This warns the program to proceed with caution, since the environment record it receives will be smaller than it expects and some of the desired fields will be missing.

4. The definition shown for the environment record is version 1, corresponding to `System` file version 4.1. For earlier versions of the `System` file, the "glue" routine for `SysEnvirons` will fill in the contents of the record and return the error code `EnvNotPresent`.

5. The constant `CurSysEnvVers` gives the current version number for the environment record (version 1 at the time this book went to print). The value of this constant will be updated as needed in future releases of the Toolbox interface files.

6. The environment record's `machineType` field identifies the model of the Macintosh hardware on which the program is running. Possible values at the time of publication include `EnvXL`, `EnvMac`, `Env512Ke`, `EnvMacPlus`, `EnvSE`, `EnvSE30`, `EnvMacII`, `EnvMacIIx`, and `EnvMacIIcx`. The value `EnvMachUnknown` denotes a hardware model unknown to this version of `SysEnvirons`.

7. A positive value for `machineType` ensures the availability of all Toolbox features included in the Macintosh Plus (128K) version of the ROM. Negative values denote "prehistoric" Macintosh models carrying the original 64K ROM.

8. `systemVersion` gives the version number of the current `System` file. The first half of the two-part version number is in the high-order byte, the second in the low, in hexadecimal form. For example, a value of $0420 denotes `System` version 4.2. Version numbers in this form can be compared directly, using the ordinary arithmetic comparison operators < (less-than) and > (greater-than).

9. `System` files earlier than version 4.1 return 0 in the `systemVersion` field.

10. `processor` identifies the type of central processor (CPU) on which the program is running. Possible values at publication time include `Env68000`, `Env68010`, `Env68020`, and `Env68030`. The value `EnvCPUUnknown` denotes a processor type unknown to this version of `SysEnvirons`.

11. The Boolean field `hasFPU` tells whether a floating-point coprocessor is present.

12. The Boolean field `hasColorQD` tells whether the Color QuickDraw graphics routines are available. (Color QuickDraw is discussed in Chapters 3 and 4.)

13. `keyboardType` identifies the type of keyboard connected to the machine. Possible values at publication time include `EnvMacKbd`, `EnvMacAndPad`, `EnvMacPlusKbd`, `EnvAExtendKbd`, and `EnvStand-ADBKbd`. The value `EnvUnknownKbd` denotes a keyboard type unknown to this version of `SysEnvirons`.

14. `atDrvrVersNum` gives the version number of the currently installed AppleTalk network driver, if any. If AppleTalk is not present, this field will be 0.

15. `sysVRefNum` is the reference number of the volume or directory in which the `System` file resides.

16. For `SysEnvirons` to work properly, it must be preceded by all of the needed Toolbox initialization calls, such as `InitGraf` [I:4.3.1], `Init-Fonts` [I:8.2.4], `InitWindows` [II:3.2.1], `InitMenus` [II:4.2.1], `TEInit` [II:5.2.1], `InitDialogs` [II:7.2.1], and `PrOpen` [III:4.2.1].

Assembly Language Information

Trap macro:

(Pascal) Routine name	(Assembly) Trap macro	Trap word
SysEnvirons	_SysEnvirons	$A090

Register usage:

Routine	Register	Contents
SysEnvirons	A0.L (in)	pointer to theEnvirons
	D0.W (in)	whichVersion
	A0.L (out)	pointer to theEnvirons
	D0.W (out)	result code

Field offsets in a system environment record:

(Pascal) Field name	(Assembly) Offset name	Offset in bytes
environsVersion	environsVersion	0
machineType	machineType	2
systemVersion	systemVersion	4
processor	processor	6
hasFPU	hasFPU	8
hasColorQD	hasColorQD	9
keyboardType	keyboardType	10
atDrvrVersNum	atDrvrVersNum	12
sysVRefNum	sysVRefNum	14

Assembly-language constants:

Name	Value	Meaning
SysEnvlSize	16	Size in bytes of environment record, version 1
CurSysEnvVers	1	Current version of SysEnvirons

Machine codes:

Name	Value	Meaning
EnvMachUnknown	0	Unrecognized hardware model
EnvXL	-2	Macintosh XL (Lisa)
EnvMac	-1	Original Skinny or Fat Mac
Env512Ke	1	Macintosh 512K enhanced
EnvMacPlus	2	Macintosh Plus
EnvSE	3	Macintosh SE
EnvMacII	4	Macintosh II
EnvMacIIx	5	Macintosh IIx
EnvMacIIcx	6	Macintosh IIcx
EnvMacSE30	7	Macintosh SE/30

CPU codes:

Name	Value	Meaning
EnvCPUUnknown	0	Unrecognized processor
Env68000	1	MC68000 processor
Env68010	2	MC68010 processor
Env68020	3	MC68020 processor
Env68030	4	MC68030 processor

Keyboard codes:

Name	Value	Meaning
EnvUnknownKbd	0	Unrecognized keyboard type
EnvMacKbd	1	Original Macintosh keyboard
EnvMacAndPad	2	Original keyboard with optional keypad
EnvMacPlusKbd	3	Macintosh Plus keyboard
EnvAExtendKbd	4	Apple Extended Keyboard
EnvStandADBKbd	5	Standard Apple Desktop Bus keyboard

2.1.2   Dispatch Table

 Definitions

```
function  GetTrapAddress
              (trapNum : INTEGER)        {Trap number of desired Toolbox routine}
                  : LONGINT;             {Address of existing routine in memory}

procedure SetTrapAddress
              (newAddr : LONGINT;        {Address of replacement routine}
              trapNum : INTEGER);        {Trap number of Toolbox routine to be replaced}

function  NGetTrapAddress
              (trapNum   : INTEGER;      {Trap number of desired Toolbox routine}
              whichType : TrapType)      {OS or Toolbox trap?}
                  : LONGINT;             {Address of existing routine in memory}
```

```
procedure NSetTrapAddress
            (newAddr    : LONGINT;        {Address of replacement routine}
             trapNum    : INTEGER;        {Trap number of Toolbox routine to be replaced}
             whichType : TrapType);       {OS or Toolbox trap?}

type
   TrapType = (OSTrap,                    {Routine resides in OS dispatch table}
               ToolTrap);                 {Routine resides in Toolbox dispatch table}

const
   UnimplTrapNum = $9F;                   {Trap number of unimplemented Toolbox trap}
```

 Notes

1. These routines manipulate the contents of the system dispatch tables, used by the Trap Dispatcher to locate Toolbox and Operating System (OS) routines accessed via the trap mechanism. The trap mechanism, Trap Dispatcher, and dispatch tables are discussed in Volume One, Chapter 2.

2. Addresses found in the dispatch table may lie either in ROM (for routines whose code is built directly into the system) or in RAM (for those loaded from the System file at startup or "patched" by a running program).

3. Each Toolbox or OS routine is identified by a *trap number*, which gives its index in the relevant dispatch table.

4. The two types of trap are distinguished by bit 11 of the trap word: 1 for Toolbox traps, 0 for OS. This determines the internal format of the trap word and the meaning of various flag bits within it; see Volume One, Chapter 2, for further discussion.

5. To find the trap number corresponding to a given Toolbox or OS routine, look up the routine's trap word in Appendix F (or in the equivalent appendix of *Inside Macintosh*). Trap words beginning with the digits $A8 or $A9 designate Toolbox traps, with the trap number in the last 9 bits of the word; those beginning with $A0 or $A1 are OS traps, with the trap number in the last 8 bits.

6. Note that in OS traps, bit 8 (the ninth from the end) is a flag affecting register usage, and is *not* part of the trap number. For example, the Toolbox routine BeginUpdate, with trap word $A922, is trap number $122; but the OS routine NewHandle, trap word $A122, is trap number $22, *not* $122.

7. In the original 64K ROM, Toolbox and OS traps share the same dispatch table; each 9-bit trap number, from 0 to 511, designates a single Toolbox or OS routine, with no overlap between the two categories. Beginning with the 128K Macintosh Plus ROM (version $75), Toolbox and OS traps are kept in separate dispatch tables; the same trap number can designate two different routines, one in each table, depending on bit 11 of the trap word.

8. GetTrapAddress and SetTrapAddress are the original forms of these routines, intended for use with the old 64K ROM and its single dispatch table. The parameter trapNum gives the trap number of the desired routine; no distinction is made between Toolbox and OS traps.

9. NGetTrapAddress and NSetTrapAddress work with newer ROMs (version $75 or greater) that maintain separate OS and Toolbox dispatch tables. An additional parameter of type TrapType selects one of the two tables and distinguishes between OS and Toolbox traps that share the same trap number.

10. On machines with the original (64K) ROM, NGetTrapAddress and NSetTrapAddress revert to the same behavior as the older versions, GetTrapAddress and SetTrapAddress. Where the same trap number is shared by both an OS and a Toolbox trap, it is taken to refer to the older of the two, whichever was present in the original ROM. Thus NGetTrapAddress and NSetTrapAddress can safely be used on any model of Macintosh, provided that the trap they are applied to is one that was included in the original ROM.

11. For more recent traps that were *not* in the original ROM, NGetTrap-Address and NSetTrapAddress *cannot* be used safely on older machines. Before attempting to call these routines for such a trap, you must first call SysEnvirons [2.1.1] to verify the presence of ROM $75 or later. This is indicated by a positive value in the machineType field of the environment record.

12. To check for the availability of a particular trap, compare the address returned for it by NGetTrapAddress with that for the unimplemented Toolbox trap, number $9F, which is guaranteed to remain forever unused. If the two addresses are different, then the desired trap is available in the dispatch table; if they're the same, then it isn't. (The constant UnimplTrapNum is not defined in some versions of the Toolbox interface files, so you may have to declare it for yourself.)

13. Replacing a Toolbox or OS routine with a substitute version of your own is hazardous and extremely tricky, and should not be attempted

unless you are certain of what you are doing. If you absolutely must patch a routine, always use `SetTrapAddress` or `NSetTrapAddress` rather than storing directly into the dispatch table yourself.

14. Instead of replacing a Toolbox or OS routine wholesale, it is generally safer to call the original routine from within your substitute version, simply adding some additional pre- or postprocessing of your own. You can obtain the original address from the dispatch table with `GetTrapAddress` or `NGetTrapAddress` and save it in an accessible location before patching the new address into the table.

15. All replacement code for patched routines should reside in your own application heap rather than in the system heap. This ensures that your patches will not affect the operation of other programs with which you may be sharing the system under MultiFinder.

16. Always be sure to remove your patches and restore the dispatch table to its original state before exiting from your program.

17. In assembly language, the newer forms, `NGetTrapAddress` and `NSet-TrapAddress`, use the same trap macros as the older ones, `_GetTrap-Address` and `_SetTrapAddress`. Bit 9 of the trap word specifies single (0) or dual (1) dispatch tables; if this bit is set, bit 10 selects one of the two tables (0 for OS, 1 for Toolbox). The trap macros accept optional parameters `NEWOS` and `NEWTOOL` to set these flags correctly for the two types of trap under the two-table scheme; omitting the parameters specifies the old, one-table scheme instead. For example,

```
_GetTrapAddress              ; GetTrapAddress
_GetTrapAddress   ,NEWOS     ; NGetTrapAddress, OS trap
_GetTrapAddress   ,NEWTOOL   ; NGetTrapAddress, Toolbox trap
```

18. In a normal Toolbox or Operating System call, issued via the trap mechanism, the contents of all processor registers are preserved except D0, A7 (the stack pointer), and sometimes A0. However, some of the preserved registers (A1, D1, and D2) are saved and restored by the Trap Dispatcher, rather than by the routine itself. When you bypass the Trap Dispatcher by fetching a routine's address from the dispatch table and calling it directly, these registers are not saved; if you need them preserved across the call, you must save and restore them for yourself.

Assembly Language Information

Trap macros:

(Pascal) Routine name	(Assembly) Trap macro	Trap word
GetTrapAddress	_GetTrapAddress	$A146
SetTrapAddress	_SetTrapAddress	$A047
———————	_Unimplemented	$A89F

Register usage:

Routine	Register	Contents
GetTrapAddress	D0.W (in)	trapNum
	A0.L (out)	function result
SetTrapAddress	A0.L (in)	newAddr
	D0.W (out)	trapNum

Masks for flag bits in trap word:

Name	Value	Meaning
NewTool	$0600	Toolbox trap
NewOS	$0200	Operating system trap

2.1.3   Memory Address Mode

Definitions

```
function  GetMMUMode
              : SignedByte;              {Current address mode}

procedure SwapMMUMode
              (var addrMode : SignedByte);   {New address mode; returns previous mode}

function  StripAddress
              (longAddr : Ptr)          {32-bit address}
                 : Ptr;                 {24-bit address}
```

```
const
    False32B = 0;                          {24-bit address mode}
    True32B  = 1;                          {32-bit address mode}
```

 Notes

1. GetMMUMode and SwapMMUMode control the width of the memory addresses in use, and hence the total amount of memory that can be addressed. (MMU stands for "memory management unit.")

2. The MC68020 and MC68030 processors, used in the Macintosh II and other advanced models, support full 32-bit addressing and can thus access a total address space of 4 gigabytes (2^{32} = 4,294,967,296 bytes). Older models, based on the MC68000 processor, are limited to 24-bit addresses for an address space of 16 megabytes (2^{24} = 16,777,216 bytes).

3. GetMMUMode returns an integer code (False32B or True32B) representing the address mode currently in effect.

4. SwapMMUMode sets the current address mode as specified by its parameter, addrMode. It also returns the previous address mode via this same variable parameter. The program can save this value and use it later to restore the system to its previous state: for example,

```
    mmuMode := True32B;        {Set new mode}
    SwapMMUMode (mmuMode);     {Swap and save old mode}
         . . . ;               {Do some work}
    SwapMMUMode (mmuMode)      {Restore previous mode}
```

5. For compatibility with earlier models, all Macintosh system software is designed to use 24-bit addresses. The Macintosh II and other models with a choice of address modes are automatically started up in 24-bit mode, and application programs ordinarily run in this mode.

6. 32-bit mode is intended mainly for use by slot-based expansion cards needing more memory than the 1 megabyte allotted to them under the standard 24-bit memory layout [2.2.1]. It is also used by A/UX, Apple's Macintosh version of the Unix operating system.

7. Some parts of the Toolbox (notably those concerned with memory management [I:3.2.4, note 5] and window and control definition functions [III:2.2.1, note 6; III:2.3.1, note 6]) use the high-order byte of a machine address to hold flags and other private data, and will not work properly in 32-bit mode.

8. When running in 24-bit mode, the Toolbox function StripAddress clears the high byte of a 32-bit pointer to zero, removing any private data the Toolbox may have stored there and converting the pointer to a usable 24-bit address. In 32-bit mode, StripAddress simply leaves the full 32-bit address unchanged.

9. Never use the high byte of a pointer for your own flags or data storage, since future versions of the Toolbox may reclaim this space for use as a full 32-bit address.

10. SwapMMUMode and StripAddress are available in assembly language via the trap mechanism, but GetMMUMode is not. To find the current address mode in assembly language, look in the global variable MMU32Bit (see "Assembly Language Information" below). This 1-byte flag will be zero in 24-bit mode, nonzero in 32-bit mode.

Assembly Language Information

Trap macros:

(Pascal) Routine name	(Assembly) Trap macro	Trap word
SwapMMUMode	_SwapMMUMode	$A05D
StripAddress	_StripAddress	$A055

Register usage:

Routine	Register	Contents
SwapMMUMode	D0.B (in)	addrMode
	D0.B (out)	addrMode
StripAddress	D0.L (in)	longAddr
	D0.L (out)	function result

Assembly-language constants:

Name	Value	Meaning
False32B	0	24-bit address mode
True32B	1	32-bit address mode

Assembly-language global variable:

Name	Address	Meaning
MMU32Bit	$CB2	Current address mode (1 byte)

2.1.4   Global Variable Access

Definitions

```
procedure SetUpA5;

procedure RestoreA5;

function  SetA5
            (newA5 : LONGINT)          {New value to be stored in A5}
                  : LONGINT;           {Previous contents of A5}

function  SetCurrentA5
                  : LONGINT;           {Previous contents of A5}
```

Notes

1. These routines are used for manipulating the contents of processor register A5, which holds the base address of a program's *application global space* (see Volume One, Chapter 3). They're useful in places such as vertical retrace (VBL) tasks and input/output completion routines, which are called via hardware interrupts and cannot assume A5 to be set up properly.

2. SetUpA5 saves the current contents of register A5 on the stack, then loads the register with the application globals pointer for the currently running program. The program can later call RestoreA5 to restore the register's previous contents from the stack.

3. The globals pointer is taken from the system variable CurrentA5 in low memory (see "Assembly Language Information" below), which always holds the correct A5 setting for the currently running program.

4. To improve code efficiency, some popular Pascal compilers (notably MPW Pascal, from Apple's own Macintosh Programmer's Workshop) manipulate the stack in unusual ways that interfere with the operation of SetUpA5 and RestoreA5. The newer routines SetA5 and SetCurrentA5 avoid using the stack and thus remain compatible with such optimizing compilers.

5. SetA5 loads register A5 with a new value, supplied as a parameter, and returns the register's previous contents as a function result. The program can save this value and use it later to restore the register to its previous state: for example,

```
globalPtr := yourA5;              {Get correct global pointer}
saveA5 := SetA5 (globalPtr);      {Load A5 and save previous}
    . . . ;                       {Do your thing}
ignore := SetA5 (saveA5)          {Restore previous contents}
```

6. SetCurrentA5 is similar to SetA5, but takes the new setting of A5 from the system global CurrentA5, rather than as a parameter. Like SetA5, it returns the register's previous contents as a function result; the program can later pass this value to SetA5 to restore the register.

7. Notice that CurrentA5 holds the application globals pointer for the *currently running program*. Under MultiFinder, this is not necessarily the same program to which an interrupt-driven routine (such as a VBL task or I/O completion routine) belongs. Recommended practice for such routines is to carry a copy of their own globals pointer in a known, accessible location, instead of relying on CurrentA5 for this information. See Macintosh Technical Note #180 for an example of this technique.

8. All of these routines are defined as part of the Pascal interface "glue," and are not available from assembly language via the trap mechanism. In assembly language, you can simply manipulate the contents of register A5 directly.

Assembly Language Information

Assembly-language global variable:

Name	Address	Meaning
CurrentA5	$904	Base pointer for application globals

2.1.5   Shutdown and Restart

 Definitions

```
procedure ShutDwnPower;

procedure ShutDwnStart;

const
    ShutDownAlert = 42;                        {System error number of shutdown alert}
```

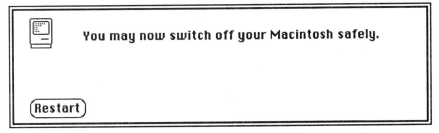

System shutdown alert

 Notes

1. ShutDwnStart restarts the system as if the power had been turned off and back on; ShutDwnPower shuts down the system without restarting.

2. On the Macintosh II (or on the Macintosh XL, née Lisa), ShutDwnPower actually turns off the power to the machine. On other models, it displays the system shutdown alert (see above), prompting the user to turn off the power manually.

3. These two routines correspond to the Finder's menu commands Restart and ShutDown, respectively.

4. Both routines perform any needed housekeeping to leave the system in an orderly, consistent state. All active drivers and desk accessories are given a "good-bye kiss" [III:3.1.2], the contents of the desk scrap are unloaded to the disk [I:7.4.4], and all mounted volumes are ejected and unmounted [II:8.1.3].

5. If several application programs are running under MultiFinder, each is sent the equivalent of a Quit command, allowing it to save files, if necessary, and exit in an orderly way.

6. If any application-defined shutdown procedures have been installed [2.1.6], they are executed at the requested times in the shutdown or restart sequence.

7. The trap macros for these routines expand to call the same machine-level trap, _Shutdown ($A895), after pushing an identifying routine selector (see table below) onto the stack.

Assembly Language Information

Trap macros and routine selectors:

(Pascal) Routine name	(Assembly) Trap macro	Trap word	Routine selector
ShutDwnPower	_SDPowerOff	$A895	1
ShutDwnStart	_SDRestart	$A895	2

Assembly-language constant:

Name	Value	Meaning
ShutDownAlert	42	System error number of shutdown alert

2.1.6   Shutdown Procedures

Definitions

```
procedure ShutDwnInstall
          (shutDownProc : ProcPtr;        {Shutdown procedure to install}
           whenToCall   : INTEGER);       {When should procedure be called?}

procedure ShutDwnRemove
          (shutDownProc : ProcPtr);       {Shutdown procedure to remove}

const
   SDOnPowerOff     = 1;                  {Call procedure before power-off}
   SDOnRestart      = 2;                  {Call procedure before restart}
   SDRestartOrPower = 3;                  {Call procedure before power-off or restart}
   SDOnUnmount      = 4;                  {Call procedure before unmounting volumes}
   SDOnDrivers      = 8;                  {Call procedure before closing drivers}
```

Notes

1. ShutDwnInstall installs an application-defined *shutdown procedure* to be called as part of the system shutdown or restart sequence [2.1.5]. ShutDwnRemove removes a previously installed shutdown procedure.

2. The shutdown procedure should accept no parameters and return no results.

3. The whenToCall parameter specifies the point in the shutdown sequence at which the procedure is to be called. Flag bits within this number denote various possible execution times:

   - before issuing good-bye kisses to active drivers and desk accessories

   - after closing drivers and before unmounting volumes

   - after unmounting volumes and before restarting the system

   - after unmounting volumes and before shutting down the system

4. The constants denoting these flag bits (SDOnDrivers, SDOnUnmount, SDOnRestart, SDOnPowerOff) can be added together to produce any needed combination of execution times. In particular, the predefined constant SDRestartOrPower represents the combination of SDOn-Restart and SDOnPowerOff, calling for execution after unmounting all online volumes during both restart and shutdown sequences.

5. The trap macros for these routines expand to call the same machine-level trap, _Shutdown ($A895), after pushing an identifying routine selector (see table below) onto the stack.

Assembly Language Information

Trap macros and routine selectors:

(Pascal) Routine name	(Assembly) Trap macro	Trap word	Routine selector
ShutDwnInstall	_SDInstall	$A895	3
ShutDwnRemove	_SDRemove	$A895	4

Assembly-language constants:

Name	Value	Meaning
SDOnPowerOff	1	Call procedure before power-off
SDOnRestart	2	Call procedure before restart
SDRestartOrPower	3	Call procedure before power-off or restart
SDOnUnmount	4	Call procedure before un-mounting volumes
SDOnDrivers	8	Call procedure before closing drivers

2.2   Memory

2.2.1   Memory Layout

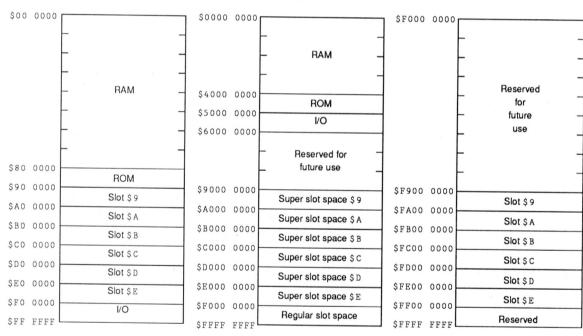

Macintosh II 24-bit
memory layout

Macintosh II 32-bit
memory layout

Macintosh II 32-bit
regular slot space

Notes

1. Earlier models of Macintosh, based on the MC68000 processor, are limited to 24-bit addresses, for a maximum address space of 16 megabytes (2^{24} = 16,777,216 bytes). The MC68020 and MC68030 processors, used in the Macintosh II and other advanced models, support full 32-bit addressing and can thus address a total space of 4 gigabytes (2^{32} = 4,294,967,296 bytes). Such models are capable of operating in either 24- or 32-bit mode.

2. In 24-bit mode, the high-order byte of each 32-bit address is ignored. The remaining 24 bits are then mapped by the memory management unit (MMU) into an equivalent 32-bit physical memory address.

3. The utility routines `GetMMUMode` and `SwapMMUMode` [2.1.3] read and change the current address mode.

4. For compatibility with earlier models, all Macintosh system software is designed to use 24-bit addresses. Models with a choice of address modes are automatically started up in 24-bit mode, and application programs ordinarily run in this mode.

5. 32-bit mode is intended mainly for use by slot-based expansion cards needing more memory than the 1 megabyte allotted to them under the standard 24-bit memory layout. It is also used by A/UX, Apple's Macintosh version of the Unix operating system.

6. In 24-bit mode, 8 megabytes ($800000 bytes) of address space are reserved for RAM, from addresses $000000 to $7FFFFF. In 32-bit mode, 1 gigabyte is available for RAM, from $00000000 to $3FFFFFFF. The 24-bit RAM addresses map into the first 8 megabytes of this space ($00000000 to $007FFFFF).

7. If less than the maximum amount of RAM is actually installed, some of the high-order address bits are ignored, causing the existing memory locations to repeat cyclically throughout the logical address space. For example, on a machine with 1 megabyte ($100000 bytes) of physical RAM, addresses $012446, $112446, $212446, and so on, all refer to the same physical byte of memory.

8. The Macintosh II's 256-kilobyte ROM occupies addresses $800000 to $83FFFF in 24-bit mode, $40000000 to $4003FFFF in 32-bit mode. In all, 1 megabyte ($800000 to $8FFFFF) is reserved for ROM in 24-bit mode, 256 megabytes ($40000000 to $4FFFFFFF) in 32-bit mode.

9. The megabyte of address space from $F00000 to $FFFFFF in 24-bit mode ($50000000 to $5FFFFFFF in 32-bit mode) is reserved for *memory-mapped input/output*. This space is further subdivided among the various interface chips: the VIAs (Versatile Interface Adapters), SCC (Serial Communications Chip), SCSI (Small Computer

Standard Interface), ASC (Apple Sound Chip), and so forth. See the *Macintosh Family Hardware Reference* for further details.

10. Each of the Macintosh II's six expansion slots is identified by a one-digit hexadecimal slot number, from $9 to $E. In 24-bit mode, all addresses beginning with that digit are reserved for memory locations residing on an expansion card plugged into the slot. (For example, slot $B is allotted addresses from $B00000 to $BFFFFF.) This allows 1 megabyte of address space for each slot.

11. In 32-bit mode, each slot is assigned 16 megabytes of *regular slot space* and 256 megabytes of *super slot space*. For slot $B, for example, the regular slot space runs from $FB000000 to $FBFFFFFF and the super slot space from $B0000000 to $BFFFFFFF. The 1 megabyte allotted to the slot in 24-bit mode maps into the first megabyte of regular slot space in 32-bit mode (in this case, from $FB000000 to $FB0FFFFF).

2.2.2   Memory Allocation

 Definitions

```
function NewHandleClear
         (blockSize : Size)          {Size of needed block in bytes}
            : Handle;                {Handle to new relocatable block}

function NewHandleSys
         (blockSize : Size)          {Size of needed block in bytes}
            : Handle;                {Handle to new relocatable block}

function NewHandleSysClear
         (blockSize : Size)          {Size of needed block in bytes}
            : Handle;                {Handle to new relocatable block}

function NewPtrClear
         (blockSize : Size)          {Size of needed block in bytes}
            : Ptr;                   {Pointer to new nonrelocatable block}

function NewPtrSys
         (blockSize : Size)          {Size of needed block in bytes}
            : Ptr;                   {Pointer to new nonrelocatable block}

function NewPtrSysClear
         (blockSize : Size)          {Size of needed block in bytes}
            : Ptr;                   {Pointer to new nonrelocatable block}
```

Notes

1. These routines are newer, specialized versions of the more general memory allocation routines NewHandle and NewPtr [I:3.2.1].

2. NewHandleClear and NewPtrClear allocate a relocatable or nonrelocatable block, respectively, and clear its contents to all zeros. (The original NewHandle and NewPtr don't initialize the block's contents in any way.)

3. NewHandleSys and NewPtrSys allocate a block from the system heap. (NewHandle and NewPtr use whatever heap zone is current at the time, normally the application heap.)

4. NewHandleSysClear and NewPtrSysClear allocate a block from the system heap and clear its contents to all zeros.

5. The blockSize parameter gives the size of the needed block in bytes. The data type of this parameter, Size, is equivalent to a long integer [I:3.1.1].

6. The block allocated by NewHandleClear, NewHandleSys, or NewHandleSysClear is initially unlocked and unpurgeable.

7. If necessary, all of these routines may compact the heap or purge blocks from it. NewHandleClear and NewPtrClear may also expand the application heap to create more space; the system heap can never be expanded.

8. Like all memory management routines, these post a result code to report the success or failure of the operation. In Pascal, you can check the result code by calling the Toolbox routine MemError [I:3.1.2] immediately after the allocation request; in assembly language, the result code is found in register D0 on return from the allocation call.

9. If a block of the requested size can't be allocated, all of these routines post the error code MemFullErr [I:3.1.2] and return a NIL handle or pointer.

10. At the machine level, these routines use the same traps as the original versions, _NewHandle and _NewPtr. Bit 9 of the trap word specifies that the new block is to be cleared to zeros on allocation; bit 10 forces allocation from the system heap. The trap macros for the new routines expand to call the original traps, setting these flag bits as required for the given combination of attributes.

Assembly Language Information

Trap macros:

(Pascal) Routine name	(Assembly) Trap macro	Trap word
NewHandleClear	_NewHandleClear	$A322
NewHandleSys	_NewHandleSys	$A522
NewHandleSysClear	_NewHandleSysClear	$A722
NewPtrClear	_NewPtrClear	$A31E
NewPtrSys	_NewPtrSys	$A51E
NewPtrSysClear	_NewPtrSysClear	$A71E

Register usage:

Routine	Register	Contents
NewHandleClear	D0.L (in)	blockSize
	A0.L (out)	function result
	D0.W (out)	result code
NewHandleSys	D0.L (in)	blockSize
	A0.L (out)	function result
	D0.W (out)	result code
NewHandleSysClear	D0.L (in)	blockSize
	A0.L (out)	function result
	D0.W (out)	result code
NewPtrClear	D0.L (in)	blockSize
	A0.L (out)	function result
	D0.W (out)	result code
NewPtrSys	D0.L (in)	blockSize
	A0.L (out)	function result
	D0.W (out)	result code
NewPtrSysClear	D0.L (in)	blockSize
	A0.L (out)	function result
	D0.W (out)	result code

2.2.3   Temporary Allocation

 Definitions

```
function  MFTempNewHandle
          (blockSize      : Size;        {Size of needed block in bytes}
           var resultCode : OSErr)       {Result code}
          : Handle;                      {Handle to temporary relocatable block}

procedure MFTempDisposHandle
          (theHandle      : Handle;      {Handle to temporary block to be deallocated}
           var resultCode : OSErr);      {Result code}

procedure MFTempHLock
          (theHandle      : Handle;      {Handle to temporary block to be locked}
           var resultCode : OSErr);      {Result code}

procedure MFTempHUnlock
          (theHandle      : Handle;      {Handle to temporary block to be unlocked}
           var resultCode : OSErr);      {Result code}
```

 Notes

1. These routines allocate and manipulate temporary memory blocks for transient uses such as file buffers and parameter blocks.

2. The letters MF stand for MultiFinder, which provides a limited amount of memory space for such purposes.

3. MFTempNewHandle allocates a relocatable temporary block; MFTempDisposHandle releases one. There are no nonrelocatable temporary blocks.

4. The blockSize parameter gives the size of the needed block in bytes. The data type of this parameter, Size, is equivalent to a long integer [I:3.1.1].

5. If a block of the requested size can't be allocated, MFTempNewHandle returns the error code MemFullErr [I:3.1.2] in its variable parameter resultCode, with a NIL handle for the function result.

6. Your program should use the temporary block and then release it immediately, before the next call to WaitNextEvent [3.1.3].

7. MFTempHLock locks a temporary block; MFTempHUnlock unlocks it.

8. Temporary blocks are initially unlocked and are permanently unpurgeable.

9. Blocks allocated with MFTempNewHandle do not reside in the same heap as those allocated with NewHandle [I:3.2.1] or related allocation calls [2.2.2]. Never attempt to apply ordinary memory-management operations to them, such as GetHandleSize, SetHandleSize [I:3.2.3], HLock, HUnlock, HPurge, HNoPurge [I:3.2.4], MoveHHi [I:3.2.5], EmptyHandle, ReallocHandle [I:3.3.3], or RecoverHandle [I:3.2.1]. Also beware of passing such blocks to Toolbox routines that may apply any of these operations to them indirectly.

10. Always use MFTempDisposHandle to release temporary blocks and DisposHandle [I:3.2.1] for ordinary blocks, never the other way around. Similarly, use MFTempHLock and MFTempHUnlock only on temporary blocks and HLock and HUnlock [I:3.2.4] only on ordinary ones.

11. At the machine level, all operations involving temporary memory are performed by a single general-purpose trap, _OSDispatch ($A88F). The trap macros all expand to call this same trap, after pushing an identifying routine selector (see table below) onto the stack.

12. These operations pass their parameters and return their results on the stack, not in registers like their counterparts for ordinary memory management [I:3.2.1, I:3.2.2, I:3.2.4, 2.2.2].

Assembly Language Information

Trap macros and routine selectors:

(Pascal) Routine name	(Assembly) Trap macro	Trap word	Routine selector
MFTempNewHandle	_MFTempNewHandle	$A88F	29
MFTempDisposHandle	_MFTempDisposHandle	$A88F	32
MFTempHLock	_MFTempHLock	$A88F	30
MFTempHUnlock	_MFTempHUnlock	$A88F	31

2.2.4   Available Temporary Space

Definitions

```
function MFFreeMem
            : LONGINT;              {Total bytes available for temporary allocation}
function MFMaxMem
            (var growBytes : Size)  {Returns maximum bytes for temporary expansion}
            : Size;                 {Size of largest available temporary block}

function MFTopMem
            : Ptr;                  {Pointer to end of memory}
```

Notes

1. These routines return information on the amount of memory space available for temporary allocation [2.2.3].

2. The letters `MF` stand for MultiFinder, which provides a limited amount of memory space for such purposes.

3. `MFFreeMem` returns the total number of free bytes available for temporary allocation.

4. `MFMaxMem` returns the size in bytes of the largest free block available for temporary allocation, after first compacting the entire temporary heap.

5. `MFTopMem` returns a pointer to the first address beyond the end of physical RAM memory (*not* the last address actually existing in memory). For example, in a 4-megabyte Macintosh II, whose last byte of physical memory is at address $3FFFFF, `MFTopMem` returns a pointer to address $400000.

6. The pointer returned by `MFTopMem` is to the end of the machine's total physical memory, not just that of the running program's MultiFinder partition.

7. At the machine level, all operations involving temporary memory are performed by a single general-purpose trap, `_OSDispatch` ($A88F). The trap macros all expand to call this same trap, after pushing an identifying routine selector (see table below) onto the stack.

8. These operations pass their parameters and return their results on the stack, not in registers like their counterparts for ordinary memory management [I:3.3.1, I:3.3.2, I:3.1.3].

Assembly Language Information

Trap macros and routine selectors:

(Pascal) Routine name	(Assembly) Trap macro	Trap word	Routine selector
MFFreeMem	_MFFreeMem	$A88F	24
MFTopMem	_MFTopMem	$A88F	22
MFMaxMem	_MFMaxMem	$A88F	21

2.3 Resources

2.3.1 Resource Types

Standard resource types:

Resource Type	Description	See Section
'PAT '	Bit pattern	[I:5.5.1]
'PAT#'	Bit pattern list	[I:5.5.2]
'ppat'	Pixel pattern	[IV:5.6.1]
'ppt#'	Pixel pattern list	
'bmap'	Bit map	
'PICT'	QuickDraw picture	[I:5.5.5]
'ICON'	Icon	[I:5.5.3]
'ICN#'	Icon list	[I:5.5.4]
'SICN'	Small icon	[IV:3.3.1]
'cicn'	Color icon	[IV:6.7.1]
'TEXT'	Any text	[I:8.4.1]
'STR '	Pascal-format string	[I:8.4.2]
'STR#'	String list	[I:8.4.3]
'FONT'	Font	[I:8.4.5]
'NFNT'	Non-menu font	[I:8.4.5]
'FWID'	Font width table	[I:8.4.6]
'FRSV'	Reserved font list	[I:8.4.7]
'FOND'	Font family definition	

Resource Type	Description	See Section
'CURS'	Cursor	[II:2.9.1]
'crsr'	Color cursor	[IV:6.7.2]
'KMAP'	Key code map	
'KCHR'	Character code map	
'KSWP'	Keyboard script table	
'FKEY'	Low-level keyboard routine	[II:2.9.2, III:6.3.1]
'WIND'	Window template	[II:3.7.1]
'MENU'	Menu	[II:4.8.1]
'MBAR'	Menu bar	[II:4.8.2]
'CNTL'	Control template	[II:6.6.1]
'ALRT'	Alert template	[II:7.6.1]
'DLOG'	Dialog template	[II:7.6.2]
'DITL'	Dialog or alert item list	[II:7.6.3]
'WDEF'	Window definition function	[III:2.5.1]
'CDEF'	Control definition function	[III:2.5.2]
'MDEF'	Menu definition procedure	[III:2.5.3]
'MBDF'	Menu bar definition function	
'LDEF'	List definition procedure	
'CODE'	Code segment	[I:7.5.1]
'PACK'	Package	[I:7.5.2]
'DRVR'	Device driver (including desk accessories)	[III:3.3.1, I:7.5.5]
'SERD'	Serial driver	
'FMTR'	Disk formatting code	
'PREC'	Print record	[III:4.6.1]
'PDEF'	Printing code	[III:4.6.2]
'FREF'	Finder file reference	[I:7.5.3]
'BNDL'	Finder bundle	[I:7.5.4]
'SIZE'	Partition size (MultiFinder)	[IV:3.3.2]
'mstr'	MultiFinder string	[IV:3.3.4]
'mst#'	MultiFinder string list	[IV:3.3.4]
'MACS'	Macintosh system autograph	
'vers'	Software version ID	
'scrn'	Screen configuration	

Resource Type	Description	See Section
`'clut'`	Color lookup table	[IV:4.7.1]
`'pltt'`	Color palette	[IV:4.7.2]
`'gama'`	Color correction table	
`'mitq'`	Color inverse table, memory requirements	
`'fctb'`	Font color table	
`'wctb'`	Window color table	[IV:6.7.3]
`'cctb'`	Control color table	[IV:6.7.4]
`'mctb'`	Menu color table	[IV:6.7.7]
`'actb'`	Alert color table	[IV:6.7.3]
`'dctb'`	Dialog color table	[IV:6.7.3]
`'ictb'`	Dialog item color table	[IV:6.7.5]
`'snth'`	Sound synthesizer	
`'snd '`	Sound definition	
`'INIT'`	Initialization resource	[I:8.4.4]
`'DSAT'`	"Dire straits" alert table	
`'PTCH'`	System patch code	
`'ptch'`	System patch	
`'boot'`	Boot blocks	
`'lmem'`	Low-memory globals	
`'ROvr'`	ROM override code	
`'ROv#'`	ROM override list	
`'CACH'`	RAM cache code	
`'ADBS'`	Apple Desktop Bus service routine	
`'MMAP'`	Mouse tracking code	
`'mcky'`	Mouse tracking data	
`'INTL'`	International localization resource	
`'itl0'`	International localization, date and time formats	
`'itl1'`	International localization, day and month names	
`'itl2'`	International localization, sort hooks	
`'itlb'`	International localization, script bundles	
`'itlc'`	International localization, script configuration	
`'NBPC'`	Name-Binding Protocol code (AppleTalk)	
`'PAPA'`	Printer Access Protocol address (AppleTalk)	
`'mppc'`	Macintosh Packet Protocol configuration (AppleTalk)	
`'atpl'`	AppleTalk private resource	

Resource Type	Description	See Section
'PRES'	Printer resource (Chooser)	
'PRER'	Printer resource, remote (Chooser)	
'RDEV'	Remote device (Chooser)	
'clst'	Cached icon list (Chooser, Control Panel)	
'cdev'	Control Panel device	
'ctab'	Control Panel device table	
'mach'	Machine compatibility list (Control Panel)	
'nrct'	Rectangle list (Control Panel)	
'KCAP'	Keyboard layout (Key Caps)	
'INT#'	Integer list (Find File)	
'APPL'	Application table (Finder)	
'FDIR'	Finder directory	
'FOBJ'	Finder object	
'FCMT'	Finder comment	
'LAYO'	Folder layout (Finder)	
'MINI'	MiniFinder resource	
'FBTN'	File button (MiniFinder)	
'insc'	Installer script	
'TMPL'	Resource type template (ResEdit)	

Notes

1. The table above supersedes the one given in [I:6.1.1] and lists all known resource types used by the Toolbox and other Macintosh system software at the time of publication.

2. New resource types are continually being invented, so this list should not be considered final or exhaustive.

3. Resource types that you invent for your own use must not conflict with those shown in the table.

4. All type names consisting entirely of lowercase letters (such as 'blob') are reserved by Apple for the private use of the Toolbox. Never give any of your own resource types a name of this form.

5. Resource types for which no section number is given in the table are not covered in this series of books. Most of these are private to the Toolbox and are of no concern to the application programmer. Some of them are described in *Inside Macintosh;* others are so private that they are not documented even there.

2.3.2   ROM-Based Resources

 Definitions

```
function RGetResource
         (rsrcType : ResType;        {Resource type}
          rsrcID   : INTEGER)        {Resource ID}
          : Handle;                  {Handle to resource}
```

Macintosh II ROM-based resources:

Resource Type	Resource ID	Description
'CURS'	1*	I-beam cursor [II:2.5.2, II:2.9.1]
	2*	Cross cursor [II:2.5.2, II:2.9.1]
	3*	Plus-sign cursor [II:2.5.2, II:2.9.1]
	4*	Wristwatch cursor [II:2.5.2, II:2.9.1]
'KMAP'	0*	Standard key code map
'KCHR'	0	Standard character code map
'FONT'	0*	Name of system font [I:8.2.1, I:8.4.5]
	12*	System font (12-point Chicago) [I:8.2.1, I:8.4.5]
	384	Name of Geneva font [I:8.2.1, I:8.4.5]
	393*	9-point Geneva font [I:8.2.1, I:8.4.5]
	396*	12-point Geneva font [I:8.2.1, I:8.4.5]
	512	Name of Monaco font [I:8.2.1, I:8.4.5]
	521*	12-point Monaco font [I:8.2.1, I:8.4.5]
'NFNT'	2	System font (12-point Chicago), 4 bits deep
	3	System font (12-point Chicago), 8 bits deep
	34	9-point Geneva font, 4 bits deep

Resource Type	Resource ID	Description
'PACK'	4*	Floating-Point Arithmetic Package [I:7.2.1, I:7.5.2]
	5*	Transcendental Functions Package [I:7.2.1, I:7.5.2]
	7*	Binary/Decimal Conversion Package [I:7.2.1, I:7.5.2]
'DRVR'	3*	Sound driver (.Sound) [III:3.3.1, I:7.5.5]
	4*	Disk driver (.Sony) [III:3.3.1, I:7.5.5]
	9*	AppleTalk driver, Macintosh Packet Protocol (.MPP) [III:3.3.1, I:7.5.5]
	10*	AppleTalk driver, AppleTalk Transaction Protocol (.ATP) [III:3.3.1, I:7.5.5]
	40*	AppleTalk driver, Extended Protocol Package (.XPP) [III:3.3.1, I:7.5.5]
'SERD'	0*	Serial drivers (.AIn, .AOut, .BIn, .BOut) [III:3.3.1, I:7.5.5]
'WDEF'	0*	Definition function for document windows [III:2.5.1]
	1*	Definition function for accessory windows [III:2.5.1]
'CDEF'	0*	Definition function for standard buttons [III:2.5.2]
	1*	Definition function for scroll bars [III:2.5.2]
'MDEF'	0*	Definition procedure for text menus [III:2.5.3]
'MBDF'	0*	Standard menu bar definition procedure
'clut'	1	Standard color table, 1 bit deep [IV:4.7.1]
	2	Standard color table, 2 bits deep [IV:4.7.1]
	4	Standard color table, 4 bits deep [IV:4.7.1]
	8	Standard color table, 8 bits deep [IV:4.7.1]
	127	Standard color table, classic color model [IV:4.7.1]
'gama'	0	Standard color correction table
'mitq'	0	Standard color inverse table memory requirements
'wctb'	0	Color table for standard windows [IV:6.7.3]
'cctb'	0	Color table for standard controls [IV:6.7.4]
'snd '	1	Standard system beep

Notes

1. The table above lists all system resources that are built into the 256K Macintosh II ROM (version $78). Those marked with an asterisk (*) are also included in the Macintosh SE ROM (version $76). See [I:6.6.3] for the contents of the 128K ROM (version $75) used in the Macintosh Plus and Macintosh 512Ke.

2. In searching for a requested resource, those in ROM are normally searched first. If the needed resource is not found there, the search then proceeds through the chain of open resource files in reverse chronological order, starting with the current resource file [I:6.2.2] and ending with the System file.

3. RGetResource searches the ROM-based resources last instead of first, only *after* exhausting the chain of open resource files without success. This allows disk-based resource files (in particular, the application resource file) to override ROM-based resources with replacement versions of their own.

4. In all other respects, RGetResource behaves exactly the same as the older routine GetResource [I:6.3.1].

Assembly Language Information

Trap macro:

(Pascal) Routine name	(Assembly) Trap macro	Trap word
RGetResource	_RGetResource	$A80C

2.4 Arithmetic

2.4.1   Small Fractions

Definitions

```
type
    SmallFract = INTEGER:

const
    MaxSmallFract = $0000FFFF:              {Largest possible small fraction}

function Fix2SmallFract
            (theNumber : Fixed)             {Fixed-point number to be converted}
                : SmallFract:               {Equivalent small fraction}

function SmallFract2Fix
            (theNumber : SmallFract)        {Small fraction to be converted}
                : Fixed:                    {Equivalent fixed-point number}
```

Notes

1. Type `SmallFract` represents a 16-bit fractional value between 0 and 1, with a binary point preceding the first bit. It is equivalent to the low-order (fractional) half of a fixed-point number of type `Fixed` [I:2.3.1].

2. The value of a small fraction is equivalent to that of the corresponding *unsigned* integer divided by 65536 (2^{16}).

3. Small fractions are used mainly for expressing the components of color values in CMY, HSV, and HSL representations [4.2.1].

4. The constant `MaxSmallFract` represents the largest possible value expressible as a small fraction, defined as a *long* integer for use in combination with full fixed-point numbers. Its value is equivalent to 65535 divided by 65536, or 0.999984741.

5. `Fix2SmallFract` and `SmallFract2Fix` convert between small fractions and fixed-point numbers.

6. These routines are implemented as part of the Color Picker Package, and are called at the machine level via the package trap `_Pack12` [I:7.2.1]. The trap macros expand to call this trap after pushing an identifying routine selector (see table below) onto the stack.

Assembly Language Information

Trap macros and routine selectors:

(Pascal) Routine name	(Assembly) Trap macro	Trap word	Routine selector
Fix2SmallFract	_Fix2SmallFract	$A82E	1
SmallFract2Fix	_SmallFract2Fix	$A82E	2

Assembly-language constant:

Name	Value	Meaning
MaxSmallFract	$0000FFFF	Largest possible small fraction

CHAPTER

Going for the Juggler

One of the more frustrating limitations in the original Macintosh software architecture was that only one application program could be run at a time. If you were using your word processor, say, and needed your graphics editor to create an illustration, you had to save your document, quit from the word processor to the Finder, start up the graphics editor, draw the illustration, save it to a disk file, select and copy it to the Clipboard, quit from the graphics editor back to the Finder, start up the word processor, reload your document, and paste in the illustration. All told, this process required four program startup cycles (counting the Finder twice); if you then decided to change the illustration, you had to go through the whole exercise all over again. Especially at the slow transfer rates of the original floppy-disk drives, this added up to a lot of finger-drumming time while waiting for programs to load from the disk.

The one limited form of program concurrency available in those early days was that offered by desk accessories, which could share the screen more or less harmoniously with any other program you happened to be running. Software developers responded with a proliferation of "mini-applications"—spreadsheets, text editors, graphics programs, terminal emulators—masquerading as lowly desk accessories. Such creations were certainly a tribute to the programmers' imagination and ingenuity, but desk accessories were really never intended for such ambitious purposes. What was needed was a way to run two or more full-scale application programs at once instead of trying to squeeze one of them into the narrow confines of a desk accessory.

Flying to the rescue with his wizard's wand at the ready came the illustrious software magician and Apple Hero, Andy Hertzfeld. Already renowned as the father of the original Toolbox, Andy bestowed yet another gift on the grateful Macintosh community in the form of Switcher, an ingeniously improvised solution to the concurrency problem. In a dazzling display of prestidigitation and legerdemain, Switcher allowed several programs to reside in memory simultaneously, giving each the illusion of having the entire system to itself. Using Switcher, you could keep that word processor and graphics editor (as well as the Finder itself) side by side in memory, switching quickly and easily from one to another with a click of the mouse.

One drawback to Switcher, though, was that it allowed programs to share the system but not the screen. Each program maintained its own independent screen display, with its own window list, menu bar, and so on. When the user switched control from one program to another, the newly activated program would take over the entire screen, displaying only its own windows and not those of the other programs. Although Switcher was a huge improvement on what had gone before, it still didn't quite have the smooth, natural "look and feel" that we've come to expect from our Macintosh software.

This time it was Apple itself that provided the solution with a new operating environment for Macintosh software, known while under development by the internal code name Juggler for its acrobatic ability to keep several balls in the air at once. Based on many of the same ideas that Andy first pioneered in Switcher, Juggler offered a similar model for concurrent program operation, but repackaged to present a more elegant, Macintosh-like appearance to the user. This system, renamed at the time of its official product release, became what we now know as MultiFinder.

Each program running under MultiFinder maintains its own independent window list, just as before. When the user activates a program, all of its windows come to the front of the screen as a single "layer," overlaying those of all other programs. The other programs' windows remain on the screen, however, and can still be seen peeking through wherever they aren't obscured by those of the active program. Clicking the mouse inside one of these other windows switches control to the program it belongs to and brings *that* program's layer of windows (including the one where the mouse was clicked) to the front. This allows the user to arrange windows freely on the screen and use them to "navigate" from one program to another in a natural, intuitive way.

Like every other significant advance in the Macintosh system software, MultiFinder is carefully designed for backward compatibility, so that programs written before its introduction can continue to work correctly without modification. On the other hand, programs written with MultiFinder in mind can use the techniques discussed in this chapter to operate more effectively in the new environment.

Memory Partitions

MultiFinder works by dividing the system's memory into separate *partitions*, one for each active application program. A program can specify the size of its partition by including a resource of type 'SIZE' [3.3.2] in its application resource file. The size resource actually contains two different size specifications—a *preferred memory size* and a *minimum memory size*—as well as a flag word [3.3.3] defining various other MultiFinder-related properties. (In particular, bit 11 of the flag word is the *MultiFinder-aware bit*, indicating that the program is prepared to take full advantage of MultiFinder's capabilities. A program that doesn't set this bit can still run properly under MultiFinder, but will be unable to use some of its more advanced features.)

The size resource defining a program's preferred and minimum memory sizes always has a resource ID of -1. When the program is started up, MultiFinder will attempt to assign it a partition of the preferred size, if possible. If this amount of space can't be found, the program will receive the largest partition currently available. If even the minimum memory requirement can't be satisfied, MultiFinder will simply post an alert message on the screen and refuse to run the program.

The user can choose to change a program's partition size (before starting the program, not after it's already running) by displaying its information window with the Finder's Get Info command and typing the new setting into the box labeled Application Memory Size (see Figure 3–1). This affects the preferred size only; the minimum size cannot be changed. The box initially shows the program's own preferred memory size, taken from its size resource number -1; this value is also displayed as static text above the box for the user's reference. If the user types in a new value, it will be stored in the program's application resource file in a separate size resource with an ID of 0; if present, this resource takes precedence over number -1, which preserves the program's original size preference unchanged. Programs with no size resource at all (such as those that predate the introduction of MultiFinder) are given a standard partition size of 384K by default.

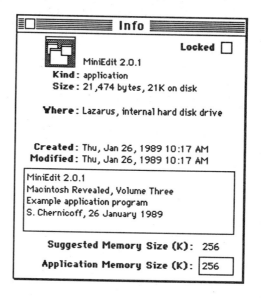

Figure 3–1 Program information window

Within its memory partition, each program has its own independent stack, application heap, and application global space ("A5 world"). Each program also has its own copy of the low-memory area where the Toolbox keeps its global variables, dispatch table, and so forth, so that one program's changes in low memory don't affect the operation of any other program. MultiFinder keeps careful track of all these memory areas and swaps them in and out as needed, so that programs won't trip over each other as control switches from one to another.

Foreground and Background

Although any number of programs can be running at once under MultiFinder (subject to the available memory), only one at a time can be in active control of the system. This active program is said to be running in the *foreground*, with all other programs in the *background*. Only the foreground program can respond to the user's mouse clicks and keystrokes. As described earlier, the foreground program's windows always appear frontmost on the screen, in front of those of all other programs. Clicking the mouse in any window belonging to another program brings all of that program's windows forward on the screen together. The program thus activated becomes the new foreground program, assuming control of the system and sending the previous program into the background.

The current foreground program is identified by a small copy of its Finder icon, reduced to half-size and displayed at the right-hand end of the menu bar. Clicking the mouse repeatedly on this menu-bar icon cycles control through all programs currently in memory, bringing each one in turn to the foreground. MultiFinder also adds the names of all available programs to the Apple menu, (along with the usual list of desk accessories), with a check mark next to the program currently in the foreground. This gives the user a choice of three ways to move from one program to another:

- Click the mouse in an exposed part of any window belonging to the desired program.
- Click repeatedly on the icon at the right of the menu bar until the desired program comes to the foreground.
- Pull down and choose the desired program from the Apple menu.

The transition from foreground to background occurs when a program asks the Toolbox for the next event to process. Old-fashioned programs that know not MultiFinder do this in the old, familiar way, by calling `GetNextEvent` [II:2.2.1]. If the user has taken any of the actions listed above to switch to another program, MultiFinder will *suspend* the current program at the point of the call, moving it to the background and transferring control to the one the user has requested. When the user eventually brings the original program back to the foreground, control will return from the `GetNextEvent` call and the program's execution will be *resumed* from that point. From the program's point of view, everything looks perfectly normal: the only way it can tell that anything unusual has happened is to call `TickCount` [II:2.7.1] before and after the `GetNextEvent` call and notice that an inordinate interval has elapsed on the system clock.

Out of respect for the preemptive nature of modal dialog windows, MultiFinder will not move a program to the background while it has such a window frontmost on the screen. MultiFinder recognizes modal dialogs by their window type: any window whose type is DBoxProc [II:3.2.2] (or Plain-DBoxProc or AltDBoxProc) is assumed to be a modal dialog. To keep MultiFinder from getting confused, you should never use these window types for anything other than modal dialogs.

Background Processing

Programs wise to the ways of MultiFinder, however, can take advantage of it to make more efficient use of the system. One of the new capabilities MultiFinder offers is that of executing a program in the background, while some other program retains nominal control of the system. To be eligible for such background processing, a program must have a size resource [3.3.2] with the *can-background bit* (bit 12) set in the resource's flag word [3.3.3]. The classic example of background processing is printing a document: once the operation is started, the user can switch control to some other program and continue to do useful work in the foreground while the original program completes the printing operation in the background.

It's even possible to write a program that runs *only* in the background and can never assume full control of the system. Bit 10 in the size resource's flag word [3.3.3] is the *background-only* bit: a program with this bit set has no user interface of its own and can operate only as an "embedded service" or "faceless background task" behind another program running in the foreground. An example might be a telecommunications program that monitors the network for incoming transmissions and buffers them to a disk file for later processing by some other program.

The can-background bit requests the opportunity to do background processing, but does not guarantee it. To receive any processor time while in the background, the program must depend on the kindness of strangers. Specifically, the foreground program running in front of it must use the new routine `WaitNextEvent` [3.1.3] to retrieve its events instead of the old standby `GetNextEvent` [II:2.2.1]. If there is no event of interest to report to the active program, `WaitNextEvent` will look for a background program able to make constructive use of the available idle time. If there is such a program, `WaitNextEvent` will suspend the foreground program that called it and resume the one requesting background time, sending it a null event as a signal to perform one cycle of its background processing task. (A program printing in the background, for instance, might use this occasion to print one line of its document.)

Notice, though, that the suspended foreground program does *not* give up active control of the system. All user events (mouse clicks and keystrokes) are still considered to be directed to the foreground program; programs running in the background can never receive such events. When a user event occurs, MultiFinder will duly report it to the foreground program by resuming the program's execution from the point of its last `WaitNextEvent` call, returning the user event as the result of the call. This, however, requires the cooperation of the background program, which in turn must call `WaitNextEvent` periodically to allow control to pass back to the foreground when necessary. If the foreground program doesn't call `WaitNextEvent` often enough, the background program won't get any processor time; if the background program doesn't call it often enough, the foreground program will appear sluggish and unresponsive to the user's actions. Apple likes to refer to this relationship of reciprocal dependence and shared responsibility as "cooperative multitasking."

Keep in mind that your program may sometimes be run on older systems that aren't equipped with MultiFinder. To ensure compatibility, you must check the dispatch table (using the technique discussed in Chapter 2) to make sure the `WaitNext-Event` trap is available before attempting to use it. If it isn't, you'll have to settle for an old-fashioned `GetNextEvent` call instead. Note, however, that `WaitNextEvent` is guaranteed to be available, with or without MultiFinder itself, under all versions of the `System` file beginning with 6.0. If your program depends for its operation on any other system feature requiring version 6.0 or later, you must of course check the current system version with `SysEnvirons` [2.1.1] and, if it isn't recent

---

enough, post an informative alert message (`Sorry, this program requires System version 6.0 or later`) and exit. Assuming the system version is acceptable, however, you may as well just assume the availability of `WaitNextEvent` without explicitly checking for it.

Even without a user event to respond to, the foreground program may still need to regain control periodically for some other task of its own—for instance, to blink the insertion point in a text document by calling `TEIdle` [II:5.4.3]. To accommodate this, `Wait-NextEvent` allows the program to request a "wakeup call" when it yields to another program for background processing. The routine's `sleepTicks` parameter [3.1.3] specifies the maximum length of time, in ticks (sixtieths of a second), for which the program is willing to relinquish control. If no user event occurs within this period, the program will be awakened with a null event so it can do its idle-time processing; if it wishes, it can then yield control again with another call to `WaitNextEvent`. Programs running in the background can use the `sleepTicks` parameter, too: for example, the telecommunications program we mentioned earlier might need to regain control no less than once per second (60 ticks) to prevent a network connection from timing out. A `sleepTicks` value of 0 requests control back as soon as possible, making `WaitNextEvent` equivalent to the old event-retrieval routine `GetNextEvent` [II:2.2.1].

Suspend and Resume Events

Programs written without any knowledge of MultiFinder can never do background processing, since they have no size resource in which to set the "can-background" flag. When such a program is switched to the background, it simply hangs in a state of suspension until it returns to the foreground, at which point it resumes execution as if nothing had happened. As we mentioned earlier, the only way for the program even to know that it has been suspended and resumed is to read the system clock and notice that an unexpectedly long time interval has elapsed—something a program ignorant of MultiFinder would have no reason to do.

For those programs able to use the information, however, MultiFinder does provide a mechanism for tracking the transitions between foreground and background. It does this by means of two new event types: *suspend events* to inform the program that it's going from the foreground to the background and *resume events* when it comes back from the background to the foreground. Such events are generated only if bit 14 (the *accept-suspend/resume bit*) is set in the flag word of the program's size resource [3.3.3]. There's also another new type of event, the *mouse-moved event*, which we'll be discussing in a later section.

All such *MultiFinder events* are identified by the type code App4Evt [II:2.1.2] in the what field of the event record [II:2.1.1]. (This was originally one of the four *application event* types reserved for application programs to use for their own private purposes; it has now been appropriated for use by MultiFinder instead.) The event's message field [II:2.1.1] distinguishes one type of MultiFinder event from another. In both suspend and resume events, the first byte of the message [3.1.1] contains the hexadecimal value $01; the last bit of the message is 0 for a suspend event, 1 for a resume. Mouse-moved events have $FA in the first byte of the message field.

MultiFinder events are not queued like ordinary user events, so you can't selectively defer them by masking out type App4Evt in the mask parameter you supply to WaitNextEvent [3.1.3]. Your program will still be suspended or resumed on schedule— you just won't know when it happens.

Program 3–1 (DoMultiEvent) shows a new routine that we might add to our MiniEdit program to handle MultiFinder events. (To call this routine on receiving such an event, we would also have to add the new clause

```
App4Evt:
    DoMultiEvent;
```

to the case statement in our existing DoEvent routine, Program II:2–5.) DoMultiEvent extracts the type code from the first byte of the event's message field and uses it to dispatch control to a more specialized routine for each specific event type. We'll examine the routine for mouse-moved events later; the one for suspend and resume events, DoSuspRes (Program 3–2), simply tests the low-order bit of the event message and passes control to a still more specialized routine, `DoSuspend` (Program 3–3) or `DoResume` (Program 3–4), to do the actual work.

Program 3–1 Handle MultiFinder event

```
{   Global variable   }

var
   TheEvent : EventRecord;                       {Current event [II:2.1.1]}

procedure DoMultiEvent;

   {   Handle MultiFinder event.   }

   const
      typeMask     = $FF000000;      {Mask for extracting event type from message field}
      suspResEvt   = $01000000;      {Event type for suspend/resume events [3.1.1]}
      mouseMovedEvt = $FA000000;     {Event type for mouse-moved events [3.1.1]}

   var
      whichType : LONGINT;                       {Type code of MultiFinder event}

   begin  {DoMultiEvent}

      with TheEvent do
         whichType := BitAnd(message, typeMask); {Extract type code from event message
                                                  [I:2.2.2, II:2.1.1]}

      case whichType of

         suspResEvt:
            DoSuspRes;                           {Handle suspend/resume event [Prog. 3-2]}

         mouseMovedEvt:
            DoMouseMoved;                        {Handle mouse-moved event [Prog. 3-5]}

         otherwise
            {Do nothing}

         end {case whichType}

   end;    {DoMultiEvent}
```

Program 3-2 Handle suspend/resume event

```
{   Global  variable   }

var
   TheEvent : EventRecord;              {Current event [II:2.1.1]}

procedure DoSuspRes;

   {   Handle  suspend/resume  event.    }

   const
     suspResBit = 31;                   {Bit number for testing suspend/resume bit [3.1.1]}

   begin {DoSuspRes}

     with  TheEvent  do
       if  not  BitTst(@message,  suspResBit)  then  {Examine suspend/resume bit
                                                      [I:2.2.1, II:2.1.1]}
         DoSuspend                       {Handle suspend event [Prog. 3-3]}
       else
         DoResume                        {Handle resume event [Prog. 3-4]}

   end;   {DoSuspRes}
```

Program 3-3 Handle suspend event

```
{   Global  variable   }

var
   InForeground : BOOLEAN;              {Currently operating in foreground?}

procedure DoSuspend;

   {   Handle  suspend  event.    }

   begin {DoSuspend}

     WriteDeskScrap;                     {Write Toolbox scrap to desk scrap [Prog. II:5–13]}

     if  TheWindow  <>  NIL  then        {Any windows on screen?}
       DeactWindow (TheWindow);          {Deactivate frontmost window [Prog. II:5–14]}
     {Hide  Clipboard  window,  if  necessary};

     InForeground := FALSE               {Set flag for background processing}

   end;   {DoSuspend}
```

A suspend event notifies you that you are about to be moved from the foreground to the background; the transition actually takes place the *next* time you request an event from the Toolbox. Program 3–3 (DoSuspend) shows how we could modify MiniEdit to respond to such an event. First we call the MiniEdit routine WriteDeskScrap (Program II:5–13), which transfers the contents of the internal Toolbox (TextEdit) scrap [II:5.5.4] to the global desk scrap [I:7.4]. This allows the user to cut or copy text in MiniEdit and paste it into another program after the MultiFinder transition. (Naturally, a program that maintains a private scrap of its own would transfer that to the desk scrap instead.)

Actually, as we'll see in Chapter 7, the latest versions of the TextEdit routines no longer maintain a separate internal scrap, but do their editing directly through the desk scrap itself. Nevertheless, you should still transfer the scrap on receiving a suspend event, for compatibility with older systems that still use the original version of TextEdit.

Moving to the background also entails deactivating our frontmost window, since some other program's windows will be moving ahead of it on the screen. However, if the MultiFinder-aware bit in our size resource is set, no separate deactivate event will be sent; so we have to remember to deactivate the window explicitly as part of our response to the suspend event itself. (MiniEdit originally handled both activate and deactivate events with a single routine, DoActivate, which appeared in Volume Two as Program II:5–14. It was split into two separate routines, ActWindow and DeactWindow, in the Version 2.0 revision of the program, listed in Appendix H of Volume Three.)

Apple's guidelines for MultiFinder behavior also recommend that programs that display a Clipboard window on the screen hide it while in the background. Although MiniEdit doesn't maintain such a window, this would be the place to hide it for those programs that do. Finally, programs that can receive events while in the background (that is, whose can-background bit is set) should use a Boolean variable to track whether they're currently operating in the foreground or the background. In MiniEdit's case, this variable is named InForeground; it is initially set to TRUE by the MiniEdit routine Initialize (Program II:2–6), then changed to FALSE on receiving a suspend event and back to TRUE on a resume event.

Program 3–4 Handle resume event

```
{   Global  variables    }

var
   TheEvent      : EventRecord;        {Current event [II:2.1.1]}
   InForeground : BOOLEAN;             {Currently operating in foreground?}

procedure DoResume;

   {   Handle  resume  event.    }

   const
      scrapDirtyBit = 30;              {Bit number for testing scrap-dirty bit [3.1.1]}

   begin  {DoResume}

      with  TheEvent  do
         if  BitTst(@message,  scrapDirtyBit)  then  {Has desk scrap changed? [I:2.2.1, II:2.1.1]}
            ReadDeskScrap;             {Read desk scrap to Toolbox scrap [Prog. II:5–12]}

      if  TheWindow  <>  NIL  then     {Any windows on screen?}
         ActWindow  (TheWindow);       {Activate frontmost window [Prog. II:5–14]}
      {Show Clipboard window, if necessary};

      InForeground  :=  TRUE           {Set flag for foreground processing}

   end;    {DoResume}
```

After receiving and responding to a suspend event, a program will be moved to the background when it calls WaitNextEvent again on the next pass of its main event loop. If the can-background bit is set in its size resource, the program may (though it is not guaranteed to) continue to receive null events, allowing it to do useful work while in the background. When the program is eventually returned to the foreground, it will be so informed with a resume event. Program 3–4 (DoResume) shows MiniEdit's response to such an event. Bit 1 (the second from the end) of the event's message field [II:2.1.1, 3.1.1] tells whether the contents of the global desk scrap have changed while we were asleep, so we can transfer them back to the Toolbox scrap if necessary. The rest of the routine is just the reverse of what we did in DoSuspend (Program 3–3) for a suspend event.

Cursor Control

As an added convenience for programs running under MultiFinder, it provides help in tracking the mouse's movements on the screen and adjusting the appearance of the cursor. Previously, you had to check the location of the mouse on every pass of your main event loop (as in MiniEdit's FixCursor routine, Program II:2–8) to find out what part of the screen it was in and set the cursor accordingly. With MultiFinder, instead of checking on every pass, you can arrange to be notified at just those times when the shape of the cursor actually needs to be changed.

The last parameter to WaitNextEvent [3.1.3] is a region of the screen within which the cursor is to keep its current appearance. Any time the mouse strays outside this region, MultiFinder will generate a *mouse-moved event* to allow you to adjust the cursor's appearance to match its new location. Like suspend and resume events, the mouse-moved event carries the type code App4Evt [II:2.1.2] in the what field [II:2.1.1] of its event record. It is distinguished from suspends and resumes by the value $FA (rather than $01, as in the other types) in the first byte of its message field [II:2.1.1, 3.1.1]. The rest of the message field is unused and reserved for future expansion.

The term *mouse-moved event* is slightly misleading, as it seems to imply that the event is generated only when the mouse actually crosses the boundary and leaves the designated region. In fact, such an event is generated *whenever* the mouse is outside the given region (and no higher-priority events are pending)—not just when it first moves outside the region. Unless you recalculate the mouse region to reflect its new location, you will keep getting the same mouse-moved event over and over again.

Program 3–5 (DoMouseMoved) shows an example of a routine MiniEdit could use to handle mouse-moved events. This routine is intended to be called from our new DoMultiEvent routine (Program 3–1), rather than from MainLoop (Program II:2–2). Besides setting the cursor to the appropriate shape, as in our original FixCursor routine (Program II:2–8), the new routine also calculates the region of the screen within which the cursor is to keep that shape:

- If the screen is empty, the cursor is the standard northwest arrow and its region is the "wide-open" region encompassing the entire QuickDraw coordinate plane.

- If one of MiniEdit's own windows is active and the cursor is inside its text rectangle, the cursor appears as an I-beam and its region is the text rectangle.

- If a MiniEdit window is active but the cursor is outside its text rectangle, the cursor is an arrow and its region is the wide-open region minus the window's text rectangle.

Program 3–5 Handle mouse-moved event

```
{   Global variables   }

var
  TheWindow  : WindowPtr;          {Pointer to currently active window [II:3.1.1]}
  TheText    : TEHandle;           {Handle to active window's edit record [II:5.1.1]}
  MouseRgn   : RgnHandle;          {Handle to current mouse region [I:4.1.5]}
  IBeam      : CursHandle;         {Handle to I-beam cursor [II:2.5.1]}


procedure DoMouseMoved;

  {   Handle mouse-moved event.   }

  var
    mousePoint  : Point;           {Current mouse position in window coordinates [I:4.1.1]}
    textRect    : Rect;            {Active window's text rectangle [I:4.1.2]}
    globalRect  : Rect;            {Text rectangle in screen coordinates [I:4.1.2]}
    textRgn     : RgnHandle;       {Region representing text rectangle [I:4.1.5]}
    wideOpen    : RgnHandle;       {Wide-open (maximum) region [I:4.1.5]}
    savePort    : GrafPtr;         {Pointer to previous current port [I:4.2.2]}

  begin  {DoMouseMoved}

    wideOpen := NewRgn;            {Create regions [I:4.1.6]}
    textRgn  := NewRgn;

    SetRectRgn (wideOpen, -32768,  -32768,   {Set wide-open region [I:4.1.7]}
                           32767,   32767);

    if FrontWindow = NIL then      {Screen empty? [II:3.3.3]}
      begin
        InitCursor;                {Set arrow cursor [II:2.5.2]}
        CopyRgn (wideOpen, MouseRgn)   {Set mouse region to wide-open [I:4.1.7]}
      end {if FrontWindow = NIL}
```

Program 3-5 Handle mouse-moved event *(continued)*

```
else if  FrontWindow = TheWindow then   {Is one of our windows active? [II:3.3.3]}
   begin

      textRect    := TheText^^.viewRect;    {Get window's text rectangle [II:5.1.1]}
      globalRect  := textRect;              {Prepare to convert}
      GetPort (savePort);                    {Save previous port [I:4.3.3]}
        SetPort (TheWindow);                 {Get into window's port [I:4.3.3]}
        with globalRect do
          begin
            LocalToGlobal (topLeft);         {Convert rectangle to global coordinates [I:4.4.2]}
            LocalToGlobal (botRight)
          end; {with globalRect}
      SetPort (savePort);                    {Restore previous port [I:4.3.3]}
      RectRgn (textRgn, globalRect);         {Set region to global text rectangle [I:4.1.7]}

      GetMouse (mousePoint);                 {Get mouse position [II:2.4.1]}
      if PtInRect (mousePoint, textRect)  then   {Is mouse in text rectangle? [I:4.4.3]}
         begin
            SetCursor   (IBeam^^);           {Set I-beam cursor [II:2.5.2]}
            CopyRgn     (textRgn,  MouseRgn) {Set mouse region to text rectangle [I:4.1.7]}
         end  {then}
      else
         begin
            InitCursor;                      {Set arrow cursor [II:2.5.2]}
            DiffRgn (wideOpen, textRgn, MouseRgn)   {Use wide-open minus text rectangle
                                                     [I:4.4.8]}
         end  {else}

   end  {if FrontWindow = TheWindow}

   else
     {Do nothing};

   DisposeRgn (wideOpen);                    {Destroy regions [I:4.1.6]}
   DisposeRgn (textRgn)

end;   {DoMouseMoved}
```

After calculating the applicable mouse region, the routine saves it in a global variable, MouseRgn. We can then use this variable as a parameter when we call WaitNextEvent from our main event loop. Thus we can replace the line

```
if GetNextEvent (EveryEvent, TheEvent) then
```

in the MiniEdit routine `DoEvent` (Program II:2–5) with

```
if InForeground then
   blinkTicks  :=  GetCaretTime
else
   blinkTicks  :=  99999999;
if WaitNextEvent (EveryEvent, TheEvent,
                    blinkTicks, MouseRgn) then
```

(The Toolbox routine `GetCaretTime` [II:5.4.3] returns the interval in ticks between blinks of the TextEdit insertion point, as set by the user with the Control Panel desk accessory. This gives us the correct value to use for the third parameter to `WaitNextEvent`, the maximum number of ticks we're willing to remain suspended before regaining control.)

It's important to keep in mind, though, that some users may be running our program on older systems that aren't equipped with MultiFinder. Before attempting to execute the code above, we must first check the dispatch table (using the technique discussed in Chapter 2) to make sure `WaitNextEvent` is available; if not, we must settle for an old-fashioned `GetNextEvent` call instead. Also notice that for this method of mouse tracking to work properly, the mouse region must be recalculated whenever a different window becomes active on the screen. Thus we must add a call to the new `DoMouseMoved` routine to our processing of activate and deactivate events in routine `DoActivate` (Program II:5–14, restructured to `ActWindow` and `DeactWindow` in Appendix III:H).

Notifications

One problem that can arise in the MultiFinder environment is how to communicate with the user while operating in the background. For example, an electronic mail program running in the background might want to notify the user, "You have new mail," whenever an incoming message arrives. Unfortunately, the time-honored method of posting an alert or dialog box won't work, because the dialog window may be obscured from the user's view by other windows belonging to the foreground program. To handle this type of situation in a convenient way, MultiFinder offers a new method of communicating with the user called a *notification.*

There are four ways a notification can capture the user's attention, any or all of which can be used in combination:

- Display a small (16-by-16) icon at the left end of the menu bar, alternating with the usual Apple symbol.
- Place a diamond mark [I:8.1.1] next to the program name on the Apple menu.
- Play a sound through the speaker.
- Post an alert box on the screen.

Unlike ordinary alerts posted by the program itself, those displayed by a notification always appear at the front of the screen, ahead of all other windows, no matter what other program may be running at the time.

Notice that all communication goes from the program to the user, not the other way around. If you need information *from* the user, post a notification to ask the user to bring your program to the foreground, then use an ordinary dialog box to request the needed information.

The exact behavior of any given notification is defined by a *notification record* [3.2.1]. The fields of this record identify the small icon to be displayed in the menu bar, the sound to be played, the menu item to be marked, and the message to be displayed in the notification box. (Any of these elements may be suppressed, if you wish; it is not necessary to use all four.) All pending notifications are kept in the *notification queue,* which is a standard Operating System queue of the form discussed in [III:3.1.6]. To issue a notification, you add it to the queue with the Toolbox routine NMInstall [3.2.2].

Another field of the notification record holds a pointer to an optional *response procedure* [3.2.3] to be executed after all the other steps (small icon, sound, menu mark, alert box) have been carried out. The response procedure should accept one parameter, a QElemPtr [III:3.1.6] pointing to the notification record that activated it, and should return no result. A procedure pointer of ProcPtr (-1) denotes the standard response procedure, which simply removes the notification from the queue; if you supply your own procedure, it can accomplish the same thing by calling NMRemove

[3.2.2]. This would make sense for a notification that just posts an alert on the screen (and perhaps plays a sound as well), but not for one that displays a small icon or marks a menu item, since it would remove these from the screen too quickly for the user to notice them. In the latter case, it's better not to remove the notification until after you've returned to the foreground.

Because notifications are typically posted at a time when some other program is in foreground control of the system, your response procedure *cannot* rely on processor register A5 being properly set up to point to your program's application global space. If you need access to any of your own global variables (or anything else in your A5 world, such as a QuickDraw global [I:4.3.1]), you can store a copy of your own A5 base address in the notification record's `nmRefCon` field for use by the response procedure.

Nuts and Bolts

Desk Accessories and MultiFinder

Desk accessories are handled somewhat differently under MultiFinder than they were in the old single-Finder (UniFinder?) environment. Previously, a desk accessory existed as a guest of the single program (called the *host program*) that happened to be running at the time the accessory was opened. The accessory's code and resources resided in the host program's application heap, and its window was part of the host program's window list. When the user decided to exit from the host program, all open desk accessories were automatically closed as part of the program's termination sequence.

Under MultiFinder, desk accessories ordinarily reside in the system heap, rather than in any one program's application heap. A special-purpose application program, named DA Handler, serves as host for all accessories, taking its place alongside all the other programs sharing the system under MultiFinder. This program maintains its own window list for all desk accessory windows, separate from that of any other program. One surprising consequence of this is that whenever the user activates any one accessory's window with a mouse click, *all* open accessories come to the front of the screen together as a single "layer."

The user can still choose to run a desk accessory the old way, under a single host program instead of DA Handler, by holding down the Option key while opening the accessory from the Apple menu. The accessory will then reside in the active program's application heap and window list, as before. This makes no difference from the accessory's point of view, and a properly written accessory should run equally well in both environments.

Before MultiFinder, application programs were expected to support the operation of desk accessories by calling the Toolbox routine `SystemTask` [II:2.7.2, III:6.2.4] at least once per tick, giving the accessories a chance to perform their periodic tasks, if necessary. Under MultiFinder, the new event-retrieval routine `WaitNextEvent` [3.1.3] calls `SystemTask` for you automatically, so you should avoid explicitly calling it yourself. If you're still retrieving your events with `GetNextEvent`, however (for instance, if you're running on an older system where `WaitNextEvent` is not available), you must still call `System-Task` as before, to give the desk accessories the processor time they need.

Faking It

The main purpose of suspend and resume events is to tell you when to transfer information between the global desk scrap and your internal Toolbox or private scrap, if you have one. It is essential for all programs running under MultiFinder to do this, to allow the user to cut and paste information from one program to another. For programs that don't accept suspend and resume events (in particular, those written before the advent of MultiFinder), a bit of trickery is needed to fool the program into transferring the scrap at the appropriate times.

When the time comes to move a program to the background, MultiFinder looks for a size resource [3.3.2] to see whether to send a suspend event. If the program has no size resource, or if its accept-suspend/resume bit [3.3.3] is off, MultiFinder instead generates a sequence of events that look to the program like the opening of a desk accessory. First it sends a mouse-down event simulating a mouse click in the title of the Apple menu. When the program responds to this event by calling MenuSelect [II:4.5.1], MultiFinder intercepts the call (by patching the dispatch table) and returns a menu ID and item number representing a choice from the menu. If the program's MultiFinder-aware bit is off as well, MultiFinder also creates an invisible dummy window to force a deactivate event for the program's frontmost window. As long as the program conforms to Macintosh standards, this sequence of events will cause it to copy its scrap to the global desk scrap. A similar sequence when the program returns to the foreground induces it to copy the desk scrap back to its internal scrap if its contents have changed while the program was suspended.

The same kind of trickery takes place when the user attempts to open one of a program's documents by double-clicking in the Finder. MultiFinder brings the program to the foreground, sends it a mouse-down event simulating a click in the title of its File menu, intercepts the resulting MenuSelect call and returns the item number of the Open command, then again intercepts the program's call to SFGetFile [II:8.3.2] and returns the name and location of the selected file. Similarly, when the user chooses the Finder's Shut Down or Restart command, MultiFinder sends each active program a sequence representing a mouse event in the program's Quit command, allowing the program to close up shop in an orderly way before the system is shut down.

To find the correct menu IDs and item numbers to denote these operations, MultiFinder looks in the program's resource file for a menu named File containing individual items named Quit and Open (or Open...). If a program uses different names from these, it can identify them to MultiFinder by using a special resource type, 'mstr' ("MultiFinder string") [3.3.4]. The internal format of such a resource is the same as for an ordinary string resource ('STR ' [I:8.4.2]). Its resource ID designates the specific item the string denotes (100 for the name of the menu containing the Quit command, 101 for the name of the Quit command itself, and so forth), as shown in the table in [3.3.4]. If, for some reason, a program uses more than one name for one of these items (for instance, if the name of a command can change dynamically during execution), it can use a resource of type 'mst#' ("MultiFinder string list") [3.3.4] instead of just 'mstr'.

MultiFinder Etiquette

Finally, we close this chapter with a few general rules of civilized behavior for programs running under MultiFinder:

- Never modify any Toolbox data structure directly; use the Toolbox routine calls provided for the purpose.

- Do not use the Window Manager port [II:3.6.1, 6.3.7] unless you're writing a window definition function or some other unusual piece of code.

- Never draw anything on the screen outside your own windows. The background "desktop" area of the screen belongs exclusively to MultiFinder.

- When operating in the background, don't draw to the screen at all or take any other user-visible action, such as changing the cursor or the menu bar. (*Exception:* See next note.)

- Be sure to respond to all update events promptly, even when in the background. This is necessary to keep the screen properly updated as the user manipulates windows in other programs.

- Don't use application-defined events (App1Evt, App2Evt, App3Evt [II:2.1.2]) for internal program communication while in the background. (Event type App4Evt, of course, is now reserved for MultiFinder events.) These are considered user events, and are never reported to background programs. If you post such an event from the background, it will be sent to the current foreground program instead, with unpredictable and possibly disastrous results. If you must send a signal to yourself from the background, try setting a global variable instead.

- Never release or detach a system resource, since other programs may be using it as well. (Under MultiFinder, resources read from the System file are always stored in the system heap, regardless of their individual ResSysHeap attributes [I:6.4.2].)

- Break time-consuming operations into smaller pieces instead of performing them all at once. For instance, when printing a document, print just one line at a time between event calls, rather than a whole page at a time. This is especially important when running in the background, to allow the foreground program to respond smoothly to the user's actions.

- It's recommended that you remember your screen layout from one session to the next. You can do this by saving all window locations in a special configuration resource in your application resource file before exiting from your program. The next time the program is started up, it can restore the exact arrangement of windows that was on the screen last time, saving the user the trouble of opening and positioning them all again.

- In general, follow Apple's recommended user interface standards and programming practices as closely as possible.

REFERENCE

3.1 Events

3.1.1   Event Messages

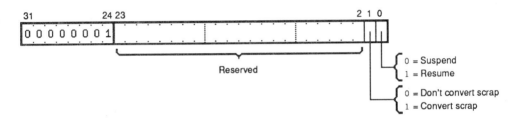

Event message for suspend/resume events

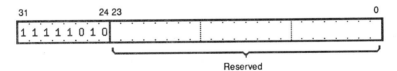

Event message for mouse-moved events

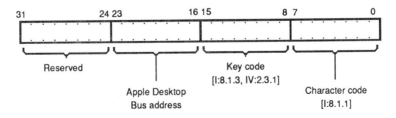

Event message for keyboard events

Definitions

```
const
   ADBAddrMask  = $00FF0000;              {Mask for ADB address}
   KeyCodeMask  = $0000FF00;              {Mask for key code}
   CharCodeMask = $000000FF;              {Mask for character code}
```

Notes

1. Event type App4Evt [II:2.1.2] is now reserved for use by MultiFinder for suspend, resume, and mouse-moved events.

2. Suspend and resume events are identified by the value $01 in the high-order byte of the event record's message field [II:2.1.1].

3. Bit 0 of the event message distinguishes suspend (0) from resume (1) events.

4. For resume events, bit 1 of the event message tells whether the contents of the desk scrap [I:7.4] have changed since the last suspend. If you are using the Toolbox text scrap or maintaining a private scrap of your own, this bit tells you to update it from the desk scrap on resuming operation.

5. For suspend events, it's up to you to keep track of changes in your own scrap and transfer its contents to the desk scrap if necessary. The simplest (though not necessarily the most efficient) policy is simply to transfer the scrap whenever you receive a suspend event.

6. If your program has a size resource [3.3.2] with the MultiFinder-aware bit set, you will not receive deactivate and activate events for your frontmost window on suspension and resumption. You must deactivate and activate the window for yourself as part of your response to suspend and resume events.

7. The value $FA in the high-order byte of a MultiFinder event's message field identifies it as a mouse-moved event, signifying that the mouse has moved outside the allowable region you specified for it in your call to WaitNextEvent [3.1.3]. The remainder of the message is reserved for future use.

8. On models equipped with the Apple Desktop Bus, the second byte of the event message for keyboard (key-down, key-up, and auto-key) events now gives the ADB address of the keyboard.

9. The third byte of the event message gives the virtual key code (not the raw key code) for the key that was pressed. The fourth byte contains the corresponding character code [I:8.1.1] under the keyboard map currently in effect.

10. The constants `ADBAddrMask`, `KeyCodeMask`, and `CharCodeMask` can be used with `BitAnd` and `BitShift` [I:2.2.2] to extract the various items from the keyboard event message.

11. The contents of the `message` field for all other event types are unchanged from earlier versions of the Toolbox [II:2.1.4].

Assembly Language Information

Masks for keyboard event messages:

Name	Value	Meaning
ADBAddrMask	$00FF0000	Mask for ADB address
KeyCodeMask	$0000FF00	Mask for key code
CharCodeMask	$000000FF	Mask for character code

3.1.2   Event Modifiers

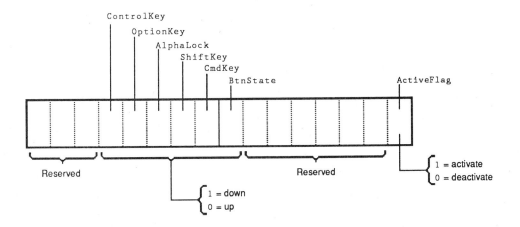

Event modifiers

Definitions

```
const
    ControlKey = $1000;              {Control key}
    OptionKey  = $0800;              {Option key}
    AlphaLock  = $0400;              {Caps Lock key}
    ShiftKey   = $0200;              {Shift key}
    CmdKey     = $0100;              {Command key}

    BtnState   = $0080;              {Mouse button}

    ActiveFlag = $0001;              {Activate or deactivate event?}
```

Notes

1. On keyboards with a Control key (such as the Macintosh II keyboard and the Apple Extended Keyboard), bit 12 of the event record's `modifiers` field [II:2.1.1] now gives the state of the Control key at the time the event was posted.

2. The remaining contents of the `modifiers` field are the same as on earlier models [II:2.1.5].

3. The assembly-language constants listed below are bit numbers within the `modifiers` field, for use with the BTST, BSET, BCLR, and BCHG instructions.

Assembly Language Information

Bit numbers in the `modifiers` *field:*

Name	Value	Meaning
ControlKey	12	Control key
OptionKey	11	Option key
AlphaLock	10	Caps Lock key
ShiftKey	9	Shift key
CmdKey	8	Command key
BtnState	7	Mouse button
ActiveFlag	0	Activate or deactivate?

3.1.3   Retrieving Events

Definitions

```
function WaitNextEvent
            (mask          : INTEGER;        {Mask designating event types of interest}
            var theEvent   : EventRecord;    {Returns information about event}
            sleepTicks     : LONGINT;        {Length of time to suspend program, in ticks}
            mouseRgn       : RgnHandle)      {Mouse-tracking region in global coordinates}
                           : BOOLEAN;        {Should application respond to event?}
```

Notes

1. WaitNextEvent requests the next available event of a specified type or types. Its operation is similar to that of GetNextEvent [II:2.2.1], except that it allows MultiFinder to switch control of the system to another program if no events of the requested types are pending.

2. To take full advantage of MultiFinder, always use WaitNextEvent to retrieve your events, if possible, rather than GetNextEvent. This allows other programs the opportunity to perform useful background work during your program's idle time. (WaitNextEvent may not always be available, however: see note 26 below.)

3. The mask parameter is an event mask [II:2.1.3] designating which event types are of interest. Event types excluded by the mask are ignored.

4. An event record describing the requested event is returned in the variable parameter theEvent. The event is then removed from the event queue.

5. Like GetNextEvent, WaitNextEvent intercepts events destined for desk accessories and passes them to the accessory for processing. It then reports such events to your program with a function result of FALSE, telling you to ignore them; a TRUE result means you must process the reported event yourself.

6. If no event of the requested types is available, WaitNextEvent may suspend your program in favor of another that is requesting processor time, either for background processing or because the user has brought it to the foreground on the screen.

7. The parameter `sleepTicks` gives the maximum length of time, in ticks, for which your program is willing to remain suspended between events. The program will resume execution when this number of ticks has elapsed or at the next reportable event of the requested types, whichever occurs first.

8. A zero value for `sleepTicks` requests control back as soon as possible. However, you may still be suspended briefly to allow other programs' minimum control requirements to be satisfied.

9. When control eventually returns to your program, your call to `Wait-NextEvent` will return either with an event of a requested type (if one has occurred in the interim) or with a null event (if the specified interval has elapsed without a reportable event).

10. If you can perform useful work while running in the background, you should do so on receiving a null event from `WaitNextEvent`. The value you supply for the `sleepTicks` parameter regulates the frequency with which you will receive such events.

11. To take advantage of MultiFinder's background processing capability, the can-background bit in your size resource [3.3.2] must be set to 1; if this bit is 0, you will receive no null events while in the background.

12. When executing in the background behind another program, you will not receive ordinary user (mouse and keyboard) events. You may receive other types of event, however, such as update events for parts of your windows that become exposed to view when another program's windows are moved on the screen.

13. Do not perform time-consuming tasks, such as garbage collection or full-page printing, while running in the background. You must make frequent, regular calls to `WaitNextEvent` to allow the foreground program the processing time it needs.

14. `WaitNextEvent` gives no direct indication of whether it has returned control immediately or after a period of suspension. The only way to find this out is to call `TickCount` [II:2.7.1] before and after `WaitNext-Event`, to see how much time has elapsed on the system clock.

15. When the user activates another program on the screen, `WaitNext-Event` will return a suspend event [3.1.1] to notify you that you are about to relinquish foreground control of the system. When you eventually return to the foreground, you will be so notified with a resume event.

16. After receiving a suspend event, you will be suspended from foreground operation at your *next* call to `WaitNextEvent`.

17. If your program has a size resource [3.3.2] with the MultiFinder-aware bit set, you will not receive deactivate and activate events for your frontmost window on suspension and resumption. You must deactivate and activate the window for yourself as part of your response to suspend and resume events.

18. If you maintain a Clipboard window on the screen, you should hide the window on receiving a suspend event and redisplay it at the subsequent resume. While in the background, you will not be able to track changes in the scrap and keep the contents of the Clipboard window current.

19. Suspend and resume events should never be masked out, either in the `mask` parameter or in the global system event mask [II:2.3.2].

20. `mouseRgn` specifies a region of the screen within which no special action is needed to respond to the mouse's movements. If the mouse position lies outside this region, `WaitNextEvent` will return a mouse-moved event [3.1.1].

21. `mouseRgn` is expressed in global coordinates.

22. The `mouseRgn` parameter and mouse-moved events are useful for adjusting the appearance of the cursor [II:2.5.2] in different regions of the screen.

23. After receiving a mouse-moved event, don't forget to change the value of `mouseRgn` for your next `WaitNextEvent` call, to reflect the new mouse position and avoid receiving the same mouse-moved event repeatedly.

24. If `sleepTicks = 0` and `mouseRgn = NIL`, `WaitNextEvent` is equivalent to `GetNextEvent`.

25. When you use `WaitNextEvent` for event retrieval instead of `GetNextEvent`, MultiFinder assumes responsibility for scheduling the periodic tasks of drivers and desk accessories. Thus you need not call `SystemTask` [II:2.7.2, III:6.2.4] regularly, as you must in the original single-Finder environment.

26. If MultiFinder is not active, the `WaitNextEvent` trap will not be available in the Toolbox dispatch table. You can test for its presence by comparing the address returned for it by `NGetTrapAddress` [2.1.2] with that of the unimplemented Toolbox trap, `UnimplTrapNum`. If the two addresses are different, you can safely call `WaitNextEvent`; if they're the same, then MultiFinder is not currently active and you should use `GetNextEvent` [II:2.2.1] (and `SystemTask` [II:2.7.2, III:6.2.4]) instead.

Assembly Language Information

Trap macro:

(Pascal) Routine name	(Assembly) Trap macro	Trap word
WaitNextEvent	_WaitNextEvent	$A860

3.2   Notifications

3.2.1   Notification Records

Definitions

```
type
  NMRec = record
           qLink       : QElemPtr;      {Pointer to next queue element}
           qType       : INTEGER;       {Queue type (= NMType)}
           nmFlags     : INTEGER;       {Private}
           nmPrivate   : LONGINT;       {Private}
           nmReserved  : INTEGER;       {Private}
           nmMark      : INTEGER;       {Item to mark on Apple menu}
           nmSIcon     : Handle;        {Handle to small icon to display in menu bar}
           nmSound     : Handle;        {Handle to sound to be played}
           nmStr       : StringPtr;     {Pointer to text to display in alert box}
           nmResp      : ProcPtr;       {Pointer to response procedure}
           nmRefCon    : LONGINT;       {Reference constant for application use}
         end;

const
  NMType = 8;                           {Queue type for a notification queue}
```

Notes

1. A notification record defines a communication to the user, typically to announce some occurrence or condition arising while running in the background under MultiFinder.

2. The letters NM stand for Notification Manager, the part of the Macintosh Operating System that deals with notifications.

3. Notification records are elements of the *notification queue,* a standard Operating System queue [III:3.1.6] maintained by the system. Use NMInstall and NMRemove [3.2.2] to add and remove elements of this queue.

4. Like all queue elements [III:3.1.6], notification records are nonrelocatable objects, referred to by pointers rather than handles.

5. qLink is a pointer to the next element in the notification queue, or NIL if this is the last element.

6. qLink is nominally of type QElemPtr [III:3.1.6], but must actually point to another notification record. Use typecasting to convert between types QElemPtr and ^NMRec.

7. qType identifies the type of queue to which this element belongs; for notification records, it must always be the constant NMType. Notice that, unlike other standard queue types, NMType is defined directly as an integer constant, not as a scalar value of the enumerated type QTypes [III:3.1.6].

8. nmMark designates an item on the Apple menu to be marked with a diamond mark [I:8.1.1] to catch the user's attention.

9. Stand-alone application programs should mark their own item on the Apple menu by setting nmMark to 1. This causes the currently running application program to be marked.

10. Desk accessories should pass their own reference number for nmMark. Any negative value is assumed to be the reference number of a desk accessory to be marked.

11. Device drivers other than desk accessories should set nmMark to 0, meaning that no item is to be marked.

12. nmSIcon is a handle to a small icon [3.3.1] to be displayed at the left of the menu bar, in rotation with the standard Apple mark [I:8.1.1].

13. nmSound is a handle to a 'snd ' resource to be played through the speaker. See *Inside Macintosh,* Volume 5, for more information.

14. The handles passed for nmSIcon and nmSound must be unpurgeable, but need not be locked.

15. A value of POINTER(-1) for nmSound denotes the standard system beep [II:2.8.1].

16. nmStr is a pointer to a text string to be displayed in an alert box on the screen.

17. The alert will be presented with only one dismissal button. No item number is returned representing a choice of dismissal actions; there is thus no way to receive information from the user about how to proceed after the notification.

18. nmResp is a pointer to a response procedure [3.2.3] to be executed after all the other steps of the notification (menu mark, small icon, sound, alert box) have been carried out.

19. An nmResp value of POINTER(-1) denotes the standard response procedure, which simply removes this notification from the notification queue.

20. Don't set nmResp to POINTER(-1) if you're using a menu mark or a small icon, since this will destroy them before the user has a chance to notice them.

21. A NIL value for nmSIcon, nmSound, nmStr, or nmResp omits the corresponding step from the notification.

22. nmRefCon is a 4-byte field reserved for the program posting the notification to use in any way it wishes.

23. Notifications are available only in version 6.0 or later of the System file. You can use SysEnvirons [2.1.1] to check the current system version and, if it is not recent enough, either use a different method of communicating with the user or post an explanatory alert message (Sorry, this program requires System version 6.0 or later) and exit.

Assembly Language Information

Assembly-language constant:

Name	Value	Meaning
NMType	8	Queue type for a notification queue

3.2.2   Posting Notifications

Definitions

```
function NMInstall
        (theRequest : QElemPtr)          {Pointer to notification request}
            : OSErr;                     {Result code}

function NMRemove
        (theRequest : QElemPtr)          {Pointer to notification request}
            : OSErr;                     {Result code}
```

```
const
  NMTypeErr = -299;                {Wrong queue type}
  QErr      =   -1;                {Element not found in queue}
```

Notes

1. NMInstall installs an entry in the notification queue; NMRemove removes one.

2. The letters NM stand for Notification Manager, the part of the Macintosh Operating System that deals with notifications.

3. The parameter theRequest is nominally of type QElemPtr [III:3.1.6], but must actually point to a notification record [3.2.1]. Use typecasting to convert between types QElemPtr and ^NMRec.

4. These routines merely install and remove an existing notification record. They perform no memory allocation or deallocation, and thus can safely be used in response procedures [3.2.3], input/output completion routines, and other routines that execute at the interrupt level.

5. Both routines return a result code [I:3.1.2] reporting the success or failure of the operation.

6. A result code of NoErr [I:3.1.2] means that all is well; no error has occurred.

7. If the designated queue element's qType field is not equal to NMType [3.2.1], both routines return the error code NMTypeErr.

8. If the designated element is not found in the notification queue, NMRemove returns the error code QErr.

9. Errors from other parts of the Toolbox can also occur in the course of these operations. See Appendix E for a complete list of Toolbox error codes.

Assembly Language Information

Trap macros:

(Pascal) Routine name	(Assembly) Trap macro	Trap word
NMInstall	_NMInstall	$A05E
NMRemove	_NMRemove	$A05F

Register usage:

Routine	Register	Contents
NMInstall	A0.L **(in)**	theRequest
	D0.W **(out)**	result code
NMRemove	A0.L **(in)**	theRequest
	D0.W **(out)**	result code

3.2.3   Response Procedures

Definitions

```
procedure YourResponse
          (theRequest : QElemPtr);        {Pointer to notification request}
```

Notes

1. A notification record [3.2.1] may contain a pointer to an optional response procedure in its nmResp field.

2. The procedure heading shown above is only a model for your response procedure. You can give your procedure any name you like; there is no Toolbox routine named YourResponse.

3. If present, the response procedure is called at the very end of the notification sequence [3.2.1], after all other steps (menu mark, small icon, sound, alert box) have been completed.

4. The response procedure receives one parameter, a pointer to the notification record that activated it, and returns no result.

5. Because the response procedure may be called during an interrupt or while executing in the background under MultiFinder, it should perform no memory allocation, mouse tracking, or drawing to the screen. If necessary, it can set a global variable that will trigger such actions when the program later resumes foreground execution.

6. Register A5 will not be properly set up to point to the program's application global space at the time the response procedure is called. If the response procedure needs access to global variables, keep a copy

of the correct A5 value in the nmRefCon field of the notification record and use SetA5 [2.1.4] to set up the register for yourself. Don't forget to restore the register's previous value before returning!

7. The standard response procedure, denoted by a value of POINTER(-1) in the notification record's nmResp field [3.2.1], simply calls NMRemove [3.2.2] to remove the record from the notification queue. The record is not deallocated and remains available for future reuse; if you have no further use for it, you must explicitly deallocate it for yourself.

3.3 Resource Formats

3.3.1 Resource Type 'SICN'

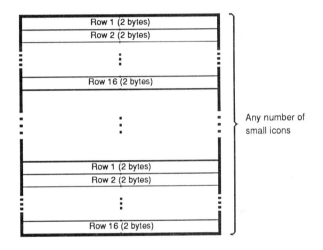

Structure of a 'SICN' resource

 Notes

1. A resource of type 'SICN' contains one or more small icons for display on the screen.

2. Each small icon is a 16-by-16 bit image, half the dimensions of a full-size icon [I:5.4.4, I:5.5.3].

3. The resource may contain any number of small icons. The number can be found from the overall size of the resource: each icon is 32 bytes long.

4. There is no defined data type representing a small icon. If you have to create one in your program, you can use an

```
array [1..16] of INTEGER
```

5. Small icons are used for a variety of purposes, including:

   • by the Finder, to represent files in a folder when viewed "by small icon"

   • by MultiFinder, to represent the currently active program at the right end of the menu bar

   • by MultiFinder, to represent other available programs on the Apple menu

   • in notifications [3.2.1], to identify the program posting the notification and requesting the user's attention

6. The Finder and MultiFinder automatically generate small icons for their own use by scaling down the full-size icon representing a program or file. It is not normally necessary to supply a small icon explicitly for these purposes. However, it is necessary to supply an explicit small icon if one is needed for use in a notification [3.2.1].

3.3.2   Resource Type 'SIZE'

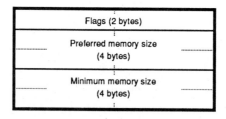

Structure of a 'SIZE' resource

Notes

1. A resource of type 'SIZE' summarizes a program's memory requirements and other information used by MultiFinder.

2. The first word of the resource contains flags [3.3.3] describing the program's MultiFinder-related properties.

3. The flags are followed by the program's preferred and minimum memory requirements, in bytes.

4. In starting up a program, MultiFinder will attempt to honor its stated memory requirements if possible:

   - If a large enough block of contiguous memory is available, MultiFinder will allocate a partition of the full preferred memory size.

   - If the largest available block is smaller than the preferred size but larger than the minimum, MultiFinder will display an alert box asking the user whether to run the program anyway, using the available memory.

   - If not even the minimum required memory is available, MultiFinder will post an appropriate error alert and refuse to start the program.

5. A program's standard memory requirements are specified by a size resource with an ID of -1.

6. The user can change the preferred memory size with the Finder's Get Info command, by typing into a text box in the resulting information window. The minimum memory size cannot be changed.

7. If the user changes a program's preferred memory size, the new value is recorded in a new size resource with an ID of 0. The original size resource (ID = -1) is retained, but resource 0 overrides it if present.

8. A program with no size resource can still run under MultiFinder, and will be given a standard memory partition of 384K.

3.3.3   MultiFinder Flags

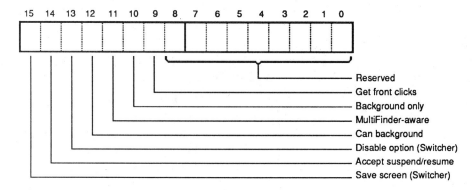

MultiFinder flags

Notes

1. The first word of a program's size resource [3.3.2] contains flags describing the program's MultiFinder-related properties.

2. Bit 11 of the flag word is the MultiFinder-aware bit. By setting this bit, the program indicates that it is prepared to take full advantage of MultiFinder's features and capabilities.

3. Bit 14 tells whether the program is prepared to accept suspend and resume events [3.1.1].

4. If bit 14 is 0, MultiFinder will instead signal the transition between foreground and background operation with a sequence of events simulating the activation or deactivation of a desk accessory, to fool the program into transferring data to or from the desk scrap [I:7.4].

5. If both bits 14 and 11 (accept-suspend/resume and MultiFinder-aware) are set, the program will *not* receive deactivate and activate events for its frontmost window on suspension and resumption. The program must deactivate and activate the window for itself as part of its response to suspend and resume events.

6. If bit 14 (accept-suspend/resume) is set but bit 11 (MultiFinder-aware) is not, the program will receive *both* suspend/resume and activate/deactivate events. To generate the latter, however, MultiFinder must create a dummy window, slowing down the transition between foreground and background. For maximum efficiency, any program that sets bit 14 to accept suspend and resume events should also set bit 11 to refuse activates and deactivates.

7. Bit 12 requests the opportunity to do useful work while running in the background behind another program. MultiFinder will comply by sending null events when the program is in the background, at the intervals specified by the `sleepTicks` parameter in the program's calls to `WaitNextEvent` [3.1.3]. If the can-background bit is 0, the program will receive no null events while in the background.

8. Bit 10 means that the program wishes to run exclusively in the background. A program with this bit set will never be switched to the foreground and can never interact directly with the user.

9. Bit 9 asks to receive the mouse clicks with which the user switches the program to the foreground. These will be reported as mouse-down and mouse-up events immediately following the resume event itself. If this bit is 0, such transitional mouse events will not be reported.

10. Bits 15 and 13 in the flag word have no meaning for MultiFinder, but were used by its predecessor, Switcher. Although MultiFinder no longer uses these bits, it continues to maintain them for the sake of backward compatibility.

11. The remaining bits in the flag word are reserved for future use.

3.3.4   Resource Types 'mstr' and 'mst#'

Resource IDs for 'mstr' and 'mst#':

Resource ID	Meaning
100	Name of menu containing Quit command
101	Name of Quit command
102	Name of menu containing Open command
103	Name of Open command

 Notes

1. Resource types 'mstr' ("MultiFinder string") and 'mst#' ("MultiFinder string list") help MultiFinder locate and identify key commands on a program's menus.

2. These resources have the same internal structure as 'STR ' [I:8.4.2] and 'STR#' [I:8.4.3], respectively.

3. When the user chooses the Finder's Restart or ShutDown command, MultiFinder sends each active program a sequence of events simulating a mouse press in the program's Quit command. The program responds by executing its normal termination sequence, just as if the user had chosen Quit directly.

4. Similarly, when the user double-clicks or opens one of a program's document files in the Finder, MultiFinder simulates a mouse press in the program's Open command, then intercepts the resulting call to SFGetFile [II:8.3.2] and returns the name and location of the selected file.

5. Ordinarily, MultiFinder assumes that both these commands reside on a menu named File, under the names Quit and Open (or Open...), respectively. 'mstr' and 'mst#' resources override these assumptions, and thus are needed only if the menu or command names differ from the standard ones.

6. In most cases, the desired menu or command will have just a single name, identified by an 'mstr' resource. If more than one name is needed (for example, if the name of the command may change in the course of program execution), use an 'mst#' resource. In either case, the table above gives the resource IDs for the various menus and commands.

7. The technique described here applies to version 6.0 of the System file. It is not available in earlier versions and may be superseded by improved methods in future versions.

CHAPTER

4

Chasing
Rainbows

Early models of Macintosh offered a range of display options something like the paint job on the old Model-T Ford: "any color you like, as long as it's black." With its built-in 9-inch screen and associated video circuitry, the classic Macintosh could support any desired display configuration, as long as it was black-and-white, 512 pixels wide by 342 high. What you saw was what you got.

The Macintosh II, with its open architecture, is more flexible in its display capabilities. Unlike earlier models, the II has no built-in display screen; instead, it must be connected to a separate *graphics device*, via a controller card plugged into one of the expansion slots. Users can now choose from a whole range of available display devices according to their needs and budget—from the old 9-inch monochrome display to 14-inch monitors with continuous gray scale to 19-inch double-page screens capable of displaying 256 distinct colors at a time. There can even be two or more different video devices connected to the system at once, displaying different portions of the same shared, "virtual" display space.

Of course, all these fancy display capabilities would be worthless if the software didn't know how to make use of them. The new, expanded version of the Toolbox includes an extensive set of added facilities to work with color displays. In this chapter, we'll learn about the general principles and concepts underlying the Toolbox's approach to color; in the next, we'll see how to put them to use on the screen.

Color Fundamentals

A really thorough conceptual discussion on the subject of color would lead us into a vast range of topics, from optics to electrodynamics to quantum theory, from electrical engineering to industrial chemistry, from physiology and psychology to esthetics and semiotics (the study of symbols). We could easily fill a whole book the size of this one and still not exhaust the subject. Still, some basic knowledge of color principles will help us to understand how the Macintosh Toolbox deals with color and how to use it in our own programs.

Physical Properties of Color

Light, as the Scottish physicist James Clerk Maxwell first recognized in the nineteenth century, is a form of electromagnetic radiation: a fluctuating energy field varying over time in the shape of a sine wave (Figure 4–1). The amplitude, or peak magnitude, of the wave determines the *brightness* or intensity of the light, the overall amount of energy it carries. The frequency of the light wave (or its inverse, the wavelength) determines the *hue*—the quality that we usually think of as "color," such as green, orange, yellow, or blue.

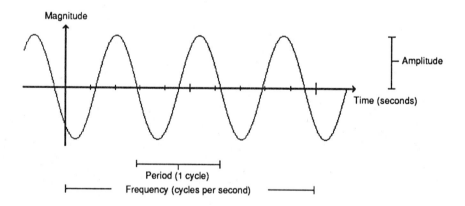

Figure 4–1 Anatomy of a light wave

A uniform mixture of all hues, with equal intensity across the spectrum of visible frequencies, produces pure white light. Adding such a mixture to light of a given frequency yields a lighter, more pastel tint. The degree to which a single, dominant hue rises above the background level of undifferentiated white is called *saturation*, and measures the vividness or purity of the color: fire-engine red is a more saturated color than rose pink, for example. A saturation level of zero represents a colorless gray tone somewhere on a scale from pure black to pure white, depending on the brightness level.

Together, these three properties of a light wave—its hue, brightness, and saturation, corresponding in physical terms to its frequency, amplitude, and what radio engineers would call its "signal-to-noise ratio"—completely characterize its color as perceived by the eye. They form the basis of the Munsell system, the most widely used method of color classification. (What we're calling brightness is commonly known in the Munsell system as the *value* of a color, and so Munsell is often referred to as hue-saturation–value, or *HSV* representation.)

A related form of color representation is *HSL*, in which the color's value (brightness) is replaced by its *lightness* level. This expresses the equivalent level of gray that would result if all trace of distinctive hue were removed (that is, if the saturation were reduced to zero). Lightness is the property that is captured by monochrome (black-and-white) video or photographic film. To understand how color (more precisely, hue) is added to a video image, we'll have to learn a little about the visual mechanisms of the human eye and brain.

Physiological Properties of Color

The retina at the back of the eye contains two types of light-sensing structures (or photoreceptors, if you like fancy words) called *rods* and *cones.* The rods are more sensitive and respond to lower levels of stimulation, but they can't distinguish one color from another. They come into play mainly under conditions of limited light, which explains why we can't perceive colors in a darkened room.

Cones need more light than rods to make them respond, but when the light level is high enough, they enable us to see colors as well as mere intensity levels. This is because the retina contains three different kinds of cone, which respond most strongly to light of different frequencies: one kind to frequencies in the red region of the color spectrum, one in the green region, and one in the blue.

Light of different hues stimulates the three types of cone to different levels of response, which the brain then recombines into a single, full-color image.

The colors at which the retinal cones exhibit their maximum levels of sensitivity are called the *additive primary colors*, because they can be added together to produce any other desired color. Mixing equal levels of blue and green, for example, yields an intermediate blue-green color called *cyan*. Similarly, red and blue combine to form the purplish shade known as *magenta*, and red and green mix together to produce plain old yellow. By presenting the eye with the right levels of the three primary colors, you can fool the brain into "seeing" any other color you wish. In fact, as we'll see in the next section, this is exactly the way color video works.

Color on the Screen

The screen of a color video tube (such as a television picture tube) is coated with three kinds of chemical phosphor, which emit red, green, and blue light, respectively, when struck by a beam of electrons from the tube's electron gun. The purest form of color video transmission consists of three independent intensity signals, one for each of the three phosphors. When the three signals are combined on the face of the tube, the result is a full-color video image. This *RGB* (red–green–blue) signal format is commonly used to drive closed-circuit monitors such as those found in television studios or connected to personal computers.

Ordinary broadcast receivers like the one in your living room, on the other hand, accept a different form of video input. When color television was first introduced, a vital concern was that the video signals it used had to be backward-compatible with the millions of black-and-white TV sets already in existence. To achieve this goal, an American industry group called the National Television Standards Committee (NTSC) established a form of *composite video* signal that could be read by both the older monochrome and the new-fangled color receivers. This is the form of video transmission used by all broadcast television receivers in the United States today.

Under the NTSC standard, all hue and saturation values are extracted from the color image, leaving only the lightness levels of the equivalent gray tones. The resulting *luminance* signal is then transmitted in exactly the same form as in a plain black-and-white transmission. The hues and saturations, in turn, are encoded into a supplementary *chrominance* signal and ingeniously inserted in the gaps between scan lines. Thus an old-fashioned monochrome receiver can simply use the luminance signal to regulate the lightness level of its black-and-white picture, while a properly equipped color receiver can decipher the additional chrominance information and use it to reconstruct the original full-color image.

Color on Paper

You may have been puzzled a few paragraphs back to read that green combines with red to produce yellow. Since when is green a primary color? Didn't we all learn in kindergarten to make green by mixing yellow and blue paint, and that red mixed with green makes black or a dark, muddy brown? Did the Color Kittens lie to us?

No, it's just that the rules for combining colors on paper aren't the same as on a video screen. Opaque coloring agents like paints and inks combine *subtractively* rather than *additively*. Instead of emitting light of their own, like the phosphors on the face of a video tube, they merely reflect the light falling on them from some other source. In the process, the chemical pigments in the paint or ink absorb some of the frequencies from the uniform mix that makes up white light. Thus the light that gets reflected back to our eyes is no longer white, because some of the original colors have been subtracted out of it.

It's the light frequencies that are left, the ones that *haven't* been absorbed by the paint, that determine what color we perceive. If the paint absorbs blue light, for example, then only the red- and green-sensing cones in our eyes will be stimulated, and we will see the color as yellow. Similarly, a paint that absorbs red but reflects blue and green will appear to us as cyan; if it absorbs green but reflects red and blue, we will perceive it as magenta.

Now suppose we mix the yellow and magenta paints together in equal proportions. The pigment molecules from the yellow paint absorb blue light, those from the magenta paint absorb green, and all that's left to reach our eyes is red. If we mix cyan and magenta, they subtract out all the red and green light and leave blue; if we mix cyan and yellow, they subtract red and blue and leave green. The Color Kittens were right after all.

Notice that the primary colors in the two systems are complementary. On a video screen, any two of the additive primaries (red, green, and blue) combine to form one of the subtractive primaries (cyan, magenta, and yellow); on paper, any pair of subtractive primaries combine to form an additive primary. On the screen, all three additive primaries combine to form pure white (all colors present); on paper, all three subtractive primaries combine to form pure black (all colors absorbed, none reflected). It all depends on which medium you're working in.

Toolbox Color Representation

Now that we know a bit about the principles and properties of color in general, we're ready to talk about how the Macintosh Toolbox represents colors internally for its own use. Naturally, to display more than just black and white on the screen, you need more than a single bit to specify the color of each pixel. This third dimension of a graphical image, the number of bits used to represent each individual pixel, is called the *pixel depth*, and determines the number of distinct colors the image can contain. Old-style monochrome images have a pixel depth of 1, allowing just two colors (normally black and white). An image 4 bits deep can contain 16 colors, an 8-bit image can contain 256 colors, and so on. Because each pixel can now occupy more than 1 bit of memory, images that include color information are no longer referred to as bit images, but rather as *pixel images.*

Actually, the Toolbox has several different formats for internal color representation, depending on the needs of a particular graphics device. In this section, we'll look at the various color formats themselves; later we'll discuss the characteristics of the graphics devices they're used with.

Planar Color

A little-known secret about the original Macintosh Toolbox is that it already included some rudimentary provisions for color graphics. Even though early Macintoshes were only equipped with a monochrome display screen, the QuickDraw graphics routines were designed right from the start to support color when it became available—as it eventually did on devices such as the ImageWriter II printer, with its optional four-color ribbon. Not many programs actually made use of this color capability, but it was there nevertheless for any program that wished to take advantage of it.

These "classic QuickDraw" color facilities are based on a *planar* model of color representation. A graphical image can consist of many separate *color planes*, each representing a single color. On each plane, a 1 bit at a given position indicates the presence of the corresponding color, a 0 denotes its absence. When all the planes are superimposed, their individual colors combine to form a single full-color image.

Every QuickDraw graphics port has a *foreground color* and a *background color* to be used in drawing operations. The current color settings are kept in the `fgColor` and `bkColor` fields of the `GrafPort` record [I:4.2.2, 4.1.2]. When a new port is created, these fields are initialized to black and white, respectively, for use in ordinary monochrome drawing. The QuickDraw routines `Fore-Color` and `BackColor` [4.1.2] change these settings, allowing you to draw with other colors instead. For example, if you set the foreground color to green and the background to yellow, all subsequent lines, shapes, patterns, and text will be drawn in green-on-yellow instead of black-on-white.

Within the `fgColor` and `bkColor` fields, each bit position corresponds to a single color plane; the value stored in the field can represent any combination of individual planes needed to produce a desired color. Drawing in the port takes place in one plane at a time, as determined by a bit number in the `colrBit` field of the port record [I:4.2.2, 4.1.3]. All drawing operations use this value to select the corresponding bits from the `fgColor` and `bkColor` fields, which tell whether the color associated with this plane is present or absent in the port's current foreground and background colors. These bits in turn determine what bit values to store into the plane's bit image.

The `colrBit` field in a newly created port is initialized to 0, denoting the black-on-white plane used in ordinary monochrome drawing. Normally this value is never changed, and only plane 0 is drawn. On color devices, however (such as the ImageWriter II with a color ribbon), the port is customized with special bottleneck routines [III:2.1] that redraw the image repeatedly, once for each plane. (The bottlenecks use the QuickDraw routine `ColorBit` [4.1.3] to switch from one plane to another; under normal circumstances, no application program should ever need to call this routine for itself.)

Since the `fgColor` and `bkColor` fields are long integers, Quick-Draw can theoretically support as many as 32 separate color planes. In practice, however, only a few of these planes are actually used. As already noted, plane 0 represents normal black-on-white monochrome; similarly, plane 1 is used for inverse monochrome (white-on-black). The next three planes, numbered 4 to 2, stand for the additive primary colors red, green, and blue, respectively. Planes 8 to 5 correspond to the four colors on the ImageWriter II ribbon: the three subtractive primaries (cyan, magenta, and yellow) plus black. The Toolbox interface includes bit-number constants representing each of these color planes, named `NormalBit`, `InverseBit`, `BlueBit`, `GreenBit`, and so on [4.1.1]; all other planes are unused.

There are also constants [4.1.1] for the eight standard colors themselves (`BlackColor`, `WhiteColor`, `RedColor`, `GreenColor`, and so on), to be used as parameters to the Toolbox routines `ForeColor` and `BackColor` [4.1.2]. The strange-looking numerical values of these constants are actually bit patterns for producing the corresponding colors in both additive and subtractive media. Notice that all of them except `WhiteColor` are odd (that is, have bit 0 set). This means that all colors except white will appear as black when displayed in a monochrome medium; in inverse monochrome (bit 1), white will appear as black and all other colors as white.

Direct Color

One drawback to the planar approach is that it allows only one bit for each plane. Even if all 32 available planes were assigned specific colors, any given color could still only be present or absent; there would be no way to mix them in varying amounts to produce a desired result. The Macintosh II version of the Toolbox takes a more straightforward approach, allowing you to specify the exact colors you want directly, in terms of the fundamental properties we discussed earlier.

The Toolbox recognizes four different formats for direct color definition: RGB (red–green–blue), CMY (cyan–magenta–yellow), HSV (hue–saturation–value), and HSL (hue–saturation–lightness). Each of the four is represented internally by a record type with three component fields: `RGBColor`, `CMYColor`, `HSVColor`, or `HSLColor` [4.2.1]. With 16 bits allotted to each field, this yields a potential range of 2^{48}, or 281,474,976,710,656 colors—even more than in your de luxe Crayola box, and far more than any existing graphics device is actually capable of displaying. As we'll see, the Toolbox includes extensive facilities for matching the abstractly defined colors you choose from this vast space to the concrete capabilities of a particular device.

In RGB format, each of the three components is expressed as an *unsigned* integer between 0 and 65535. In the other three formats, the component values are given instead as small fractions [2.4.1] between 0.00000 and 1.00000. The distinction is only an illusion, however, created by the Pascal interface definitions themselves. At the underlying machine level, it's the same 16 bits either way: the only difference is at which end of the number the imaginary binary point is considered to lie.

In both RGB and CMY, any color with three equal components represents a pure gray level, with no predominant hue. Notice, however, that the scales go in opposite directions for the two formats: a color with all components equal to 0 represents black in RGB (no illumination on the screen), whereas in CMY it represents white (no ink on the paper; all frequencies reflected, none absorbed). At the opposite extreme, an RGB color with all components equal to the maximum value of 65535 represents white; a similar color in CMY format (all components equal to 1.00000) stands for black. In HSV and HSL formats, saturation and lightness or brightness are measured on a closed scale, but the hue value represents a position on a "color wheel" whose ends wrap around cyclically. Both ends of the scale, 0.00000 and 1.00000, correspond to red, with .33333 standing for green and .66667 for blue.

Because it deals primarily with colors displayed on a video screen, the Toolbox uses RGB as its standard format for device-independent color representation. Most parts of the Toolbox that deal with device-independent colors expect them to be given in RGB form: for instance, when you draw into a color graphics port, you normally specify your foreground and background colors in RGB. If for some reason you prefer one of the other formats instead, you must convert it to RGB before passing it to the Toolbox, using one of the conversion routines [4.2.2] provided for this purpose.

Notice that all the conversion routines have RGB as either their source or target format. Thus if you wanted to convert from, say, HSV to CMY, you would have to do it in two stages: first from HSV to RGB, then from RGB to CMY.

Mapped Color

Theoretically, a display device could accept a full RGBColor record for each pixel and display precisely that color on the screen. But at 48 bits per pixel, the screen image for even a dinky 9-inch screen like the one on the original Macintosh would take up more than a megabyte of memory; today's roomier screens would need even more. And since no existing device can actually produce so many fine gradations of color anyway, there's really no point in using up such extravagant amounts of memory.

To reduce the memory requirements to less gargantuan proportions, most graphics devices use a form of *mapped* color representation. Out of the trillions of possible colors in RGB space, only a limited number are available on the device at any given time. The current selection of colors is kept in a *color lookup table* (often referred to, briefly if not euphoniously, as a *CLUT*).

Instead of direct RGB color values, the pixel image for such a mapped device contains a *color index* for each pixel, identifying the position in the device's color table where the actual color is to be found. The device driver reads out the color index for each pixel in the image and looks up the corresponding entry in the table to find what color to display on the screen. The size of the color table determines the pixel depth of the image in memory: 4 bits for a table of 16 colors, 8 bits for 256 colors, and so on.

The Color Picker

As a convenience to the user in selecting colors for use on the screen, the Toolbox provides a standard dialog box called the Color Picker (Figure 4–2). Any time your program needs to specify a color for any purpose, you can call the Toolbox routine GetColor [4.2.3] to put up the Color Picker dialog and leave the choice to the user. You supply a prompting string to be displayed in the dialog box ("Please pick a color:" in the figure) and propose an initial color for the user to consider. The GetColor routine handles all interactions with the user until the dialog is dismissed, then returns the color the user has picked via the variable parameter pickedColor. You can then use this color in any way you consider appropriate.

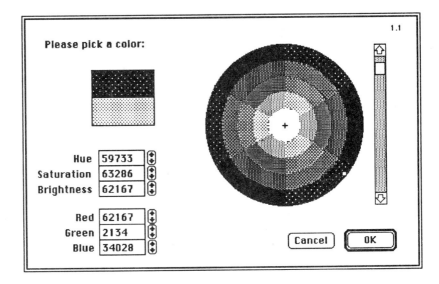

Figure 4–2 Color Picker dialog

Like the Standard File dialogs [II:8.3] for selecting file names, the Color Picker is technically not part of the Toolbox proper, but instead resides in a new disk-based package, the Color Picker Package. This package also includes the routines for converting color formats [4.2.2] that we referred to earlier.

The user can specify a color in any of three ways:

- Use the mouse to designate a position on the color wheel and the scroll-bar-style brightness control.

- Type the color's HSV parameters directly into the upper set of three text boxes or manipulate their contents with the up and down arrows.

- Set the color's RGB components in a similar way in the lower three text boxes.

The angular position of the color wheel's indicator defines the hue of the selected color, and the radial distance from the center gives the saturation. The brightness is determined by the scroll-bar-style control at the right.

Any change in any of the three methods of color selection is automatically reflected in the others as well: for instance, changing any of the RGB components also changes the HSV values and repositions the indicators on the color wheel and brightness control. In addition, the currently selected color is displayed in the upper of the two color boxes near the top-left of the dialog box, just below the prompting string. The lower box always displays the initial color you proposed when you first posted the dialog; clicking in this box with the mouse resets the upper box (and all the other settings) to match it.

When the user dismisses the dialog, `GetColor` returns a Boolean value telling whether it was dismissed with the `OK` or the `Cancel` button. If the function result is `TRUE`, then the dialog was confirmed and you should use the color value returned in the parameter `pickedColor`. If the result is `FALSE`, then the user canceled the dialog and you should use your own default color choice instead (presumably the one you initially proposed as `startColor`).

Graphics Devices

Unlike earlier models, the Macintosh II is not limited to a single display screen of a predetermined size. Any number of separate display devices can be connected via controller cards in the system's expansion slots, each with its own screen dimensions, pixel depth, and other characteristics. Since the pixel image defining the contents of the screen can vary in size from one device to another, it no longer occupies a fixed block of locations in the computer's main memory. Instead, it resides in the controller card's slot space, in memory chips physically located on the card itself. The card can support a screen of any size it wishes, so long as it provides enough memory capacity to hold the required screen image.

Each time the system is started up, it scans through all of its slots looking for installed display devices. For each one it finds, it creates a *device record* of type `GDevice` [4.3.1], containing all the information the Toolbox needs to carry out its drawing operations on that device. In particular, the record's `gdRect` field holds a *boundary rectangle* giving the dimensions of the device's screen image and its location on the QuickDraw coordinate plane.

The screen image itself is kept in a *pixel map* (analogous to an old-style QuickDraw bit map) located via a handle in the device record's `gdPMap` field. As we'll see in the next chapter [5.1.1], the pixel map also defines the image's pixel depth, color table, and other important properties. The record's `gdType` field holds an integer code identifying the form of color representation this device expects to find in its pixel map:

- A *direct device* accepts colors in explicit RGB format and reproduces them directly on the screen. The present version of the Toolbox doesn't support this type of device; it's included purely for the sake of future compatibility.

- A *fixed device* uses a color table to map color indices from the pixel map into the actual color values they stand for. However, the selection of available colors is predefined by the device itself and cannot be changed.

- A *variable CLUT device* also uses a color table, but the contents of the table can be changed as needed by the running program. This is the type of device with which the present version of the Toolbox is primarily designed to operate, and to which all discussions in this book are understood to apply unless otherwise stated.

Devices records are created and destroyed by the Toolbox routines `NewGDevice` and `DisposGDevice` [4.3.2]. These chores are normally handled by the system, though, and you'll rarely have any occasion to worry about them yourself. Ordinarily the only time you'll need to create a device record of your own is for drawing to an offscreen pixel map rather than directly to a display device.

There are a variety of reasons for offscreen drawing: to present smoothly animated graphics on the screen, to avoid flickers and other unwanted visual effects when drawing overlapping objects, to draw into a window that crosses the boundary from one display screen to another (possibly with differing color environments), or to prepare an image for a printer or other device whose color environment doesn't match that of any existing display. In each of these cases, you must use the Toolbox routine `NewGDevice` [4.3.2] to create a dummy device record that isn't associated with any actual graphics device in the system. Offscreen drawing is an unusual and rather tricky operation, however; if you really need to attempt it, see the chapter on graphics devices in *Inside Macintosh* for details.

The device records for all true graphics devices (but not those you create yourself for offscreen drawing) are linked together into a global *device list*. The list begins in the system global variable DeviceList [4.3.3] (accessible only in assembly language) and continues through the gdNextGD fields of the individual records [4.3.1]; a NIL handle marks the end of the list. You can get a handle to the first device in the list from the Toolbox routine GetDevice- List [4.3.3] and move from one device to the next with GetNext- Device [4.3.3].

A device can have one or more display modes that determine the way it presents an image on the screen. Different display modes typically correspond to different pixel depths, and hence control the number of distinct colors that can appear on the screen; but they may also affect other aspects of the device's operation, such as the use of gray scale instead of full color. The possible modes in which the device can operate are defined by slot resources in declaration ROM on its controller card; the ID numbers of these resources also serve as identifying numbers for the modes themselves.

The gdMode field in the device record [4.3.1] always contains the number of the mode in which the device is currently operating. By convention, mode number 128 denotes the device's default mode, which is normally monochrome (1-bit) video; if there are any additional modes, they are numbered sequentially from 129 up. The Toolbox routine InitGDevice [4.3.2] reinitializes an existing device record for a specified display mode.

Using the Control Panel desk accessory, the user can set a *screen configuration* that includes the display mode for each screen and, if there's more than one, their spatial arrangement relative to one another. This information is then saved in a special resource of type 'scrn' for future reference. If a 'scrn' resource is present the next time the system is started, and if the same set of devices are still connected, they will automatically be initialized to the previous configuration. Otherwise, the device in the lowest-numbered slot will be placed in its standard (monochrome) mode and all others will be made inactive (unavailable for use).

The user's screen configuration also designates one particular device as the *main device* or *main screen*, the one on which the menu bar is to appear. This device's boundary rectangle establishes the global coordinate system in which those of all other devices (if any) are expressed. If no screen configuration is present at system startup, the device in the lowest-numbered slot automatically becomes the main device. The assembly-language global variable `MainDevice` holds a handle to the device record defining the main device; you can get a copy of this handle with the Toolbox routine `GetMainDevice` [4.3.4].

At any given time, exactly one graphics device is singled out as the *current device*, whose color table and other attributes establish the color environment for all color drawing operations. A handle to the current device record is kept in the system global `TheGDevice`, where you can read or change it with the Toolbox routines `Get-GDevice` and `SetGDevice` [4.3.4]. It isn't usually necessary to manipulate the current device yourself, however, since the Toolbox does it for you automatically when you draw into a given window or graphics port. Even if a window spans the boundary from one screen to another, the Toolbox will see to it that all drawing operations are directed to the proper graphics device.

Color Tables

The mapping from the color indices used in a pixel map to the actual color values they stand for is defined by a Toolbox data structure called a *color table* [4.4.1]. Every mapped device has its own color table defining the selection of colors currently available; a handle to the color table is kept in a field of the device's pixel map [5.1.1], which in turn is located via the `gdPMap` field of the device record [4.3.1]. On a fixed device, the contents of the table are predefined and unchangeable, while on a variable device (the usual type) you can modify them to tailor the color environment to your own needs. The color table belonging to the current graphics device is the *current color table*, which defines the color mapping currently in effect for all drawing operations.

An individual pixel map can also have its own color table, separate from that of the device on which it is displayed. In this case, the color table defines the exact RGB colors that the index values in the pixel map are intended to represent. When displayed on a particular device, these colors are matched against those in the device's own color table and replaced with the closest approximations currently available. Thus the actual appearance of the image may vary, depending on the device, the display mode the user has chosen, and the dynamic state of the device's color environment.

Structure of Color Tables

Structurally, a color table [4.4.1] consists of a few bytes of header information followed by an array of *color specifications*. The `ctFlags` field is reserved for flag bits describing various attributes of the table; the only one currently defined is the high-order bit, which is 1 for a table belonging to a graphics device or 0 for one associated with a device-independent pixel map. The `ctSeed` field is used to coordinate the contents of the color table with those of its matching inverse table, so we'll postpone discussing it until later in this chapter when we talk about inverse tables.

The main body of the table is the array `ctTable`, which contains an indefinite number of entries; the `ctSize` field tells how many. Each entry is a record of type `ColorSpec` [4.4.1], which in turn has two fields, `value` and `rgb`. In a color table belonging to a device-independent pixel map, each entry's `rgb` field defines a desired or intended color and the associated `value` field gives the index number that stands for that color in the body of the map. In a table belonging to a graphics device, the `rgb` fields define the colors currently available on the device and are indexed positionally by their location within the table; the `value` fields are used internally for other purposes, and are nobody's business but the Toolbox.

Color tables can be stored as resources of type `'clut'` ("color lookup table") [4.7.1] and read in with the Toolbox routine `Get-CTable` [4.4.3]. Resource IDs from 0 to 127 are reserved for system use; in particular, the Macintosh II ROM contains built-in `'clut'` resources numbered 1, 2, 4, and 8, which define default color sets for the corresponding standard pixel depths. There's also another built-in resource, number 127, which holds a table of RGB equivalents to the eight standard colors of the "classic QuickDraw" planar color model. Any `'clut'` resources you create for yourself should have ID numbers between 128 and 1023.

Inverse Tables

The Toolbox routines `Index2Color` and `Color2Index` [4.4.4] convert in either direction between a color index and the corresponding RGB value. The results in both cases are based on the current state of the color environment (that is, on the color table of the current graphics device). `Index2Color` just does a simple table lookup, but the inverse mapping, `Color2Index`, is less straightforward. This is an important operation, because the Toolbox uses it to convert your requested drawing colors into the corresponding pixel values to be written into the screen image—so it's worth going to some trouble to implement as efficiently as possible.

To avoid having to do a lengthy table search each time you ask for a new drawing color, the Toolbox builds an auxiliary data structure, the *inverse table* [4.4.2], based on the contents of the color table itself. Every graphics device has its own inverse table, located via a handle in the `gdITable` field of the device record [4.3.1]. Entries in the inverse table are indexed according to the RGB color they represent, and in turn yield the index of the entry in the color table most closely approximating that color. Once the inverse table is built, the Toolbox can simply look up your color requests directly instead of searching the entire color table for a match.

The Toolbox routine `MakeITable` [4.4.2] builds an inverse table corresponding to a given color table. Both the color table and the inverse table (or at least the memory block to hold it) must already exist; `MakeITable` accepts handles to both as parameters. (For convenience, a `NIL` value for either or both of these parameters designates the color or inverse table belonging to the current graphics device.) The third parameter to `MakeITable` is the desired *bit resolution*, which determines the size and precision of the inverse table. The `gdResPref` field of a device record [4.3.1] gives the preferred bit resolution for that device's inverse table; the actual resolution for a given table is kept in the table's `iTabRes` field [4.4.2].

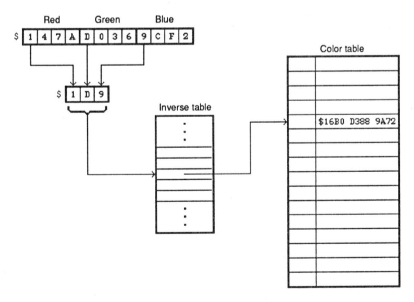

Figure 4-3 Inverse color mapping

To look up a given color in the inverse table, the Toolbox constructs a table index by concatenating together the most significant (high-order) bits from each of the color's three RGB components. The table's bit resolution tells how many bits to take from each: for example, at 4-bit resolution, the first 4 bits of each color component (red, green, and blue in that order) combine to form a 12-bit table index, as shown in Figure 4–3. The entry at that position in the inverse table gives, in turn, the index of the closest available matching color in the color table itself. (Notice in the figure that the match is not exact, but is merely the best approximation among the colors currently contained in the color table. The Toolbox routine RealColor [4.4.4] tests whether a given exact color is available in the current color environment.)

Higher bit resolutions yield more precise color mappings, but at the expense of exponentially increasing table size. For example, at 3-bit resolution, each table index is 9 bits long (3 bits for each of three color components); thus the table must contain 2^9, or 512 entries. At a resolution of 4 bits, the table size is 2^{12}, or 4K entries; at 5 bits, it grows to 2^{15}, or 32K. These are the only three bit resolutions the Toolbox currently supports: anything less than 3 bits would give results too coarse to be meaningful, while more than 5 bits would require table indices longer than a single 16-bit word. In general, 4-bit resolution is sufficient for most practical purposes.

Once an inverse table is built, it remains valid only as long as the contents of the underlying color table remain the same. Any change in the color table invalidates the inverse table, which must then be rebuilt before it can be used again. Instead of rebuilding the table immediately, however, the Toolbox simply marks it as invalid, postponing the actual rebuilding until the next time it needs the table for a color lookup.

To coordinate this rebuilding process, the Toolbox maintains a long-integer *seed* for every color and inverse table. The Toolbox routine GetCTable [4.4.3], which creates a color table from a 'clut' resource, initializes the table's ctSeed field [4.4.1] to the resource ID. (If you create a color table in some other way, you should call GetCTSeed [4.4.3] to get an initial seed value and store it into the ctSeed field "by hand.") Thereafter, any operation that changes the contents of the color table automatically changes its seed value as well.

When MakeITable builds an inverse table corresponding to a given color table, it copies the color table's current seed value into the iTabSeed field of the inverse table [4.4.2]. Then, whenever it needs to use the inverse table for color mapping, the Toolbox first compares its seed with that of the color table it's based on. If the two seed values agree, then the inverse table is still valid and can be used as is; if they don't, the contents of the color table have changed and the inverse table must be rebuilt.

Color Table Management

As you might expect, the Toolbox includes a variety of routines for maintaining and manipulating the contents of color tables. In practice, however, you'll seldom need to use these facilities directly. We'll be learning in the next section about *color palettes*, a handy mechanism for managing your color environment in a controlled, flexible way. Although the lower-level routines described here are always available for direct color table management, you'll generally find it more convenient to work with palettes instead.

The main routine for setting the contents of a color table directly is SetEntries [4.4.5]. You supply an array of color specifications [4.4.1], newColors, giving the RGB values to be entered in the current color table; the nEntries parameter tells how many. (Actually, nEntries must be set to the number of colors minus 1.) There are two ways of specifying the color indices under which the colors are to be entered. If you set the startIndex parameter to -1, each color's index is given by the value field of its color specification in the newColors array. If startIndex is positive, the value fields are ignored and the colors are simply entered at consecutive indices starting from the given value. In either case, notice that all index numbers refer to *logical* color indices and do not necessarily correspond to physical positions within the color table.

Before making any change in the color environment, you can save its current state with SaveEntries and restore it later with RestoreEntries [4.4.5]. Both routines take a *request list* as a parameter, an array of index numbers identifying the entries to be saved or restored. (In this case, just to keep you on your toes, the indices are physical rather than logical.) SaveEntries copies the requested entries from the main color table into a smaller, auxiliary table; RestoreEntries copies them back from the auxiliary table to the main table. Just as for the MakeITable routine we discussed earlier, a NIL value for the mainTable parameter implicitly refers to the current color table.

One thing to bear in mind is that in the MultiFinder environment, space in the color table is a limited resource that you may have to share with other programs. The Toolbox routines `ProtectEntry` and `ReserveEntry` [4.4.6] allow you to claim some of this precious real estate for your own private use. Protecting a color table entry prevents any other program from changing its color value; reserving it makes it unavailable as a match for other programs' color requests, even if it is the nearest color in the table to the one they asked for. Both routines accept a color index referring to an entry in the current color table, along with a Boolean parameter telling whether you wish to apply or remove the protection or reservation on that entry. These routines are particularly useful in allocating table entries for *color table animation*, a technique we'll be talking about in the next chapter [5.4.3].

Color Palettes

By far the most convenient way to manage your program's color environment is with *color palettes*. A palette is a predefined collection of colors that you wish to use for your drawing operations. Whenever the palette is activated, the Toolbox will automatically update the current color table to try to ensure that the colors requested in the palette are available for use. Palettes save you the trouble of manipulating the color environment for yourself: you just place the colors you want in a palette and let the Toolbox take care of the details.

The most common way of using palettes is in connection with windows. Every color window has its own palette. When the user brings a window to the front of the screen, its palette is automatically activated and the color table stocked with its preferred selection of colors. We'll have more to say on this subject when we take up color windows in Chapter 6.

The internal description of a palette is a *palette record* [4.5.1]. The palette can include as many colors as you wish; the Toolbox will do its best to make them all available (subject of course to the capacity of the color table on the device you're drawing on). Each color in the palette is identified positionally by its *palette index*. It's sort of like one of those paint-by-numbers kits you can buy at the hobby store—1 for red, 2 for purple, 3 for brown—except that you get to choose the numbers and the colors.

Note that a color's palette index is not the same as the color index used to represent it in pixel images. A color index refers to a position in a color table, a palette index to a position in a palette. As the color environment varies over time or from one device to another, the color index most nearly approximating a given color may change, but its palette index never does. That's what makes palettes so convenient.

Color Usage

The heart of a palette record is an array of subrecords of type `ColorInfo` [4.5.1] defining the individual colors. Each `ColorInfo` record includes the desired RGB value along with a *usage level* that determines how the color is to be matched against those available in the color table. The current Toolbox recognizes five possible usage levels, known as tolerant, courteous, animating, explicit, and dithered colors.

Tolerant colors are the standard form of color usage. This type of color will match an existing value in the current color table if there is one close enough. If no such match can be found, the Toolbox will choose an existing entry in the table and set it to the exact RGB value requested in the palette. (This may spoil the appearance of other windows on the screen, but only until those windows are activated and their own palettes come back into effect.)

Just what constitutes "close enough" is defined by a *tolerance* value that's included in the `ColorInfo` record. The tolerance expresses the margin of error the color is willing to accept: an existing color is considered to match if each of its three RGB components differs from that of the requested color by less than the specified tolerance. A tolerance level of $5000 is suggested for most ordinary purposes, but of course you can vary this according to your specific needs. A tolerance of 0 yields what might be called an "intolerant color," which demands perfection and won't settle for anything less than an exact match.

At the opposite extreme are *courteous colors*, which don't like making a fuss and will accept any old value you care to give them. (This makes them equivalent to tolerant colors with the maximum possible tolerance level, $FFFF.) A courteous color will still look for the best available match in the current color table, but it will always be satisfied with *some* available color and will never cause any change in the existing color environment.

The main use of courteous colors is to avoid having your favorite colors dropped from the color table in favor of someone else's. Recall that if the Toolbox can't find a suitable match for a tolerant color, it will throw some other color out of the table to make room. If you have expressed a fondness for a particular color, the Toolbox will attempt to keep it available and kick out some other color instead. This kindness is not guaranteed, and you may sometimes find your colors getting stolen anyway— but at least you stand a chance if you keep the Toolbox informed of your preferences by declaring them courteously in a palette.

Animating colors reserve entries in a device's color table for use in color table animation [5.4.3]. As we learned earlier, such reserved entries become unavailable for use in other drawing operations and will not match any color request issued by another program. We'll learn more about color table animation in the next chapter.

Explicit colors bypass the color-matching process entirely and use the entry's palette index directly as an index into the current color table. (This is the one time that a color's palette index and color index are guaranteed to be the same.) They always use the color currently associated with the given index in the color table, without reference to the RGB value specified in the palette entry itself.

The last type of color usage a palette entry can specify is a *dithered color*. If the requested RGB value is not explicitly available in the color table, it will be simulated by "dithering" together two or more other colors in a pattern of dots that blend visually to approximate the desired color—sort of like the colored dots on the Sunday comics page. This capability is not yet supported in the current version of the Toolbox, but is included for possible future implementation.

Creating and Destroying Palettes

Before the Toolbox can perform any operation involving palettes, it must be prepared for the task with InitPalettes [4.5.2]. This initializes its internal palette-related data structures and performs other bits of miscellaneous housekeeping. However, in all versions of the Toolbox that support palettes at all, this routine is called automatically by InitWindows [II:3.2.1], so there should never be any need for you to call it directly yourself.

The usual way of creating a new palette is from a template resource of type 'pltt' [4.7.2]. In the common case where the palette is to be associated with a window on the screen, you should give the palette template the same resource ID as the window template it belongs with. The Toolbox routine GetNewCWindow [6.3.4], which creates a color window from a template, will then automatically create the palette as well. In other cases, you can call GetNewPalette [4.5.3] to create the palette explicitly.

You can also build a new palette "from scratch" with New-Palette [4.5.3]. The nEntries parameter tells how many colors it should hold. For the color values themselves, you can either supply a color table, entryColors, or else initialize them all to black by passing NIL for this parameter and then set each color individually with SetEntryColor [4.5.4]. All colors in the new palette will be given the same usage and tolerance levels, as specified by the NewPalette parameters entryUsage and entryTolerance; if necessary, you can then use SetEntryUsage [4.5.4] to adjust these settings for individual palette entries.

Once a palette is built, SetEntryColor [4.5.4] returns the RGB value of an individual entry and SetEntryUsage [4.5.4] returns its usage and tolerance values. Other utility routines that are occasionally useful are CTab2Palette and Palette2CTab [4.5.5], which copy the contents of a color table to a palette and vice versa, and CopyPalette [4.5.5], which copies all or part of one palette to another. When you have no further need for a palette, Dispose-Palette [4.5.3] destroys it and recycles its memory space for other uses. (Needless to say, this operation also converts all existing handles to the palette into lethal weapons, so don't leave them lying around for your kids to play with.)

REFERENCE

4.1 Classic Color Model

4.1.1 Color Values

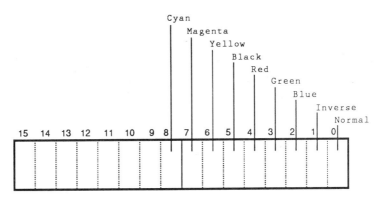

Classic QuickDraw color bits

![icon] **Definitions**

```
const
                              {Bit numbers for color planes: }
  NormalBit  = 0;               {Normal monochrome (black-on-white)}
  InverseBit = 1;               {Inverse monochrome (white-on-black)}
```

```
BlueBit      = 2;                              {Blue}
GreenBit     = 3;                              {Green}
RedBit       = 4;                              {Red}

BlackBit     = 5;                              {Black}
YellowBit    = 6;                              {Yellow}
MagentaBit   = 7;                              {Magenta}
CyanBit      = 8;                              {Cyan}

                                               {Color values for drawing operations: }
BlackColor     = $0021;                        {Black}
WhiteColor     = $001E;                        {White}

RedColor       = $00CD;                        {Red}
GreenColor     = $0155;                        {Green}
BlueColor      = $0199;                        {Blue}

CyanColor      = $0111;                        {Cyan}
MagentaColor   = $0089;                        {Magenta}
YellowColor    = $0045;                        {Yellow}
```

 Notes

1. The planar color model used in "classic" QuickDraw provides two planes for monochrome drawing (normal and inverse), three for additive color (red, green, blue), and four for subtractive color (cyan, magenta, yellow, black).

2. The constants `NormalBit`, `InverseBit`, and so on, are bit numbers representing the various color planes, for use with the Toolbox routine `ColorBit` [4.1.3].

3. The constants `BlackColor`, `WhiteColor`, and so on, are actual color values for use in QuickDraw drawing operations.

4. The numerical values of the color constants represent the appropriate combinations of individual color bits for planar imaging.

5. Standard monochrome graphics devices, such as the original Macintosh screen, use only the low-order bit (`NormalBit`) of the color value. Since all the color constants except `WhiteColor` are odd, this causes all colors except white to appear as black.

6. To draw with a given color, use ForeColor or BackColor [4.1.2] to make it the foreground or background color of the current graphics port. The color will then be used in place of black or white, respectively, in all of the port's subsequent drawing operations.

Assembly Language Information

Bit numbers for color planes:

Name	Value	Meaning
NormalBit	0	Normal monochrome (black-on-white)
InverseBit	1	Inverse monochrome (white-on-black)
BlueBit	2	Blue
GreenBit	3	Green
RedBit	4	Red
BlackBit	5	Black
YellowBit	6	Yellow
MagentaBit	7	Magenta
CyanBit	8	Cyan

Color values for drawing operations:

Name	Value	Meaning
BlackColor	$0021	Black
WhiteColor	$001E	White
RedColor	$00CD	Red
GreenColor	$0155	Green
BlueColor	$0199	Blue
CyanColor	$0111	Cyan
MagentaColor	$0089	Magenta
YellowColor	$0045	Yellow

4.1.2   Foreground and Background Colors

Definitions

```
type
   GrafPort = record
            . . . :
               fgColor : LONGINT;          {Current foreground color}
               bkColor : LONGINT;          {Current background color}
            . . .
         end;

procedure ForeColor
         (newColor : LONGINT);             {New foreground color}

procedure BackColor
         (newColor : LONGINT);             {New background color}
```

Notes

1. `ForeColor` and `BackColor` set the foreground and background colors of an old-style graphics port.

2. The foreground and background colors are kept in the `fgColor` and `bkColor` fields of the `GrafPort` record [I:4.2.2].

3. The value of `newColor` should be one of the constants `BlackColor`, `WhiteColor`, and so on, defined in [4.1.1].

4. In a newly created graphics port, the foreground color is initialized to black and the background color to white.

5. In the discussions of classic QuickDraw drawing operations in earlier volumes of this series, all references to black and white pixels actually apply to the port's current foreground and background colors, respectively.

6. `ForeColor` and `BackColor` are intended for use in old-style graphics ports only.   In a color port [5.1.3], use `RGBForeColor` and `RGBBackColor` (or `PMForeColor` and `PMBackColor`) [5.4.1] instead.

Assembly Language Information

Field offsets in a graphics port:

(Pascal) Field name	(Assembly) Offset name	Offset in bytes
fgColor	fgColor	80
bkColor	bkColor	84

Trap macros:

(Pascal) Routine name	(Assembly) Trap macro	Trap word
ForeColor	_ForeColor	$A862
BackColor	_BackColor	$A863

4.1.3   Color Plane

Definitions

```
type
   GrafPort = record
               . . . ;
             colrBit : INTEGER;        {Current color plane}
               . . .
           end;

procedure ColorBit
         (whichPlane : INTEGER);      {New color plane}
```

Notes

1. The `colrBit` field of the `GrafPort` record [I:4.2.2] controls which color plane the port draws into.

2. The Toolbox routine `ColorBit` sets the color plane for the current port. Subsequent drawing operations will take place in the designated plane.

3. The value of whichPlane should be one of the constants NormalBit, InverseBit, and so on, defined in [4.1.1].

4. ColorBit is meaningful for old-style graphics ports only, and should never be used in a color port [5.1.3].

5. This routine is intended to be used by low-level printing and video imaging software; ordinary application programs normally have no need for it.

Assembly Language Information

Field offset in a graphics port:

(Pascal) Field name	(Assembly) Offset name	Offset in bytes
colrBit	colrBit	88

Trap macro:

(Pascal) Routine name	(Assembly) Trap macro	Trap word
ColorBit	_ColorBit	$A864

4.2 Color Representation

4.2.1   Color Formats

Definitions

```
type
  RGBColor = record
              red    : INTEGER;      {Level of red component}
              green  : INTEGER;      {Level of green component}
              blue   : INTEGER       {Level of blue component}
            end;

  CMYColor = record
              cyan    : SmallFract;  {Level of cyan component}
              magenta : SmallFract;  {Level of magenta component}
              yellow  : SmallFract   {Level of yellow component}
            end;
```

```
HSVColor = record
            hue         : SmallFract;  {Hue}
            saturation  : SmallFract;  {Saturation}
            value       : SmallFract   {Value (brightness)}
        end;

HSLColor = record
            hue         : SmallFract;  {Hue}
            saturation  : SmallFract;  {Saturation}
            lightness   : SmallFract   {Lightness}
        end;
```

 ## Notes

1. These data structures all represent alternative methods of specifying colors in a device-independent way.

2. RGB (red–green–blue) is the standard form of device-independent color representation used by the Macintosh Toolbox. The three components give the relative levels of the additive primary colors used in color video.

3. CMY (cyan–magenta–yellow) format expresses colors in terms of the subtractive primaries used in hardcopy printing.

4. HSV (hue–saturation–value) is the most widely known form of color representation, and is used by the Color Picker Package [4.2.3] to allow users to specify colors interactively on the screen.

5. HSL (hue–saturation–lightness) is an alternative format similar to HSV.

6. RGB components are expressed as *unsigned* integers, from 0 to 65535.

7. In all other forms of color representation, the components are expressed as small fractions [2.4.1] with values between 0 and 1.

8. *Hue* values wrap around cyclically to denote positions on a circular "color wheel." Values of both 0 and 1 correspond to red, .33333 to green, and .66667 to blue.

9. *Saturation* denotes the purity or vividness of a color, from 0 (pure gray, no color) to 1 (pure color, no gray).

10. *Value* (also called brightness) measures the strength or intensity of a color, from 0 (pure black, no color) to 1 (maximum intensity).

11. *Lightness* expresses the depth of a color's shade as an equivalent gray level, from 0 (pure black) to 1 (pure white).

12. To convert colors from one format to another, use the conversion routines in [4.2.2].

Assembly Language Information

Field offsets in color records:

(Pascal) Field name	(Assembly) Offset name	Offset in bytes
red	red	0
green	green	2
blue	blue	4
cyan	cyan	0
magenta	magenta	2
yellow	yellow	4
hue	hue	0
saturation	saturation	2
value	value	4
lightness	lightness	4

Assembly-language constant:

Name	Value	Meaning
RGBColor	6	Size of color records, in bytes

4.2.2   Color Conversion

Definitions

```
procedure RGB2CMY
        (fromColor    : RGBColor;      {Color to be converted, in RGB format}
     var toColor  : CMYColor);     {Equivalent color in CMY format}

procedure CMY2RGB
        (fromColor    : CMYColor;      {Color to be converted, in CMY format}
     var toColor  : RGBColor);     {Equivalent color in RGB format}

procedure RGB2HSV
        (fromColor    : RGBColor;      {Color to be converted, in RGB format}
     var toColor  : HSVColor);     {Equivalent color in HSV format}
```

```
procedure HSV2RGB
            (fromColor   : HSVColor;      {Color to be converted, in HSV format}
             var toColor : RGBColor);     {Equivalent color in RGB format}

procedure RGB2HSL
            (fromColor   : RGBColor;      {Color to be converted, in RGB format}
             var toColor : HSLColor);     {Equivalent color in HSL format}

procedure HSL2RGB
            (fromColor   : HSLColor;      {Color to be converted, in HSL format}
             var toColor : RGBColor);     {Equivalent color in RGB format}
```

RGB values of standard primary colors:

Table Index	Color	Red Dec.	Red Hex.	Green Dec.	Green Hex.	Blue Dec.	Blue Hex.
0	Black	0	$0000	0	$0000	0	$0000
1	Yellow	64512	$FC00	62333	$F37D	1327	$052F
2	Magenta	62167	$F2D7	2134	$0856	34028	$84EC
3	Red	56683	$DD6B	2242	$08C2	1698	$06A2
4	Cyan	577	$0241	43860	$AB54	60159	$EAFF
5	Green	0	$0000	32768	$8000	4528	$11B0
6	Blue	0	$0000	0	$0000	54272	$D400
7	White	65535	$FFFF	65535	$FFFF	65535	$FFFF

Notes

1. These routines convert colors among the alternative representation formats defined in [4.2.1].

2. The standard format used by the Toolbox itself is RGB. All the conversion routines convert between this form and one of the others.

3. The table shows the equivalent RGB values of the standard additive and subtractive primary colors.

4. The assembly-language global variable QDColors (see "Assembly Language Information" below) holds a handle to a table of these values.

5. Each color's index in the table is taken from bits 4–2 of the corresponding color constant [4.1.1].

6. The RGB values for the standard colors are based on those produced by an ImageWriter II printer with a color ribbon.

7. The conversion routines are implemented as part of the Color Picker Package, and are called at the machine level via the package trap _Pack12 [I:7.2.1]. The trap macros expand to call this trap after pushing an identifying routine selector (see table below) onto the stack.

Assembly Language Information

Trap macros and routine selectors:

(Pascal) Routine name	(Assembly) Trap macro	Trap word	Routine selector
RGB2CMY	_RGB2CMY	$A82E	4
CMY2RGB	_CMY2RGB	$A82E	3
RGB2HSV	_RGB2HSV	$A82E	8
HSV2RGB	_HSV2RGB	$A82E	7
RGB2HSL	_RGB2HSL	$A82E	6
HSL2RGB	_HSL2RGB	$A82E	5

Assembly-language global variable:

Name	Address	Meaning
QDColors	$8B0	Handle to table of primary color values

4.2.3 The Color Picker

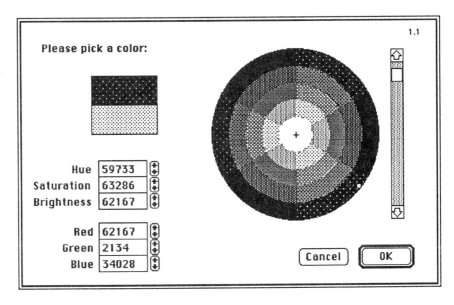

Color Picker dialog

Definitions

```
function GetColor
        (topLeft       : Point;          {Top-left corner of dialog in screen coordinates}
        promptString   : Str255;         {Prompting string}
        startColor     : RGBColor;       {Initial color to propose in dialog box}
        var pickedColor : RGBColor)      {Returns color selected by user}
        : BOOLEAN;                       {Did user confirm color selection?}
```

Notes

1. GetColor displays the dialog box shown in the figure, allowing the user to specify a color interactively on the screen.

2. GetColor handles all events until the user dismisses the dialog box, either by clicking the OK or Cancel button or by pressing the Return or Enter key.

3. The `topLeft` parameter gives the location of the dialog box in *global (screen) coordinates.*

4. The point designated by `topLeft` should lie on the screen of the main graphics device [4.3.4].

5. If `topLeft = (0, 0)`, the dialog box will automatically be centered horizontally on the main screen, with half as much empty space above as below.

6. `startColor` specifies an initial color value to be proposed to the user when the dialog first appears on the screen. This color will remain permanently displayed in the lower of the two color boxes, while the color in the upper box changes in response to the user's actions.

7. The `promptString` parameter is displayed as a static text item above the two color boxes.

8. The currently selected color is displayed simultaneously in four different ways:

    • as a direct visual sample in the upper of the two color boxes

    • as an indicator position on the color wheel and the sliding brightness control (scroll bar)

    • as a set of digital HSV parameters in the upper three text boxes

    • as a set of digital RGB components in the lower three text boxes

9. The angular position of the indicator on the color wheel determines the hue of the selected color, the radial distance from the center determines the saturation, and the height of the indicator box in the scroll bar determines the value (brightness).

10. All digital (HSV and RGB) parameters range from a minimum of 0 to a maximum of 65535. Hue values wrap around from 65535 to 0, allowing the hue to cycle continuously around the color wheel; all other values pin at 0 or 65535.

11. The user can vary the selected color either by moving the indicators on the color wheel and scroll bar, manipulating the HSV or RGB parameters with the up and down arrows, or typing new parameter values directly into the text boxes. All changes in any one form of color display are automatically reflected in the others as well.

12. Clicking the mouse in the lower color box automatically restores all color settings to the color initially proposed via the `startColor` parameter.

13. When satisfied with the selected color, the user confirms the selection by clicking the OK button or pressing the Return or Enter key. The

selected color is then returned as an RGB value in the variable parameter `pickedColor`.

14. Clicking the `Cancel` button dismisses the dialog and rejects the selected color. The value returned for `pickedColor` is then undefined; the program should presumably use the original `startColor` instead.

15. The Boolean function result tells whether the user confirmed (`TRUE`) or canceled (`FALSE`) the dialog.

16. `GetColor` does not change the current color environment in any way. It is up to your program to use the selected color in whatever way it considers appropriate.

17. `GetColor` is part of the Color Picker Package, and is called at the machine level via the package trap `_Pack12` [I:7.2.1]. The trap macro expands to call this trap after pushing an identifying routine selector (see table below) onto the stack.

Assembly Language Information

Trap macro and routine selector:

(Pascal) Routine name	(Assembly) Trap macro	Trap word	Routine selector
GetColor	_GetColor	$A82E	9

4.3 Graphics Devices

4.3.1   Device Records

Definitions

```
type
  GDHandle = ^GDPtr;
  GDPtr    = ^GDevice;

  GDevice = record
              gdRefNum    : INTEGER;     {Driver reference number}
              gdID        : INTEGER;     {Client ID for matching routines [4.6.2]}
              gdType      : INTEGER;     {Device type}
              gdITable    : ITabHandle;  {Inverse table [4.4.2]}
```

```
        gdResPref      :  INTEGER;          {Preferred inverse table resolution [4.4.2]}
        gdSearchProc   :  SProcHndl;        {List of custom search functions [4.6.1]}
        gdCompProc     :  CProcHndl;        {List of custom complement procedures [4.6.1]}
        gdFlags        :  INTEGER;          {Attribute flags [4.3.5]}
        gdPMap         :  PixMapHandle;     {Pixel map to hold displayed image}
        gdRefCon       :  LONGINT;          {CalcCMask and SeedCFill parameters [5.4.5]}
        gdNextGD       :  GDHandle;         {Next device in device list}
        gdRect         :  Rect;             {Boundary rectangle}
        gdMode         :  LONGINT;          {Current display mode}
        gdCCBytes      :  INTEGER;          {Private}
        gdCCDepth      :  INTEGER;          {Private}
        gdCCXData      :  Handle;           {Private}
        gdCCXMask      :  Handle;           {Private}
        gdReserved     :  LONGINT           {Reserved for future expansion}
      end;

const
  CLUTType    = 0;                          {Mapped device with color lookup table}
  FixedType   = 1;                          {Fixed device, no lookup table}
  DirectType  = 2;                          {Direct RGB device}
```

Notes

1. A device record summarizes the characteristics of a graphics device.

2. A device record is created at system startup for each installed video graphics card. Additional device records can be created as needed (for example, for drawing into an offscreen pixel map whose pixel depth or other properties differ from those of the screen).

3. All device records reside in the system heap.

4. gdRect is the device's boundary rectangle, in the coordinate system established by the main graphics device [4.3.4]. For devices other than the main device, the relative positioning of this rectangle is set by the user via the Control Panel desk accessory.

5. gdType identifies the device's general method of color specification. Currently defined device types are CLUTType, FixedType, and DirectType.

6. The device's pixel depth, color table [4.4.1], and other specific display characteristics are defined by the pixel map [5.1.1] containing its displayed image. The gdPMap field of the device record holds a handle to this pixel map.

7. `gdRefNum` is the reference number of the device's driver.

8. `gdMode` is the display mode in which the device is currently operating. The available modes are defined in declaration ROM on the device's controller card; the user chooses among them with the Control Panel.

9. By convention, mode number `128` designates the device's default mode, which is normally monochrome (1-bit) video. Additional modes are numbered sequentially from `129` up.

10. `gdFlags` is a word of flag bits describing the device's attributes; see [4.3.5] for details.

11. `gdNextGD` is a handle to the next device record in the global device list [4.3.3]. A `NIL` handle marks the end of the list.

12. `gdITable` is a handle to the device's inverse table [4.4.2], used for mapping RGB color values to their corresponding color table index or other concrete representation. `gdResPref` is the preferred bit resolution for the inverse table, as discussed in [4.4.2].

13. `gdSearchProc` and `gdCompProc` are handles to lists of custom color-matching routines [4.6.1] (search functions and complement procedures, respectively). `NIL` values denote the standard matching routines only. The `gdID` field holds a client ID [4.6.2] for use with custom matching routines.

14. The `gdRefCon` field is used to pass parameter information to the special graphics operations `CalcCMask` and `SeedCFill` [5.4.5]. Application programs should never store directly into this field.

15. The `gdCCBytes`, `gdCCDepth`, `gdCCXData`, and `gdCCXMask` fields are used privately by the Toolbox to maintain the device's color cursor [6.2].

16. The `gdReserved` field is reserved for future expansion, and should always be set to `0`.

Assembly Language Information

Field offsets in a device record:

(Pascal) Field name	(Assembly) Offset name	Offset in bytes
gdRefNum	gdRefNum	0
gdID	gdID	2
gdType	gdType	4
gdITable	gdITable	6
gdResPref	gdResPref	10

(Pascal) Field name	(Assembly) Offset name	Offset in bytes
gdSearchProc	gdSearchProc	12
gdCompProc	gdCompProc	16
gdFlags	gdFlags	20
gdPMap	gdPMap	22
gdRefCon	gdRefCon	26
gdNextGD	gdNextGD	30
gdRect	gdRect	34
gdMode	gdMode	42
gdCCBytes	gdCCBytes	46
gdCCDepth	gdCCDepth	48
gdCCXData	gdCCXData	50
gdCCXMask	gdCCXMask	54
gdReserved	gdReserved	58

Assembly-language constant:

Name	Value	Meaning
GDRec in bytes	62	Size of a graphics device record

Graphics device types:

Name	Value	Meaning
CLUTType lookup table	0	Mapped colors with color
FixedType table	1	Fixed color mapping, no lookup
DirectType	2	Direct RGB representation

4.3.2   Creating and Destroying Devices

 Definitions

```
function  NewGDevice
              (dRefNum  : INTEGER;          {Driver reference number}
               initMode : LONGINT)          {Initial display mode}
                : GDHandle;                 {Handle to device record}
```

```
procedure InitGDevice
         (dRefNum   : INTEGER;        {Driver reference number}
          newMode   : LONGINT;        {New display mode}
          theDevice : GDHandle);      {Handle to device record}

procedure DisposGDevice
         (theDevice : GDHandle);      {Handle to device record}
```

 Notes

1. NewGDevice creates and initializes a new device record [4.3.1] and all of its subsidiary data structures; InitGDevice reinitializes an existing device record for a specified display mode.

2. dRefNum is the reference number of the driver for the desired device.

3. initMode or newMode specifies the display mode to which the device is to be set. The fields of the device record are set to reflect the characteristics of the requested mode.

4. A color table for the specified mode is allocated and initialized, either from a 'clut' resource [4.7.1] (for mapped devices) or directly from the controller card's ROM (for fixed devices). MakeITable [4.4.2] is then called to build a corresponding inverse table.

5. A device's possible display modes are defined in declaration ROM on its controller card. By convention, mode number 128 designates the device's default mode, which is normally monochrome (1-bit) video. Additional modes are numbered sequentially from 129 up.

6. If initMode or newMode ≠ 128, the device is assumed to be capable of displaying color and its GDDevType attribute [4.3.5] is set to TRUE. All other device attributes are initialized to FALSE.

7. To create a device record for an offscreen pixel map, set dRefNum to 0 and initMode to -1. The contents of the record will then not be initialized for a particular device and display mode; it's up to you to initialize them for yourself.

8. Newly created device records are *not* added to the global device list [4.3.3]. The contents of the device list are maintained entirely by the Toolbox; do not attempt to add new devices to the list yourself.

9. All device records and their associated data structures reside in the system heap.

10. If a new device record cannot be successfully allocated or initialized, NewGDevice returns NIL.

11. `DisposGDevice` deallocates and destroys a device record and all of its associated data structures.

12. Device records for all installed graphics devices are created automatically by the Toolbox at system startup and can be reinitialized to a new display mode by the user via the Control Panel desk accessory. You don't ordinarily need to call these routines yourself unless you're doing something unusual, such as drawing to an offscreen pixel map.

Assembly Language Information

Trap macros:

(Pascal) Routine name	(Assembly) Trap macro	Trap word
NewGDevice	_NewGDevice	$AA2F
InitGDevice	_InitGDevice	$AA2E
DisposGDevice	_DisposGDevice	$AA30

4.3.3   Device List

Definitions

```
function GetDeviceList
            : GDHandle;                          {First device in list}

function GetNextDevice
            (thisDevice : GDHandle)              {Handle to a device}
            : GDHandle;                          {Next device in list}
```

Notes

1. All graphics devices in the system are kept in a global device list, linked together through the `gdNextGD` fields of their device records [4.3.1].

2. A handle to the first device in the list is kept in the assembly-language global variable `DeviceList`; `GetDeviceList` returns a copy of this handle.

3. `GetNextDevice` returns a handle to the next device following a given one, or `NIL` for the last device in the list.

4. The list only includes true graphics devices, whose controller cards are found installed in the system at startup time. New device records created dynamically with NewGDevice [4.3.2] are *not* added to the list.

5. The contents of the device list are maintained entirely by the Toolbox; do not attempt to add new devices to the list yourself.

Assembly Language Information

Trap macros:

(Pascal) Routine name	(Assembly) Trap macro	Trap word
GetDeviceList	_GetDeviceList	$AA29
GetNextDevice	_GetNextDevice	$AA2B

Assembly-language global variable:

Name	Address	Meaning
DeviceList	$8A8	Handle to first graphics device in device list

4.3.4 Current Device

Definitions

```
procedure SetGDevice
            (newDevice : GDHandle);        {Handle to device to be made current}

function  GetGDevice
            : GDHandle;                    {Handle to current device}

function  GetMaxDevice
            (globalRect : Rect)            {Rectangle to intersect with, in global coordinates}
            : GDHandle;                    {Deepest device that intersects with this rectangle}

function  GetMainDevice
            : GDHandle;                    {Handle to main device}
```

Notes

1. SetGDevice makes a designated graphics device the current device; GetGDevice returns a handle to the current device.

2. The Toolbox uses the color table, inverse table, and matching routines associated with the current device to find the best available matches to the colors you specify for your drawing operations.

3. When you draw into a window, the Toolbox automatically finds which screen(s) the window lies on and handles the setting of the current device for you. You don't ordinarily need to call SetGDevice yourself unless you're doing something unusual, such as drawing to an offscreen pixel map.

4. GetMaxDevice finds the device with the greatest pixel depth whose boundary rectangle intersects with a given rectangle. This is useful, for instance, in determining the appropriate depth for an image that may span two or more separate screens.

5. The rectangle to be intersected is given in global coordinates.

6. GetMainDevice returns a handle to the main graphics device (the one on which the menu bar is displayed).

7. The graphics device installed in the lowest-numbered slot at system startup becomes the main device, unless the user designates some other device with the Control Panel desk accessory.

8. The assembly-language global variables TheGDevice and Main-Device hold handles to the current and main devices, respectively.

Assembly Language Information

Trap macros:

(Pascal) Routine name	(Assembly) Trap macro	Trap word
SetGDevice	_SetGDevice	$AA31
GetGDevice	_GetGDevice	$AA32
GetMainDevice	_GetMainDevice	$AA2A
GetMaxDevice	_GetMaxDevice	$AA27

Assembly-language global variables:

Name	Address	Meaning
TheGDevice	$CC8	Handle to current graphics device
MainDevice	$8A4	Handle to main screen device

4.3.5 Device Attributes

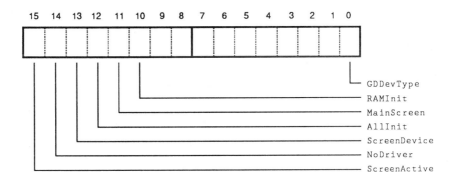

Graphics device attribute flags

Definitions

```
function  TestDeviceAttribute
              (theDevice : GDHandle;        {Handle to device record}
               whichAttr : INTEGER)         {Bit number of desired attribute}

                        : BOOLEAN;          {Current    value    of    attribute}

procedure SetDeviceAttribute
              (theDevice : GDHandle;        {Handle to device record}
               whichAttr : INTEGER;         {Bit number of desired attribute}
               newValue  : BOOLEAN);        {New value of attribute}
```

```
const
    GDDevType    =  0;                  {Supports color}
    RAMInit      = 10;                  {Initialized from RAM}
    MainScreen   = 11;                  {Is main device (contains menu bar)}
    AllInit      = 12;                  {Initialized from a 'scrn' resource}
    ScreenDevice = 13;                  {Is a screen device}
    NoDriver     = 14;                  {Has no driver}
    ScreenActive = 15;                  {Available for drawing}
```

 Notes

1. `TestDeviceAttribute` and `SetDeviceAttribute` test and set the attribute flags in the `gdFlags` field of a device record [4.3.1].

2. The desired attribute is identified by its bit number within the flag word, using one of the constants shown.

3. The `GDDevType` attribute tells whether the device is capable of displaying color. For monochrome devices, this attribute is `FALSE`.

4. The `RAMInit` attribute tells whether the device was initialized from RAM.

5. The `MainScreen` attribute marks the main graphics device (the one on which the menu bar is displayed).

6. The `AllInit` attribute is `TRUE` if the modes and arrangement of the system's screens were initialized from a screen configuration ('`scrn`') resource.

7. The `ScreenDevice` attribute tells whether the device is a video display screen. This attribute would be `FALSE`, for example, for a printer or for a device record representing an offscreen pixel map.

8. The `NoDriver` attribute is `TRUE` for devices, such as an offscreen pixel map, that have no associated device driver.

9. The `ScreenActive` attribute tells whether the device is currently active (available for drawing).

10. The remaining bits in the flag word are reserved for future use.

Assembly Language Information

Bit numbers for device attribute flags:

Name	Value	Meaning
GDDevType	0	Supports color
RAMInit	10	Initialized from RAM
MainScreen	11	Is main device (contains menu bar)
AllInit	12	Initialized from a 'scrn' resource
ScreenDevice	13	Is a screen device
NoDriver	14	Has no driver
ScreenActive	15	Is current device

Trap macros:

(Pascal) Routine name	(Assembly) Trap macro	Trap word
TestDeviceAttribute	_TestDeviceAttribute	$AA2C
SetDeviceAttribute	_SetDeviceAttribute	$AA2D

4.4   Color Tables

4.4.1   Color Table Structure

Definitions

```
type
    CTabHandle = ^CTabPtr;
    CTabPtr    = ^ColorTable;
    ColorTable = record
                    ctSeed  : LONGINT;      {Seed value for coordinating inverse table}
                    ctFlags : INTEGER;      {Attribute flags}
                    ctSize  : INTEGER;      {Number of entries minus 1}
                    ctTable : CSpecArray    {Array of color specifications}
                 end;
```

```
CSpecArray = array [0..0] of ColorSpec;
ColorSpec  = record
                    value : INTEGER;          {Color index}
                    rgb   : RGBColor          {True color value}
             end;
```

 Notes

1. A color table maps the index numbers used to represent colors in a pixel image into the corresponding actual color values.

2. Each mapped or fixed-color graphics device has its own color table defining the colors the device is currently configured to display. A handle to the device's color table is kept in the pmTable field of its pixel map [5.1.1], which in turn is located via a handle in the gdPMap field of the device record [4.3.1].

3. For fixed devices, the color table is read from ROM on the device's controller card and cannot be changed. For mapped devices, the table's contents are initialized from a 'clut' resource [4.7.1], but can then be modified to vary the range of colors presented.

4. Individual pixel maps can also have their own tables of intended color values, independent of the device on which the pixel map is displayed.

5. The high-order bit of the color table's ctFlags field tells whether this table belongs to a graphics device (1) or a device-independent pixel map (0).

6. All remaining bits of ctFlags are reserved for future use.

7. ctSeed is the color table's current seed value, used to coordinate its contents with those of its matching inverse table [4.4.2].

8. For color tables created from 'clut' resources [4.7.1] with Get-CTable [4.4.3], ctSeed is initialized to the resource ID, which is always between 0 and 1023. For tables created any other way, call GetCTSeed [4.4.3] to obtain an initial seed value, which will always be greater than 1023.

9. All Toolbox routines that change the contents of a color table also change its seed value. This invalidates the corresponding inverse table, forcing the Toolbox to rebuild it before it can be used. (*Exception:* RestoreEntries [4.4.5] does not change the seed and thus does not force rebuilding of the inverse table.)

10. ctTable is a variable-length array of color specifications (not directly accessible in Pascal) containing the actual entries in the color table.

11. ctSize is the index of the last element in the ctTable array, and is equal to the total number of entries in the color table minus 1.

12. In a color table belonging to a graphics device, each color specification represents a color currently available for display on the device. The rgb field gives the actual value of the color; the use of the value field is private to the Toolbox.

13. In a color table belonging to a device-independent pixel map, each color specification represents a desired or intended color. The value field gives the index number used to denote the color in the map's pixel image; the rgb field gives the exact color value that index is intended to represent. When the image is displayed on a given graphics device, this color will be matched to the closest approximation available on the device.

14. By convention, the first and last entries in a color table should always be white (red = green = blue = $FFFF) and black (red = green = blue = $0000), respectively.

Assembly Language Information

Field offsets in a color table:

(Pascal) Field name	(Assembly) Offset name	Offset in bytes
ctSeed	ctSeed	0
ctFlags	ctFlags	4
ctSize	ctSize	6
ctTable	ctTable	8

Field offsets in a color specification:

(Pascal) Field name	(Assembly) Offset name	Offset in bytes
value	value	0
rgb	rgb	2

Assembly-language constants:

Name	Value	Meaning
CTRec	8	Size of a color table record in bytes, excluding `ctTable`
CTEntrySize	8	Size of a color table entry in bytes
ColorSpecSize	8	Size of a color specification in bytes

4.4.2 Inverse Tables

Definitions

```
type
   ITabHandle = ^ITabPtr;
   ITabPtr    = ^ITab;
   ITab       = record
                   iTabSeed : LONGINT;                          {Seed value}
                   iTabRes  : INTEGER;                          {Bit resolution}
                   itTable  : array [0..0] of SignedByte        {Array of color indices}
                end;

procedure MakeITable
           (colorTab   : CTabHandle;                            {Handle to color table}
            inverseTab : ITabHandle;                            {Handle to inverse table}
            bitRes     : INTEGER);                              {Desired bit resolution}
```

Notes

1. An inverse table maps RGB color values into the corresponding color indices relative to a given color table.

2. `iTabSeed` is the seed value for the version of the color table on which this inverse table is based. If the color table's current seed value doesn't match, then the inverse table is invalid and must be rebuilt before it can be used.

3. iTabRes is the *bit resolution* of the inverse table. A color's index in the table is constructed by concatenating this many high-order bits from each of its three RGB components.

4. The length of each inverse table index in bits is thus three times the bit resolution, and the total number of entries in the table is 2 to this power. For example, 3-bit resolution produces 9-bit table indices and a table size of 512 (2^9) entries.

5. The only bit resolutions currently supported are 3, 4, and 5 bits. The corresponding table sizes are 512, 4096, and 32,768 entries, respectively. The standard resolution is 4 bits.

6. itTable is a variable-length array of signed bytes (not directly accessible in Pascal) containing the actual entries in the inverse table. Each array element gives the index of the color table entry best approximating the corresponding RGB color.

7. MakeITable constructs an inverse table of a given bit resolution based on a given color table.

8. A NIL value for either colorTab or inverseTab denotes the color or inverse table associated with the current graphics device [4.3.1].

9. If bitRes = 0, the inverse table will be built to the current device's preferred bit resolution, taken from the gdResPref field of its device record [4.3.1].

10. Reserved entries [4.4.6] in the color table are ignored, and are never included in the inverse table.

11. If bitRes is less than 3 or greater than 5, the error code CResErr is posted. (You can check for this error with the Toolbox routine QDError [5.1.7].)

12. The inverse table format described here may change in future versions of the Toolbox or for nonstandard color-matching routines [4.6.1]. This information is given for your background understanding only; never write code based on it.

Assembly Language Information

Field offsets in an inverse table:

(Pascal) Field name	(Assembly) Offset name	Offset in bytes
iTabSeed	iTabSeed	0
iTabRes	iTabRes	4
itTable	itTable	6

Trap macro:

(Pascal) Routine name	(Assembly) Trap macro	Trap word
MakeITable	_MakeITable	$AA39

4.4.3   Creating and Destroying Color Tables

Definitions

```
function  GetCTable
              (cTabID : INTEGER)          {Resource ID of color table resource}
                  : CTabHandle;           {Handle to new color table}

function  GetCTSeed
                  : LONGINT;              {Seed value for color table}

procedure DisposCTable
              (theTable : CTabHandle);    {Handle to color table to destroy}
```

Notes

1. GetCTable creates a new color table from a resource of type 'clut' [4.7.1] and returns a handle to it.

2. The new table's seed value is initialized to the resource ID from which it was created.

3. If no 'clut' resource exists with the given ID, the function result will be NIL.

4. GetCTSeed returns an initial seed value for a color table not created from a 'clut' resource. This value will always be greater than 1023, and is guaranteed to be different from that of any other existing color table.

5. DisposCTable destroys a color table and deallocates the storage space it occupies.

Assembly Language Information

Trap macros:

(Pascal) Routine name	(Assembly) Trap macro	Trap word
GetCTable	_GetCTable	$AA18
GetCTSeed	_GetCTSeed	$AA28
DisposCTable	_DisposCTable	$AA24

Assembly-language constant:

Name	Value	Meaning
MinSeed	1023	Minimum seed value for color and inverse tables

4.4.4   Color Mapping

Definitions

```
procedure Index2Color
         (theIndex    : LONGINT;          {Color index}
          var theColor : RGBColor);        {Returns corresponding color value}

function  Color2Index
         (theColor : RGBColor)            {Color value}
             : LONGINT;                   {Corresponding color index}

function  RealColor
         (theColor : RGBColor)            {Color value}
             : BOOLEAN;                   {Exact match available?}

procedure InvertColor
         (var theColor : RGBColor);       {Color to be inverted; returns complement}

procedure GetSubtable
         (theSubtable : CTabHandle;       {Subtable of matched colors}
          iTabRes     : INTEGER;          {Bit resolution for matching}
          sourceTable : CTabHandle);      {Color table to be searched}
```

Notes

1. `Index2Color` finds the RGB color value corresponding to a given color index; `Color2Index` finds the index most nearly approximating a given color value.

2. Both routines use the color table of the current graphics device.

3. Notice that because `Color2Index` only produces the nearest available approximation, the two operations are not necessarily direct inverses. That is, applying `Color2Index` to a given color and then `Index2Color` to the result does not necessarily yield back the same color you originally started with.

4. `RealColor` tests whether an exact match to a given color is available in the current device's color table.

5. The test is limited by the current bit resolution of the device's inverse table: that is, if the inverse table resolution is 3 bits, `RealColor` tests for a color that matches the given color in the three most significant bits of each RGB component.

6. `InvertColor` finds the complement of a given RGB color.

7. The color to be complemented is passed as the value of the parameter `theColor`; the resulting complement is returned via the same variable parameter.

8. `Color2Index` and `InvertColor` use the current device's list of search functions and complement procedures [4.6.1], respectively.

9. `GetSubtable` accepts a pair of color tables as parameters and builds a subtable of the best available matches from one table to the colors in the other.

10. The colors given in the `rgb` fields of `theSubtable`'s color specifications [4.4.1] are matched against the contents of `sourceTable`; the color indices of the best available approximations are returned in the `value` fields of `theSubtable`.

11. A NIL value for `sourceTable` denotes the color table belonging to the current graphics device.

12. A temporary inverse table is built for `sourceTable`, at the bit resolution specified by `iTabRes`, and immediately discarded on completion of the operation. (If `sourceTable` = NIL, the current device's existing inverse table is used instead of building a new one.)

Assembly Language Information

Trap macros:

(Pascal) Routine name	(Assembly) Trap macro	Trap word
Index2Color	_Index2Color	$AA34
Color2Index	_Color2Index	$AA33
RealColor	_RealColor	$AA36
InvertColor	_InvertColor	$AA35
GetSubtable	_GetSubtable	$AA37

4.4.5 Color Table Management

Definitions

```
procedure SetEntries
        (startIndex : INTEGER;          {First color index to be set}
         nEntries   : INTEGER;          {Number of colors minus 1}
         newColors  : CSpecArray);      {Array of color specifications}

procedure SaveEntries
        (mainTable       : CTabHandle;   {Color table to copy from}
         saveTable       : CTabHandle;   {Color table to copy to}
         var whichEntries : ReqListRec); {List of entries to copy}

procedure RestoreEntries
        (saveTable       : CTabHandle;   {Color table to copy from}
         mainTable       : CTabHandle;   {Color table to copy to}
         var whichEntries : ReqListRec); {List of entries to copy}

type
  ReqListRec = record
               reqLSize : INTEGER;                    {Number of entries to copy}
               reqLData : array [0..0] of INTEGER     {Array of index numbers}
             end;
```

Notes

1. SetEntries enters a specified set of colors in the current device's color table.

2. newColors is an array of color specifications [4.4.1] whose rgb fields define the colors to be entered. nEntries gives the number of colors minus 1.

3. If startIndex = -1, the color indices to be set are given by the value fields of the color specifications [4.4.1] in the newColors array. These indices must be in the proper range for the current device's pixel depth (for example, from 0 to 255 for a pixel depth of 8).

4. If startIndex ≥ 0, it specifies the first color index to be set. Colors taken from the newColors array are loaded into the color table with consecutive color indices, starting from this point; the value fields in the array are ignored.

5. Notice that all index values, whether taken from the startIndex parameter or from the value fields in the newColors array, refer to logical color indices, not to physical positions within the color table.

6. SaveEntries copies a specified set of entries from a main color table, mainTable, to an auxiliary table, saveTable. RestoreEntries copies them back from saveTable to mainTable.

7. Notice that the parameters to the two routines are given in opposite orders, so that the source table always comes first and the destination table second.

8. A NIL value for mainTable denotes the color table belonging to the current graphics device.

9. whichEntries is a *request list* specifying which entries from mainTable to save or restore. The contents of these entries are copied to or from consecutive positions starting at the beginning of save-Table.

10. The number of entries in saveTable must be the same as the size of the request list (reqLSize).

11. Entries are identified in the request list by their physical positions within the main table, *not* by the logical color indices given in the value fields of their color specifications [4.4.1].

12. If any of the indices specified in the request list lie outside the range of mainTable, the corresponding elements of the request list are set

to a (negative) error value and the error code CRangeErr is posted. (You can check for this error with the Toolbox routine QDError [5.1.7].) All valid indices in the request list will be correctly saved or restored.

13. SaveEntries and RestoreEntries are not affected by the protection or reservation [4.4.6] of any color table entry.

14. All changes made in the current device's color table by SetEntries or RestoreEntries will directly affect the colors appearing on the screen.

15. RestoreEntries does not change the value of mainTable's seed [4.4.1] and thus does not invalidate the corresponding inverse table, even though the contents of the two tables no longer match. This may cause inverse color-mapping operations such as Color2Index, RealColor, InvertColor, GetSubtable [4.4.4], RGBForeColor, RGBBackColor [5.4.1], and SetCPixel [5.1.6] to produce erroneous results. If necessary, you must explicitly rebuild the inverse table with MakeITable [4.4.2].

16. SaveEntries and RestoreEntries are intended only for very limited, special purposes. In general, it's safer and more convenient to use palettes [4.5] to manage your color environment instead.

Assembly Language Information

Trap macros:

(Pascal) Routine name	(Assembly) Trap macro	Trap word
SetEntries	_SetEntries	$AA3F
SaveEntries	_SaveEntries	$AA49
RestoreEntries	_RestoreEntries	$AA4A

Field offsets in a request list:

(Pascal) Field name	(Assembly) Offset name	Offset in bytes
reqLSize	reqLSize	0
reqLData	reqLData	2

4.4.6 Protecting and Reserving Entries

Definitions

```
procedure ProtectEntry
          (colorIndex : INTEGER;        {Color index}
           onOrOff    : BOOLEAN);       {Protect or release?}

procedure ReserveEntry
          (colorIndex : INTEGER;        {Color index}
           onOrOff    : BOOLEAN);       {Reserve or relinquish?}
```

Notes

1. ProtectEntry and ReserveEntry protect or reserve a specified color table entry, preventing other programs from using it.

2. Both routines operate on the color table of the current graphics device.

3. The onOrOff parameter tells whether to apply protection or reservation to the specified entry (TRUE) or remove it (FALSE).

4. A protected entry cannot be changed by other programs; any operation that attempts to do so will fail with the error code CProtectErr. (You can check for this error with the Toolbox routine QDError [5.1.7].)

5. A reserved entry cannot be matched by another program's color requests. This is particularly useful for setting aside specific indices for color table animation [5.4.3].

6. Both routines will themselves post the error code CProtectErr [5.1.7] if you attempt to protect an already protected entry or reserve an already reserved one. However, you can freely release or relinquish any entry.

Assembly Language Information

Trap macros:

(Pascal) Routine name	(Assembly) Trap macro	Trap word
ProtectEntry	_ProtectEntry	$AA3D
ReserveEntry	_ReserveEntry	$AA3E

4.5 Color Palettes

4.5.1   Palette Records

Definitions

```
type
  PaletteHandle = ^PalettePtr;
  PalettePtr    = ^Palette;
  Palette       = record
                    pmEntries    : INTEGER;                        {Number of colors}
                    pmDataFields : array [0..6] of INTEGER;        {Private}
                    pmInfo       : array [0..0] of ColorInfo       {Array of colors}
                  end;

  ColorInfo = record
                ciRGB        : RGBColor;                           {RGB color value}
                ciUsage      : INTEGER;                            {Usage level}
                ciTolerance  : INTEGER;                            {Color tolerance}
                ciDataFields : array [0..2] of INTEGER             {Private}
              end;

const
  PMCourteous = 0;                        {Courteous color}
  PMDithered  = 1;                        {Dithered color (not yet implemented)}
  PMTolerant  = 2;                        {Tolerant color}
  PMAnimated  = 4;                        {Animated color}
  PMExplicit  = 8;                        {Explicit color}
```

Notes

1. A palette represents a selection of colors requested by a program for use in its drawing operations.

2. Each individual window can have its own palette [6.3.6]. The Toolbox will do its best to ensure that the colors in the palette are available whenever that window becomes active on the screen.

3. The letters pm (or PM) stand for Palette Manager, the part of the Toolbox that deals with color palettes.

4. The variable-length array `pmInfo` (not directly accessible in Pascal) contains a *color info record* for each color in the palette, specifying the color's RGB value, usage level, and tolerance.

5. `pmEntries` gives the number of colors in the palette, and thus defines the true size of the `pmInfo` array.

6. `pmDataFields` holds information used privately by the Toolbox, including a pointer to the window to which this palette belongs.

7. The `ciRGB` field of the color info record specifies the requested RGB color value.

8. `ciUsage` gives the color's usage level, and must be one of the constants shown.

9. *Tolerant colors* (`PMTolerant`) will match an existing color in the current color environment if there is one that approximates the requested RGB value (`ciRGB`) to within a specified tolerance (`ciTolerance`). If no such color exists, the current device's color table will be modified to make the exact requested color available.

10. An existing color will be considered to match if it differs from the requested color by less than the given tolerance in each of the three RGB components independently. A tolerance value of 0 requires an exact match.

11. *Courteous colors* (`PMCourteous`) always use the best available approximation in the existing color environment, without changing the environment in any way. They are thus equivalent to tolerant colors with a tolerance value of `$FFFF`.

12. *Explicit colors* (`PMExplicit`) refer directly to the corresponding color index in the current device's color table. They always use the RGB value currently associated with the given color index, without reference to the value of `ciRGB`.

13. *Animating colors* (`PMAnimated`) reserve [4.4.6] entries in the current device's color table for use in color table animation [5.4.3]. Such reserved entries become unavailable for use in other drawing operations and will not match any color request issued by another program.

14. *Dithered colors* (`PMDithered`) can be simulated by a pixel pattern [5.2] constructed of other colors that blend visually to approximate the requested color. This capability is not yet supported in the current version of the Toolbox.

Assembly Language Information

Field offsets in a palette record:

(Pascal) Field name	(Assembly) Offset name	Offset in bytes
pmEntries	pmEntries	0
pmDataFields	pmWindow	2
————————	pmPrivate	6
————————	pmDevices	8
————————	pmSeeds	12
pmInfo	pmInfo	16

Field offsets in a color info record:

(Pascal) Field name	(Assembly) Offset name	Offset in bytes
ciRGB	ciRGB	0
ciUsage	ciUsage	6
ciTolerance	ciTolerance	8
ciDataFields	ciFlags	10
————————	ciPrivate	12

Assembly-language constants:

Name	Value	Meaning
pmHdrSize	16	Size of a palette record in bytes, excluding pmInfo
ciSize	16	Size of a color info record in bytes

Color usage levels:

Name	Value	Meaning
PMCourteous	0	Courteous color
PMDithered	1	Dithered color
PMTolerant	2	Tolerant color
PMAnimated	4	Animated color
PMExplicit	8	Explicit color

4.5.2   Initializing the Toolbox for Palettes

Definitions

```
procedure InitPalettes;
```

Notes

1. InitPalettes initializes the Toolbox's internal data structures for working with color palettes.

2. This routine must be called before any other operation involving palettes.

3. InitPalettes is called automatically by the Toolbox routine Init-Windows [II:3.2.1]. There is normally no need for you to call it directly yourself.

Assembly Language Information

Trap macro:

(Pascal) Routine name	(Assembly) Trap macro	Trap word
InitPalettes	_InitPalettes	$AA90

4.5.3   Creating and Destroying Palettes

Definitions

```
function NewPalette
        (nEntries       : INTEGER;        {Number of colors in palette}
         entryColors    : CTabHandle;     {Table of colors}
         entryUsage     : INTEGER;        {Usage level for all entries}
         entryTolerance : INTEGER)        {Tolerance value for all entries}
          : PaletteHandle;                {Handle to new palette}
```

```
function  GetNewPalette
              (paletteID : INTEGER)        {Resource ID of palette}
                  : PaletteHandle;         {Handle to new palette}

procedure DisposePalette
              (thePalette : PaletteHandle);  {Handle to palette to be destroyed}
```

 ## Notes

1. NewPalette and GetNewPalette both create a new color palette and return a handle to it.

2. NewPalette receives its initialization information as parameters; GetNewPalette gets it from a resource.

3. entryColors is a handle to a color table defining the colors to be included in the new palette.

4. Colors from the color table are entered sequentially in the palette, using only their rgb values; the value fields of their color specifications [4.4.1] are ignored.

5. If the color table contains more than the specified number of colors (nEntries), unneeded entries from the end of the table are unused; if there are not enough colors in the table to fill the palette, the remaining palette entries are initialized to black.

6. By convention, the first two colors in a palette should always be white (red = green = blue = $FFFF) and black (red = green = blue = $0000).

7. For compatibility with a range of graphics devices, the first four colors in the palette should be the preferred colors for use on devices with 2-bit pixel depth, the first 16 for 4-bit devices, and so on.

8. If entryColors = NIL, all colors in the palette are initialized to black. You can then set their values explicitly with SetEntryColor [4.5.4].

9. The entryUsage and entryTolerance parameters give the initial usage level and tolerance for all entries in the palette. If necessary, you can change these settings for individual entries with SetEntryUsage [4.5.4].

10. paletteID is the ID number of a palette resource of type 'pltt' [4.7.2].

11. The Toolbox routine GetNewCWindow [6.3.4], which creates a color window from a template in a resource file, automatically loads the corresponding palette resource as well. As long as the window and its palette have the same resource ID, there is no need to call GetNew-Palette explicitly.

12. `DisposePalette` destroys a palette and frees the storage space it occupies.

13. Any color table entries the palette has reserved for animating colors are relinquished.

14. All handles to the palette become invalid and must not be used again.

Assembly Language Information

Trap macros:

(Pascal) Routine name	(Assembly) Trap macro	Trap word
NewPalette	_NewPalette	$AA91
GetNewPalette	_GetNewPalette	$AA92
DisposePalette	_DisposePalette	$AA93

4.5.4   Setting Palette Colors

Definitions

```
procedure GetEntryColor
        (thePalette       : PaletteHandle;     {Handle to palette}
         entryIndex    : INTEGER;          {Palette index of desired entry}
         var entryColor : RGBColor);       {Returns current color value}

procedure SetEntryColor
        (thePalette : PaletteHandle;          {Handle to palette}
         entryIndex : INTEGER;                {Palette index of desired entry}
         newColor   : RGBColor);              {New color value}

procedure GetEntryUsage
        (thePalette            : PaletteHandle;  {Handle to palette}
         entryIndex         : INTEGER;        {Palette index of desired entry}
         var entryUsage     : INTEGER;        {Returns current usage level}
         var entryTolerance : INTEGER);       {Returns current tolerance value}

procedure SetEntryUsage
        (thePalette    : PaletteHandle;       {Handle to palette}
         entryIndex    : INTEGER;             {Palette index of desired entry}
         newUsage      : INTEGER;             {New usage level}
         newTolerance  : INTEGER);            {New tolerance value}
```

Notes

1. These routines read or change the current color, usage, and tolerance settings of a palette entry.

2. The desired entry is identified by the palette it belongs to and its index within the palette.

3. The value you supply for newUsage must be one of the usage constants (PMCourteous, PMTolerant, and so on) defined in [4.5.1].

4. A value of -1 for either newUsage or newTolerance leaves that property of the palette entry unchanged from its previous value.

5. Changes in the contents of a palette are *not* immediately reflected in the current color environment. Call ActivatePalette [6.3.6] after any change to put it into effect on the screen.

Assembly Language Information

Trap macros:

(Pascal) Routine name	(Assembly) Trap macro	Trap word
GetEntryColor	_GetEntryColor	$AA9B
SetEntryColor	_SetEntryColor	$AA9C
GetEntryUsage	_GetEntryUsage	$AA9D
SetEntryUsage	_SetEntryUsage	$AA9E

4.5.5 Palette Conversion

Definitions

```
procedure CTab2Palette
        (fromCTab       : CTabHandle;      {Color table to convert from}
         toPalette      : PaletteHandle;   {Palette to convert to}
         entryUsage     : INTEGER;         {Usage level for all entries}
         entryTolerance : INTEGER);        {Tolerance value for all entries}

procedure Palette2CTab
        (fromPalette : PaletteHandle;      {Palette to convert from}
         toCTab      : CTabHandle);        {Color table to convert to}
```

```
procedure CopyPalette
         (fromPalette : PaletteHandle;      {Palette to copy from}
          toPalette   : PaletteHandle;      {Palette to copy to}
          fromEntry   : INTEGER;            {Index of first entry to copy from}
          toEntry     : INTEGER;            {Index of first entry to copy to}
          nEntries    : INTEGER);           {Number of entries to copy}
```

Notes

1. CTab2Palette and Palette2CTab copy colors from a color table to a palette or vice versa.

2. No new data structures are created; colors are simply copied from one existing data structure (color table or palette) to another.

3. The destination data structure is resized, if necessary, to match the number of colors in the source structure.

4. CTab2Palette first relinquishes any color table entries that were previously reserved [4.4.6] for animating colors in the palette.

5. All entries in the palette are set to the values given by the entryUsage and entryTolerance parameters. If necessary, you can then change these settings for individual entries with SetEntryUsage [4.5.4].

6. CopyPalette copies a specified range of entries from one palette to another.

7. fromEntry is the index of the first entry to copy from the source palette; toEntry is the index of the first entry to copy to in the destination palette; nEntries tells how many entries to copy.

8. Changes in the contents of a palette as a result of CTab2Palette or CopyPalette are *not* immediately reflected in the current color environment. If necessary, call ActivatePalette [6.3.6] to put the palette's new contents into effect on the screen.

Assembly Language Information

Trap macros:

(Pascal) Routine name	(Assembly) Trap macro	Trap word
CTab2Palette	_CTab2Palette	$AA9F
Palette2CTab	_Palette2CTab	$AAA0
CopyPalette	_CopyPalette	$AAA1

4.6 Nuts and Bolts

4.6.1   Custom Matching Routines

Definitions

```
type
    SProcHndl = ^SProcPtr;
    SProcPtr  = ^SProcRec;
    SProcRec  = record
                    nxtSrch  : Handle;      {Handle to next list element}
                    srchProc : ProcPtr      {Pointer to search function}
                end;

    CProcHndl = ^CProcPtr;
    CProcPtr  = ^CProcRec;
    CProcRec  = record
                    nxtComp  : CProcHndl;   {Handle to next list element}
                    compProc : ProcPtr      {Pointer to complement procedure}
                end;

function   YourSearchProc
            (colorValue      : RGBColor;    {Color to be matched}
            var colorIndex : LONGINT)       {Returns corresponding color index}
                : BOOLEAN;                  {Was color matched?}

procedure  YourCompProc
            (var colorValue : RGBColor);    {Color to be inverted; returns complement}
```

Notes

1. Custom color-matching routines allow a program to provide its own nonstandard algorithms for approximating colors or their complements on a given graphics device.

2. The lists of search functions and complement procedures begin in the `gdSearchProc` and `gdCompProc` fields, respectively, of the device record [4.3.1] and are linked through the `nxtSrch` or `nxtComp` fields of the individual list elements.

3. For unknown reasons, the Pascal interface defines `nxtSrch` as an untyped `Handle` instead of a typed `SProcHndl`.

4. Use AddSearch and AddComp [4.6.2] to add new routines to the lists, DelSearch and DelComp to remove them.

5. The routine headings shown are merely models for your own matching routines. There are no Toolbox routines named YourSearchProc and YourCompProc.

6. Search and complement routines recognize their own program's color-matching requests via a unique *client ID* in the gdID field of the device record [4.3.1]. The program must set this field with the Toolbox routine SetClientID [4.6.2] before issuing any color requests.

7. The color to be matched is passed to the routine in the parameter colorValue.

8. To satisfy a color request (presumably after recognizing its own program's client ID in the device record's gdID field), a search function should set its colorIndex parameter to the index of the nearest match available on the device and return a TRUE function result.

9. A FALSE result refuses the request, passing it on to the next search function in the list.

10. If all functions in the list return FALSE, the standard search function is used, which simply looks up the requested color in the device's inverse table [4.4.2].

11. Complement procedures receive the color to be complemented in the variable parameter colorValue and return the complement via the same parameter.

12. The standard complement procedure simply replaces each of the specified color's RGB components with its bitwise complement.

Assembly Language Information

Field offsets in matching-procedure records:

(Pascal) Field name	(Assembly) Offset name	Offset in bytes
nxtSrch	nxtSrch	0
srchProc	srchProc	4
nxtComp	nxtComp	0
compProc	compProc	4

Assembly-language constants:

Name	Value	Meaning
SProcSize	8	Size of a search procedure record in bytes
CProcSize	8	Size of a complement procedure record in bytes

4.6.2   Installing Matching Routines

Definitions

```
procedure AddSearch
         (searchFunc : ProcPtr);        {Search function to be added}

procedure AddComp
         (compProc : ProcPtr);          {Complement procedure to be added}

procedure DelSearch
         (searchFunc : ProcPtr);        {Search function to be deleted}

procedure DelComp
         (compProc : ProcPtr);          {Complement procedure to be deleted}

procedure SetClientID
         (clientID : INTEGER);          {Client ID to be set}
```

Notes

1. `AddSearch` and `AddComp` add new routines to the current graphics device's list of search functions and complement procedures, respectively; `DelSearch` and `DelComp` delete them.

2. New routines are always added at the head of the relevant list.

3. List elements of types `SProcRec` and `CProcRec` [4.6.1] pointing to the specified routines are automatically allocated and deallocated as needed.

4. SetClientID sets the value of the client ID in the gdID field of the current device record [4.3.1], allowing search and complement routines to recognize their own program's color requests.

Assembly Language Information

Trap macros:

(Pascal) Routine name	(Assembly) Trap macro	Trap word
AddSearch	_AddSearch	$AA3A
AddComp	_AddComp	$AA3B
DelSearch	_DelSearch	$AA4C
DelComp	_DelComp	$AA4D
SetClientID	_SetClientID	$AA3C

4.7   Color-Related Resources

4.7.1   Resource Type 'clut'

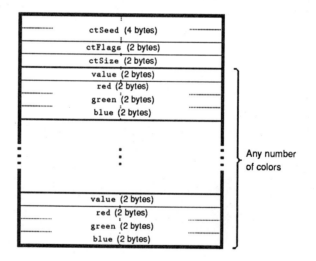

Structure of a 'clut' resource

Definitions

```
const
    DefQDColors = 127;
```
{Resource ID of "classic QuickDraw" color table}

Notes

1. A resource of type 'clut' defines the contents of a color table [4.4.1].

2. When the color table is read into memory, its seed (ctSeed) will be initialized to the resource ID. The ID must be ≤ 1023, since seed values of 1024 and above denote color tables built from scratch rather than from a resource.

3. Resource IDs from 0–127 are reserved for use by the Toolbox; your own color tables should be numbered in the range 128–1023.

4. In the resource file, the table's ctSeed field should be set to 0.

5. The high-order bit of ctFlags should be 1 for a color table belonging to a graphics device, 0 for one belonging to a device-independent pixel map. All remaining flag bits should be set to 0.

6. ctSize gives the number of entries in the color table minus 1.

7. In a color table for a pixel map, each color's value field gives the index number by which that color is identified in the map. In a table for a graphics device, all value fields should be 0; a color's index number is defined instead by its position within the table.

8. By convention, the first and last entries in a color table should always be white (red = green = blue = $FFFF) and black (red = green = blue = $0000), respectively.

9. The Macintosh II ROM contains built-in 'clut' resources [2.3.2] with IDs of 1, 2, 4, and 8, each defining the standard array of colors for the corresponding pixel depth.

10. There is also a built-in 'clut' resource numbered 127, containing the RGB values of the eight standard "classic QuickDraw" colors [4.1.1, 4.2.2]. The constant DefQDColors defines the resource ID for this table.

11. Use GetCTable [4.4.3] to load resources of this type.

Assembly Language Information

Assembly-language constant:

Name	Value	Meaning
DefQDColors	127	Resource ID of "classic Quick-Draw" color table

4.7.2 Resource Type 'pltt'

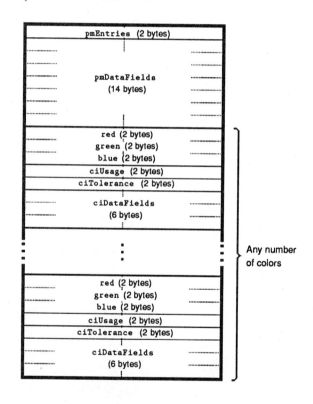

Structure of a 'pltt' resource

Standard system palette:

Palette Index	Color	Red Dec.	Red Hex.	Green Dec.	Green Hex.	Blue Dec.	Blue Hex.
0	White	65535	$FFFF	65535	$FFFF	65535	$FFFF
1	Black	0	$0000	0	$0000	0	$0000
2	Yellow	64512	$FC00	62333	$F37D	1327	$052F
3	Orange	65535	$FFFF	25738	$648A	652	$028C
4	Blue-green	881	$0371	50943	$C6FF	40649	$9EC9
5	Green	0	$0000	40960	$A000	0	$0000
6	Blue	0	$0000	0	$0000	54272	$D400
7	Red	56683	$DD6B	2242	$08C2	1698	$06A2
8	Light gray	49152	$C000	49152	$C000	49152	$C000
9	Medium gray	32768	$8000	32768	$8000	32768	$8000
10	Beige	65535	$FFFF	50140	$C3DC	33120	$8160
11	Brown	37887	$93FF	10266	$281A	4812	$12CC
12	Olive green	25892	$6524	49919	$C2FF	0	$0000
13	Bright green	0	$0000	65535	$FFFF	1265	$04F1
14	Sky blue	26078	$65DE	44421	$AD85	65535	$FFFF
15	Violet	32768	$8000	0	$0000	65535	$FFFF

 Notes

1. A resource of type 'pltt' defines the contents of a color palette [4.5.1].

2. The fields of the 'pltt' resource have the same meanings as in a palette record [4.5.1] in memory.

3. By convention, the first two colors in a palette should always be white (red = green = blue = $FFFF) and black (red = green = blue = $0000).

4. For compatibility with a range of graphics devices, the first four colors in the palette should be the preferred colors for use on devices with 2-bit pixel depth, the first 16 for 4-bit devices, and so on.

5. A palette belonging to a color window should have the same resource ID as the window template itself, so that the Toolbox routine Get-NewCWindow [6.3.4] will read it in automatically at the time the window is created.

6. Noncolor windows and those without assigned palettes of their own use the standard system palette, stored in the system resource file as 'pltt' resource number 0.

7. `'pltt'` resource number 0 holds the standard system palette, used for old-style (monochrome) windows and for color windows without explicit palettes of their own.

8. The table shows the RGB values for the entries in the system palette. All entries are tolerant, with a tolerance level of 0.

9. Use `GetNewPalette` [4.5.3] to load resources of this type.

CHAPTER

Showing Your Colors

Now that we know how to mix our paints, it's time to start painting some pictures. In this chapter, we'll learn about the extensions to the QuickDraw graphics routines that allow you to add color to your creations. You'll find the additions involve nothing radically new, just straightforward generalizations of old familiar concepts. Once you get the hang of them, you'll be ready to set up your electronic easel and let your true colors shine through.

Pixel Maps

The canvas you spread on your Color QuickDraw easel is a *pixel map* [5.1.1]. Just as an old-fashioned bit map [I:4.2.1] contains a bit image along with the additional information needed to interpret it, a pixel map does the same for a pixel image. All color drawing operations take place within the context of a pixel map.

Like bit maps, two or more pixel maps can share the same underlying image in memory. In particular, every graphics device has its own *screen map* representing the image displayed on its screen, located via the gdPMap field in the device record [4.3.1]. This map's pixel image, the *screen image*, is then shared by all other pixel maps (those belonging to windows, for instance) whose contents appear on the screen.

The first few fields of a pixel map are exactly the same as those of a bit map. There's a pointer (baseAddr) to the start of the pixel

171

image, followed by its row width (rowBytes) and boundary rectangle (bounds). The row width tells the Toolbox how many bytes to skip to get from the beginning of one row of pixels to the beginning of the next; the boundary rectangle delimits the extent of the pixel image and establishes its system of coordinates. The high-order bit of the rowBytes field serves as a flag to distinguish the two types of map: it's set to 1 for a pixel map, 0 for a bit map. The Toolbox, of course, strips off this bit before attempting to use the contents of rowBytes as an integer row width.

Notice that a pixel map's row width varies with the pixel depth of its image (since it depends on the number of pixels that are packed into each byte of the image), while the boundary rectangle, which is expressed directly in pixels, is independent of the depth.

In theory, a pixel image can be stored in any of three different *storage formats* in memory, known as *planar, chunky,* and *chunky/ planar.* (In practice, only chunky format is supported by the current version of the Toolbox; the others are included for possible future implementation.)

- *Planar* format corresponds to the "classic QuickDraw" model of color representation that we discussed in Chapter 4. Each color plane has its own separate image in memory, with just 1 bit per pixel in each plane. Together, these individual bit images combine to form the complete pixel image.

- In *chunky* format, the bits representing each pixel in the image are grouped or "chunked" together into a single image, rather than distributed into separate bit images as in the planar model. Depending on the needs of a particular graphics device, the bits may represent either a direct color value or (more commonly) an index into a mapped color table.

- *Chunky/planar* is a hybrid format consisting of some number of planes (normally three, one for each color component), with a separate chunky representation for each plane. Typically these would represent color intensities in the three primary colors, to be used to drive the color circuitry of a direct video device.

The `pixelType` field in the pixel map record [5.1.1] holds an integer code identifying the storage format in use. The `cmpCount` ("component count") field specifies the number of separate planes, with `cmpSize` giving the depth of each plane in bits per pixel. For the time being, at least, `pixelType` must always be 0 (for chunky format), `cmpCount` must be 1, and `cmpSize` is simply the image's overall pixel depth. In principle, this logical pixel depth need not exactly equal `pixelSize`, the physical number of bits allotted per pixel. In the present implementation, however, both the logical and physical depths are restricted to powers of 2 (allowing a whole number of pixels to be packed efficiently within an 8-bit byte or a 16-bit word), and thus they are, in fact, always equal.

To help the Toolbox navigate its way around in the pixel image, the pixel map's `planeBytes` field gives the *plane offset*, the distance in bytes from the beginning of one plane in memory to the beginning of the next. (In chunky format, this field is simply set to 0 and ignored.) Our old friend the row width (`rowBytes`) refers to the offset from one row to the next *within* each individual plane. `hRes` and `vRes` give the image's horizontal and vertical resolution in pixels per inch, allowing it to be scaled, if necessary, to the physical resolution of the device it's drawn on. There's also a pair of fields, `packType` and `packSize`, to be used in compressing the image for more efficient storage, but the present Toolbox doesn't yet take advantage of this capability.

One of the most important fields in the pixel map is `pmTable`, which holds a handle to the map's color table. The color table assigns an actual, concrete color value to each abstract color index used in the map's pixel image. (Only chunky images on mapped devices need such a table, of course, but those are also the only kind the Toolbox currently supports.) In a graphics device's screen map—or in other pixel maps based on it, such as those belonging to windows on the screen—`pmTable` points to the device's own color table, which controls the colors it displays on the screen. In device-independent pixel maps, `pmTable` is a table of desired or intended colors, to be matched to the existing color environment when the image is displayed on a given device.

When you open a color graphics port—such as, in particular, a color window—on the screen of a graphics device, the Toolbox automatically creates a new pixel map for you and initializes all of its fields from the corresponding fields of the device's screen map. It then stores a handle to the pixel map into a field of the graphics port. (We'll be discussing color graphics ports in detail in the next section.) There's also a Toolbox routine, `SetPortPix` [5.1.2], for explicitly setting the current port's pixel map. This operation works only for color ports, and has no effect if an old-style (monochrome) port is current; in that case, use `SetPortBits` [I:4.3.4] instead.

Should you ever need to create a pixel map that isn't associated with a window (for offscreen drawing, for instance), you can use the Toolbox routine `NewPixMap` [5.1.2]. Again the fields of the new pixel map are initialized from those of the current device's screen map, but in this case the color table handle, `pmTable`, is not copied, but simply set to an empty handle. It's then up to you to initialize this field yourself by creating a new color table, copying the handle from the device's screen map, or whatever else may be appropriate.

Another Toolbox routine, `CopyPixMap` [5.1.2], treats the color table in yet a different way. Instead of just copying the color table handle from one pixel map to another, it makes a brand-new copy of the entire color table and gives the new pixel map a handle to the copy. Thus the new and original pixel maps initially have the same set of colors to work with, but subsequent changes in one map's color table will not affect the other. The two maps *do* share the same pixel image in memory, however, since only the `baseAddr` pointer is copied and not the underlying image itself. Thus drawing operations in one map *will* affect the contents of the other.

When you're through with a pixel map, use `DisposPixMap` [5.1.2] to destroy it and deallocate its memory space. Don't forget to drop any remaining handles in the handle shredder, lest they fall into the wrong hands and come back to haunt you later.

Color Graphics Ports

To accommodate the needs of the full-color drawing environment, the old-style graphics port has been expanded into a new structure, the *color graphics port*. Actually, "expanded" is not quite the right word, since the new port record is exactly the same size as the old, 108 bytes, with most of the same fields in the same relative locations as before. What's different is that several of the larger data structures that formerly were embedded directly in the port record have been moved elsewhere and replaced by their handles, freeing some additional space in the body of the record itself.

Structure of Color Ports

If you compare the definition of the old `GrafPort` record [I:4.2.2] with that of the new `CGrafPort` [5.1.3], you'll see that four such embedded structures—one bit map (`portBits`) and three patterns (`bkPat`, `fillPat`, `pnPat`)—have been removed in favor of handles to the corresponding pixel-based structures (`portPixMap`, `bkPixPat`, `fillPixPat`, `pnPixPat`). Since a bit map is 14 bytes long and the bit patterns 8 bytes each, this means that a total of 38 bytes have been reduced to 16, making 22 extra bytes available for other uses.

The first of the new fields added to the port record is `portVersion`, which identifies the version of Color QuickDraw that created the port. As the Toolbox continues to evolve over time, this version number will be used to track the changes and maintain compatibility. The two high-order bits of the `portVersion` field are set to 1, identifying this as a color port. (In an old-style port, this same relative position within the record is occupied by the field `portBits.rowBytes`, the row width of the port's bit map. Since this is always a positive integer comfortably less than 16,384, its first two bits are always 0.)

As we learned in Chapter 4, the original type of graphics port already has a pair of fields, `fgColor` and `bkColor`, to hold its current foreground and background drawing colors. The QuickDraw routines `ForeColor` and `BackColor` [4.1.2] set the contents of these two fields. Colors are represented in planar form, which means they are limited in practice to the eight color constants of the classic QuickDraw color interface [4.1.1].

In the new color port, these same two fields hold the pixel values for the foreground and background colors as they will appear in the port's pixel image. Since the current version of Color QuickDraw only supports chunky pixel images for mapped devices, these pixel values are always indices into a color table, which defines the actual colors that will appear on the screen. These are not necessarily the exact drawing colors you originally requested, but merely the best available matches in the current color environment. The exact requested RGB values are kept in a new pair of fields in the port record, `rgbFgColor` and `rgbBkColor`.

When you use a color palette [4.5] to set your drawing colors, the Toolbox also saves a handle to the palette, along with the color's index within it, for future reference. This information lives in a new data structure, the *auxiliary port record* [5.1.4], which in turn is located via a handle in a new field (`grafVars`) of the main port record. The other two fields of the auxiliary port record, rgbOpColor and rgbHiliteColor, are used in connection with some of the new color transfer modes, which we'll be discussing later in this chapter.

The last two new fields in the color port are both concerned with text drawing. When drawing a line of text, the Toolbox maintains a fractional pen location for more accurate character placement on high-resolution devices such as the LaserWriter printer. The pnLocHFrac field of the port record is nominally defined as an integer, but is actually a fraction between 0 and 1, to be added to the horizontal coordinate of the pen location, pnLoc. The other new field, chExtra, specifies an extra width to be added to all characters except spaces (which are still governed by the old spExtra field, as before). Again the number is nominally an integer, but this time it is interpreted as a fixed-point quantity with 4 bits before the binary point and 12 after it.

Opening and Closing Color Ports

Color ports, like their monochrome predecessors, are nonrelocatable objects and are always referred to with simple pointers instead of handles. Also like their predecessors, they form the basis for other, more extended structures: color windows, color dialog boxes, and so forth. Most of the ports you use will be opened implicitly as part of these other structures, and you'll rarely need to create one for yourself. If you do, you can use the Toolbox routine OpenCPort [5.1.5] to initialize the port and open it for use. This routine accepts a pointer to an existing color port as a parameter, so you must first allocate the space for the new port with NewPtr [I:3.2.1] and typecast the resulting untyped pointer into a port pointer:

```
rawPtr     := NewPtr(SIZE(CGrafPort));
colorPort  := CGrafPtr(rawPtr);
OpenCPort  (colorPort)
```

OpenCPort allocates space for the port's internal data structures—its pixel map, auxiliary port record, visible and clipping regions, and pen, fill, and background patterns—then calls another Toolbox routine, InitCPort [5.1.5], to initialize its fields.

The one subsidiary structure that isn't allocated fresh from the heap when you open a new port is the color table: its handle (along with all the other fields of the port's pixel map) is simply copied from the screen map of the current graphics device. Thus the port shares the device's own color table in memory, and is directly affected by all changes in the device's color environment.

  When the time comes to close a color port, the Toolbox routine `CloseCPort` [5.1.5] deallocates all of its internal structures except the color table, on the assumption that the table really belongs to a graphics device and that the rightful owner will not take kindly to its premature demise. If for some reason you've provided your own color table, not associated with any device, you'll have to dispose of it yourself before closing the port. Notice also that `CloseCPort` only destroys the port's internal structures, not the port record itself—so you have to follow it with a call to `DisposPtr` [I:3.2.2] to finish the demolition job:

```
{Deallocate color table if appropriate};
CloseCPort (colorPort);
rawPtr := Ptr(colorPort);
DisposPtr (rawPtr)
```

Pixel Patterns

The classic QuickDraw bit pattern [I:5.1.1] was a simple structure: just an array of 8 bytes representing an 8-by-8 square arrangement of black and white (or foreground and background) pixels. In Color QuickDraw, this is generalized to a more flexible (and consequently more complex) structure, the *pixel pattern*. Like its monochrome counterpart, a pixel pattern is a rectangular "tile" that can be laid end to end and repeated indefinitely to fill an arbitrary area in a graphics port.

  Instead of just a simple array, a pixel pattern is represented by a relocatable record of type `PixPat` [5.2.1], referred to by a handle of type `PixPatHandle`. The heart of this structure is a pixel map, `patMap`, which defines the pattern's graphical characteristics. The map's color table assigns RGB values to the color indices used in the pattern's pixel image. Because the map has a boundary rectangle to define its dimensions, the pattern can be of any size and is not limited to 8 pixels wide by 8 high, like an old-style bit pattern. The only restriction is that, for speed and storage efficiency, both its width and height must be powers of 2.

  Surprisingly, however, the pixel map's `baseAddr` field does *not* point to the pixel image defining the pattern's content. Instead, a handle to the image is stored as a separate field, `patData`, in the pattern record itself; the pixel map's base address is simply ignored.

The pattern record also includes a field for a monochrome bit pattern, `pat1Data`, to be substituted for the full-color pattern when drawing in a monochrome port.

When drawing a pattern in a given color environment, the Toolbox creates a private copy of the pattern, specifically tailored to the current pixel depth and color table. The pixel map and image for this "expanded" version of the pattern are kept in the `patXMap` and `patXData` fields of the pattern record. The `patXValid` field flags whether the expanded pattern is valid for the current color environment: a value of -1 in this field means that the environment has changed and the pattern must be rebuilt.

Every color graphics port [5.1.3] has fields for three pixel patterns: a *pen pattern*, a *background pattern*, and a *fill pattern*. The pen pattern is used for drawing lines and for painting shapes with the QuickDraw operations `PaintRect`, `PaintOval`, and so on; the background pattern is used in operations like `EraseRect` and `EraseOval`. The new QuickDraw routines `PenPixPat` and `Back-PixPat` [5.2.4] assign new pixel patterns to these fields of the current (color) port. The third field, the fill pattern, is used internally by the new color shape-filling operations, such as `FillCRect` and `FillCOval` [5.4.2], to hold the pixel pattern you supply as a parameter.

It's still possible to use the old-fashioned monochrome bit patterns, even in a color graphics port. When a color port is current, the old bit-oriented routines like `PenPat` [I:5.2.2], `BackPat` [I:5.1.1], `FillRect` [I:5.3.2], `FillOval` [I:5.3.4], and so on, will construct a special type of pixel pattern that simulates a simple bit pattern. Patterns of this type are identified by a code value of 0 in the `patType` field of the pattern record [5.2.1]. (In a full-color pixel pattern, this field is set to 1.) The `patMap` and `patData` fields are ignored; the `pat1Data` field holds the pattern's bit image. The pattern's dimensions are always understood to be 8-by-8, and it is always drawn in the port's current foreground and background colors.

As usual, the recommended way of creating a new pixel pattern is from a resource. In this case, the resource type is `'ppat'` [5.6.1] and the Toolbox routine for reading it in is `GetPixPat` [5.2.2]. You can also build a pixel pattern from scratch, using `NewPixPat` [5.2.2].

Besides creating the pattern record itself, this routine also creates the pattern's pixel map and initializes its fields from those of the current device's screen map. Empty handles are created for the rest of the pattern's subsidiary structures, but no storage is allocated for the structures themselves. It's up to you to create the pixel image (`patData`) and color table (`patMap^^.pmTable`) and store their handles in the appropriate fields; the expanded map (`patXMap`) and image (`patXData`) are the Toolbox's responsibility. The pattern's monochrome equivalent (`pat1Data`) is initialized to the standard medium gray [I:5.1.2], but you can change it, if you wish, to something else more to your liking.

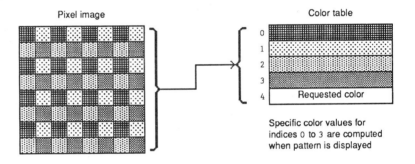

Figure 5–1 A dithered pattern

One interesting way of creating a pixel pattern is with `MakeRGBPat` [5.2.3]. This routine constructs a *dithered pattern* of colored dots that blend to create the visual illusion of a specified color. The pattern record must already exist, presumably having been created previously with `NewPixPat` [5.2.2]; `MakeRGBPat` merely sets its internal fields to approximate the given color. The pattern's `patType` field is set to 2, denoting a dithered pattern. A pattern of this type has no explicit pixel image; its `patData` field is NIL. The pattern is implicitly understood to consist of an 8-by-8 arrangement of four alternating colors, as shown in Figure 5–1. The RGB color value the pattern stands for is stored in its color table under index 4, but the four colors making up the image itself, numbered 0 to 3, are left unspecified in the table. The actual values of these colors are not filled in until the pattern is drawn, using the available color environment then in effect.

Dithered patterns are most effective for filling relatively large areas, less so for smaller areas or narrow lines. In particular, they don't work at all for lines only 1 pixel wide, since these use only half of the pattern's four-color pixel arrangement.

When you no longer need a pixel pattern, `DisposPixPat` [5.2.2] disposes of it and all its subsidiary data structures—its pixel image, pixel map, expanded image, expanded map, and color table. Notice, though, that if some graphics port happens to be holding a handle to this pattern as its pen, background, or fill pattern, the handle will be left pointing into Never-Never-Land. To protect you from the crocodile, the Toolbox automatically checks all existing ports for handles to the vanishing pattern and clears them safely to `NIL`. In spite of this built-in protection, destroying patterns before their time is frowned upon in polite society and will get you ostracized from the best programming circles.

Color Transfer Modes

Just as in monochrome, all color drawing is governed by a *transfer mode,* which controls the way the new pixels you draw combine with the old ones already existing in the pixel map. In monochrome QuickDraw, there are four basic drawing modes—`Copy`, `Or`, `Bic` ("bit clear"), and `XOr` [I:5.1.3]—each with a variant that inverts the source pixels before drawing them (`NotCopy`, `NotOr`, `NotBic`, `NotXOr`). In the color environment, these "classic" monochrome modes are supplemented by a new set [5.3.1] designed specifically for color operation.

You may recall that the original QuickDraw had two versions of each transfer mode—a *source mode* for transferring images from one bit map to another (including text characters from a font's character strike) and a *pattern mode* for drawing lines and shapes or filling areas with a pattern. On the Macintosh II, this distinction is no longer maintained: all drawing operations automatically perform correctly with either type of mode. Thus

---

it's no longer necessary to distinguish, for example, `SrcCopy` from `PatCopy` or `NotSrcOr` from `NotPatOr`. However, for compatibility with earlier versions of QuickDraw that still observe the distinction, you should continue to use the correct type of mode for any given operation. For simplicity, we will use short forms such as `Copy` and `NotOr` to refer to the old modes in this chapter, even though these names are not valid in an actual program.

Color graphics ports have the same two mode fields as their monochrome counterparts: a *pen mode* (`pnMode`) for drawing lines and shapes and a *text mode* (`txMode`) for characters. The old QuickDraw routines `PenMode` [I:5.2.2] and `TextMode` [I:8.3.2] still set these two fields of the current port record, whether color or monochrome. The low-level transfer routine `CopyBits` [I:5.1.4], which now works on pixel maps as well as bit maps, also accepts a transfer mode as a parameter. To use the new color modes, you simply pass them to these routines in the usual way. As we'll see later, you can also still use the old monochrome modes in a color port, though the results may not always be useful or pleasing to look at.

All the color transfer modes operate on a pair of pixels at a time: a new one from the pattern or pixel map being drawn (the *source*) and an existing one from the map it's being drawn to (the *destination*). Since the "raw" pixel values are normally mapped indices into a color table, QuickDraw first looks in the table for their current RGB values. It then combines the two colors arithmetically, component by component, according to whatever rule the given mode calls for. Finally, it finds the nearest available match to the RGB result in the destination color table and stores the corresponding color index back into the destination pixel map as the result of the operation.

Additive and Subtractive Modes

The most obvious way to combine two colored pixels is simply to add their respective components together. This mixes the two colors additively and raises the overall brightness level, something like mixing colored spotlights on a stage or double-exposing a photographic slide. Color QuickDraw has two such additive modes [5.3.2]. The first, `AddOver`, allows the component values to overflow and "wrap around" from the maximum value ($FFFF, or 65535) back to 0. This can sometimes produce anomalous or unexpected results.

Usually you'll want to use AddPin instead, which limits ("pins") the components to a maximum value to prevent wraparound. The pin limits for the three components are specified by a field, rgbOp-Color, in the current port's auxiliary port record. This is initially set to black (all components equal to 0), but you can then change it with the Toolbox routine OpColor [5.3.2]. For additive drawing, you'll almost always want to use pure white, pinning all components at the top of the scale ($FFFF). If you need to achieve some other oddball effect—photographing through a colored filter, perhaps—you can use different pin limits instead.

There are also a pair of analogous subtractive modes, SubOver and SubPin [5.3.2]. These combine the source and destination colors subtractively and darken the overall color level, like mixing watercolor paints. Again, SubOver allows underflow from 0 to $FFFF, while SubPin limits all components to the minimum values given in the port's rgbOpColor field. (In this case, you'll usually want to use the default setting of pure black, pinning all color components at 0.) Drawing a color subtractively is like painting with its RGB complement: for example, subtracting blue on a cyan background is like painting in yellow, and will yield a green result.

Other Arithmetic Modes

Another obvious idea for combining colors is to average their components, producing a result that falls somewhere between the two original colors. This is what the transfer mode Blend [5.3.3] does. Once again, the rgbOpColor field in the auxiliary port record provides additional information on how to perform the operation: in this case, it gives the weights to be used in averaging the original colors. Each component of rgbOpColor gives the relative weight of the corresponding component from the source pixel, on a scale from 0 to 65535 ($FFFF). Dividing this value by 65536 normalizes it to a fraction between 0 and 1 (let's call it w), which is then subtracted from 1 to get the complementary weight for the destination pixel. Thus each component in the result is given by the formula

```
result = w*source + (1-w)*destination
```

As always, you use the Toolbox routine OpColor [5.3.2] to set the value of rgbOpColor. Ordinarily you'll want to make it medium gray (all components equal to $8000, or 32768), to obtain an equally-weighted blend midway between the source and destination colors.

In unusual cases, you may want to use a different value to weight the result more toward one or the other of the original colors. If you're feeling *really* eccentric, you can even use different weights for each of the three RGB components.

Rather less useful are the comparative modes ADMax and ADMin [5.3.3]. (The letters AD stand for "arithmetic drawing.") These modes compare the two operand pixels, one component at a time, and choose the larger or smaller of the two values for each component independently; notice that this may produce a result that doesn't match either of the two original colors. These modes are useful mainly for certain specialized purposes, such as drawing text in an "anti-aliased" font that uses gray-scale pixels, rather than just black and white, to increase the effective resolution. If you think anti-aliasing is a police technique for catching criminals operating under assumed names, you'll probably never have any use for these transfer modes.

Transparency and Highlighting

Perhaps the most useful color transfer mode of all is Transparent [5.3.4]. This copies all pixels directly from the source to the destination unless they match the current background color. In the latter case, it leaves the existing destination pixels unchanged, producing an overlay or "see-through" effect. If you set the port's background color to one that doesn't occur anywhere in the source, Transparent mode will simply copy all source pixels exactly as they are, without modification.

The last of the color transfer modes is Hilite [5.3.4]. As the name implies, this one is particularly useful for highlighting selected text or other objects in a window. On the old black-and-white screen, highlighting was usually done by color inversion with the monochrome mode XOr, changing black pixels to white and vice versa. XOr doesn't work very well in a color environment, however, so Hilite mode is provided as a full-color equivalent.

Hilite mode produces a color reversal similar to that of XOr in monochrome by exchanging the port's background color with a second *highlighting color*, read from the rgbHiliteColor field of the auxiliary port record [5.1.4]. The effect is similar to marking with a colored highlighting pen. The user can set a preferred highlighting color with the Control Panel desk accessory, which saves it in battery-powered parameter RAM where it will be retained even when the machine's power is turned off. At system startup, this value is copied into a low-memory global, HiliteRGB, which in turn is used to initialize the `rgbHiliteColor` field for all newly created ports. You can change the highlighting color with the Toolbox routine `HiliteColor` [5.3.4], but normally you should just honor the user's preference.

Although you can use `Hilite` mode in the usual way, by passing it as a parameter to `PenMode` [I:5.2.2], `TextMode` [I:8.3.2], or `CopyBits` [I:5.1.4], there's also another way to activate it. The low-memory global variable `HiliteMode`, at address `$938`, is a flag that causes the old monochrome mode `XOr` to do color highlighting instead of simple bit inversion. (Actually, the flag is just the high-order bit at this address; the other 7 bits are reserved for future use, and should not be disturbed.) When this flag is 0, any drawing operation that would otherwise use `XOr` (or `NotXOr`) mode will in effect use `Hilite` mode instead. This applies not only to routine line- or shape-drawing operations with `XOr` as an explicit pen or fill mode, but also to the standard shape-inverting operations `InvertRect`, `InvertOval`, and so on, all of which use `XOr` mode implicitly. The advantage to this method is that it allows older, existing code that uses `XOr` mode for monochrome highlighting to work properly in color as well.

Setting the `HiliteMode` flag is fairly straightforward in assembly language, where you can manipulate single bits directly. The assembly-language constant `HiliteBit` is the bit number of the flag bit within the byte, for use with the machine instruction `BCLR` (Bit Clear):

```
BCLR        #HiliteBit,HiliteMode
```

Following the standard M68000 convention, the bits are numbered from right to left within a byte, so the high-order bit, the one that actually contains the flag, is bit 7.

In Pascal, on the other hand, you need the Toolbox utility routine `BitClr` [I:2.2.1] to get your hands on the single flag bit. Since this routine defies the normal convention and numbers the bits from left to right, you have to identify the flag as bit number 0 instead of 7, using the constant `PHiliteBit` instead of `HiliteBit`. Notice also that the constant `HiliteMode` (defined in the Pascal interface file `SysEqu`) is an integer representing the *address* of the flag, so you have to typecast it to a pointer before passing it to `BitClr`:

```
flagPtr := Ptr(HiliteMode);
BitClr (flagPtr, PHiliteBit)
```

One more wrinkle to be aware of is that the highlighting flag is a "one-shot" flag that automatically gets set back to 1 after every drawing operation. If you want it to remain in effect, you have to clear it again explicitly before each drawing operation.

Mixing Color and Monochrome

Color and monochrome transfer modes are compatible in both directions: that is, you can use color modes to draw in a monochrome port and vice versa. QuickDraw will attempt to do something sensible in such hybrid situations, though its idea of sensible may not always coincide with yours. Mixing color and monochrome modes can produce useful results, but only if you're careful and observe some restrictions in the way you use them.

When used in a color port, the old monochrome modes perform the same bit-level operations as before, but on multibit pixel values rather than single bits. In place of simple black and white, they use the current foreground and background colors, taken from fields `fgColor` and `bkColor` of the port record. Notice that these are direct pixel representations, presumably color table indices, and *not* the absolute RGB values they stand for. These are combined bitwise with the existing pixel values found in the destination pixel map. The source map or pattern serves as a mask, telling where to use the bits from the port's drawing color and where to use the ones from the destination.

Because the raw pixel values bear no direct relation to the RGB colors they denote, it makes no sense to combine them partially, using some bits from one pixel and some from another. For the results to be useful, they should consist only of whole pixels—either the drawing color or the destination pixel, but not a mixture of the two—meaning that the source pixels that control the operation must each be either all 0s or all 1s. These two pixel values refer to the first and last entries in the color table, which by convention are always pure white and black, respectively. (Notice that this is the opposite of RGB representation, in which all 0s stand for black and all 1s for white.) Thus the monochrome modes produce meaningful results in a color port only when the source pixels that control them are restricted solely to black and white.

Table 5–1 Monochrome modes in a color port

Mode	Effect of Black Source Pixels	Effect of White Source Pixels
Copy	Foreground color	Background color
NotCopy	Background color	Foreground color
Or	Foreground color	No change
NotOr	No change	Foreground color
Bic	Background color	No change
NotBic	No change	Background color
XOr	Invert bits	No change
NotXOr	No change	Invert bits

Subject to this restriction, the effects of the monochrome modes are reasonably orderly and predictable (see Table 5–1). Copy mode, for instance, copies the source image to the destination in the port's current drawing colors, using the foreground color in place of black and the background color for white; NotCopy reverses the two colors. Or and Bic each paint one of the drawing colors (the foreground color for Or, background for Bic) wherever the source image has a black pixel, leaving the destination image unchanged where the source is white. NotOr and NotBic do the same, but reverse the roles of black and white in the source: that is, they paint the color where the source is white and leave the destination alone where the source is black.

XOr and NotXOr are a bit trickier. These modes invert the bits of selected destination pixels, using the source pixels as a mask to determine which ones to invert. Since the effects of bitwise inversion on raw pixel values are unpredictable, XOr and NotXOr yield meaningful results only when the destination pixels, as well as those in the source, are limited to black and white; in that case, they do simple black-and-white inversion, just as before. If the destination includes colors other than black and white, use the HiliteMode flag to make XOr and NotXOr do color highlighting instead of bit inversion, as described in the preceding section.

Similarly, you can use the new color modes in an old-style port. If you're drawing in color under the classic QuickDraw planar model [4.1], the new modes will do their best to carry out their intended functions, using the limited range of eight colors available in that model. Since the port has no auxiliary port record, those modes that ordinarily depend on fields of the auxiliary record have to use standard default values instead: AddPin pins to pure white, SubPin to black, Blend averages all colors equally, and Hilite uses the preferred highlighting color set by the user with the Control Panel.

Table 5-2 Color modes in a monochrome port

Color Mode	Equivalent Monochrome Mode
AddOver	XOr
AddPin	Bic
SubOver	XOr
SubPin	Or
ADMax	Bic
ADMin	Or
Blend	Copy
Transparent	Or
Hilite	XOr

If you're drawing in true monochrome, all the color modes default to monochrome equivalents that best approximate their intended functions, as shown in Table 5-2. These substitutions apply even in a color port if the pixel depth happens to be 1. Another problem that can arise at low pixel depths is that both the foreground and background colors may map into the same pixel value. Recall, in particular, that in 1-bit mode, anything that isn't white maps to black. You may think you're drawing in, say, dark blue on a yellow background, only to have the results appear on a 1-bit screen as black on black. At pixel depths of 1 or 2, QuickDraw will check for this problem and automatically invert one of the drawing colors, if necessary, to make sure the results are plainly visible.

Drawing in Color

When it comes to actually putting pixels on the screen, everything you already know about drawing in monochrome still holds true in color. You use a color port in just the same way as the old-fashioned kind: make it the current port and draw into it. To make a color port current, you simply use the old QuickDraw routine SetPort [I:4.3.3], just as you always have. First, though, you have to typecast its pointer into an old-style `GrafPtr` to propitiate the Pascal type-checking deities:

```
plainPort := GrafPtr(colorPort);
SetPort (plainPort)
```

Once you've made the port current, you can go ahead and scribble in it to your heart's content.

Don't let the ease with which you can typecast one kind of port into the other lull you into a false sense of security. The two are still distinct record types with different internal structures. Never try to use an old-style port pointer (like `plainPort` in the example above) to access the internal fields of a color port, lest the shade of Blaise Pascal descend on you in a howling fury and dispatch your program to the nether regions.

This can be especially hazardous if you use `GetPort` [I:4.3.3] to obtain a pointer to the current port. This routine has never heard of color ports and always returns an old-style `GrafPtr`, no matter which type the port may actually be. If it matters, you have to test the port's type yourself and typecast it to a color port:

```
colorMask := $C000;
GetPort (plainPort);
with plainPort^ do
    colorFlag := BitAnd(portBits.rowBytes, colorMask);

if colorFlag = colorMask then
    begin
        colorPort := CGrafPtr(plainPort);
        with colorPort^ do
            {Treat as color port}
    end
else
    with plainPort^ do
        {Treat as monochrome port}
```

Because the two types of port record are the same size and have most of the same fields, you can use them more or less interchangeably. All the old monochrome drawing routines from Volume One will still work in a color port, and will use the port's foreground and background colors instead of boring old black and white. The nifty new color drawing routines will also work in a monochrome port, though naturally the results won't be as pretty as in a full-color port.

Setting Drawing Colors

One difference between the two kinds of port is the way you set their drawing colors. In an old-style port, you normally do all your drawing in plain black and white. If you wish, you can use the old ForeColor and BackColor routines [4.1.2] to choose other drawing colors instead, but your selection is limited to the eight colors offered by the classic planar model [4.1.1].

In a color port, you set your drawing colors with the new routines RGBForeColor and RGBBackColor [5.4.1]. You can ask for any color you like, over the full range of 281 trillion RGB possibilities, but QuickDraw doesn't promise to deliver exactly the shade you ask for—you have to settle for the best approximation available in the current color environment. The color index you actually get is stored in the port's fgColor or bkColor field [5.1.3], to be used for drawing into the pixel image. The exact RGB value you originally requested is saved in the rgbFgColor or rgbBkColor field; if the color environment later changes, QuickDraw can try again and perhaps find you a better (or worse) match. The QuickDraw routines GetForeColor and GetBackColor [5.4.1] return these exact RGB values for the current foreground and background colors, respectively.

If you're using a palette to manage your color environment (as you usually do in a color window), you can use PMForeColor and PMBackColor [5.4.1] to set your drawing colors. Instead of giving an RGB value directly, you identify the desired color by its palette index; the Toolbox will look up the corresponding color value in the palette record and use it to set the port's drawing color. It also saves the palette handle and palette index in the auxiliary port record [5.1.4] for future reference, using the pmFgColor and pmFgIndex fields for the foreground color, pmBkColor and pmBkIndex for the background color.

Line and Shape Drawing

Once you've set your foreground and background colors, drawing in a color port is pretty much the same as in a monochrome port. All the old line- and shape-drawing operations we learned about in Volume One [I:5.2, I:5.3] still work, and are still governed by the port's pen and background patterns, pen mode, and pen size. Of course, these can now include the new multicolored pixel patterns and color transfer modes that we've been discussing in this chapter as well as the old monochrome patterns and modes.

By using a solid black, monochrome pen pattern with a pen mode of `PatCopy` [I:5.1.3], you can do simple line drawing in the port's current foreground color. (These are the standard pattern and mode settings that you get by default when you open a new port [5.1.5], so you needn't do anything to disturb them.) You position the pen and draw with it the same way as always, using the old QuickDraw routines `Move`, `MoveTo`, `Line`, and `LineTo` [I:5.2.4]. You can still make the pen visible and invisible with `HidePen` and `ShowPen` [I:5.2.3], set its dimensions with `PenSize` [I:5.2.2], or save and restore its drawing characteristics wholesale with `GetPen-State` and `SetPenState` [I:5.2.1]. (The latter save and restore the old `pnPat` [I:4.2.2] field, among others. This field no longer exists in a color port, but since its place is taken by the new `pnPixPat` and `fillPixPat` handles [5.1.3], everything should still work correctly.)

You can also use `PenPixPat` [5.2.4] to switch to a multicolored pen pattern and do your line drawing with that instead of just a solid foreground color. Remember, though, that the old monochrome transfer modes [I:5.1.3] don't work properly on a colored source, so be sure to use one of the new color modes instead. Unfortunately, there is no simple color copy mode corresponding to the monochrome `PatCopy`. To achieve the same effect in color, you have to use `Transparent` mode and set the port's background color to one that doesn't occur in the pen pattern.

Shape drawing, too, works more or less the same as it always has. The same five drawing operations (frame, paint, fill, erase, and invert [I:5.3.1]) are still available, and can be applied to rectangles [I:5.3.2], rounded rectangles [I:5.3.3], ovals [I:5.3.4], arcs and wedges [I:5.3.5], polygons [I:5.3.6], and regions [I:5.3.7]. As always, framing and painting use the port's current pen pattern and mode, erasing uses the background pattern. If the pen and background are set to monochrome bit patterns, all black and white pixels in the patterns will be replaced with the current foreground and background colors, respectively. Thus under the standard settings (solid black pen pattern, solid white background, `PatCopy` mode), shapes will be framed or painted in the foreground color and erased in the background color.

The old shape-filling routines like `FillRect` and `FillOval`, which accept a fill pattern as an explicit parameter, operate on bit patterns only and can't be applied to pixel patterns. Instead, there's a set of alternate routines [5.4.2] designed specifically for pixel patterns, named `FillCRect`, `FillCOval`, and so on (C for "color," of course). The fifth operation, inverting a shape, is really a monochrome operation that forms the bitwise complement of each pixel within the shape's boundary. In a color port with mapped representation, the results are unpredictable and usually quite peculiar. Recall, however, that this operation implicitly uses `PatXOr` mode and thus is governed by the `HiliteMode` flag that we learned about earlier. Clearing this flag to 0 before inverting a shape yields a much more pleasing result by exchanging the port's background and highlighting colors instead of complementing bits.

Direct Pixel Transfer

The fundamental drawing operation `CopyBits` [I:5.1.4], on which all others are based, has been modified [5.4.4] to operate on pixel maps as well as bit maps. For both its source and destination maps, `CopyBits` examines the two high-order bits of the `rowBytes` field [I:4.2.1, 5.1.1] to see which kind of map it is. If these two flag bits are 00, the map is understood to be an old-fashioned bit map; if they're 10, it is a pixel map. Either way, the new version of `CopyBits` is prepared to deal with it properly.

A third possibility is that the map's two flag bits are 11. This indicates that it isn't really a bit or pixel map at all, but the part of a color port record [5.1.3] occupying the same relative position as the bit map, `portBits`, in an old-style port [I:4.2.2]. The field containing the flag bits is not really `rowBytes` but `portVersion`, and what looks like the `baseAddr` field is really `portPixMap`, the handle to the port's pixel map. `CopyBits` will follow this handle and use the real pixel map instead of the fake bit map it actually received. Thus, to operate on the pixel map belonging to a color port, you can just typecast it to an old-style port and pass its fictitious `portBits` field as a parameter:

```
dummyPort := GrafPtr(colorPort);
CopyBits (...dummyPort^.portBits...)
```

(You can get away with this because `CopyBits` already dwells in the nether regions, safely beyond the reach of Pascal's ghost.)

The source and destination maps need not be the same kind: you can copy between a bit map and a pixel map, or between pixel maps of different depths, and `CopyBits` will automatically adjust the results to the depth of the destination map. Similarly, if the source and destination rectangles are of different sizes, `CopyBits` will scale the source rectangle to the dimensions of the destination, and if the two maps have different color tables, it will convert all source colors to their nearest available matches in the destination. (Such color mapping is always done through the inverse table of the current graphics device, however, so it won't work correctly unless the destination pixel map is based on that device's color table.)

Like the old monochrome version, this new color version of `CopyBits` accepts a transfer mode as a parameter. You can use either a monochrome or a color mode, depending on the nature of the pixel source. Monochrome modes give useful results only if the source is either a bit map or a pixel map containing black and white pixels exclusively. For a full-color source, use one of the new color transfer modes instead.

The alternate transfer routine `CopyMask` [I:5.1.4] has likewise been extended [5.4.4] to handle both pixel and bit maps. This routine works similarly to `CopyBits`, but accepts an additional bit map to use as a mask. Although the source and destination maps may be of either kind, the mask must be a bit map, not a pixel map, and must have the same width and height as the source. Pixels are copied from the source to the destination only in those positions where the mask has a black (1) bit.

`CopyMask` is useful for transferring icons [I:5.4.4, 6.1.1] into a bit map and also for implementing on-screen drawing tools like the "lasso" and "paint bucket." In the former case, the mask normally comes from an icon resource of type `'ICN#'` [I:5.5.4, I:7.5.3] (for monochrome icons) or `'cicn'` [6.7.1] (for color icons). In the latter, the mask is generated by the special-purpose QuickDraw routines `CalcCMask` and `SeedCFill` [5.4.5], for the lasso and paint bucket, respectively.

These routines work essentially the same as their old monochrome counterparts `CalcMask` and `SeedFill` [I:5.1.6], but on pixel maps as well as bit maps. `CalcCMask` starts from a given rectangle within the source map and finds the largest closed boundary lying entirely within the rectangle, representing the area "roped" by the lasso. `SeedCFill` starts from a given seed point and finds the smallest closed boundary surrounding that point, representing the area filled by the paint bucket. Both routines then build a mask to be passed to CopyMask, with 1 bits corresponding to the identified boundary and the area inside it.

The difference between these routines and their older counterparts lies in the way they define what constitutes a boundary. By default, both of the new color-oriented routines look for a closed boundary or a contiguous area of one single color: CalcCMask accepts the color as a parameter and SeedCFill takes it from the source map itself at the designated seed coordinates. Thus if the edge color specified to CalcCMask is cobalt blue, it looks for the largest closed chain of cobalt blue pixels completely enclosed within the given rectangle; if the pixel at SeedCFill's seed point is lemon yellow, it finds the region of all lemon yellow pixels contiguous to that one. If this simple one-color approach isn't what you need, you can customize it to suit yourself: see the "Nuts and Bolts" section at the end of this chapter for further information.

Color Table Animation

One interesting technique that the new color environment makes possible is *color table animation.* Instead of changing the contents of a pixel map to produce the illusion of motion on the screen, you can leave the map fixed and change the color values of its pixels. Depending on how you set things up, this can produce a variety of unusual and useful effects.

Figure 5–2 shows an example, going eyeball to eyeball with our old friend Big Brother from Volume One and finally making him blink. (Now that we have color available, we've given him an iris instead of just a solid black pupil; picture it as blood red.) Figure 5–2a shows the old boy in his normal vigilant state; in 5–2b, he's caught napping. By changing quickly from one image to the other, you can make him visibly blink on the screen.

As Figure 5–2c shows, the eyeball is actually made up of five separate regions with different pixel values, representing various color transitions from one image to the other. One region includes the eyelids and pupil, which remain black both before and after the transition. The white of the eye is divided into two regions, one that changes from white to black and another that remains white throughout; similarly, the iris has one region that goes from blood red to black and another that goes from red to white. When all these color transitions are made simultaneously, the eye changes from open to closed.

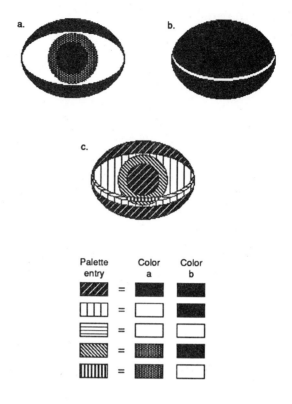

Figure 5–2 Color table animation

It's possible to do this kind of animation by manipulating the contents of the color table directly with `SetEntries` [4.4.5], but it's generally much more convenient to use a palette instead. The palette contains a separate animating entry [4.5.1] for each color region in the animated image (Figure 5–2c in our example). As we'll see, for effective animation the entries should occupy consecutive positions within the palette. Each animating entry reserves an index in the device color table and sets it to the specified initial color (presumably the one shown in the first column in the figure). Once such a color index has been reserved [4.4.6], it becomes unavailable for use as an ordinary drawing color, via `RGBForeColor` or `RGBBackColor` [5.4.1]: you can use it only through the palette, by passing its palette index to `PMForeColor` or `PMBackColor` [5.4.1].

If you're drawing in a window that spans more than one display screen, a separate index will be reserved in each device's color table for each palette entry you use. In general, the same palette entry will correspond to different color indices on different devices, but all the appropriate color settings will be maintained for you automatically and won't affect the way you do your drawing at the application level.

Once you've drawn the image in terms of your animating palette entries, you have to change the colors associated with those entries to produce the animation. The Toolbox routine `Animate-Entry` [5.4.3] changes the color of a single palette entry, but if you change one entry at a time, the intermediate results will be visible on the screen and will ruin the effect. For the animation to be effective, you have to change the entries all at once with `AnimatePalette` [5.4.3]. This routine sets the color values for a whole group of palette entries simultaneously, taking the new colors from a color table passed as a parameter. A sequence of consecutive colors are copied from the color table to the palette: that's why we said earlier that the entries for an animated image should occupy consecutive positions within the palette. To make Big Brother blink, we would call `AnimatePalette` with an auxiliary color table containing the five colors shown in the second column in the figure: black, black, white, black, white. To open his eye again, we would use another color table with the colors from the first column: black, white, white, red, red.

Nuts and Bolts

The `CalcCMask` and `SeedCFill` routines [5.4.5], which build bit masks for use with `CopyMask` [5.4.4] to implement the lasso and paint bucket drawing tools, ordinarily use a single color to define the lasso boundary or fill region (specified either by the `edgeColor` parameter to `CalcCMask` or by the pixel color at the seed point supplied to `SeedCFill`). If your needs are different, you can customize these routines to use some other search algorithm instead. Before learning how, we'll have to understand a little about how these routines work internally.

Both routines build the required bit mask by calling `CopyBits` to convert the source pixel map to 1-bit depth, after first installing their own custom search function [4.6.1] in the current device record. For each pixel in the source map, `CopyBits` looks in the map's color table to find the pixel's RGB color. It then calls `Color2Index` [4.4.4] to convert the color to an equivalent 1-bit "color index" for the destination (mask) map. This in turn activates the search function to perform the actual color-to-index conversion.

Before issuing the call to `CopyBits`, the `CalcCMask` and `SeedCFill` routines create a special parameter record of type `MatchRec` [5.4.5], containing the RGB components of the reference (edge or seed) color, and place a pointer to this record in the `gdRefCon` field of the current device record [4.3.1]. The standard search function simply compares each pixel's color against this reference color, generating a 1 bit in the mask if the two colors match, a 0 bit otherwise. This is the function that's used if the `searchFunc` parameter to `CalcCMask` or `SeedCFill` is NIL.

To customize the operation of these routines, you can supply your own search function in place of the standard one. The function receives the RGB color of a pixel and returns the resulting mask bit via a variable parameter, along with a Boolean function result of TRUE to signal that it has accepted and processed the request. The value of the edge or seed color (which the search function is free to ignore if it wishes) is available in the match record [5.4.5], which is pointed to by the current device's `gdRefCon` field. The match record also contains an additional utility field, `matchData`, to be used in any way the search function wishes. You supply the contents of this field as a parameter in your call to `CalcCMask` or `SeedCFill`, and the parameter value is copied into the match record for use by the search function.

For example, suppose you want to copy a six-colored banana from one place to another on the screen. In order to "lasso" the banana for copying, you need to call `CalcCMask` with a search function that recognizes all six of the banana's colors instead of just a single edge color. You can accomplish this by building a color table containing the six colors and passing a handle to the table (typecast to a long integer) as the `searchParam` parameter to `CalcCMask`. This handle will be copied into the `matchData` field of the match record, where your search function can find it. The function can then search the table for each pixel color it receives and generate a mask bit telling whether the table includes that color.

REFERENCE

5.1 Graphical Foundations

5.1.1 Pixel Maps

 Definitions

```
type
  PixMapHandle = ^PixMapPtr;
  PixMapPtr    = ^PixMap;

  PixMap       = record
                   baseAddr   : Ptr;         {Pointer to pixel image}
                   rowBytes   : INTEGER;     {Row width in bytes}
                   bounds     : Rect;        {Boundary rectangle}
                   pmVersion  : INTEGER;     {Color QuickDraw version number}
                   packType   : INTEGER;     {Format of packed image}
                   packSize   : LONGINT;     {Size of packed image in bytes}
                   hRes       : Fixed;       {Horizontal resolution in pixels per inch}
                   vRes       : Fixed;       {Vertical resolution in pixels per inch}
                   pixelType  : INTEGER;     {Storage format}
                   pixelSize  : INTEGER;     {Physical pixel size in bits}
                   cmpCount   : INTEGER;     {Number of color planes}
                   cmpSize    : INTEGER;     {Logical pixel size per plane, in bits}
                   planeBytes : LONGINT;     {Plane offset in bytes}
                   pmTable    : CTabHandle;  {Handle to color table}
                   pmReserved : LONGINT      {Reserved for future expansion}
                 end;
```

Notes

1. A pixel map contains the information needed to interpret a given pixel image in memory.

2. Each graphics device has its own *screen map*, defining the image to be displayed on the screen of the device. The gdPMap field of the device record [4.3.1] holds a handle to the screen map.

3. baseAddr is a pointer to the map's pixel image. The pixels of the image define the contents of the pixel map.

4. rowBytes is the *row width*, the number of bytes in each row of the pixel image.

5. The row width should always be even, representing a whole number of 16-bit words.

6. The high-order bit (bit 15) of rowBytes must be 1, to distinguish the pixel map from an old-style bit map [I:4.2.1]. Bits 14 and 13 are reserved for future use as flags, and for now should be set to 0.

7. bounds is the pixel map's *boundary rectangle*, which defines its extent and coordinate system.

8. The first pixel in the pixel image lies just inside the top-left corner of the boundary rectangle.

9. The width of the boundary rectangle must not exceed the image's row width in pixels (that is, 8/cmpSize * rowBytes). Its height must not exceed the number of rows in the pixel image.

10. Any pixels of the image that lie beyond the right or bottom edge of the boundary rectangle are ignored.

11. pmVersion identifies the version of Color QuickDraw that created this pixel map.

12. hRes and vRes give the horizontal and vertical resolution of the image in pixels per inch.

13. pixelSize is the physical number of bits occupied by each pixel in the image.

14. pixelSize is always a power of 2, allowing efficient packing of pixels within an 8-bit byte or a 16-bit word.

15. pixelSize is not necessarily equal to the image's logical pixel depth. However, in the current version of the Toolbox, pixel depths are also restricted to powers of 2, so the two quantities are in fact always equal.

16. pixelType is an integer code denoting the format in which the pixel image is stored in memory. A value of 0 stands for chunky format, 1 for chunky/planar, and 2 for planar. At present, only chunky format is supported; the others are included for possible future expansion.

17. In planar and chunky/planar formats, `cmpCount` is the number of components (planes) and `cmpSize` the number of bits per pixel in each plane (1 for pure planar representation). In chunky format, `cmpCount` = 1 and `cmpSize` = `pixelSize`.

18. `planeBytes` is the size of each plane's pixel image in bytes, and thus defines the offset from the beginning of one plane to the beginning of the next. Note that `rowBytes` refers to the row width *within* each plane. In chunky format, `planeBytes` = 0.

19. `packType` and `packSize` are included for future use with compressed pixel images. `packType` identifies the packing format used; `packSize` gives the size of the compressed image in bytes. At present, no packing formats are supported and both fields should be set to 0.

20. `pmTable` is a handle to a color table defining the colors used in the pixel image. This may be either the hardware color table for a particular graphics device or a table of intended color values for a device-independent pixel map.

21. The field `pmReserved` is reserved for future expansion and should be set to 0.

Assembly Language Information

Field offsets in a pixel map:

(Pascal) Field name	(Assembly) Offset name	Offset in bytes
baseAddr	pmBaseAddr	0
—————	pmNewFlag	4
rowBytes	pmRowBytes	4
bounds	pmBounds	6
pmVersion	pmVersion	14
packType	pmPackType	16
packSize	pmPackSize	18
hRes	pmHRes	22
vRes	pmVRes	26
pixelType	pmPixelType	30
pixelSize	pmPixelSize	32
cmpCount	pmCmpCount	34
cmpSize	pmCmpSize	36
planeBytes	pmPlaneBytes	38
pmTable	pmTable	42
pmReserved	pmReserved	46

Assembly-language constant:

Name	Value	Meaning
PMRec bytes	50	Size of a pixel map record in

5.1.2   Creating and Destroying Pixel Maps

Definitions

```
function  NewPixMap
              : PixMapHandle;            {Handle to new pixel map}

procedure CopyPixMap
          (fromPix : PixMapHandle;      {Pixel map to be copied}
           toPix   : PixMapHandle);     {Pixel map to copy it to}

procedure SetPortPix
          (thePix : PixMapHandle);      {New pixel map for current port}

procedure DisposPixMap
          (thePix : PixMapHandle);      {Pixel map to be destroyed}
```

Notes

1. NewPixMap creates a new pixel map and returns a handle to it.

2. An empty handle is created for the pixel map's color table (pmTable). No memory is actually allocated for the table.

3. All other fields are initialized from those of the pixel map belonging to the current graphics device.

4. CopyPixMap copies the contents of one pixel map record [5.1.1] to another.

5. The destination pixel map shares the same physical pixel image in memory with the source map. Only the baseAddr pointer is copied, not the underlying image itself.

6. The destination pixel map receives a *copy* of the source map's color table, not just a handle to the same table. The two pixel maps are thus left with separate color tables, rather than sharing the same table.

7. SetPortPix assigns a new pixel map to the current graphics port.

8. The pixel map thePix is stored into the port's portPixMap field [5.1.3].

9. The rectangle thePix.bounds becomes the port's boundary rectangle and establishes a new local coordinate system for the port.

10. If the current port is not a color graphics port, SetPortPix has no effect. Similarly, if the port *is* a color port, the old QuickDraw routine SetPortBits [I:4.3.4] has no effect.

11. DisposPixMap destroys a pixel map and frees its storage for other uses.

12. The pixel map's color table is deallocated as well as the pixel map itself. If a pixel map is using the color table associated with a graphics device, be sure to clear its pmTable field [5.1.1] to NIL before disposing of it.

Assembly Language Information

Trap macros:

(Pascal) Routine name	(Assembly) Trap macro	Trap word
NewPixMap	_NewPixMap	$AA03
CopyPixMap	_CopyPixMap	$AA05
SetPortPix	_SetPortPix	$AA06
DisposPixMap	_DisposPixMap	$AA04

5.1.3 Color Graphics Ports

Definitions

```
type
    CGrafPtr  = ^CGrafPort:

    CGrafPort = record
                device      : INTEGER;        {Device code for font selection [I:8.3.1]}
                portPixMap  : PixMapHandle;   {Pixel map for this port [5.1.1]}
                portVersion : INTEGER;        {Color QuickDraw version number}
                grafVars    : Handle;         {Handle to auxiliary port record [5.1.4]}
                chExtra     : INTEGER;        {Extra character width}
```

```
           pnLocHFrac  : INTEGER;          {Fractional pen location}
           portRect    : Rect;             {Port rectangle}
           visRgn      : RgnHandle;        {Visible region}
           clipRgn     : RgnHandle;        {Clipping region}
           bkPixPat    : PixPatHandle;     {Background pixel pattern [5.2.1]}
           rgbFgColor  : RGBColor;         {RGB value of foreground color [5.4.1]}
           rgbBkColor  : RGBColor;         {RGB value of background color [5.4.1]}
           pnLoc       : Point;            {Current pen location [I:5.2.1]}
           pnSize      : Point;            {Dimensions of graphics pen [I:5.2.1]}
           pnMode      : INTEGER;          {Transfer mode for graphics pen [5.3.1]}
           pnPixPat    : PixPatHandle;     {Pixel pattern for line drawing [5.2.1]}
           fillPixPat  : PixPatHandle;     {Pixel pattern for area fill [5.2.1]}
           pnVis       : INTEGER;          {Pen visibility level [I:5.2.3]}
           txFont      : INTEGER;          {Font number for text [I:8.2.1, I:8.3.1]}
           txFace      : Style;            {Type style for text [I:8.3.1]}
           txMode      : INTEGER;          {Transfer mode for text [5.3.1, I:8.3.1]}
           txSize      : INTEGER;          {Type size for text [I:8.3.1]}
           spExtra     : Fixed;            {Extra space between words [I:8.3.1]}
           fgColor     : LONGINT;          {Color index of foreground color [5.4.1]}
           bkColor     : LONGINT;          {Color index of background color [5.4.1]}
           colrBit     : INTEGER;          {Current color plane [4.1.3]}
           patStretch  : INTEGER;          {Private}
           picSave     : Handle;           {Private}
           rgnSave     : Handle;           {Private}
           polySave    : Handle;           {Private}
           grafProcs   : QDProcsPtr        {Pointer to bottleneck procedures [5.5.1]}
      end;
```

Notes

1. A color graphics port is a complete color drawing environment containing all the information needed for Color QuickDraw drawing operations.

2. The CGrafPort record is the same size as an old-style GrafPort record [I:4.2.2] and (with the exceptions noted below) has most of the same fields in the same locations within the record.

3. Like old-style graphics ports, color ports are nonrelocatable objects in the heap and are always referred to by simple pointers rather than handles.

4. portPixMap is a handle to the pixel map [5.1.1] that this port draws into.

5. The port's *boundary rectangle* is the same as that of its pixel map, portPixMap^^.bounds [5.1.1].

6. portVersion identifies the version of Color QuickDraw that created this port.

7. The first two bits (bits 15 and 14) of portVersion are set to 1. This distinguishes color graphics ports from old-style ports, in which the field portBits.rowBytes (occupying the same relative position within the port record) always has 0 in these two bits.

8. grafVars is a handle to an *auxiliary port record* [5.1.4] containing additional information about the port.

9. The bkPat, fillPat, and pnPat fields of the old-style graphics port [I:4.2.2] are replaced by bkPixPat, fillPixPat, and pnPixPat. Notice that these are now *handles* to pixel patterns [5.2.1], rather than old-style bit patterns [I:5.1.1] embedded directly in the port record.

10. rgbFgColor and rgbBkColor are the exact RGB values [4.2.1] requested for the port's foreground and background colors [5.4.1]. fgColor and bkColor are the corresponding actual pixel values, normally the color indices of the best available matches in the current device's color table.

11. colrBit is the current color plane [4.1.3] for drawing under the "classic QuickDraw" planar color model.

12. chExtra is a new field specifying the additional character width to be used in proportional spacing. All text characters except spaces are widened by this number of pixels; space characters are still governed by the spExtra field, as before [I:8.3.1].

13. chExtra is nominally defined as an integer, but is actually a fixed-point number with 4 bits before the binary point and 12 after it.

14. pnLocHFrac is a fractional pen location maintained by the Toolbox for more precise character placement when drawing text.

15. All other fields of the color graphics port have the same meanings as in an old-style port [I:4.2.2].

Assembly Language Information

Field offsets in a color graphics port:

(Pascal) Field name	(Assembly) Offset name	Offset in bytes
device	device	0
portPixMap	portPixMap	2
portVersion	portVersion	6
grafVars	grafVars	8
chExtra	chExtra	12
pnLocHFrac	pnLocHFrac	14
portRect	portRect	16
visRgn	visRgn	24
clipRgn	clipRgn	28
bkPixPat	bkPixPat	32
rgbFgColor	rgbFgColor	36
rgbBkColor	rgbBkColor	42
pnLoc	pnLoc	48
pnSize	pnSize	52
pnMode	pnMode	56
pnPixPat	pnPixPat	58
fillPixPat	fillPixPat	62
pnVis	pnVis	66
txFont	txFont	68
txFace	txFace	70
txMode	txMode	72
txSize	txSize	74
spExtra	spExtra	76
fgColor	fgColor	80
bkColor	bkColor	84
colrBit	colrBit	88
patStretch	patStretch	90
picSave	picSave	92
rgnSave	rgnSave	96
polySave	polySave	100
grafProcs	grafProcs	104

Assembly-language constant:

Name	Value	Meaning
PortRec	108	Size of a color port record in bytes

5.1.4 Auxiliary Port Record

Definitions

```
type
    GVarHandle = ^GVarPtr;
    GVarPtr    = ^GrafVars;

    GrafVars   = record
                    rgbOpColor     : RGBColor;    {Reference color for transfer modes}
                    rgbHiliteColor : RGBColor;    {Highlighting color}
                    pmFgColor      : Handle;      {Palette containing foreground color}
                    pmFgIndex      : INTEGER;     {Palette index of foreground color}
                    pmBkColor      : Handle;      {Palette containing background color}
                    pmBkIndex      : INTEGER;     {Palette index of background color}
                    pmFlags        : INTEGER      {Private flags for palette usage}
                 end;
```

Notes

1. The auxiliary port record contains additional information associated with a graphics port, beyond what is contained in the port record itself.

2. The grafVars field in the main port record [5.1.3] holds a handle to the auxiliary port record.

3. rgbOpColor is an RGB color value used in connection with the transfer modes AddPin, SubPin [5.3.2], and Blend [5.3.3]. See the sections on these transfer modes for further discussion.

4. rgbHiliteColor is the port's *highlighting color;* see [5.3.4] for further discussion.

5. The values of rgbOpColor and rgbHiliteColor are set by the Toolbox routines OpColor [5.3.2] and HiliteColor [5.3.4], respectively.

6. The remaining fields are used internally by the Toolbox when the port's drawing colors are set from a palette with the routines

PMForeColor and PMBackColor [5.4.1]. The letters pm stand for Palette Manager, the part of the Toolbox that deals with color palettes.

7. pmFgColor and pmBkColor are handles to the palettes containing the port's foreground and background colors, respectively. pmFgIndex and pmBkIndex are the colors' palette indices within these palettes.

8. pmFlags contains private flags relating to the port's use of palettes.

Assembly Language Information

Field offsets in an auxiliary port record:

(Pascal) Field name	(Assembly) Offset name	Offset in bytes
rgbOpColor	rgbOpColor	0
rgbHiliteColor	rgbHiliteColor	6
pmFgColor	pmFgColor	12
pmFgIndex	pmFgIndex	16
pmBkColor	pmBkColor	18
pmBkIndex	pmBkIndex	22
pmFlags	pmFlags	24

Assembly-language constant:

Name	Value	Meaning
GrafVarRec	26	Size of an auxiliary port record in bytes

5.1.5   Creating and Destroying Color Ports

Definitions

```
procedure OpenCPort
        (whichPort : CGrafPtr);        {Pointer to port to open}

procedure InitCPort
        (whichPort : CGrafPtr);        {Pointer to port to initialize}

procedure CloseCPort
        (whichPort : CGrafPtr);        {Pointer to port to close}
```

Initial values of `CGrafPort` fields:

Field	Initial Value
device	0 (screen)
portPixMap	Copy of current device's pixel map
portVersion	$C000
chExtra	0
pnLocHFrac	0.5
portRect	portPixMap^^.bounds
visRgn	Rectangular region equal to portRect
clipRgn	Rectangular region (-32768, -32768) to (+32767, +32767)
bkPixPat	Solid white
rgbFgColor	Black
rgbBkColor	White
pnLoc	(0, 0)
pnSize	(1, 1)
pnMode	PatCopy [I:5.1.3]
pnPixPat	Solid black
fillPixPat	Solid black
pnVis	0 (visible) [I:5.2.3]
txFont	0 (system font) [I:8.2.1]
txFace	Plain [I:8.3.1]
txMode	SrcOr [I:5.1.3]
txSize	0 (standard size) [I:8.3.1]
spExtra	0
fgColor	Black
bkColor	White
colrBit	0
patStretch	0
picSave	NIL
rgnSave	NIL
polySave	NIL
grafProcs	NIL (standard bottlenecks) [III:2.1, 5.5.1]

Notes

1. `OpenCPort` initializes a color graphics port and opens it for use; `InitCPort` reinitializes a color port that has already been opened.

2. Both routines set the fields of the `CGrafPort` record to their standard initial values, as shown in the table.

3. The `CGrafPort` record representing the port must already have been allocated previously with `NewPtr` [I:3.2.1]. Use typecasting to convert the resulting pointer from type `Ptr` [I:3.1.1] to `CGrafPtr` [5.1.3].

4. In both cases, the designated port becomes the current port.

5. In addition to the port record itself, `OpenCPort` allocates space for the port's internal data structures (pixel map; pen, fill, and background pixel patterns; visible and clipping regions; auxiliary port record), but not for the pixel map's color table. `InitCPort` allocates no storage, but merely initializes the contents of the existing port record and internal structures.

6. All fields of the port's pixel map are initialized from those of the current device's pixel map. In particular, the map's color table handle (`portPixMap^^.pmTable`) is set to point to the device's color table (`gdPMap^^.pmTable`). Thus the port and the device share the identical color table in memory.

7. The `rgbOpColor` field in the auxiliary port record [5.1.4] is initialized to black, and `rgbHiliteColor` to the default highlight color taken from the system global `HiliteRGB` [5.3.4]. All other fields of the auxiliary port record are initialized to 0.

8. To create a port for drawing into an offscreen pixel map, call `NewGDevice` [4.3.2] with a `dRefNum` parameter of 0 to create a device record that is not initialized for any existing device. Set the record's `gdPMap` field [4.3.1] to point to your offscreen map and initialize its other fields "by hand" as necessary. Then use `SetGDevice` [4.3.4] to make it the current device before calling `OpenCPort` to create a port based on it.

9. `CloseCPort` destroys a port's internal data structures, but not the `CGrafPort` record itself. Use this routine to deallocate the internal structures, then `DisposPtr` [I:3.2.2] to dispose of the port itself.

10. Since a port's pixel map commonly shares the color table belonging to a graphics device, `CloseCPort` does not deallocate the color table along with the pixel map itself. If you have supplied your own color table and wish to dispose of it, you must do so explicitly before calling `CloseCPort`.

11. These routines have no effect on an old-style graphics port; similarly, the old routines `OpenPort`, `InitPort`, and `ClosePort` [I:4.3.2] have no effect on a color port.

Assembly Language Information

Trap macros:

(Pascal) Routine name	(Assembly) Trap macro	Trap word
OpenCPort	_OpenCPort	$AA00
InitCPort	_InitCPort	$AA01
CloseCPort	_CloseCPort	$A87D

5.1.6   Pixel Access

Definitions

```
procedure GetCPixel
          (hCoord       : INTEGER;     {Horizontal coordinate of pixel}
           vCoord       : INTEGER;     {Vertical coordinate of pixel}
           var pixelColor : RGBColor);  {Returns current color of pixel}

procedure SetCPixel
          (hCoord     : INTEGER;       {Horizontal coordinate of pixel}
           vCoord     : INTEGER;       {Vertical coordinate of pixel}
           pixelColor : RGBColor);     {Desired new color of pixel}
```

Notes

1. GetCPixel returns the color of a designated pixel in the current graphics port; SetCPixel sets a pixel to a specified color.

2. hCoord and vCoord are expressed in the local coordinate system of the current port. The pixel affected will be the one immediately below and to the right of these coordinates.

3. SetCPixel accepts an RGB color value and sets the designated pixel to the nearest available color in the current color environment. GetCPixel returns the pixel's exact RGB color.

4. For a graphics port on the screen (such as a window), the result is meaningful only if the given coordinates lie within the port's visible region.

Assembly Language Information

Trap macros:

(Pascal) Routine name	(Assembly) Trap macro	Trap word
GetCPixel	_GetCPixel	$AA17
SetCPixel	_SetCPixel	$AA16

5.1.7   Error Reporting

Definitions

```
function QDError
          : INTEGER;                    {Result code of last QuickDraw or color operation}

const
  NoErr       =    0;                   {No error; all is well}
  CMatchErr   = -150;                   {Unable to match requested color}
  CTempMemErr = -151;                   {Unable to allocate temporary memory}
  CNoMemErr   = -152;                   {Unable to allocate memory}
  CRangeErr   = -153;                   {Color index out of range}
  CProtectErr = -154;                   {Color table protection violation}
  CDevErr     = -155;                   {Invalid type for graphics device}
  CResErr     = -156;                   {Invalid resolution for inverse table}
```

Notes

1. QDError returns the result code posted by the last QuickDraw or color-related routine call.

2. The result code returned in the normal case is 0 (NoErr). Any nonzero result code denotes an error.

3. Error codes listed here are only those directly related to color. Errors from other parts of the Toolbox can also occur in the course of color-related operations, and will be reported by QDError. See Appendix E for a complete list of Toolbox error codes.

Assembly Language Information

Trap macro:

(Pascal) Routine name	(Assembly) Trap macro	Trap word
QDError	_QDError	$AA40

Result codes:

Name	Value	Meaning
NoErr	0	No error; all is well
CMatchErr	-150	Unable to match requested color
CTempMemErr	-151	Unable to allocate temporary memory
CNoMemErr	-152	Unable to allocate memory
CRangeErr	-153	Color index out of range
CProtectErr	-154	Color table protection violation
CDevErr	-155	Invalid type for graphics device
CResErr	-156	Invalid resolution for inverse table

5.2 Pixel Patterns

5.2.1 Pixel Pattern Structure

Definitions

```
type
    PixPatHandle = ^PixPatPtr:
    PixPatPtr    = ^PixPat:

    PixPat       = record
                     patType  : INTEGER;        {Pattern type}
                     patMap   : PixMapHandle;   {Characteristics of pixel image}
                     patData  : Handle;         {Pixel image}
                     patXData : Handle;         {Expanded pixel image}
```

```
        patXValid : INTEGER;        {Is expanded image valid?}
        patXMap   : Handle;         {Characteristics of expanded image}
        pat1Data  : Pattern         {Bit pattern for old-style ports}
end;
```

Notes

1. A pixel pattern is the color analog of an old-style (monochrome) bit pattern [I:5.1.1]: a colored "tile" that can be repeated indefinitely to draw lines or fill areas in a graphical image.

2. Unlike bit patterns, which are limited to a fixed size (8-by-8), a pixel pattern's height and width may be any power of 2.

3. When drawn in a graphics port, a pixel pattern is aligned with the coordinates of the port rectangle, so that adjacent patterned areas will blend continuously without creating "seams."

4. `patType` is an integer code denoting the type of pattern. A value of 0 stands for a monochrome pattern (equivalent to an old-style bit pattern), 1 for a full-color pixel pattern, and 2 for a dithered pattern approximating a given RGB color.

5. The assembly-language interface to the Toolbox includes constants `OldPat`, `NewPat`, and `DitherPat`, representing the three pattern types (see "Assembly Language Information" below). These constants have been inadvertently omitted from the Pascal version of the interface.

6. `patData` is a handle to the pixel image defining the pattern.

7. `patMap` is a pixel map defining the pattern's dimensions, pixel depth, color table, and other properties. The map's `baseAddr` field is ignored, since the pixel image is defined by `patData` instead.

8. In a monochrome pattern (`patType = 0`), `patMap` is ignored. The pattern's dimensions are always 8-by-8, its pixel depth is 1, and it is always drawn in the port's current foreground and background colors [5.4.1].

9. When a pixel pattern is drawn in a given color environment, the Toolbox builds a private copy to match the current pixel depth and color table. The pixel image and map defining this private copy are stored in the `patXData` and `patXMap` fields.

10. patXValid is a flag indicating whether patXData and patXMap represent a valid expansion of the pattern for the current color environment. After changing the pattern's pixel image, color table, or other properties, set this field to -1 to mark the expanded pattern as invalid and force it to be rebuilt.

11. pat1Data is a monochrome bit pattern [I:5.1.1] for use in drawing the pattern into old-style graphics ports. Like all bit patterns, it is limited to the standard fixed dimensions, 8 bits by 8.

12. In a newly created pixel pattern, pat1Data is initialized to the standard medium gray pattern [I:5.1.2]. To use a different pattern instead, you must explicitly store it into this field yourself.

Assembly Language Information

Field offsets in a pixel pattern:

(Pascal) Field name	(Assembly) Offset name	Offset in bytes
patType	patType	0
patMap	patMap	2
patData	patData	6
patXData	patXData	10
patXValid	patXValid	14
patXMap	patXMap	16
pat1Data	pat1Data	20

Assembly-language constant:

Name	Value	Meaning
PPRec	28	Size of a pixel pattern in bytes

Pattern types:

Name	Value	Meaning
OldPat	0	Monochrome (bit) pattern
NewPat	1	Full-color pixel pattern
DitherPat	2	Dithered pixel pattern

5.2.2   Creating and Destroying Pixel Patterns

Definitions

```
function  NewPixPat
             : PixPatHandle;              {Handle to new pixel pattern}

function  GetPixPat
             (patternID : INTEGER)        {Resource ID of desired pixel pattern}
             : PixPatHandle;              {Handle to pattern in memory}

procedure DisposPixPat
             (thePixPat : PixPatHandle);  {Pixel pattern to be destroyed}
```

Notes

1. NewPixPat creates a new pixel pattern [5.2.1] and initializes its fields.

2. The pattern's patType field is set to 1, denoting a standard, full-color pixel pattern.

3. A new pixel map (patMap) is created, with its fields (row width, boundary rectangle, pixel depth, and so forth) initialized from those of the current graphics device. If these settings are not the ones you want for the pattern, you must change them yourself.

4. Empty handles are created for the pattern's pixel image (patData), color table (patMap^^.pmTable), expanded image (patXData), and expanded pixel map (patXMap), but no memory is actually allocated for these structures. The patXValid field is set to -1, marking the expanded image as invalid.

5. The pattern's monochrome equivalent (pat1Data) is initialized to the standard medium gray pattern [I:5.1.2]. To use a different pattern instead, you must explicitly store it into this field yourself.

6. GetPixPat creates a new pixel pattern from a 'ppat' resource [5.6.1].

7. DisposPixPat disposes of a pixel pattern and all of its subsidiary data structures (pixel image, pixel map, expanded image, expanded map, and color table).

8. If the pattern you're destroying is the current pen, background, or fill pattern of any existing graphics port, the port's handle to the pattern is automatically cleared to NIL to avoid leaving it dangling. In general, you should be careful not to dispose of a pattern while it is still in use by a port.

Assembly Language Information

Trap macros:

(Pascal) Routine name	(Assembly) Trap macro	Trap word
NewPixPat	_NewPixPat	$AA07
GetPixPat	_GetPixPat	$AA0C
DisposPixPat	_DisposPixPat	$AA08

5.2.3   Filling Pixel Patterns

Definitions

```
procedure MakeRGBPat
          (toPixPat   : PixPatHandle;      {Pixel pattern to be filled}
           fromColor  : RGBColor);         {Color value to be approximated}

procedure CopyPixPat
          (fromPixPat : PixPatHandle;      {Pixel pattern to be copied}
           toPixPat   : PixPatHandle);     {Pixel pattern to copy it to}
```

Notes

1. MakeRGBPat builds a dithered pixel pattern approximating a given RGB color.

2. The pixel pattern data structure [5.2.1] must already exist; MakeRGBPat merely sets its fields to represent the desired pattern.

3. The pattern's patType field is set to 2, denoting a dithered pattern.

4. A dithered pattern has no explicit pixel image; its patData field is set to NIL. The pattern is implicitly understood to consist of four (not necessarily different) colors in a 2-by-2 grid, which blend visually to give the appearance of the requested color.

5. Entries 0 to 3 in the pattern's color table are allotted to the four dithered colors, but MakeRGBPat does not fill in any color values. The colors are computed when the pattern is actually drawn, using the color environment current at that time.

6. Entry 4 in the color table holds the exact RGB value the pattern is intended to represent, as specified by the `fromColor` parameter to `MakeRGBPat`.

7. `CopyPixPat` copies the contents of one pixel pattern to another.

8. All of the pattern's subsidiary data structures are copied, including its pixel image, pixel map, expanded image, expanded map, and color table. The resulting copy shares none of these structures with the original.

Assembly Language Information

Trap macros:

(Pascal) Routine name	(Assembly) Trap macro	Trap word
MakeRGBPat	_MakeRGBPat	$AA0D
CopyPixPat	_CopyPixPat	$AA09

5.2.4   Using Pixel Patterns

Definitions

```
procedure PenPixPat
          (newPenPat : PixPatHandle);    {New pen pattern}

procedure BackPixPat
          (newBackPat : PixPatHandle);   {New background pattern}

procedure SetDeskCPat
          (newDeskPat : PixPatHandle);   {New desk pattern}
```

Notes

1. `PenPixPat` and `BackPixPat` set the current port's pen pattern (`pnPixPat`) and background pattern (`bkPixPat`), respectively.

2. The port's fill pattern (`FillPixPat`) is set implicitly by shape-filling operations such as `FillCRect` [5.4.2].

3. If the current port is an old-style graphics port, the pixel pattern's monochrome equivalent, pat1Data [5.2.1] is used instead.

4. The old routines PenPat [I:5.2.2] and BackPat [I:5.1.1] can still be used in a color port, and will construct a monochrome pattern (patType = 0) equivalent to the specified bit pattern.

5. SetDeskCPat sets the desktop pattern for drawing the screen background to a given pixel pattern.

6. The screen is immediately repainted with the new desktop pattern.

7. This routine is intended for use by the Control Panel desk accessory, and should not normally be called by an application program.

Assembly Language Information

Trap macros:

(Pascal) Routine name	(Assembly) Trap macro	Trap word
PenPixPat	_PenPixPat	$AA0A
BackPixPat	_BackPixPat	$AA0B
SetDeskCPat	_SetDeskCPat	$AA47

5.3   Color Transfer Modes

5.3.1   Mode Constants

Definitions

```
const
  Blend        = 32;          {Blend colors [5.3.3]}
  AddPin       = 33;          {Add with maximum [5.3.2]}
  AddOver      = 34;          {Add with wraparound [5.3.2]}
  SubPin       = 35;          {Subtract with minimum [5.3.2]}
  Transparent  = 36;          {Copy with transparency [5.3.4]}
  ADMax        = 37;          {Arithmetic maximum [5.3.3]}
  SubOver      = 38;          {Subtract with wraparound [5.3.2]}
  ADMin        = 39;          {Arithmetic minimum [5.3.3]}
  Hilite       = 50;          {Highlight background [5.3.4]}
```

Notes

1. Color transfer modes control the transfer of pixels between pixel maps, or between a pixel pattern and a pixel map.

2. Each transfer mode denotes a way of combining pixels from the source (pixel map, character, or pattern) with the corresponding pixels from the destination pixel map. The resulting pixels are then stored back into the destination. See [5.3.2] to [5.3.4] for details of specific color modes.

3. Two transfer modes are associated with each graphics port [I:4.2.2, 5.1.3]:

    • a *pen mode* (pnMode) for drawing lines and shapes

    • a *text mode* (txMode) for drawing text characters

4. To set a port's pen mode, use PenMode [I:5.2.2]; to set the text mode, use TextMode [I:8.3.2]. The low-level transfer routine CopyBits [I:5.1.4] also requires a mode as a parameter. All of these routines will accept the new color modes shown here as well as the older monochrome modes [I:5.1.3].

5. Monochrome modes can still be used in a color graphics port, but are useful only when all source pixels are restricted to black and white. Other colors in the source produce unpredictable results and should be avoided.

6. On the Macintosh II, the QuickDraw routines no longer distinguish between source and pattern transfer modes; the right type is chosen automatically according to the operation being performed. (For this reason, the following notes refer simply to Copy mode, for example, rather than SrcCopy and PatCopy.) Earlier versions of QuickDraw still observe the source–pattern distinction, however, so you should continue to use the correct type of mode for the sake of compatibility.

7. The monochrome modes Copy and NotCopy completely replace the pixels of the destination with those of the source, drawn in the port's current drawing colors. Copy uses the port's foreground color where the source has a black pixel, the background color where the source is white; NotCopy does the reverse.

8. To copy a multicolored source rather than black-and-white, use Transparent mode [5.3.4] instead.

9. The monochrome modes Or, NotOr, Bic ("bit clear"), and NotBic replace selected pixels in the destination with one of the port's current drawing colors, while leaving the remaining pixels unchanged. Or and

NotOr use the port's foreground color, Bic and NotBic the background color. Or and Bic paint the given color where the source has a black pixel, leaving the destination unchanged where the source is white; NotOr and NotBic do the reverse.

10. The monochrome modes XOr and NotXOr yield unpredictable results unless the destination, as well as the source, is limited to black and white pixels only. To achieve the effect of color inversion in a multicolored pixel map, use Hilite mode [5.3.4] instead.

Assembly Language Information

Color transfer modes:

Name	Value	Meaning
Blend	32	Blend colors
AddPin	33	Add with maximum
AddOver	34	Add with wraparound
SubPin	35	Subtract with minimum
Transparent	36	Copy with transparency
ADMax	37	Arithmetic maximum
SubOver	38	Subtract with wraparound
ADMin	39	Arithmetic minimum

5.3.2   Additive and Subtractive Modes

Definitions

```
const
    AddOver = 34;              {Add with wraparound}
    AddPin  = 33;              {Add with maximum}
    SubOver = 38;              {Subtract with wraparound}
    SubPin  = 35;              {Subtract with minimum}

procedure OpColor
             (newColor : RGBColor);    {Color to pin to}
```

Notes

1. These modes combine colored pixels by arithmetically adding or subtracting their respective RGB components, then finding the nearest available approximation to the RGB result.

2. AddOver and SubOver ignore arithmetic overflow or underflow and allow the component values to "wrap around" from $FFFF to 0 or vice versa.

3. AddPin and SubPin limit the results to a specified maximum or minimum value. Component values that would otherwise go above the maximum (for AddPin) or below the minimum (for SubPin) are instead "pinned" to the limiting value.

4. Because of the additional check for overflow or underflow, AddPin and SubPin are slightly slower than AddOver and SubOver.

5. Maximum or minimum values for the three RGB components are specified by the rgbOpColor field in the current port's auxiliary port record [5.1.4].

6. In a newly created graphics port, rgbOpColor is initialized to black; it can then be changed, if necessary, with the Toolbox routine OpColor.

7. In an old-style graphics port, AddPin always pins to pure white (all components equal to $FFFF) and SubPin to pure black (all components equal to 0).

8. When drawn at 1-bit depth, AddOver and SubOver are both equivalent to XOr, AddPin to Bic, and SubPin to Or.

Assembly Language Information

Trap macro:

(Pascal) Routine name	(Assembly) Trap macro	Trap word
OpColor	_OpColor	$AA21

5.3.3   Comparative and Combinative Modes

Definitions

```
const
    ADMax = 37;                          {Arithmetic maximum}
    ADMin = 39;                          {Arithmetic minimum}
    Blend = 32;                          {Blend colors}
```

Notes

1. The modes ADMax and ADMin combine colored pixels by arithmetically comparing their respective RGB components, choosing the maximum or minimum value for each, then finding the nearest available approximation to the RGB result.

2. The letters AD stand for "arithmetic drawing."

3. Since each color component is compared separately, the result may differ from both of the original colors.

4. In some versions of the Pascal interface files, the constant ADMax is incorrectly spelled AddMax.

5. Blend mode combines colored pixels by computing a weighted average of their respective RGB components, then finding the nearest available approximation to the RGB result.

6. Weights for averaging the three color components are specified by the rgbOpColor field in the current port's auxiliary port record [5.1.4].

7. For each component, rgbOpColor gives the relative weight of the source pixel on a scale from 0 to 65535 ($FFFF). This value is first divided by 65536, normalizing it to a fractional weight w between 0 and 1; the result is then subtracted from 1 to obtain the complementary destination weight. Thus the result value for each component is given by the formula

```
result = w*source + (1-w)*dest
```

8. In a newly created graphics port, rgbOpColor is initialized to black; it can then be changed, if necessary, with the Toolbox routine OpColor [5.3.2].

9. In an old-style graphics port, source and destination pixels are always averaged with equal weights.

10. When drawn at 1-bit depth, `ADMax` is equivalent to `Bic`, `ADMin` to `Or`, and `Blend` to `Copy`.

5.3.4   Transparency and Highlighting

Definitions

```
const
    Transparent = 36;                    {Copy with transparency}
    Hilite      = 50;                    {Highlight background}

    HiliteMode  = $938;                  {Address of highlighting flag}
    PHiliteBit  =    0;                  {Bit number of highlight bit for BitClr [I:2.2.1]}

procedure HiliteColor
          (newColor : RGBColor);         {New highlight color}
```

Notes

1. `Transparent` mode copies all pixels from the source to the destination except those of the current port's background color. The latter leave the corresponding destination pixels unchanged, producing a transparent or "see-through" effect.

2. `Hilite` mode exchanges a given *highlighting color* in the destination with the current port's background color at all positions where the source has a black pixel. The effect is similar to marking with a colored highlighting pen.

3. Source pixels other than black and white will produce unpredictable results and should be avoided.

4. The `rgbHiliteColor` field of the current port's auxiliary port record [5.1.4] defines the highlighting color to be used.

5. The user can specify a preferred highlighting color with the Control Panel desk accessory. This value is then saved in parameter RAM, copied into the low-memory global `HiliteRGB` at system startup, and used to initialize the `rgbHiliteColor` field for all newly created graphics ports.

6. You can change the current port's `rgbHiliteColor`, if you wish, with the Toolbox routine `HiliteColor`, but ordinarily you should simply honor the user's preferred setting.

7. The low-memory global `HiliteMode` is a flag that converts the monochrome transfer mode `XOr` [I:5.1.3] to `Hilite`. When the high-order bit at this address is 0, all drawing operations nominally using `XOr` or `NotXOr` mode actually perform color highlighting instead. This also affects shape-inverting operations such as `InvertRect`, `InvertOval`, and so forth, which use `XOr` mode implicitly.

8. The constant `PHiliteBit` is a bit number for clearing the highlighting flag with the Toolbox routine `BitClr` [I:2.2.1], which numbers bits from left to right within a byte:

```
BitClr (Ptr(HiliteMode), PHiliteBit)
```

In assembly language, use the constant `HiliteBit` with the machine instruction `BCLR`, which numbers the bits from right to left according to the usual M68000 convention:

```
BCLR    #HiliteBit,HiliteMode
```

9. All remaining bits of `HiliteMode` are reserved for future use and should never be changed.

10. The highlighting flag is a "one-shot" flag: it is automatically set to 1 after every drawing operation, and must be explicitly cleared again before the next operation if it is to remain in effect.

11. When drawn at 1-bit depth, `Transparent` is equivalent to `Or` and `Hilite` to `XOr`.

Assembly Language Information

Assembly-language global variables:

Name	Address	Meaning
HiliteMode	$938	Highlighting flag
HiliteRGB	$DA0	Initial highlighting color

Assembly-language constant:

Name	Value	Meaning
HiliteBit	7	Bit number of highlight bit for BCLR

Trap macro:

(Pascal) Routine name	(Assembly) Trap macro	Trap word
HiliteColor	_HiliteColor	$AA22

5.4 Color Drawing Operations

5.4.1   Foreground and Background Colors

Definitions

```
procedure GetForeColor
          (var theColor : RGBColor);        {Current foreground color}

procedure GetBackColor
          (var theColor : RGBColor);        {Current background color}

procedure RGBForeColor
          (newColor : RGBColor);            {New foreground color}

procedure RGBBackColor
          (newColor : RGBColor);            {New background color}

procedure PMForeColor
          (paletteEntry : INTEGER);         {Palette index of new foreground color}

procedure PMBackColor
          (paletteEntry : INTEGER);         {Palette index of new background color}
```

Notes

1. GetForeColor and GetBackColor return the RGB value of the current port's foreground and background colors, respectively.

2. In a color port, the RGB value is taken directly from the rgbFgColor or rgbBkColor field in the port record [5.1.3].

3. In an old-style port, the RGB value is taken from the global table QDColors [4.2.2] for the color specified by the port's fgColor or bkColor field [4.1.2].

4. RGBForeColor and RGBBackColor set the foreground and background colors for the current port.

5. The exact RGB color requested is stored into the port's rgbFgColor or rgbBkColor field.

6. The port's fgColor or bkColor field is set to the color index of the nearest available match in the current color table. This is the pixel value that will actually be used in the port's drawing operations.

7. In an old-style graphics port, the high-order bits of the three requested RGB components are used to find the nearest match among the eight colors of the classic planar model [4.1.1]. The port's fgColor or bkColor field is then set to the corresponding color constant [4.1.1].

8. You can also set the drawing colors for an old-style port directly to a desired color constant with the old routines ForeColor and BackColor [4.1.2].

9. PMForeColor and PMBackColor set a window's foreground or background color from an entry in its color palette. (The letters PM stand for Palette Manager, the part of the Toolbox that deals with palettes.)

10. If the current port is not a color window or has no assigned palette of its own, the standard system palette [4.7.2] is used.

11. For tolerant or courteous palette entries, the entry's RGB value is stored into the port's rgbFgColor or rgbBkColor field, with the color index of the nearest available match in fgColor or bkColor.

12. For animating palette entries, the entry's reserved color index is stored into the port's fgColor or bkColor field, with the corresponding RGB value from the current color table in rgbFgColor or rgbBkColor.

13. For explicit palette entries, the requested palette index is stored directly into the port's fgColor or bkColor field as a color index, with the corresponding RGB value from the current color table in rgbFgColor or rgbBkColor. If the designated index exceeds the size of the color table, its remainder modulo the table size is used.

14. In all cases, the palette handle and palette index are saved in the auxiliary port record [5.1.4], either in fields pmFgColor and pmFgIndex or in pmBkColor and pmBkIndex.

Assembly Language Information

Trap macros:

(Pascal) Routine name	(Assembly) Trap macro	Trap word
GetForeColor	_GetForeColor	$AA19
GetBackColor	_GetBackColor	$AA1A
RGBForeColor	_RGBForeColor	$AA14
RGBBackColor	_RGBBackColor	$AA15
PMForeColor	_PMForeColor	$AA97
PMBackColor	_PMBackColor	$AA98

5.4.2   Shape Drawing

Definitions

```
procedure FillCRect
        (theRect : Rect;              {Rectangle to be filled}
         fillPat : PixPatHandle);     {Pixel pattern to fill with}

procedure FillCRoundRect
        (theRect      : Rect;         {Body of rectangle}
         cornerWidth  : INTEGER;      {Width of corner oval}
         cornerHeight : INTEGER;      {Height of corner oval}
         fillPat      : PixPatHandle); {Pixel pattern to fill with}

procedure FillCOval
        (inRect  : Rect;              {Rectangle defining oval}
         fillPat : PixPatHandle);     {Pixel pattern to fill with}

procedure FillCArc
        (inRect     : Rect;           {Rectangle defining oval}
         startAngle : INTEGER;        {Starting angle}
         arcAngle   : INTEGER;        {Extent of arc}
         fillPat    : PixPatHandle);  {Pixel pattern to fill with}

procedure FillCPoly
        (thePolygon : PolyHandle;     {Handle to polygon to be filled}
         fillPat    : PixPatHandle);  {Pixel pattern to fill with}
```

```
procedure FillCRgn
            (theRegion : RgnHandle;          {Handle to region to be filled}
             fillPat   : PixPatHandle);      {Pixel pattern to fill with}
```

 Notes

1. These routines fill a specified shape with a pixel pattern. They are analogous to the old routines FillRect [I:5.3.2], FillRoundRect [I:5.3.3], and so on.

2. The letter C in the routine names stands for "color."

3. The specified pattern handle, fillPat, is stored into the current port's fillPixPat field [5.1.3]. The port's pen pattern (pnPixPat) is unaffected.

4. In an old-style graphics port, the fill pattern's monochrome equivalent, pat1Data [5.2.1], will be used instead.

5. These operations do not change the location of the graphics pen; however, they have no effect if the pen is hidden.

6. All drawing is clipped to the intersection of the current port's boundary rectangle, port rectangle, clipping region, and visible region. Only those portions of shapes that fall within all of these boundaries will actually be filled.

7. Pixels outside the boundaries of the shape being drawn are not affected.

 Assembly Language Information

Trap macros:

(Pascal) Routine name	(Assembly) Trap macro	Trap word
FillCRect	_FillCRect	$AA0E
FillCRoundRect	_FillCRoundRect	$AA10
FillCOval	_FillCOval	$AA0F
FillCArc	_FillCArc	$AA11
FillCPoly	_FillCPoly	$AA13
FillCRgn	_FillCRgn	$AA12

5.4.3   Color Table Animation

Definitions

```
procedure AnimateEntry
        (inWindow      : WindowPtr;        {Window the palette belongs to}
         paletteIndex  : INTEGER;          {Palette index of entry to be set}
         newColor      : RGBColor);        {Color to set it to}

procedure AnimatePalette
        (inWindow      : WindowPtr;        {Window the palette belongs to}
         newColors     : CTabHandle;       {Color table containing new color values}
         firstColor    : INTEGER;          {Color table index of first new color}
         firstEntry    : INTEGER;          {Palette index of first entry to be set}
         nColors       : INTEGER);         {Number of entries to be set}
```

Notes

1. These routines set the color values of animating entries in a window's color palette [4.5.1].

2. The palette itself is not identified directly, but only implicitly via the window it belongs to.

3. All requested color settings are made in the color table of the device on which the window is displayed.

4. The requested color for each palette entry is stored into the color table under that entry's reserved color index.

5. If the window spans more than one device, the requested colors are stored into each device's color table independently. Notice that, in general, the color index associated with a given palette entry will be different for each device.

6. If a designated palette entry is not an animating entry, or if no color index is reserved for it in the device's color table, no color setting is made for that entry. If inWindow is not a color window or has no assigned palette of its own, the color environment is not affected at all.

7. AnimateEntry sets the color of a single palette entry, designated by its index within the palette.

8. AnimatePalette sets a range of consecutive entries, beginning at palette index firstEntry and continuing for nColors entries.

9. The new color values to be set are taken from consecutive indices in the color table `newColors`, beginning at color index `firstColor` and continuing for `nColors` entries.

10. If the end of the `newColors` table is reached before all designated palette entries have been set, the remaining entries are left unchanged from their previous color values.

Assembly Language Information

Trap macros:

(Pascal) Routine name	(Assembly) Trap macro	Trap word
AnimateEntry	_AnimateEntry	$AA99
AnimatePalette	_AnimatePalette	$AA9A

5.4.4   Low-Level Pixel Transfer

Definitions

```
procedure CopyBits
        (sourceMap  : BitMap;        {Bit or pixel map to copy from}
         destMap    : BitMap;        {Bit or pixel map to copy to}
         sourceRect : Rect;          {Rectangle to copy from}
         destRect   : Rect;          {Rectangle to copy to}
         transMode  : INTEGER;       {Transfer mode}
         clipTo     : RgnHandle);    {Region to clip to}

procedure CopyMask
        (sourceMap  : BitMap;        {Bit or pixel map to copy from}
         maskMap    : BitMap;        {Bit map containing mask}
         destMap    : BitMap;        {Bit or pixel map to copy to}
         sourceRect : Rect;          {Rectangle to copy from}
         maskRect   : Rect;          {Rectangle containing mask}
         destRect   : Rect);         {Rectangle to copy to}
```

Notes

1. These old QuickDraw routines, formerly used to transfer images from one bit map to another [I:5.1.4], can now operate on pixel maps as well.

2. `CopyBits` transfers pixels from one bit or pixel map to another, in any transfer mode and with any specified scaling and clipping. `CopyMask` transfers pixels under the control of a third bit map used as a mask.

3. `sourceMap` is the bit or pixel map that is the source of the transfer, `destMap` the destination. For `CopyMask`, `maskMap` is the mask controlling which pixels to transfer from source to destination.

4. The source and destination maps can each be either a monochrome bit map or a color pixel map. If the two high-order bits of the map's `rowBytes` field [I:4.2.1] are 00, it is treated as a bit map; if 10, as a pixel map. If these bits are 11, the "map" is understood to be part of a color port record [5.1.3] instead: its `baseAddr` field is interpreted as the port's pixel map handle, `portPixMap`, and the operation is applied to the pixel map. Thus you can operate on a color port's pixel map by typecasting to an old-style graphics port [I:4.2.2] and passing its (fictitious) `portBits` field as a parameter:

    ```
    dummyPort := GrafPtr(colorPort);
    CopyBits (...dummyPort^.portBits...)
    ```

5. Pixel and bit maps, or pixel maps of different depths, can be mixed as source and destination in the same call; the results are adjusted automatically to the depth of the destination map.

6. The `maskMap` parameter to `CopyMask` must be a bit map rather than a pixel map. Bits set to 1 in the mask cause the corresponding source pixel to be transferred to the destination; 0 bits leave the existing destination pixel unchanged.

7. `sourceRect` tells what portion of the source map to transfer; `destRect` tells where in the destination map to transfer it to; `maskRect` tells what portion of the mask map to use as the mask.

8. Each rectangle is expressed in the local coordinate system of its own map.

9. The source and destination maps may be the same, but the rectangles must not overlap. There is no error checking for this condition; the transfer simply will not work correctly.

10. The source and destination rectangles need not be the same size. If they aren't, the contents of the source rectangle will be scaled to the

width and height of the destination. (For CopyMask, this represents a change from the earlier version, which performed no scaling [I:5.1.4, note 12]; however, the source and mask rectangles must still have the same dimensions.)

11. The source and destination pixel maps may have different color tables; all source colors are converted to their nearest available matches in the destination color table.

12. Color conversion from source to destination always uses the inverse table [4.4.2] of the current graphics device. To work correctly, the destination pixel map must be based on the current device's color table.

13. Before calling CopyBits or CopyMask, set the current port's foreground and background colors [5.4.1] to black and white, respectively, to avoid spurious coloring of the pixels being transferred.

14. The transMode parameter to CopyBits specifies the transfer mode to be used, and may be either a monochrome [I:5.1.3] or color [5.3.1] mode.

15. When applied to a pixel map, monochrome modes are useful only when all source pixels are restricted to black and white. Other colors in the source produce unpredictable results and should be avoided.

16. The source and pattern varieties of monochrome mode [I:5.1.3] are no longer distinguished; CopyBits and CopyMask always use a source mode automatically, no matter which type you specify. However, for compatibility with earlier versions of QuickDraw, you should still be sure to specify a source mode with these routines.

17. All transfer operations are clipped to the destination map's boundary rectangle. If the destination is the bit or pixel map belonging to the current port, the transfer is clipped to the port rectangle and the port's visible and clipping regions as well.

18. clipTo is an additional clipping region to be used by CopyBits for this transfer only, expressed in the coordinate system of the destination map. If clipTo = NIL, no additional clipping region will be used. CopyMask never performs such additional clipping.

19. Calls to CopyBits are recorded in picture definitions [I:5.4.2], but those to CopyMask are not.

20. CopyMask is useful for drawing icons, particularly those that are stored with their masks in resources of type 'ICN#' [I:5.5.4, I:7.5.3] or 'cicn' [6.7.1]. It can also be used in connection with CalcCMask and SeedCFill [5.4.5] (or the older monochrome versions, CalcMask and SeedFill [I:5.1.6]) to implement the MacPaint "lasso" and "paint bucket" tools.

Assembly Language Information

Trap macros:

(Pascal) Routine name	(Assembly) Trap macro	Trap word
CopyBits	_CopyBits	$A8EC
CopyMask	_CopyMask	$A817

5.4.5   Special Operations

Definitions

```
procedure CalcCMask
          (sourceMap   : BitMap;          {Bit or pixel map to operate on}
           maskMap     : BitMap;          {Bit map to hold result mask}
           sourceRect  : Rect;            {Rectangle to operate on}
           maskRect    : Rect;            {Rectangle to hold result mask}
           edgeColor   : RGBColor;        {Color defining edge of masked region}
           searchFunc  : ProcPtr;         {Pointer to custom search function}
           searchParam : LONGINT);        {Parameter for custom search function}

procedure SeedCFill
          (sourceBits  : BitMap;          {Bit or pixel map to operate on}
           maskBits    : BitMap;          {Bit map to hold result mask}
           sourceRect  : Rect;            {Rectangle to operate on}
           maskRect    : Rect;            {Rectangle to hold result mask}
           seedHoriz   : INTEGER;         {Horizontal coordinate of starting point}
           seedVert    : INTEGER;         {Vertical coordinate of starting point}
           searchFunc  : ProcPtr;         {Pointer to custom search function}
           searchParam : LONGINT);        {Parameter for custom search function}

type
  MatchRec = record
               red       : INTEGER;       {Red component of seed or edge color}
               green     : INTEGER;       {Green component of seed or edge color}
               blue      : INTEGER;       {Blue component of seed or edge color}
               matchData : LONGINT        {Value passed for searchParam}
             end;
```

Notes

1. These routines are color versions of the old QuickD aw routines `CalcMask` and `SeedFill` [I:5.1.6], used to implement specialized MacPaint-style drawing operations.

2. The letter `C` in the routine names stands for "color."

3. Both routines operate on an existing bit or pixel map and produce a mask to be passed to the pixel-transfer routine `CopyMask` [5.4.4].

4. `CalcCMask` finds the largest closed boundary lying entirely within the given rectangle (like the MacPaint "lasso") and produces a mask representing the area inside this boundary. `SeedCFill` does the same for the smallest closed boundary surrounding a given starting point (the *seed*), like the MacPaint "paint bucket."

5. For both routines, `sourceMap` may be either a monochrome bit map or a color pixel map. If the two high-order bits of the map's `rowBytes` field [I:4.2.1] are `00`, it is treated as a bit map; if `10`, as a pixel map. If these bits are `11`, the "map" is understood to be part of a color port record [5.1.3] instead: its `baseAddr` field is interpreted as the port's pixel map handle, `portPixMap`, and the operation is applied to the pixel map. Thus you can operate on a color port's pixel map by typecasting to an old-style graphics port [I:4.2.2] and passing its (fictitious) `portBits` field as a parameter:

   ```
   dummyPort := GrafPtr(colorPort);
   CalcCMask (...dummyPort^.portBits...)
   ```

6. `maskMap` must be a bit map rather than a pixel map. Pixels falling within the desired boundary will be set to `1` in the mask; those falling outside the boundary will be set to `0`.

7. `sourceRect` tells what portion of the source map to operate on; `maskRect` tells what portion of the mask map will receive the mask.

8. The source and mask rectangles must have the same dimensions.

9. Each rectangle is expressed in the local coordinate system of its own map.

10. No clipping is performed either to map's boundary rectangle or to the current port's port rectangle, visible region, or clipping region.

11. The `seedHoriz` and `seedVert` parameters to `SeedCFill` give the seed location in the local coordinate system of the source map.

12. By default, the desired boundary is defined by an unbroken edge (for CalcCMask) or a contiguous area (for SeedCFill) composed of pixels of a single color. For CalcCMask, the color is given by the parameter edgeColor; for SeedCFill, it is the color of the pixel at the given seed location.

13. The default method of determining the boundary can be overridden by supplying a non-NIL value for the parameter searchFunc. This should be a pointer to a search function of the form given in [4.6.1]. It will be installed in the current device record [4.3.1] and used to convert the colors in the source pixel map to 1-bit depth for inclusion in the mask.

14. The search function will be called once for each pixel in the source rectangle, with the color of the pixel passed directly as a parameter. It should return a color index of 1 for pixels lying on the lasso boundary (for CalcCMask) or within the fill region (for SeedCFill), 0 for all other pixels.

15. At the time the search function is called, the gdRefCon field of the current device record [4.3.1] will point to a record of type MatchRec containing the RGB components of the seed or edge color, for comparison with the given source pixel.

16. The calling program can pass an arbitrary long-integer value to the search function via the parameter searchParam. This value will be copied into the matchData field of the match record for use by the search function. A program might use it, for example, to hold a handle to a color table containing several colors, rather than just one, to be included in the lasso boundary or fill region.

17. Calls to CalcCMask and SeedCFill are not recorded in picture definitions [I:5.4.2].

Assembly Language Information

Trap macros:

(Pascal) Routine name	(Assembly) Trap macro	Trap word
CalcCMask	_CalcCMask	$AA4F
SeedCFill	_SeedCFill	$AA50

Field offsets in a match record:

(Pascal) Field name	(Assembly) Offset name	Offset in bytes
red	red	0
green	green	2
blue	blue	4
matchData	matchData	6

Assembly-language constant:

Name	Value	Meaning
MatchRecSize	10	Size of a match record in bytes

5.5 Nuts and Bolts

5.5.1   Color Bottleneck

 Definitions

```
type
   CQDProcsPtr = ^CQDProcs;

   CQDProcs    = record
                   textProc    : Ptr;      {Draw text}
                   lineProc    : Ptr;      {Draw lines}
                   rectProc    : Ptr;      {Draw rectangles}
                   rRectProc   : Ptr;      {Draw rounded rectangles}
                   ovalProc    : Ptr;      {Draw ovals}
                   arcProc     : Ptr;      {Draw arcs and wedges}
                   polyProc    : Ptr;      {Draw polygons}
                   rgnProc     : Ptr;      {Draw regions}
                   bitsProc    : Ptr;      {Copy bit images}
                   commentProc : Ptr;      {Process picture comments}
                   txMeasProc  : Ptr;      {Measure text}
                   getPicProc  : Ptr;      {Retrieve picture definitions}
                   putPicProc  : Ptr;      {Save picture definitions}
                   opCodeProc  : Ptr;      {Process unknown picture operation}
```

```
            newProc1    : Ptr;      {Reserved for future expansion}
            newProc2    : Ptr;      {Reserved for future expansion}
            newProc3    : Ptr;      {Reserved for future expansion}
            newProc4    : Ptr;      {Reserved for future expansion}
            newProc5    : Ptr;      {Reserved for future expansion}
            newProc6    : Ptr       {Reserved for future expansion}
        end;

procedure SetStdCProcs
        (var theProcs : CQDProcs);    {Color bottleneck record to initialize}
```

Notes

1. A CQDProcs record holds pointers to the low-level "bottleneck" routines on which all Color QuickDraw operations are based.

2. Each color graphics port can have its own set of bottleneck routines, identified via the grafProcs field of the CGrafPort record [5.1.3].

3. A NIL value for grafProcs designates the standard, built-in bottleneck routines, described below and in sections [III:2.1.2] to [III:2.1.6].

4. SetStdCProcs initializes a CQDProcs record to the standard bottleneck routines. Always use this routine to initialize the bottlenecks in a color port, the older routine SetStdProcs [III:2.1.1] in an old-style port. You can then selectively change individual fields of the bottleneck record to install your own routines in place of the standard ones.

5. The color bottleneck record is identical to the old one [III:2.1.1], but with several extra fields added at the end.

6. opCodeProc is a new routine for processing pictures [I:5.4.1] in the new, expanded color format. Any unknown operation code encountered in a picture definition will be passed to this routine for handling. As previously unused op codes are assigned meanings and added to the picture protocol, this routine will be modified to process them.

7. The Color QuickDraw picture format and op codes are described in detail in *Inside Macintosh*, Volume V.

8. The standard version of the opCodeProc routine, StdOpCodeProc, simply ignores all op codes passed to it and returns without doing anything.

9. StdOpCodeProc is defined in the assembly-language trap interface and listed as a trap macro in the table below, but has been inadvertently omitted from the Pascal interface to the Toolbox.

10. The remaining fields of the CQDProcs record, newProc1 to newProc6, are reserved for future expansion.

Assembly Language Information

Field offsets in a color bottleneck record:

(Pascal) Field name	(Assembly) Offset name	Offset in bytes
textProc	textProc	0
lineProc	lineProc	4
rectProc	rectProc	8
rRectProc	rRectProc	12
ovalProc	ovalProc	16
arcProc	arcProc	20
polyProc	polyProc	24
rgnProc	rgnProc	28
bitsProc	bitsProc	32
commentProc	commentProc	36
txMeasProc	txMeasProc	40
getPicProc	getPicProc	44
putPicProc	putPicProc	48
opCodeProc	opCodeProc	52
newProc1	newProc1	56
newProc2	newProc2	60
newProc3	newProc3	64
newProc4	newProc4	68
newProc5	newProc5	72
newProc6	newProc6	76

Assembly-language constant:

Name	Value	Meaning
CQDProcsRec	80	Size of a color bottleneck record in bytes

Trap macros:

(Pascal) Routine name	(Assembly) Trap macro	Trap word
SetStdCProcs	_SetStdCProcs	$AA4E
———————	_StdOpCodeProc	$ABF8

5.6 Resource Formats

5.6.1   Resource Type `'ppat'`

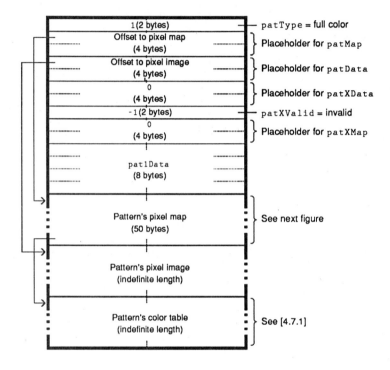

Structure of a `'ppat'` resource

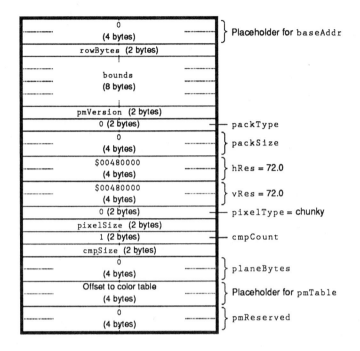

Detail of pixel map in a 'ppat' resource

Notes

1. A resource of type 'ppat' contains a pixel pattern for color drawing.

2. The resource includes not only the pattern record [5.2.1] itself, but also its associated pixel map [5.1.1], pixel image, and color table [4.4.1].

3. The first figure above shows the overall structure of the 'ppat' resource, the second the detailed structure of the pixel map embedded within it.

4. The pattern's `patMap` and `patData` fields contain the offset in bytes from the beginning of the resource to the start of the pixel map and pixel image, respectively. Similarly, the `pmTable` field of the pixel map holds the offset from the beginning of the resource to the start of the color table. When the resource is loaded from a file, these fields are replaced by handles to the corresponding actual data structures in memory.

5. The pattern's `patXMap` and `patXData` fields and the pixel map's `baseAddr` field are set to 0 in the resource as placeholders for the actual handles and pointer that these fields will contain in memory.

6. The `patType` field is always set to 1, denoting a standard, full-color pixel pattern.

7. The `patXValid` field is set to -1, marking the pattern's expanded map and image as invalid so that they will be built and installed in the pattern record the first time the pattern is used.

8. In the current version of the Toolbox, the pixel map's `pixelType`, `planeBytes`, `packType`, and `packSize` fields are always set to 0, denoting chunky format with no packing of the pixel image. `cmpCount`, the number of color planes, is always 1, and `cmpSize`, the pixel depth per plane, is equal to `pixelSize`.

9. The pattern's horizontal and vertical pixel resolution, `hRes` and `vRes`, are always set to 72 pixels per inch.

10. The structure of the color table within the `'ppat'` resource is the same as that of a `'clut'` resource, shown in [4.7.1].

11. `'ppat'` resource number 16 in the system resource file holds the standard pixel pattern for the screen's desktop background.

12. Use `GetPixPat` [5.2.2] to load resources of this type.

CHAPTER

6

Through Rose-Colored Windows

One area where you can apply the use of color to interesting effect is in the Macintosh user interface itself. The new color Toolbox includes facilities for coloring all the familiar features of the standard interface: windows, menus, controls, cursors, and dialog boxes. In this chapter we'll learn how to liven up our program's personality with a touch of color.

A word of caution, though: when it comes to user interfaces, a small dash of color goes a long way. Red text on a blue background is neither as legible nor as pleasing to look at as plain old black-on-white. Green windows with pink titles and purple scroll bars add nothing but noise to the user interface and make your program look more like a video arcade game than a serious piece of software. Try to use color sparingly for visual accents and highlights instead of spraying it all over your screen like a graffiti artist.

Bear in mind, too, that not all users have a color monitor. Never use color as the sole means of conveying information to the user; always provide some other cue as well, using color purely as an additional or supplementary indication. Finally, unless you have some strong reason for using a particular color for a given purpose (such as a well-established color-coding convention in your application domain), let the user choose a color with the Color Picker [4.2.3] and then honor that choice—don't impose your own preferences against the user's will. Always remember that on the Macintosh, the user controls the computer and not the other way around.

241

Color Icons and Cursors

The old monochrome icon and cursor structures have been updated and expanded to operate in the color environment. The new color versions of these data structures are CIcon [6.1.1] and CCrsr [6.2.1]. Both are normally stored as resources (of types 'cicn' [6.7.1] and 'crsr' [6.7.2], respectively) and loaded into memory with the Toolbox routines GetCIcon [6.1.2] and GetCCursor [6.2.2]. The routines DisposCIcon and DisposCCursor destroy the two structures and recycle their heap space for other uses.

GetCIcon and GetCCursor work a little differently than most Toolbox resource-loading routines. Usually, if the resource you request has already been loaded into memory, the Toolbox will simply give you a handle to the existing copy instead of reading in the same resource again. These two routines, however, always create a fresh copy of the requested resource, as well as all its subsidiary data structures (pixel image, color table, and so forth). To avoid wasting substantial amounts of memory for no reason, be careful to call these routines just once for each resource and save the handle for later use, rather than call them again each time you need the resource.

Color Icons

The original Toolbox didn't even have a defined data type to represent an icon—just an array of 128 bytes (32 long integers) containing a bit image of fixed dimensions, 32 wide by 32 high [I:5.4.4]. To draw an icon on the screen normally required a second bit image of the same dimensions to serve as a mask, defining which bits of the icon to transfer and which to leave transparent to the existing screen image. The icon and its mask were typically stored together in an *icon list* resource of type 'ICN#' [I:5.5.4].

In the brave new world of Color QuickDraw, icons are no longer second-class citizens without a data type to call their own. The *color icon record* [6.1.1] holds a complete pixel map (iconPMap) defining the icon's dimensions, pixel depth, color table, and other properties, along with a matching bit map (iconMask) containing its transfer mask. As in a pixel pattern [5.2.1], the pixel map's `baseAddr` field is ignored and a handle to the icon's pixel image is instead kept in a separate field of the icon record, `iconData`. There's also a monochrome bit map, `iconBMap`, to be used instead of the pixel map at shallow pixel depths of only 1 or 2 bits.

Because the dimensions of a color icon are defined by the boundary rectangle of its pixel map, they are not limited to a fixed 32-by-32, as they are in the monochrome case. It is essential, however, that the icon's pixel map (`iconPMap`), bit map (`iconBMap`), and mask (`iconMask`) all have the same dimensions.

The Toolbox routine `PlotCIcon` [6.1.2] draws a color icon in the current graphics port at a location specified by the parameter `inRect`. The dimensions of this rectangle need not match those of the icon itself: if necessary, it will be scaled to fit. The icon is also adjusted automatically to the port's pixel depth, and all of its colors are mapped to their best matches in the current color table. In a monochrome port (or a color port only 1 or 2 bits deep), the icon is drawn in the port's current foreground and background colors, using the icon's bit map in place of its full pixel map.

Color Cursors

The record representing a color cursor [6.2.1] is actually a sort of hybrid between a pixel pattern [5.2.1] and a monochrome cursor [II:2.5.1]. The first seven fields (`crsrType` through `crsr1Data`) are nearly identical in form and function to those of a pixel pattern and are handled internally in much the same way. The Toolbox distinguishes between the two types of record by the high-order bit of the type code in their first field, which is 1 for a cursor, 0 for a pattern. Like a pattern, a cursor has a pixel map to define its graphical characteristics, but the map's base address is ignored in favor of a handle to the pixel image kept directly in a field (`crsrData`) of the cursor record itself. The image must always be exactly 16 pixels wide by 16 high, the same as an old-style monochrome cursor.

When you make a color cursor current with `SetCCursor` [6.2.2], its pixel image is automatically expanded to match the current pixel depth and color table. The crsrXData field of the cursor record holds a handle to this expanded image, allowing it to be drawn quickly to track the mouse in real time. Two other fields help coordinate the expanded image with the current color environment: crsrXValid holds the pixel depth of the expanded image and crsrID the seed value of the color table on which it is based. If either of these values doesn't match the current environment, then the expanded image is invalid and must be rebuilt.

If you ever have occasion to change either the cursor's image or its color table, you should invalidate the cursor by setting its crsrXValid to 0, obtain a new seed value from GetCTSeed [4.4.3] and store it into the crsrID field, and call SetCCursor to rebuild and redisplay the cursor.

Also embedded in the color cursor record are three fields corresponding to those of an old-style cursor [II:2.5.1]. crsr1Data holds a 16-by-16 bit image to be used in place of the full pixel image when drawing the cursor on a monochrome device or at 1- or 2-bit depth. (If the type code in the crsrType field is $8000, denoting a monochrome cursor, this bit image is simply used all the time and the pixel image is ignored entirely.) crsrMask is a bit mask defining which pixels of the cursor to draw and which to leave transparent to the existing screen image. The mask must always be 16-by-16, and is used with both the color (pixel) and monochrome (bit) images. Finally, the field crsrHotSpot defines the point within the cursor's image that corresponds to the actual mouse position on the screen. The point is expressed relative to the cursor's own coordinate system, with (0, 0) denoting the top-left corner.

Color Windows

To draw anything in color on the screen, you need a *color window* [6.3.1] to draw it in. Remember that at the machine level, a window is just a port with some extra fields appended at the end. The only difference between a color window record and the old-fashioned monochrome kind [II:3.1.1] is that it's based on a color graphics port [5.1.3] instead of a monochrome port [I:4.2.2]. Thus the Toolbox can tell one kind of window from the other by looking at the high-order flag bit in its portVersion (or portBits.rowBytes) field.

Like all structures based on graphics ports, color windows are nonrelocatable objects and are referred to with simple pointers rather than handles. Just as for monochrome windows, there are two different pointer types [6.3.1] for referring to them. The first, `CWindowPtr`, is equivalent to a `CGrafPtr`—a pointer to a color graphics port. The second, `CWindowPeek`, is defined specifically as a pointer to a color window record, allowing you to "peek" at the window-specific fields beyond the end of the port record.

Because color and monochrome ports are the same size in memory, all the window-specific fields that follow them are in the same relative places in both types of window record, allowing all the old Toolbox window operations from Volume Two, Chapter 3, to work equally well on both. They all accept parameters of type `WindowPtr`, though, so you'll have to typecast your color windows from `CWindowPtr` first:

```
dummyWindow := WindowPtr(colorWindow);
BringToFront (dummyWindow)
```

The Toolbox routines for creating color windows are perfectly analogous to the ones for monochrome windows. One routine, `NewCWindow`, accepts descriptive information about the window as direct parameters; another, `GetNewCWindow`, reads the same information from a window template in a resource file. In both cases, the parameters are the same as for the old monochrome routines `NewWindow` and `GetNewWindow` [II:3.2.2]. So much so, in fact, that there isn't even a separate resource type for color windows: both `GetNewWindow` and `GetNewCWindow` use exactly the same template resource, `'WIND'` [II:3.7.1]. The only thing different about the new routines is the internal structure of the graphics port on which they build the new window record. They don't even bother to return a different pointer type: although they create a color window, they return it as a plain `WindowPtr` that you can pass directly to any other Toolbox routine without typecasting.

Window Color Tables

Recall from Volume Two that every window has a *frame*, which is drawn automatically by the Toolbox, and a *content region* that your program must draw for itself. The frame normally includes those structural features that are common to all windows, such as the title bar, close box, and zoom box. In the color environment, you can supply a *window color table* to specify colors for these features instead of the normal black and white.

Window color tables are normally built from resources of type `'wctb'` [6.7.3]. Their structure [6.3.3] is essentially the same as that of an ordinary color table [4.4.1], but the first couple of fields are ignored. The only fields that matter are `ctSize`, which gives the number of entries (minus 1) in the table, and `ctTable`, an array containing the entries themselves. As in an ordinary color table, each entry is a color specification [4.4.1]: its `value` field holds an integer *part identifier* designating the part of the window to which this specification applies, with the corresponding color value in the `rgb` field.

The specific values and meanings of a window's part identifiers are determined by its window definition function [III:2.2], and can vary from one type of window to another. Figure 6–1 shows the ones for the standard type of Toolbox document window; their numerical values are given in [6.3.3]. The part identifier `WFrameColor` denotes the color in which the outline of the window's frame is drawn, as well as the borders defining the title bar, close box, and zoom box. `WTitleBarColor` gives the title bar's background color, `WHilite-Color` the accent color for the inside of the close and zoom boxes, and `WTextColor` the color in which the text of the window title is drawn. Finally, `WContentColor` defines the background color for the interior of the window's content region; this value is used to initialize the window's background color [5.4.1] for all `Erase` operations in the content region.

Since a window's scroll bars are part of its content region rather than its frame, they are not governed by the window's color table. Instead, their colors are defined by a *control color table* that we'll be learning about later in this chapter.

Auxiliary Window Records

The connection between a window and its color table is established by an *auxiliary window record* [6.3.2], a new data structure maintained by the color Toolbox. The auxiliary record holds information on a window's color-related properties, supplementing the more general information in the main window record itself. Although it has several other fields as well, the auxiliary record's main purpose is to hold a handle (`awCTable`) to the window's color table.

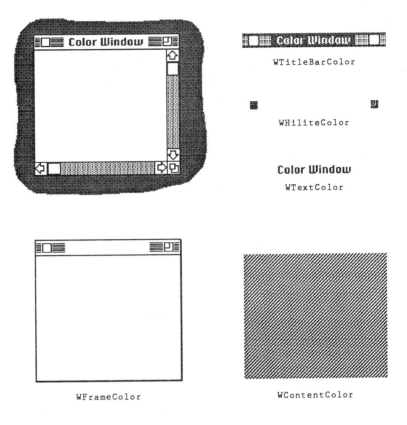

Figure 6-1 Part identifiers in a document window

Although the auxiliary record contains a pointer (awOwner) back to the window it belongs to, there is no forward pointer or handle from the window to its auxiliary record. Instead, all auxiliary window records are kept in a separate *auxiliary window list*, linked together through a chain of handles in their awNext fields. To locate a window's auxiliary record, the Toolbox scans through this list looking for a record whose awOwner field points to the desired window. No two windows can share the same auxiliary record, though two different auxiliary records can point to the same underlying color table.

It isn't necessary to have a separate auxiliary record and color table for every window you open on the screen. If an auxiliary record doesn't exist for a given window, the Toolbox uses the program's default color table, pointed to by the last record in the auxiliary window list. The default table is read from 'wctb' resource [6.7.3] number 0 when you call InitWindows [II:3.2.1] at the start of your program. The standard, system-wide version of this resource (kept in ROM or in the system resource file) simply specifies the same black-and-white colors for a window's frame as in the old monochrome environment. If you wish, you can override these colors for your own program by including a substitute color table under the same resource type and ID in your application resource file.

When you create a new window from a template with Get-NewCWindow [6.3.4], the Toolbox looks for a 'wctb' resource with the same ID number as the window template itself. If it finds one, it reads it into memory (if it isn't already there), creates an auxiliary window record pointing to it, and adds the record to the auxiliary window list. If not, the window will not be given an auxiliary record and will use the standard color table (found in the last record of the list) by default.

Instead of using a 'wctb' resource, you can explicitly assign a color table to a window with SetWinColor [6.3.5]. If the window already has an auxiliary record, this simply replaces the previous color table handle with a new one; if it hasn't, a new auxiliary record is created pointing to the designated color table. Passing a handle to the standard color table destroys a window's existing auxiliary record, causing it to revert to the standard colors by default. Finally, by passing a NIL window pointer, you can redefine the standard color table itself in the last record of the auxiliary window list.

There is no Toolbox routine for obtaining a window's color table directly, but you can use GetAuxWin [6.3.5] to get its auxiliary record and then look in the record's awCTable field for the color table handle. GetAuxWin returns a handle to the auxiliary record via a variable parameter; if the window has no auxiliary record of its own, a handle to the standard record is returned instead. The Boolean function result tells whether the handle returned is to the window's own auxiliary record (TRUE) or to the standard one from the end of the list (FALSE). Passing a NIL window pointer specifically requests the standard auxiliary record rather than one belonging to any individual window; in this case, the function returns TRUE, since it's giving you the record you asked for.

One more piece of information that's sometimes found in the auxiliary window record is the window's *variation code.* This code, taken from the last 4 bits of the window definition ID [II:3.2.2] when the window is first created, distinguishes among several different types of window implemented by the same definition function [III:2.2]. As we learned in Volume Three, it was originally kept in the high-order byte of the window record's `windowDefProc` field [II:3.1.1, 6.3.1].

Now that some Macintosh models can run in 32-bit memory mode [2.1.3], however, the handle to the definition function can take up the entire `windowDefProc` field all by itself, leaving no room there for the variation code. In that case, the variation code must be moved elsewhere—to the `awFlags` field of the auxiliary window record. A new routine, `GetWVari-ant` [6.3.5], has been added to the Toolbox to return a window's variation code wherever it may live. Always use this routine to access the variation code; never assume you know where to find it or attempt to read it directly from the window record.

Window Palettes

The natural way to manage a window's color environment is with a color palette [4.5]. Each window you open can have its own palette, defining the colors you wish to be made available whenever that window is active on the screen. This, in fact, is just what palettes were invented for.

The easiest way to associate a palette with a window is to include it in your resource file as a `'pltt'` resource [4.7.2] with the same ID as the `'WIND'` template. `GetNewCWindow` [6.3.4] will then use it to build the window's palette automatically at the same time it creates the window itself. Alternatively, you can build the palette yourself with `NewPalette` [4.5.3], `SetEntryColor`, and `SetEn-tryUsage` [4.5.4] and assign it to the window explicitly with `SetPal-ette` [6.3.6]. In any case, you can use `GetPalette` [6.3.6] to get a handle to the palette belonging to a given window.

Every time the window comes to the front of the screen and becomes the active window, the Toolbox will automatically call `ActivatePalette` [6.3.6] for its palette as well. This routine examines and, if necessary, modifies the color table for the device on which the window appears, doing its best to provide the color environment called for in the palette. (If the window spans more than one graphics device, `ActivatePalette` operates on each one independently.)

    `ActivatePalette` first attempts to reserve a color table index for each animating entry in the palette, then looks for an acceptable match for each tolerant entry. If no such match can be found, it selects an entry in the color table and forces it to the requested tolerant color. After repeating these steps for all entries in the palette, it generates update events for all other windows that are affected by the changes, causing them to redraw their contents under the new color environment. The important thing to notice about this process is that it happens automatically: once you've associated a palette with a window, you can just take it for granted that the requested color environment is present whenever the window becomes active on the screen.

Color Controls

The mechanism for specifying the colors in which controls (pushbuttons, scroll bars, and so forth) are drawn on the screen is nearly identical to the one for windows. Each control can have an optional *auxiliary control record* [6.4.1] pointing to a *control color table* [6.4.2]. The color table is usually taken from a resource of type `'cctb'` [6.7.4] with the same resource ID as the `'CNTL'` template [II:6.5.1] defining the control itself. The Toolbox routine `GetNewControl` [II:6.2.1] now looks for such a resource and, if it finds one, uses it to build an auxiliary record and color table for the new control. Alternatively, you can construct the color table yourself and assign it to the control "by hand" with `SetCtlColor` [6.4.3].

Unlike a window's frame, which is always drawn in the Color Window Manager port [6.3.7] even for a monochrome window, controls (including scroll bars) are part of the window's content region and thus are governed by the color properties of the window's own port. Although it's possible to include color controls in a monochrome window, they are then limited to the eight "classic QuickDraw" colors [4.1.1] only. Color controls are most effective when they belong to a color window.

All of a program's auxiliary control records (not just the ones for a given window) are chained together through their acNext fields to form an *auxiliary control list.* The last record in the list points to the default control color table, which defines the drawing colors for all controls that don't have a table of their own. The Toolbox routine GetAuxCtl [6.4.3] returns a handle to a control's auxiliary record, or to the last record in the list if the control doesn't have one of its own.

The default color control table is read in from 'cctb' resource number 0 at program initialization time by the Toolbox routine InitWindows [II:3.2.1]. The standard version of this table, found in ROM or in the system resource file, contains the same black-and-white colors that are used on a monochrome screen; a program can override these settings, if it wishes, with an alternate 'cctb' 0 resource in its own application resource file.

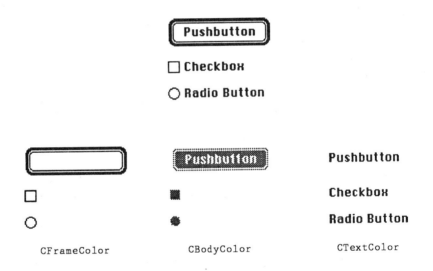

Figure 6–2 Part identifiers in button controls

Each entry in a control color table carries a *part identifier* in its value field. Just as for windows, the meanings of the part identifiers are determined by the control definition function and can vary from one type of control to another. Figures 6–2 and 6–3 show the part identifiers for the standard Toolbox button controls (pushbuttons, checkboxes, radio buttons) and scroll bars, respectively.

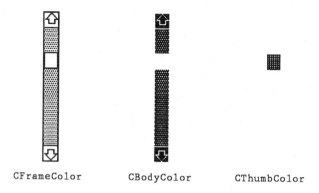

CFrameColor   CBodyColor   CThumbColor

Figure 6–3 Part identifiers in a scroll bar

Color Dialogs

There is no special data type for color dialog and alert windows—just our old friend `DialogRecord` [II:7.1.1] and her pointer sisters, `DialogPtr` and `DialogPeek`. Recall that every dialog record includes a complete window record in its `window` field, and that the window record in turn includes a complete graphics port. In a color dialog, the embedded window record is a color window [6.3.1], based on a color port [5.1.3]. Thus the Toolbox can tell color and monochrome dialogs apart by looking at the flag bits in the port's `portVersion` (or `portBits.rowBytes`) field.

The old Toolbox routines `GetNewDialog` [II:7.2.2] and `Alert` [II:7.4.2] (as well as the more specialized variants `NoteAlert`, `CautionAlert`, and `StopAlert` [II:7.4.2]), which create a new dialog or alert window from a template of type `'DLOG'` [II:7.6.2] or `'ALRT'` [II:7.6.1], now also look for a matching color table resource with the same resource ID as the template itself. If they find one, they build the new dialog record around a color graphics port, with a window color table [6.3.3] read from the resource and an auxiliary window record [6.3.2] to point to it. If no color table resource exists, a monochrome dialog will be created instead. (There's also a new Toolbox routine, `NewCDialog` [6.5.1], that explicitly builds a color dialog from scratch. This routine doesn't give the new dialog an auxiliary record or color table, however: you have to assign these by

hand with `SetWinColor` [6.3.5]. As always, it's much more convenient to use resource-based templates instead.)

Even if you want your dialog to use the standard window colors
without modification, you must still give it a color table resource to mark it as a color dialog. A value of `-1` in the color
table's `ctSize` field, with an empty `ctTable` array [6.7.3], calls
for the standard window colors as defined by the last entry in
your program's auxiliary window list [6.3.2].

The resources defining a dialog's or alert's color table have the
same form as an ordinary window color table [6.7.3], but are
distinguished by the special resource types `'dctb'` and `'actb'`
instead of the usual `'wctb'`. The `GetNewDialog` and `Alert` routines also look for an *item color list* of type `'ictb'` [6.7.5], again with
the same resource ID as the main dialog or alert template. (Notice
that it's an item color *list*, not a color *table*—the spelling of the
resource type notwithstanding—because its structure is not the
same as a true color table [4.4.1].) If present, the color list defines
the colors (and also the text styles) for the dialog's items; if there is
no item color list, the items will be displayed in standard black-and-
white.

The item color list begins with a table of 2-word entries that
parallel the dialog's main item list itself (resource type `'DITL'`
[II:7.6.3]). The first word for each item is an *item header* whose
contents vary depending on the item type; the second is an offset in
bytes from the beginning of the color list to the *item data* for this
item. Only control items, static text items, and editable text boxes
[7.1.2] are actually affected by the color list, but there must still be
a 2-word placeholder for every item, regardless of type. For those
that have no item data, the header and offset are simply equal to 0.

For control items, the item data consists of a control color table
in exactly the same form as in a `'cctb'` resource [6.7.4]. The item
header gives the length of the data in bytes. For text items (both
static and editable), the item data includes not only color information but also text style attributes (typeface, size, and so forth), in the
form shown in [6.7.6]. This is basically a text style record such as
we'll be learning about in the next chapter [7.2.1], with two extra
fields added for the background color and transfer mode.

Not every field of a text item's style attributes need necessarily apply: the item header at the beginning of the item color list contains flag bits telling the Toolbox which attributes to use and which to ignore. These flags are in the same format used for the `whichAttrs` parameter to the styled text-editing routines `TESetStyle`, `TE-ReplaceStyle` [7.3.4], and `TEContinuousStyle` [7.3.3], but with some extra bits added to account for the additional fields in the style record. For style attributes whose flag bit is 0, the standard settings will be used: 12-point system font, plain character style, `SrcCopy` transfer mode [I:5.1.3], black-on-white. Where the flag bit is 1, the value from the item data overrides the standard setting.

If you just want to use the standard style settings for a text item, you can omit the item data entirely and just set the item header and offset to 0. But to override even one of the style attributes, you must include all fields in the item data and use the flags in the header to mask out those that don't apply.

A couple of the flags in the item header have special meanings worth mentioning. If bit 4 is set, the value given in the item data for the type size is not to be used directly, but rather as a positive or negative adjustment to the standard 12-point type size. (For example, a value of -3 would denote a type size of 9 points.) Bit 15 causes the typeface to be identified by name rather than by font number [I:8.2.1]. In this case, the last item data in the color list [6.7.5] is followed by a series of Pascal-format strings giving the names of the typefaces for the various text items; instead of a font number, an item's typeface field gives the offset in bytes from the start of the color list to that of the typeface name. (This is the recommended way of identifying typefaces for universal compatibility, since the Font/DA Mover utility program may renumber a font when installing it in the `System` file.) All other bits of the header are straightforward on-or-off flags for the corresponding fields of the item data.

Color Menus

A new data structure, the *menu color information table* [6.6.1], holds the information the Toolbox needs to display your menus in color on the screen. (It isn't just a "menu color table" because, unlike those for windows, dialogs, and controls, it doesn't have the same structure as a true color table [4.4.1].) The Toolbox maintains a single current version of this table (located via a handle in the low-memory global `MenuCInfo`), which defines the colors to be used for drawing the menu bar and the titles and contents of all the menus it contains.

The entries in the menu color information table form a hierarchy, with one entry for the menu bar as a whole, one for each menu title, and one for each individual item. The fields `mctID` and `mctItem` in each entry designate the menu ID and item number to which it applies. The entry for a menu's title carries that menu's ID with a zero item number; the one for the menu bar itself has a zero menu ID. A given entry may be missing from the table, but there must never be duplicate entries with the same menu ID and item number. A special entry with a menu ID of -99 (defined as the Toolbox constant `MCTLastIDIndic`) marks the end of the table.

An entry's color settings are held in four fields named `mctRGB1` to `mctRGB4`, whose meanings vary depending on the type of entry (menu bar, menu title, or menu item) [6.6.1]. Entries at each level of the hierarchy establish the default colors for those missing at lower levels. The menu bar entry defines the standard text and background colors for menu titles and items with no table entries of their own; a given menu can override these settings with a title entry specifying different colors for just that menu's items; and these, in turn, can be overridden by an explicit entry for any single item.

Recall from Volume Two that besides its text, a menu item can display an optional mark character [II:4.6.4], icon [II:4.6.5], and keyboard alias. The item's entry in the color information table can define separate colors for the text, mark, and alias. For items that have no table entry of their own, however, these all default to a single foreground text color, defined either in the title entry for the item's menu or in the entry for the menu bar as a whole.

The display colors for an item's icon, if any, are not included in the menu color information table. Recall [II:4.6.5] that such an icon is identified by an *icon number* between 1 and 255, which is added to 256 to arrive at the resource ID (from 257 to 511) under which the icon is stored in the application resource file. In a color environment, the Toolbox will look for a color icon

---

resource of type `'cicn'` [6.7.1] with the required resource ID. If no such resource exists, it will next look for a monochrome icon of type `'ICON'` [I:5.5.3] and display it in the item's text and background colors as defined in the color information table.

Remember, too, that although color icons (unlike their monochrome counterparts) can vary in size, those used in menus must always be of the standard dimensions, 32 pixels wide by 32 high. Icons larger than this will not be displayed on the menu.

Menu color information is stored in resources of type `'mctb'` [6.7.7]. Such a resource is simply a collection of entries of the same form as in a menu color information table [6.6.1], preceded by a 2-byte count giving the number of entries. `'mctb'` resource number 0 contains the table entry for the menu bar, which is read into memory to start the color information table when you call `Init-Menus` [II:4.2.1] at the beginning of your program. This entry contains the standard menu colors set by the user with the Control Panel; you should normally just honor these settings without alteration.

Each time you build a menu from a `'MENU'` resource [II:4.8.1] with `GetMenu` [II:4.2.2], the Toolbox automatically reads in the matching `'mctb'` resource, if any, and adds its contents to the global menu color information table. Removing a menu from the menu bar with `DeleteMenu` [II:4.4.1] removes its entries from the color information table as well. Emptying the entire menu bar with `ClearMenuBar` [II:4.4.1] automatically clears the color information table and disposes of its previous contents; you can do the same thing explicitly with `DispMCInfo` [6.6.2], though this would be an unusual action for an application program.

You can also add and remove table entries explicitly with `SetMCEntries` and `DelMCEntries` [6.6.3]. `SetMCEntries` accepts a pointer to a separate color information table and copies its contents into the main table. (For menus and items that are already included in the main table, `SetMCEntries` simply updates the existing entry to the new color settings; for those that aren't already present, it adds a new entry to the table.) `DelMCEntries` accepts a menu ID and item number and deletes the corresponding entry from the global table; if the item number is `-98` (Toolbox constant

MCTAllItems), it deletes all entries associated with the designated menu. Neither of these routines redraws the menu bar automatically, so you have to follow them with a call to DrawMenuBar [II:4.4.3] if you want the color changes to become visible immediately on the screen.

If you need to, you can get a copy of the current color information table with GetMCInfo or replace its contents wholesale with SetMCInfo [6.6.2]. The main purpose of these routines is for saving the previous contents of the table before making changes and then restoring them later. They're particularly useful in conjunction with the older routines GetMenuBar and SetMenuBar [II:4.4.4], which save and restore the contents of the menu bar itself.

Another routine, GetMCEntry [6.6.3], returns a pointer to the table entry for a given menu ID and item number. Beware, though: this isn't a pointer to a copy, but directly to the relevant entry within the global color information table itself. Since the table is a relocatable heap object, it's liable to slither out from under the pointer without asking your permission. To be on the safe side, it's a good idea to make a copy of the table entry immediately and then work with the copy instead of the original:

```
entrySize  := SIZE(MCEntry);
copyHandle := NewHandle  (entrySize);
origPtr    := GetMCEntry (menuID, theItem);
BlockMove (origPtr, copyHandle^, entrySize);
{Work with copyHandle instead of origPtr}
```

Notice that the memory block to hold the copy must be preallocated *before* the call to GetMCEntry; otherwise, the allocation call might cause the table to move in the heap and trigger the very catastrophe we're trying to avoid.

Another tricky point to watch out for concerns the old Toolbox routine GetNewMBar [II:4.4.2], which creates a new menu bar from a template resource of type 'MBAR' [II:4.8.2]. This routine works by temporarily "borrowing" the main system menu bar and using it to build the new one. That is, it saves the previous contents of the menu bar with GetMenuBar [II:4.4.4], clears it to empty with ClearMenuBar [II:4.4.1], then builds the new menu bar by reading in its menus one at a time with GetMenu [II:4.2.2]. Once the new menu bar is built, it restores the old one with SetMenuBar [II:4.4.4] and returns the handle to the new one as its function result. Thus the net effect is to leave the main menu bar unchanged from its original state; the whole operation is invisible to the user, since none of the temporary changes become visible on the screen without an explicit call to `DrawMenuBar` [II:4.4.3].

This neat little scheme breaks down, however, when menu color information is added to the picture. The calls to `ClearMenuBar` and `GetMenu` to clear and rebuild the menu bar operate on the color information table as well, but those to `GetMenuBar` and `SetMenuBar` do not. Thus, although the `GetNewMBar` operation doesn't change the previous contents of the menu bar, it does change the color information table to the colors for the newly built menu bar instead of the original (saved and restored) one. Of course, `GetNewMBar` could use `GetMCInfo` and `SetMCInfo` [6.6.2] to save and restore the color information along with the menu bar itself, but then the new menu bar's color information would be lost (since `GetNewMBar` returns only the menu bar to the calling program and not the color information to go with it). So the only feasible solution is to leave it up to you to do the saving and restoring for yourself:

```
    saveColors := GetMCInfo;
       newMBar   := GetNewMBar (mBarID);
       newColors := GetMCInfo;
    SetMCInfo (saveColors)
```

Naturally, if you're making the new menu bar current immediately, there's no need for this little juggling act: you can just follow `GetNewMBar` directly with `SetMenuBar`—

```
    newMBar := GetNewMBar (mBarID);
    SetMenuBar (newMBar)
```

—since the color information table is now already set up for the new menu bar.

REFERENCE

6.1 Color Icons

6.1.1 Color Icon Structure

 Definitions

```
type
    CIconHandle = ^CIconPtr;
    CIconPtr    = ^CIcon;

    CIcon       = record
                    iconPMap     : PixMap;                      {Full pixel map}
                    iconMask     : BitMap;                      {Bit mask}
                    iconBMap     : BitMap;                      {Substitute bit map}
                    iconData     : Handle;                      {Handle to pixel image}
                    iconMaskData : array [0..0] of INTEGER      {Private}
                  end;
```

 Notes

1. A color icon is the color analog of an old-style (monochrome) icon [I:5.4.4]: a small pixel image, commonly (but not necessarily) used to represent an object on the screen.

2. Color icons are usually stored in resource files under resource type 'cicn' [6.7.1] and read in with GetCIcon [6.1.2].

3. `iconData` is a handle to the pixel image defining the icon.

4. `iconPMap` is a pixel map [5.1.1] defining the icon's dimensions, pixel depth, color table, and other properties. The map's `baseAddr` field is ignored, since the pixel image is defined by `iconData` instead.

5. `iconBMap` is a monochrome bit map [I:4.2.1] for use in drawing the icon at 1- or 2-bit pixel depths.

6. If the bit map's `rowBytes` field is zero, the bit map is ignored and the pixel map is used to draw the icon at all depths.

7. `iconMask` is a monochrome bit map defining which pixels to transfer in plotting the icon, like the second part of a monochrome 'ICN#' resource [I:5.5.4].

8. Unlike monochrome icons, which are limited to a fixed size (32-by-32), a color icon's height and width are defined by the boundary rectangle of its pixel map. The pixel map, bit map, and mask must all have the same dimensions.

9. Notice that the pixel map and bit maps themselves, not just their handles, are embedded directly within the color icon record.

10. The `iconMaskData` field holds the actual data for the icon's mask, bit image, color table, and pixel image, and is meaningful only for icons residing in a resource file. After the icon has been read into memory for use, this field is ignored.

Assembly Language Information

Field offsets in a color icon:

(Pascal) Field name	(Assembly) Offset name	Offset in bytes
iconPMap	iconPMap	0
iconMask	iconMask	50
iconBMap	iconBMap	64
iconData	iconData	78

Assembly-language constant:

Name	Value	Meaning
IconRec	82	Size of a color icon in bytes, excluding `iconMaskData`

6.1.2 Using Color Icons

Definitions

```
function  GetCIcon
            (iconID : INTEGER)          {Resource ID of desired icon}
                : CIconHandle;          {Handle to icon in memory}

procedure PlotCIcon
            (inRect  : Rect;            {Rectangle to plot in}
             theIcon : CIconHandle);    {Handle to icon}

procedure DisposCIcon
            (theIcon : CIconHandle);    {Handle to icon to be destroyed}
```

Notes

1. GetCIcon reads a color icon [6.1.1] from a resource file into memory and returns a handle to it.

2. iconID is the resource ID of the desired icon; its resource type is 'cicn' [6.7.1].

3. Space is allocated from the heap for the icon's pixel image, bit image, mask, and color table, as well as for the color icon record itself.

4. Unlike other resource-loading operations, GetCIcon always creates a new copy of the requested icon instead of just returning a handle to an existing copy already in memory. Call it just once for any given icon, rather than repeatedly before each use.

5. PlotCIcon draws a color icon in the current graphics port, under the control of the icon's mask and scaled to a specified rectangle.

6. The rectangle inRect is expressed in the local coordinate system of the current port.

7. The icon is automatically converted to the current port's pixel depth; at depths of 1 or 2 bits, the icon's bit map (iconBMap) is used in place of its full pixel map (iconPMap) [6.1.1].

8. All of the icon's colors are mapped to their nearest matches in the current color environment.

9. Calls to PlotCIcon are not recorded in picture definitions [I:5.4.2].

10. DisposCIcon destroys a color icon and all of its subsidiary data structures, and deallocates the space they occupy in the heap.

Assembly Language Information

Trap macros:

(Pascal) Routine name	(Assembly) Trap macro	Trap word
GetCIcon	_GetCIcon	$AA1E
PlotCIcon	_PlotCIcon	$AA1F
DisposCIcon	_DisposCIcon	$AA25

6.2 Color Cursors

6.2.1   Color Cursor Structure

Definitions

```
type
   CCrsrHandle = ^CCrsrPtr;
   CCrsrPtr    = ^CCrsr;

   CCrsr       = record
                     crsrType    : INTEGER;      {Cursor type}
                     crsrMap     : PixMapHandle;  {Characteristics of pixel image}
                     crsrData    : Handle;        {Pixel image}
                     crsrXData   : Handle;        {Expanded pixel image}
                     crsrXValid  : INTEGER;       {Depth of expanded image}
                     crsrXHandle : Handle;        {Reserved for future use}
                     crsr1Data   : Bits16;        {Bit image for old-style ports}
                     crsrMask    : Bits16;        {Transfer mask}
                     crsrHotSpot : Point;         {Point coinciding with mouse}
                     crsrXTable  : LONGINT;       {Reserved for future use}
                     crsrID      : LONGINT        {Seed value for color table}
                 end;

   Bits16      = array [0..15] of INTEGER;       {16 rows of 16 bits each}
```

Notes

1. The first seven fields of the color cursor record are identical in form to those of a pixel pattern [5.2.1]. However, the crsrXHandle field (corresponding to patXMap in a pixel pattern) is unused and reserved for future expansion, and crsrXValid is used in a slightly different way than its counterpart patXValid (see note 9 below).

2. crsrType is an integer code denoting the type of cursor. The high-order bit must be 1, to distinguish the cursor from a pixel pattern. A value of $8000 stands for a monochrome cursor (equivalent to an old-style bit cursor [II:2.5.1]), $8001 for a full-color cursor.

3. The assembly-language interface to the Toolbox includes constants OldCrsrPat and CCrsrPat, representing the two cursor types (see "Assembly Language Information," below). These constants have been inadvertently omitted from the Pascal version of the interface.

4. crsrData is a handle to the pixel image defining the cursor.

5. crsrMap is a pixel map defining the cursor's dimensions, pixel depth, color table, and other properties. The map's baseAddr field is ignored, since the pixel image is defined by crsrData instead.

6. The cursor is always 16 pixels wide by 16 high.

7. In a monochrome cursor (crsrType = $8000), crsrMap is ignored. The cursor's pixel depth is 1 by definition, and it is always drawn in the port's current foreground and background colors [5.4.1].

8. When a color cursor is drawn in a given color environment, the Toolbox builds a private copy to match the current pixel depth and color table. A handle to the pixel image defining this private copy is stored in the crsrXData field.

9. crsrXValid holds the pixel depth of the expanded pixel image. After changing the cursor's pixel image, color table, or other properties, set this field to 0 to mark the expanded cursor as invalid and force it to be rebuilt.

10. crsr1Data is a monochrome bit image, 16 bits by 16, for use in drawing the pattern into old-style graphics ports or at depths of 1 or 2 bits per pixel.

11. crsrMask is another bit image, also 16-by-16, that defines how the cursor's pixel or bit image is transferred to the screen.

12. The same mask is used for both the monochrome bit image (crsr1Data) and the full-color pixel image (crsrData).

13. 1 bits in the mask cause the corresponding pixels of the cursor's image to be copied directly to the screen.

14. Where the mask has a 0 bit, the corresponding pixel of the image will be "exclusive-or'ed" with the existing pixel value already on the screen. Image pixels at such positions should always be set to white, causing the cursor to overlay the screen transparently; other pixel values will produce peculiar and unpredictable results.

15. `crsrHotSpot` defines the point in the cursor that coincides with the mouse position on the screen.

16. The hot spot is expressed in the cursor's own coordinate system, not that of the screen. The top-left corner of the cursor has coordinates (0, 0).

17. Notice that the fields `crsr1Data`, `crsrMask`, and `crsrHotSpot` have exactly the same contents and form as the fields of an old-style cursor record [II:2.5.1].

18. `crsrID` holds a seed value for coordinating the cursor's colors with those of the current color table. After changing the cursor's pixel image, color table, or other properties, obtain a new seed value with `GetCTSeed` [4.4.3] and store it into this field, then call `SetCCursor` [6.2.2] to redisplay the cursor.

19. Color cursors are usually stored in resource files under resource type `'crsr'` [6.7.2] and read in with `GetCCursor` [6.2.2].

Assembly Language Information

Field offsets in a color cursor:

(Pascal) Field name	(Assembly) Offset name	Offset in bytes
crsrType	crsrType	0
crsrMap	crsrMap	2
crsrData	crsrData	6
crsrXData	crsrXData	10
crsrXValid	crsrXValid	14
crsrXHandle	crsrXHandle	16
crsr1Data	crsr1Data	20
crsrMask	crsrMask	52
crsrHotSpot	crsrHotSpot	84
crsrXTable	crsrXTable	88
crsrID	crsrID	92

Assembly-language constant:

Name	Value	Meaning
CrsrRec	96	Size of a color cursor in bytes

Cursor types:

Name	Value	Meaning
OldCrsrPat	$8000	Monochrome cursor
CCrsrPat	$8001	Full-color cursor

6.2.2   Using Color Cursors

Definitions

```
function  GetCCursor
              (cursorID : INTEGER)          {Resource ID of desired color cursor}
                : CCrsrHandle;              {Handle to cursor in memory}

procedure SetCCursor
              (newCursor : CCrsrHandle);    {Color cursor to be made current}

procedure DisposCCursor
              (oldCursor : CCrsrHandle);    {Color cursor to be destroyed}
```

Notes

1. GetCCursor reads a color cursor [6.2.1] from a resource file into memory and returns a handle to it.

2. cursorID is the resource ID of the desired cursor; its resource type is 'crsr' [6.7.2].

3. Space is allocated from the heap for the cursor's pixel map, pixel image, and color table, as well as for the color cursor record itself.

4. Unlike other resource-loading operations, GetCCursor always creates a new copy of the requested cursor instead of just returning a handle to an existing copy already in memory. Call it just once for any given cursor, rather than repeatedly before each use.

5. `SetCCursor` makes a designated color cursor the current cursor.

6. If the cursor's `crsrXValid` and `crsrID` fields [6.2.1] don't match the current pixel depth and color table seed, the cursor's expanded pixel image (`crsrXData`) is rebuilt.

Assembly Language Information

Trap macros:

(Pascal) Routine name	(Assembly) Trap macro	Trap word
GetCCursor	_GetCCursor	$AA1B
SetCCursor	_SetCCursor	$AA1C
DisposCCursor	_DisposCCursor	$AA26

6.3   Color Windows

6.3.1   Color Window Records

Definitions

```
type
   CWindowPtr    = CGrafPtr;
   CWindowPeek   = ^CWindowRecord;

   CWindowRecord = record
                port          : CGrafPort;     {Color graphics port for this window}
                windowKind    : INTEGER;       {Window class}
                visible       : BOOLEAN;       {Is window visible?}
                hilited       : BOOLEAN;       {Is window highlighted?}
                goAwayFlag    : BOOLEAN;       {Does window have close region?}
                spareFlag     : BOOLEAN;       {Is zooming enabled?}
                strucRgn      : RgnHandle;     {Handle to structure region}
                contRgn       : RgnHandle;     {Handle to content region}
                updateRgn     : RgnHandle;     {Handle to update region}
                windowDefProc : Handle;        {Handle to window definition function}
                dataHandle    : Handle;        {Handle to definition function's data}
                titleHandle   : StringHandle;  {Handle to window's title}
                titleWidth    : INTEGER;       {Private}
```

```
        controlList   : ControlHandle;    {Handle to start of control list}
        nextWindow    : CWindowPeek;      {Pointer to next window in window list}
        windowPic     : PicHandle;        {Picture for drawing window's contents}
        refCon        : LONGINT           {Reference constant}
    end;
```

Notes

1. A color window record is identical in form to an old-style window record [II:3.1.1], except that it is based on a color, instead of a monochrome, graphics port.

2. Use a `CWindowPtr` to refer to the window as a color graphics port (to draw into it with Color QuickDraw) and a `CWindowPeek` to refer to it as a window (to access the remaining fields of the color window record).

3. `port` is a complete color graphics port record [5.1.3] (not just a pointer) embedded within the color window record.

4. The declared type of the `nextWindow` field has been changed from `WindowPeek`, as in a monochrome window record, to `CWindowPeek`.

5. All other fields have the same meanings as in a monochrome window; see [II:3.1.1] for details.

6. All old Toolbox routines for working with monochrome windows [II:3] can operate on color windows as well. At the Pascal level, you must typecast the window pointer from type `CWindowPtr` to `WindowPtr` before passing it to such routines.

Assembly Language Information

Field offsets in a color window record:

(Pascal) Field name	(Assembly) Offset name	Offset in bytes
port	port	0
windowKind	windowKind	108
visible	wVisible	110
hilited	wHilited	111
goAwayFlag	wGoAway	112
spareFlag	wZoom	113

(Pascal) Field name	(Assembly) Offset name	Offset in bytes
strucRgn	structRgn	114
contRgn	contRgn	118
updateRgn	updateRgn	122
windowDefProc	windowDef	126
dataHandle	wDataHandle	130
titleHandle	wTitleHandle	134
titleWidth	wTitleWidth	138
controlList	wControlList	140
nextWindow	nextWindow	144
windowPic	windowPic	148
refCon	wRefCon	152

Assembly-language constant:

Name	Value	Meaning
WindowSize	156	Size of color window record in bytes

6.3.2   Auxiliary Window Records

 Definitions

```
type
    AuxWinHndl = ^AuxWinPtr;
    AuxWinPtr  = ^AuxWinRec;

    AuxWinRec  = record
                awNext      : AuxWinHndl;    {Next record in auxiliary window list}
                awOwner     : WindowPtr;     {Window this record belongs to}
                awCTable    : CTabHandle;    {Window color table}
                dialogCItem : Handle;        {Dialog item color list}
                awFlags     : LONGINT;       {Private}
                awReserved  : CTabHandle;    {Reserved for future use}
                awRefCon    : LONGINT        {Reference constant for application use}
            end;
```

Notes

1. An auxiliary window record holds information about a window's color-related properties, supplementing the more general information in the main window record [6.3.1].

2. A window need not have its own auxiliary window record unless its color properties differ from the standard ones the program uses for all its windows.

3. Two windows may not share the same auxiliary record, but two auxiliary records may share the same underlying color table.

4. awOwner is a pointer to the window to which this auxiliary record belongs. There is no corresponding forward pointer or handle from the window itself to its auxiliary record.

5. awOwner is declared as a plain WindowPtr, rather than a CWindowPtr, so that it can be passed directly to window-related Toolbox routines without typecasting.

6. awCTable is a handle to the window color table [6.3.3] for this window.

7. For alert and dialog windows, dialogCItem holds a handle to the dialog item color list [6.7.5].

8. awFlags holds flags and other information for private use by the Toolbox. In particular, in 32-bit address mode [2.1.3], this field includes the window's variation code [III:2.2.1] (formerly kept in the high-order byte of the windowDefProc field in the main window record [II:3.1.1, 6.3.1]).

9. awRefCon is a 4-byte reference "constant" (actually a variable) that your program can use in any way it chooses. awReserved is reserved for future use by the Toolbox, and should always be set to 0.

10. All auxiliary window records are kept in an *auxiliary window list*, linked together through their awNext fields.

11. In assembly language, the beginning of the auxiliary window list is accessible in the global variable AuxWinHead.

12. The last record in the auxiliary window list defines the program's standard window colors, to be used by default for all windows that have no auxiliary record of their own.

13. The default record at the end of the list is identified by NIL values for both awNext and awOwner.

14. CloseWindow and DisposeWindow [II:3.2.3] automatically dispose of the auxiliary window record along with the window itself.

Assembly Language Information

Field offsets in an auxiliary window record:

(Pascal) Field name	(Assembly) Offset name	Offset in bytes
awNext	awNext	0
awOwner	awOwner	4
awCTable	awCTable	8
dialogCItem	dialogCItem	12
awFlags	awFlags	16
awReserved	awResrv	20
awRefCon	awRefCon	24

Assembly-language constant:

Name	Value	Meaning
AuxWinSize	28	Size of auxiliary window record in bytes

Assembly-language global variable:

Name	Address	Meaning
AuxWinHead	$CD0	Pointer to first record in auxiliary window list

6.3.3   Window Color Tables

Definitions

```
type
  WCTabHandle = ^WCTabPtr;
  WCTabPtr    = ^WinCTab;

  WinCTab     = record
                  wcSeed     : LONGINT;                {Reserved for future use}
                  wcReserved : INTEGER;                {Reserved for future use}
                  ctSize     : INTEGER;                {Number of entries minus 1}
                  ctTable    : array [0..4] of ColorSpec  {Array of color specifications}
                end;
```

```
const
    WContentColor   = 0;                    {Background fill color for content region}
    WFrameColor     = 1;                    {Frame and border color}
    WTextColor      = 2;                    {Text color for window title}
    WHiliteColor    = 3;                    {Background color for close and zoom boxes}
    WTitleBarColor  = 4;                    {Background color for title bar}
```

Notes

1. A window color table specifies the colors to be used in displaying a window on the screen.

2. The colors in the table apply only to the window's frame, which is drawn automatically by the Toolbox. The window's contents are the application program's responsibility.

3. A window color table has the same general structure as an ordinary color table [4.4.1], but its first two fields (renamed from ctSeed and ctFlags to wcSeed and wcReserved) are unused and reserved for future use. For now, these fields should always be set to 0.

4. ctSize is the index of the last element in the ctTable array, and is equal to the total number of entries in the color table minus 1. For standard document windows, this value is normally 4.

5. ctTable is an array of color specifications [4.4.1] containing the actual entries in the color table.

6. Each color specification's value field contains an integer *part identifier* designating the part of the window to which it applies; the rgb field gives the color in which that part of the window is to be drawn.

7. The meanings of the part identifiers are determined by the window definition function [III:2.2] and can vary for different types of window. The constants shown (WContentColor, WFrameColor, and so on) are for the standard Toolbox document window.

8. Because the color specifications are identified by their value fields, they need not all be present and need not appear in any particular order. The table's first color entry is used for any window part that is missing from the table.

9. A window's color table is normally stored as a resource of type 'wctb' [6.7.3] with the same resource ID as that of the window template ('WIND' [II:3.7.1]) itself.

10. The standard system window color table, defined by 'wctb' resource number 0 in ROM, contains the same color values as an ordinary monochrome window: black for WFrameColor and WTextColor, white for WContentColor, WHiliteColor, and WTitleBarColor.

11. The assembly-language Toolbox interface doesn't define offset constants specifically for the fields of a window color table; use the ones for an ordinary color table [4.4.1] instead, as shown in the table below.

Assembly Language Information

Field offsets in a window color table:

(Pascal) Field name	(Assembly) Offset name	Offset in bytes
wcSeed	ctSeed	0
wcReserved	ctFlags	4
ctSize	ctSize	6
ctTable	ctTable	8

Assembly-language constants:

Name	Value	Meaning
CTRec	8	Size of a window color table record in bytes, excluding ctTable
CTEntrySize	8	Size of a window color table entry in bytes

Standard indices in a window color table:

Name	Value	Meaning
WContentColor	0	Background and fill color for content region
WFrameColor	1	Frame and border color
WTextColor	2	Text color for window title
WHiliteColor	3	Highlight color for close and zoom boxes
WTitleBarColor	4	Background color for title bar

6.3.4 Creating Color Windows

Definitions

```
function NewCWindow
        (wStorage      : Ptr;          {Storage for window record}
        windowRect     : Rect;         {Window's port rectangle in screen coordinates}
        title          : Str255;       {Window's title}
        visible        : BOOLEAN;      {Is window initially visible?}
        windowType     : INTEGER;      {Window definition ID}
        behindWindow   : WindowPtr;    {Window in front of this one}
        hasClose       : BOOLEAN;      {Does window have a close region?}
        refCon         : LONGINT)      {Window's reference constant}
         : WindowPtr;                  {Pointer to new window}

function GetNewCWindow
        (templateID    : INTEGER;      {Resource ID of window template}
        wStorage       : Ptr;          {Storage for window record}
        behindWindow   : WindowPtr)    {Window in front of this one}
         : WindowPtr;                  {Pointer to new window}
```

Notes

1. Both these routines create a new color window, enter it in the window list, and return a pointer to it.

2. NewCWindow takes its initialization information as parameters, GetNewCWindow gets it from a window template in a resource file.

3. All parameters have the same meanings as for the old monochrome routines NewWindow and GetNewWindow; see [II:3.2.2] for details.

4. Both routines return a plain WindowPtr instead of a CWindowPtr, so that it can be passed directly to other window-related Toolbox routines without typecasting. To access the internal fields of the window record, typecast this pointer to a CWindowPeek [6.3.1].

5. The new window is based on a color graphics port [5.1.3] and supports the full use of color for drawing in its content region.

6. If 'wctb' [6.7.3] and 'pltt' [4.7.2] resources exist with the same resource ID as the window template itself (templateID), GetNewCWindow uses them to define the new window's color table [6.3.3]

and palette [4.5.1, 6.3.6]. An auxiliary window record [6.3.2] is created pointing to the given color table, and the contents of this table determine the colors in which the window's frame will be drawn.

7. NewCWindow (or GetNewCWindow, if the required 'wctb' and 'pltt' resources don't exist) does not create an auxiliary window record or assign the window a color table or palette of its own. If necessary, you can assign them explicitly with SetWinColor [6.3.5] and SetPalette [6.3.6]; otherwise, the window will use the standard color table and palette by default, as defined by 'wctb' and 'pltt' resources number 0.

Assembly Language Information

Trap macros:

(Pascal) Routine name	(Assembly) Trap macro	Trap word
NewCWindow	_NewCWindow	$AA45
GetNewCWindow	_GetNewCWindow	$AA46

6.3.5   Color Window Properties

Definitions

```
procedure SetWinColor
          (theWindow : WindowPtr;        {Pointer to the window}
           newCTab   : WCTabHandle);     {New color table}

function  GetAuxWin
          (theWindow     : WindowPtr;    {Pointer to the window}
           var theAuxRec : AuxWinHndl)   {Returns handle to auxiliary window record}
              : BOOLEAN;                 {Does window have an auxiliary record?}

function  GetWVariant
          (theWindow : WindowPtr)        {Pointer to the window}
              : INTEGER;                 {Window's variation code}
```

Notes

1. SetWinColor sets a window's color table, defining the colors in which its frame is drawn on the screen.

2. The window's frame is immediately redrawn in the new colors.

3. The background color [5.4.1] of the window's port is set to the color designated by the part identifier WContentColor [6.3.3] in the new color table.

4. If an auxiliary window record [6.3.2] already exists for the given window, it is modified to point to the new color table; if the window has no auxiliary record, a new one is created.

5. If newCTab contains the standard window colors (defined by the last record in the auxiliary window list [6.3.2]), the window's existing auxiliary record is destroyed; the window will use the standard auxiliary record and color table instead.

6. If theWindow = NIL, the standard color table itself is redefined to newCTab.

7. GetAuxWin returns a handle to a window's auxiliary window record, if any, via the variable parameter theAuxRec.

8. If the window has no auxiliary record, the standard record (last in the auxiliary window list) is returned instead.

9. The function result tells whether the record returned as theAuxRec actually belongs to the designated window (TRUE) or is merely the standard one (FALSE).

10. If theWindow = NIL, the standard auxiliary record is returned as theAuxRec and the function result is TRUE.

11. GetWVariant returns a window's variation code, taken from the window definition ID [II:3.2.2] at the time the window is created.

12. The variation code, formerly stored in the high-order byte of the window's windowDefProc field [II:3.1.1, 6.3.1], now resides elsewhere on some systems and in some memory modes. Always use GetWVariant to obtain it, rather than trying to read it directly from the window record.

Assembly Language Information

Trap macros:

(Pascal) Routine name	(Assembly) Trap macro	Trap word
SetWinColor	_SetWinColor	$AA41
GetAuxWin	_GetAuxWin	$AA42
GetWVariant	_GetWVariant	$A80A

6.3.6   Window Palettes

Definitions

```
procedure SetPalette
          (theWindow   : WindowPtr;        {Pointer to the window}
           thePalette : PaletteHandle;     {Handle to new palette}
           doUpdates   : BOOLEAN);         {Automatic updates?}

function  GetPalette
          (theWindow : WindowPtr)          {Pointer to the window}
             : PaletteHandle;              {Handle to current palette}

procedure ActivatePalette
          (theWindow : WindowPtr);         {Pointer to the window}
```

Notes

1. SetPalette sets a window's color palette; GetPalette returns its current palette.

2. If doUpdates is TRUE, an update event will automatically be generated for the window whenever its color environment changes, allowing you to redraw the window's contents in the new colors.

3. If theWindow has no palette or is not a color window, GetPalette returns NIL.

4. ActivatePalette puts a window's palette into effect, modifying the color environment if necessary to make the colors in the palette available for drawing.

5. If the window spans more than one device, each device's color environment is modified independently.

6. Update events are generated for all windows that have requested them (via the doUpdates parameter to SetPalette).

7. A window's palette is activated automatically whenever the window itself becomes active (frontmost) on the screen. You should also call it explicitly after making any change in the contents of the palette.

Assembly Language Information

Trap macros:

(Pascal) Routine name	(Assembly) Trap macro	Trap word
SetPalette	_SetPalette	$AA95
GetPalette	_GetPalette	$AA96
ActivatePalette	_ActivatePalette	$AA94

6.3.7 Screen Properties

Definitions

```
procedure GetCWMgrPort
          (var cwMgrPort : CGrafPtr);      {Returns pointer to Color Window Manager port}

function  GetGrayRgn
          : RgnHandle;                     {Handle to desktop region}
```

Notes

1. GetCWMgrPort returns a pointer to the Color Window Manager port, the color graphics port in which the Toolbox draws all window frames.

2. All drawing in the Color Window Manager port is done by the Toolbox itself and by window definition functions [III:2.2]. Application programs should never draw into this port themselves, particularly when running under MultiFinder.

3. GetGrayRgn returns a handle to the *desktop region*, defining the size and shape of the total area in which drawing can take place on all available screens combined.

4. In assembly language, a handle to the desktop region is available in the global variable GrayRgn.

Assembly Language Information

Trap macro:

(Pascal) Routine name	(Assembly) Trap macro	Trap word
GetCWMgrPort	_GetCWMgrPort	$AA48

Assembly-language global variable:

Name	Address	Meaning
GrayRgn	$9EE	Handle to desktop region

6.4   Color Controls

6.4.1   Auxiliary Control Records

Definitions

```
type
   AuxCtlHndl = ^AuxCtlPtr;
   AuxCtlPtr  = ^AuxCtlRec;

   AuxCtlRec  = record
                  acNext     : AuxCtlHndl;    {Next record in auxiliary control list}
                  acOwner    : ControlHandle; {Control this record belongs to}
                  acCTable   : CCTabHandle;   {Control color table}
                  acFlags    : INTEGER;       {Private}
                  acReserved : LONGINT;       {Reserved for future use}
                  acRefCon   : LONGINT        {Reference constant for application use}
                end;
```

Notes

1. An auxiliary control record holds information about a control's color-related properties, supplementing the more general information in the main control record [II:6.1.1].

2. A control need not have its own auxiliary control record unless its color properties differ from the standard ones the program uses for all its controls.

3. Two controls may not share the same auxiliary record, but two auxiliary records may share the same underlying color table.

4. acOwner is a handle to the control to which this auxiliary record belongs. There is no corresponding forward pointer or handle from the control itself to its auxiliary record.

5. acCTable is a handle to the control color table [6.4.2] for this control.

6. acFlags holds flags and other information for private use by the Toolbox. In particular, in 32-bit address mode [2.1.3], this field includes the control's variation code [III:2.3.1] (formerly kept in the high-order byte of the contrlDefProc field in the main control record [II:6.1.1]).

7. acRefCon is a 4-byte reference "constant" (actually a variable) that your program can use in any way it chooses. acReserved is reserved for future use by the Toolbox, and should always be set to 0.

8. All auxiliary control records are kept in an *auxiliary control list*, linked together through their acNext fields.

9. There is only one auxiliary control list for the entire program, *not* a separate one for each window.

10. In assembly language, the beginning of the auxiliary control list is accessible in the global variable AuxCtlHead.

11. The last record in the auxiliary control list defines the program's standard control colors, to be used by default for all controls that have no auxiliary record of their own.

12. The default record at the end of the list is identified by NIL values for both acNext and acOwner.

13. DisposeControl and KillControls [II:6.2.2] automatically dispose of the auxiliary control record along with the control itself.

Assembly Language Information

Field offsets in an auxiliary control record:

(Pascal) Field name	(Assembly) Offset name	Offset in bytes
acNext	acNext	0
acOwner	acOwner	4
acCTable	acCTable	8
acFlags	acFlags	12
acReserved	acReserved	14
acRefCon	acRefCon	18

Assembly-language constant:

Name	Value	Meaning
ACSize	22	Size of auxiliary control record in bytes

Assembly-language global variable:

Name	Address	Meaning
AuxCtlHead	$CD4	Handle to first record in auxiliary control list

6.4.2   Control Color Tables

Definitions

```
type
  CCTabHandle = ^CCTabPtr;
  CCTabPtr    = ^CtlCTab;

  CtlCTab     = record
                  ccSeed  : LONGINT;     {Reserved for future use}
                  ccRider : INTEGER;     {Reserved for future use}
                  ctSize  : INTEGER;     {Number of entries minus 1}
                  ctTable : array [0..3] of ColorSpec  {Array of color specifications}
                end;
```

```
const
    CFrameColor = 0;          {Frame and border color}
    CBodyColor  = 1;          {Background fill color}
    CTextColor  = 2;          {Text color for control title}
    CThumbColor = 3;          {Fill color for scroll box}
```

 Notes

1. A control color table specifies the colors to be used in displaying a control on the screen.

2. A control color table has the same general structure as an ordinary color table [4.4.1], but its first two fields (renamed from `ctSeed` and `ctFlags` to `ccSeed` and `ccRider`) are unused and reserved for future use. For now, these fields should always be set to 0.

3. Yes, the second field is really named `ccRider` (see what you have done . . .).

4. `ctSize` is the index of the last element in the `ctTable` array, and is equal to the total number of entries in the color table minus 1. For standard controls, this value is normally 3.

5. `ctTable` is an array of color specifications [4.4.1] containing the actual entries in the color table.

6. Each color specification's `value` field contains an integer *part identifier* designating the part of the control to which it applies; the `rgb` field gives the color in which that part of the control is to be drawn.

7. The meanings of the part identifiers are determined by the control definition function [III:2.3] and can vary for different types of control. The constants shown (`CFrameColor`, `CBodyColor`, and so on) are for the standard Toolbox control types.

8. Because the color specifications are identified by their `value` fields, they need not all be present and need not appear in any particular order. The table's first color entry is used for any control part that is missing from the table.

9. A control's color table is normally stored as a resource of type `'cctb'` [6.7.4] with the same resource ID as that of the control template (`'CNTL'` [II:6.5.1]) itself.

10. The standard control color table, read from `'cctb'` resource number 0, contains the same color values as for ordinary monochrome (black-and-white) controls: black for `CFrameColor` and `CTextColor`, white for `CBodyColor` and `CThumbColor`.

11. The assembly-language Toolbox interface doesn't define offset constants specifically for the fields of a control color table; use the ones for an ordinary color table [4.4.1] instead, as shown in the table below.

Assembly Language Information

Field offsets in a control color table:

(Pascal) Field name	(Assembly) Offset name	Offset in bytes
ccSeed	ctSeed	0
ccRider	ctFlags	4
ctSize	ctSize	6
ctTable	ctTable	8

Assembly-language constants:

Name	Value	Meaning
CTRec	8	Size of a control color table record in bytes, excluding ctTable
CTEntrySize	8	Size of a control color table entry in bytes

Standard indices in a control color table:

Name	Value	Meaning
CFrameColor	0	Frame and border color
CBodyColor	1	Background fill color
CTextColor	2	Text color for control title
CThumbColor	3	Fill color for scroll box

6.4.3   Color Control Properties

Definitions

```
procedure SetCtlColor
          (theControl : ControlHandle;    {Handle to the control}
           newCTab    : CCTabHandle);     {New color table}
```

```
function  GetAuxCtl
          (theControl     : ControlHandle;   {Handle to the control}
          var theAuxRec : AuxCtlHndl)        {Returns handle to auxiliary control record}
              : BOOLEAN;                      {Does control have an auxiliary record?}

function  GetCVariant
          (theControl : ControlHandle)       {Handle to the control}
              : INTEGER;                       {Control's variation code}
```

 Notes

1. SetCtlColor sets a control's color table, defining the colors in which it is drawn on the screen.

2. The control is immediately redrawn in the new colors.

3. If an auxiliary control record [6.4.1] already exists for the given control, it is modified to point to the new color table; if the control has no auxiliary record, a new one is created.

4. If newCTab contains the standard control colors (defined by the last record in the auxiliary control list [6.4.1]), the control's existing auxiliary record is destroyed; the control will use the standard auxiliary record and color table instead.

5. If theControl = NIL, the standard color table itself is redefined to newCTab.

6. GetAuxCtl returns a handle to a control's auxiliary control record, if any, via the variable parameter theAuxRec.

7. If the control has no auxiliary record, the standard record (last in the auxiliary control list) is returned instead.

8. The function result tells whether the record returned as theAuxRec actually belongs to the designated control (TRUE) or is merely the standard one (FALSE).

9. If theControl = NIL, the standard auxiliary record is returned as theAuxRec and the function result is TRUE.

10. GetCVariant returns a control's variation code, taken from the control definition ID [II:6.2.1] at the time the control is created.

11. The variation code, formerly stored in the high-order byte of the control's contrlDefProc field [II:6.1.1], now resides elsewhere on some systems and in some memory modes. Always use GetCVariant to obtain it, rather than trying to read it directly from the control record.

Assembly Language Information

Trap macros:

(Pascal) Routine name	(Assembly) Trap macro	Trap word
SetCtlColor	_SetCtlColor	$AA43
GetAuxCtl	_GetAuxCtl	$AA44
GetCVariant	_GetCVariant	$A809

6.5 Color Dialogs

6.5.1 Creating Color Dialogs

Definitions

```
function NewCDialog
        (dStorage     : Ptr;          {Storage for dialog record}
        windowRect    : Rect;         {Dialog window's port rectangle}
        title         : Str255;       {Title of dialog window}
        visible       : BOOLEAN;      {Is dialog window initially visible?}
        windowType    : INTEGER;      {Dialog window's definition ID}
        behindWindow  : WindowPtr;    {Window in front of this one}
        hasClose      : BOOLEAN;      {Does dialog window have a close box?}
        refCon        : LONGINT;      {Dialog window's reference constant}
        itemList      : Handle)       {Handle to item list}
            : DialogPtr;              {Pointer to new dialog record}
```

Notes

1. NewCDialog creates a new color dialog window, enters it in the window list, and returns a pointer to it.

2. All parameters have the same meanings as for the old monochrome routine NewDialog; see [II:7.2.2] for details.

3. This routine is for creating modal and modeless dialogs only; alerts are always created implicitly by the alert routines [II:7.4.2].

4. There is no separate data type for color dialogs. They are simply old-style dialog records [II:7.1.1] whose `window` field contains a color window record [6.3.1], based on a color graphics port [5.1.3].

5. `NewCDialog` returns an old-style `DialogPtr` that can be passed directly to other dialog-related Toolbox routines without typecasting. To access the internal fields of the dialog record, typecast this pointer to a `DialogPeek` [II:7.1.1].

6. The old Toolbox routines `GetNewDialog` [II:7.2.2], `Alert`, `NoteAlert`, `CautionAlert`, and `StopAlert` [II:7.4.2] now look for a dialog or alert color table (resource type `'dctb'` or `'actb'` [6.7.3]) with the same resource ID as the dialog or alert template (`'DLOG'` [II:7.6.2] or `'ALRT'` [II:7.6.1]) itself. If they find one, they create a color dialog window with an auxiliary window record [6.3.2] and color table [6.3.3] based on the `'dctb'` or `'actb'` resource. If an item color list (resource type `'ictb'` [6.7.5]) is also present, it is used to color the dialog's items and its handle is saved in the `dialogCItem` field of the auxiliary window record [6.3.2].

7. `NewCDialog` does *not* give the new dialog window an auxiliary window record or color table; you must assign these explicitly with `SetWin-Color` [6.3.5].

8. The old Toolbox routines `CouldDialog`, `CouldAlert`, `FreeDialog`, and `FreeAlert` [II:7.5.3] now operate on the dialog's or alert's color table and item color list resources as well as on the template resource itself.

Assembly Language Information

Trap macro:

(Pascal) Routine name	(Assembly) Trap macro	Trap word
NewCDialog	_NewCDialog	$AA4B

6.6   Color Menus

6.6.1   Menu Color Information Tables

   Definitions

```
type
  MCTableHandle = ^MCTablePtr;
  MCTablePtr    = ^MCTable;
  MCTable       = array [0..0] of MCEntry;      {Any number of entries}

  MCEntryPtr    = ^MCEntry;
  MCEntry       = record
                      mctID       : INTEGER;    {Menu ID number}
                      mctItem     : INTEGER;    {Item number within the menu}
                      mctRGB1     : RGBColor;   {Color information (see table below)}
                      mctRGB2     : RGBColor;   {Color information (see table below)}
                      mctRGB3     : RGBColor;   {Color information (see table below)}
                      mctRGB4     : RGBColor;   {Color information (see table below)}
                      mctReserved : INTEGER     {Private}
                  end;

const
  MCTLastIDIndic = -99;                         {Dummy menu ID for last entry in table}
```

Menu color information:

Field Name	Menu Bar	Menu Title	Menu Item
mctID	0	Menu ID	Menu ID
mctItem	0	0	Item number
mctRGB1	Default text color for menu titles	Text color for menu title	Text color for mark character
mctRGB2	Default background color for menus	Background color for menu title	Text color for item text
mctRGB3	Default text color for menu items	Default text color for menu items	Text color for keyboard alias
mctRGB4	Background color for menu bar	Background color for menu	Background color for item

Notes

1. A menu color information table defines the colors to be used in displaying a program's menus.

2. Color information for each menu is stored in a resource of type 'mctb' [6.7.7]. As the menu bar is built, the colors for the individual menus are accumulated into a single information table in memory.

3. In each information table entry, fields `mctID` and `mctItem` give the menu ID and item number to which the entry refers.

4. There is at most one entry for the menu bar as a whole (`mctID` = 0), one for the title of each menu (`mctID` = menu ID, `mctItem` = 0), and one for each individual menu item (`mctID` = menu ID, `mctItem` = item number).

5. Fields `mctRGB1` to `mctRGB4` contain the entry's RGB color values. The exact meanings of these fields vary depending on the type of entry, as shown in the table.

6. `mctReserved` is a private field for use by the Toolbox itself.

7. The information table entry for the menu bar is read from 'mctb' resource number 0 by the initialization routine `InitMenus` [II:4.2.1].

8. The title and item entries for a given menu are read by `GetMenu` [II:4.2.2] from the 'mctb' resource with the same ID number as the menu itself.

9. If there is no table entry for a given item, it uses the default colors from its menu's title entry; if there is no title entry, it uses those from the menu bar entry; if there is no menu bar entry, it defaults to black text on a white background. Similarly, the default colors for a menu title are taken from the menu bar entry, or black-on-white if there is none.

10. When used as a menu title at pixel depths of 4 bits and above, the Apple mark character [I:8.1.1] is always displayed in six colors.

11. For missing item entries, the default text color from the menu title or menu bar governs the item's keyboard alias and mark character [II:4.6.4] as well as the text of the item itself.

12. To define the colors for an item's icon [II:4.6.5], use a resource of type 'cicn' [6.7.1] with the appropriate resource ID (256 plus the icon number [II:4.6.5]). If present, such a color icon resource takes precedence over any monochrome icon resource ('ICON' [I:5.5.3]).

13. A color icon will not be displayed if it is larger than the standard monochrome size, 32 pixels by 32.

14. If a monochrome icon is used, it is displayed in the same foreground and background colors as the item's text, keyboard alias, and mark character.

15. The end of the menu color information table is marked by a special entry with a menu ID of -99 (constant MCTLastIDIndic). All other fields of this final entry are reserved by the Toolbox for its private use.

16. In assembly language, the global variable MenuCInfo holds a handle to the current menu color information table.

Assembly Language Information

Field offsets in a menu color information table entry:

(Pascal) Field name	(Assembly) Offset name	Offset in bytes
mctID	mctID	0
mctItem	mctItem	2
mctRGB1	mctRGB1	4
mctRGB2	mctRGB2	10
mctRGB3	mctRGB3	16
mctRGB4	mctRGB4	22
mctReserved	mctReserved	28

Assembly-language constants:

Name	Value	Meaning
MCTEntrySize	30	Size of a menu color information table entry in bytes
MCTLastIDIndic	-99	Dummy menu ID for last entry in table

Assembly-language global variable

Name	Address	Meaning
MenuCInfo	$D50	Handle to current menu color information table

6.6.2   Access to Menu Colors

 Definitions

```
function  GetMCInfo
          : MCTableHandle;              {Copy of current menu color info table}

procedure SetMCInfo
          (newMCTab : MCTableHandle);   {New menu color info table}

procedure DispMCInfo
          (oldMCTab : MCTableHandle);   {Menu color info table to be destroyed}
```

 Notes

1. GetMCInfo returns the contents of the current menu color information table [6.6.1]; SetMCInfo replaces the current table with a new one.

2. The handle returned by GetMCInfo refers to a *copy* of the current color information table, not to the actual table itself. Similarly, SetMCInfo makes the new current table a *copy* of the one supplied as parameter newMCTab.

3. After installing a new menu color information table, SetMCInfo automatically disposes of the old one.

4. Always follow SetMCInfo with a call to DrawMenuBar [II:4.4.3] to redraw the menu bar on the screen in its new colors.

5. You can use GetMCInfo and SetMCInfo in conjunction with the old routines GetMenuBar and SetMenuBar [II:4.4.4] to save and restore the contents of the menu color information table along with those of the menu bar itself.

6. The old Toolbox routine GetNewMBar [II:4.4.2], which builds a new menu bar from a resource of type 'MBAR' [II:4.8.2], now also builds a corresponding color information table. However, although this routine does not change the contents of the current menu bar by making the new one current, it *does* replace the previous color information table with the one belonging to the new menu bar. If you aren't immediately making the new menu bar current, you must bracket

GetNewMBar with calls to GetMCInfo and SetMCInfo to save and restore the previous contents of the table:

```
saveColors := GetMCInfo;
   newMBar   := GetNewMBar (mBarID);
   newColors := GetMCInfo;
SetMCInfo (saveColors)
```

Notice that it isn't necessary to save and restore the menu bar itself, since GetNewMBar does this automatically.

7. DispMCInfo destroys a designated menu color information table and releases the space it occupies in the heap.

8. Emptying the menu bar with ClearMenuBar [II:4.4.1] also automatically disposes of the current color information table.

Assembly Language Information

Trap macros:

(Pascal) Routine name	(Assembly) Trap macro	Trap word
GetMCInfo	_GetMCInfo	$AA61
SetMCInfo	_SetMCInfo	$AA62
DispMCInfo	_DispMCInfo	$AA63

6.6.3   Managing Menu Colors

Definitions

```
function GetMCEntry
        (menuID  : INTEGER;          {Menu ID of desired menu}
         theItem : INTEGER)          {Item number within the menu}
            : MCEntryPtr;            {Pointer to item's color information entry}

procedure SetMCEntries
        (nEntries  : INTEGER;        {Number of entries in table}
         newColors : MCTablePtr);    {Table of new menu colors}
```

```
procedure DelMCEntries
            (menuID  : INTEGER;          {Menu ID of desired menu}
             theItem : INTEGER);         {Item number within the menu}

const
   MCTAllItems = -98;                    {Delete all items in menu}
```

Notes

1. GetMCEntry returns a pointer to the menu color information table entry [6.6.1] for a given menu item.

2. The item is identified by its menu ID and its item number within the menu.

3. An item number of 0 requests the table entry for the title of the given menu; a menu ID of 0 requests the entry for the menu bar.

4. Notice that the function result is a *pointer* to the item's table entry, not a handle. This pointer points directly into the global menu color information table.

5. If the requested entry doesn't exist in the color information table, the function returns a NIL result.

6. *BEWARE:* The menu color information table is a relocatable object and may move in the heap, invalidating the pointer returned by GetMC-Entry. Safest practice is to copy the underlying table entry immediately and then work with the copy instead of the original.

7. SetMCEntries accepts a *pointer* (not a handle) to a table of new menu colors and copies its contents into the global menu color information table.

8. For menus and items that are already included in the global table, the existing entry is updated to the color values given in newColors. For those that are not already included, a new entry is added to the table.

9. The table designated by newColors must be locked or nonrelocatable.

10. nEntries gives the size of the newColors table.

11. DelMCEntries deletes one or all of a menu's entries from the global menu color information table.

12. The entry to be deleted is identified by menu ID and item number.

13. An item number of -98 (constant MCTAllItems) deletes all entries associated with the designated menu.

14. Deleting a menu from the menu bar with DeleteMenu [II:4.4.1] also automatically deletes all of its entries from the color information table.

Assembly Language Information

Trap macros:

(Pascal) Routine name	(Assembly) Trap macro	Trap word
GetMCEntry	_GetMCEntry	$AA64
SetMCEntries	_SetMCEntries	$AA65
DelMCEntries	_DelMCEntries	$AA60

Assembly-language global constant:

Name	Value	Meaning
MCTAllItems	-98	Delete all items in menu

6.7   Resource Formats

6.7.1   Resource Type 'cicn'

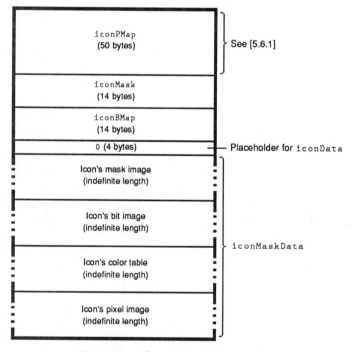

Structure of a 'cicn' resource

Notes

1. A resource of type 'cicn' contains a color icon to be displayed on the screen.

2. The resource includes not only the color icon record [6.1.1] itself (with embedded pixel map, bit map, and mask map), but also its associated pixel image, bit image, mask image, and color table.

3. When the icon is loaded into memory for use, its pixel image, bit image, mask image, and color table are read into separate blocks and the appropriate pointers and handles within the main structure are set to point to them.

4. The icon's iconData field, the baseAddr fields of both bit maps, and the pixel map's pmTable field are all set to 0 in the resource as placeholders for the actual handles and pointers that these fields will contain in memory.

5. The pixel map, bit map, and mask must all have the same dimensions.

6. See the second figure in section [5.6.1] for the detailed structure of the pixel map (iconPMap) embedded within the resource.

7. In the current version of the Toolbox, the pixel map's pixelType, planeBytes, packType, and packSize fields are always set to 0, denoting chunky format with no packing of the pixel image. cmpCount, the number of color planes, is always 1, and cmpSize, the pixel depth per plane, is equal to pixelSize.

8. The pattern's horizontal and vertical pixel resolution, hRes and vRes, are always set to 72 pixels per inch.

9. The structure of the color table within the 'cicn' resource is the same as that of a 'clut' resource, shown in [4.7.1].

10. 'cicn' resources should normally be purgeable.

11. Use GetCIcon [6.1.2] to load resources of this type.

6.7.2   **Resource Type 'c r s r'**

$8001 (2 bytes)	─ crsrType = full color
Offset to pixel map (4 bytes)	─ Placeholder for crsrMap
Offset to pixel image (4 bytes)	─ Placeholder for crsrData
0 (4 bytes)	─ Placeholder for crsrXData
0 (2 bytes)	─ crsrXValid = invalid
0 (4 bytes)	─ Placeholder for crsrXHandle
crsr1Data (32 bytes)	
crsrMask (32 bytes)	
crsrHotSpot (4 bytes)	
0 (4 bytes)	─ Placeholder for crsrXTable
0 (4 bytes)	─ Placeholder for crsrID
Cursor's pixel map (50 bytes)	} See [5.6.1]
Cursor's pixel image (indefinite length)	
Cursor's color table (indefinite length)	} See [4.7.1]

Structure of a 'crsr' resource

Notes

1. A resource of type 'crsr' contains a color cursor to be displayed on the screen.

2. The resource includes not only the color cursor record [6.2.1] itself, but also its associated pixel map [5.1.1], pixel image, and color table [4.4.1].

3. The figure above shows the overall structure of the 'crsr' resource; see the second figure in section [5.6.1] for the detailed structure of the pixel map embedded within it.

4. The cursor's crsrMap and crsrData fields contain the offset in bytes from the beginning of the resource to the start of the pixel map and pixel image, respectively. Similarly, the pmTable field of the pixel map holds the offset from the beginning of the resource to the start of the color table. When the resource is loaded from a file, these fields are

replaced by handles to the corresponding actual data structures in memory.

5. The cursor's `crsrXData` field and the pixel map's `baseAddr` field are set to 0 in the resource as placeholders for the actual handle and pointer that these fields will contain in memory.

6. The `crsrType` field is always set to $8001, denoting a full-color cursor.

7. The `crsrXValid` field is set to 0, marking the cursor's expanded image as invalid so that it will be built and installed in the cursor record the first time the cursor is used.

8. In the current version of the Toolbox, the pixel map's `pixelType`, `planeBytes`, `packType`, and `packSize` fields are always set to 0, denoting chunky format with no packing of the pixel image. `cmpCount`, the number of color planes, is always 1, and `cmpSize`, the pixel depth per plane, is equal to `pixelSize`.

9. The cursor's horizontal and vertical pixel resolution, `hRes` and `vRes`, are always set to 72 pixels per inch.

10. The structure of the color table within the `'crsr'` resource is the same as that of a `'clut'` resource, shown in [4.7.1].

11. `'crsr'` resources should normally be purgeable.

12. Use `GetCCursor` [6.2.2] to load resources of this type.

6.7.3   Window Color Table Resources

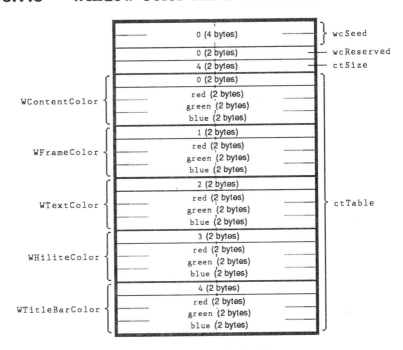

Structure of window color table resources

Notes

1. Three resource types share the structure shown: 'wctb' (window color table), 'dctb' (dialog color table), and 'actb' (alert color table).

2. The structure of the resource is the same as that of a window color table in memory. All fields have the same form and meaning described in [6.3.3].

3. The first two fields (wcSeed and wcReserved) are unused and reserved for future use. For now, these fields should always be set to 0.

4. 'wctb' resource number 0 defines the standard colors for windows with no color table of their own. The system-wide, ROM-based [2.3.2] version of this resource contains the same color values as an ordinary monochrome window: black for WFrameColor and WTextColor, white for WContentColor, WHiliteColor, and WTitleBarColor. A program can substitute its own set of standard window colors by including a 'wctb' resource number 0 in its own application resource file.

5. Color table resources are typically paired in the resource file with corresponding window templates under the same resource ID: 'wctb' resources with those of type 'WIND' [II:3.7.1], 'dctb' with 'DLOG' [II:7.6.2], 'actb' with 'ALRT' [II:7.6.1].

6. If a 'wctb' resource exists with the same ID as the main 'WIND' template, GetNewCWindow [6.3.4] will use it to build the window's color table [6.3.3] and create an auxiliary window record [6.3.2] pointing to it. If no such resource exists, the window will have no auxiliary record and will use the standard window colors from 'wctb' number 0 instead.

7. If a 'dctb' or 'actb' resource exists with the same ID as the 'DLOG' or 'ALRT' template, the old Toolbox routines GetNewDialog [II:7.2.2], Alert, NoteAlert, CautionAlert, and StopAlert [II:7.4.2] will now build a color dialog record, based on a color graphics port. If no such resource exists, an old-style monochrome dialog [II:7.1.1] will be created.

8. To create a color dialog or alert box using the standard window colors defined in 'wctb' number 0, use a 'dctb' or 'actb' resource with a value of -1 in the ctSize field and no color specifications of its own.

6.7.4   Resource Type 'cctb'

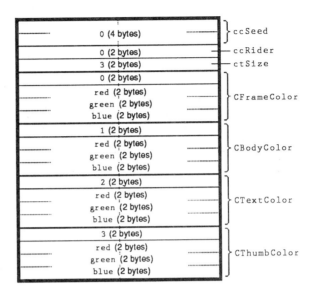

Structure of a 'cctb' resource

Notes

1. A resource of type 'cctb' defines the color table for a control.

2. The structure of the resource is the same as that of a control color table in memory. All fields have the same form and meaning described in [6.4.2].

3. The first two fields (ccSeed and ccRider) are unused and reserved for future use. For now, these fields should always be set to 0.

4. 'cctb' resource number 0 defines the standard colors for controls with no color table of their own. The system-wide, ROM-based [2.3.2] version of this resource contains the same color values as ordinary monochrome controls: black for CFrameColor and CTextColor, white for CBodyColor and CThumbColor. A program can substitute its own set of standard control colors by including a 'cctb' resource number 0 in its own application resource file.

5. 'cctb' resources are typically paired in the resource file with the corresponding control template ('CNTL' [II:6.5.1]) under the same resource ID.

6. If a 'cctb' resource exists with the same ID as the main 'CNTL' template, GetNewControl [II:6.2.1] will use it to build the control's color table [6.4.2] and create an auxiliary control record [6.4.1] pointing to it. If no such resource exists, the control will have no auxiliary record and will use the standard control colors from 'cctb' number 0 instead.

6.7.5   Resource Type 'ictb'

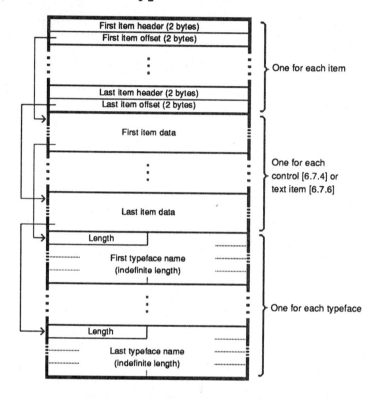

Structure of an 'ictb' resource

Notes

1. A resource of type 'ictb' defines the colors and text styles for a dialog's or alert's items.

2. The resource ID must match that of the dialog or alert itself ('DLOG' [II:7.6.2] or 'ALRT' [II:7.6.1]), as well as its item list ('DITL' [II:7.6.3]) and color table ('dctb' or 'actb' [6.7.3]).

3. A handle to the item color list is kept in the `dialogCItem` field of the dialog's auxiliary window record [6.3.2].

4. The item color list affects control items, static text items, and editable text boxes [II:7.1.2] only. However, there must be an item header and offset for *every* item in the corresponding item list, regardless of type. For items not covered in the list (including controls and text items using the standard colors and styles), set these fields to 0.

5. For controls, static text, and text boxes, the item offset gives the location of the corresponding item data, expressed in bytes relative to the start of the color list.

6. The item data for control items consists of a control color table [6.4.2] in exactly the same form as in a `'cctb'` resource [6.7.4]. The item header gives the length of the item data in bytes.

7. Two or more control items can share the same color table within the resource.

8. The item data for text items (both static text and editable boxes) has the form shown in [6.7.6]. The item header contains flags [6.7.6] specifying which fields of the data to apply.

9. Following the last item's data is an optional series of typeface names for the dialog's text items. These are needed only for typefaces designated by name in the item data [6.7.6].

10. To define the colors for an icon item [II:7.1.2], include a resource of type `'cicn'` [6.7.1] in your resource file under the ID given in the dialog's item list [II:7.6.3]. If present, such a color icon resource will take precedence over any monochrome resource of type `'ICON'` [I:5.5.3].

11. You can use an item color list just to define the styles for a dialog's text items, without any color information as such. For the list to be honored, however, you must still include a dialog or alert color table (`'dctb'` or `'actb'` [6.7.3]) in your resource file, even in a monochrome environment.

6.7.6   Text Style for Dialog Items

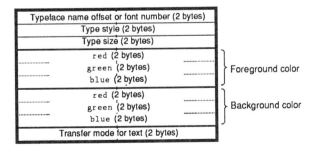

Text item data in an `'ictb'` resource

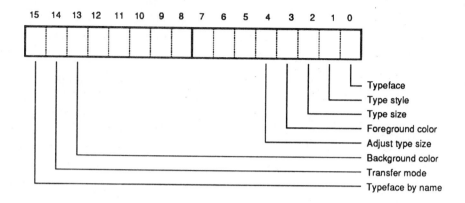

Flag bits for dialog text styles

Notes

1. The first figure shows the form of the item data for a text item (static text or editable text box [II:7.1.2]) in an 'ictb' resource [6.7.5].

2. The data has the same form as a text style record [7.2.1], with two extra fields (background color and transfer mode) added at the end.

3. The item header [6.7.5] for a text item contains flags specifying which fields of the item data to apply to the item's text. The format of the header is shown in the second figure.

4. For style attributes whose flag bits are 0, the contents of the item data are ignored and the standard settings used instead: system font, 12 points, plain type style, black-on-white, SrcCopy mode [I:5.1.3].

5. All style attributes must be present for each item, even if not all are actually used. However, for items that use only the standard colors and styles, you can set both the item header and offset [6.7.5] to 0 and omit the item data entirely.

6. Bits 0 to 4 have the same meanings as in the whichAttrs parameter to the TextEdit routines TESetStyle, TEReplaceStyle [7.3.4], and TEContinuousStyle [7.3.3]. Bits 13 and 14 refer to the two additional style attributes, background color and transfer mode.

7. If bit 15 is 1, the first field of the item data contains the offset in bytes from the beginning of the item color list to the name of the typeface. If bit 15 is 0, this field holds the typeface's font number [I:8.2.1] instead.

8. Two or more text items can point to the same copy of the typeface name.

9. To ensure compatibility in all system environments, always specify typefaces by name rather than font number.

10. The type style is given as a Pascal set of type `Style` [I:8.3.1].

11. If bit 4 is 1, the type size field in the item data is an incremental adjustment (positive or negative) to be added to the standard type size of 12 points. If bit 4 is 0, this field gives the type size directly.

12. The foreground and background colors are given in RGB form [4.2.1].

13. The text transfer mode can be any monochrome [I:5.1.3] or color [5.3.1] mode.

14. You can use an item color list [6.7.5] just to define the styles for a dialog's text items, without any color information as such. For the list to be honored, however, you must still include a dialog or alert color table ('dctb' or 'actb' [6.7.3]) in your resource file, even in a monochrome environment.

6.7.7 Resource Type 'mctb'

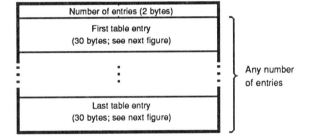

Structure of an 'mctb' resource

Table entry in an 'mctb' resource

Notes

1. A resource of type 'mctb' defines the colors for displaying a menu on the screen.

2. The structure of the resource is the same as that of a menu color information table in memory, with an additional 2-byte field at the beginning giving the number of table entries the resource contains. All other fields have the same form and meaning described in [6.6.1].

3. The resource ID should be the same as the menu ID to which it applies. This is also the resource ID of the corresponding 'MENU' resource [II:4.8.1].

4. Each entry's mctID field should contain the menu ID.

5. The mctItem field holds the item number of the menu item to which the entry refers.

6. An item number of 0 refers to the menu title.

7. Fields mctRGB1 to mctRGB4 each contain an RGB color value [4.2.1]. For the specific meanings of these fields, see the table in [6.6.1].

8. Field mctReserved is for private use by the Toolbox and should always be set to 0.

9. 'mctb' resource number 0 defines the table entry for the menu bar and establishes the standard colors for menus with no color information of their own.

10. If an 'mctb' resource exists with the requested menu ID, GetMenu [II:4.2.2] will read it in and add its contents to the global menu color information table [6.6.1]. If no such resource exists, the menu will have no color information and will use the standard colors from the menu bar entry instead.

11. The standard menu colors in 'mctb' resource number 0 are set by the user with the Control Panel desk accessory and ordinarily should not be overridden.

CHAPTER

7

Editing with Style

One of the handier features of the original Toolbox was its extensive facilities for on-screen text editing. A set of built-in routines, known collectively as TextEdit, provided full Toolbox support for performing Macintosh-style editing on the screen, including text display, point-and-click selection, keyboard text entry, cutting and pasting, word wrap, justification, and scrolling. Although intended primarily for light editing tasks such as entering text in interactive dialog boxes, TextEdit was also powerful enough to support full-scale, stand-alone editing programs like our Mini-Edit example from Volume Two.

The original TextEdit routines did suffer from one serious limitation, however: they could display text in only one format at a time. If one character was in boldface, they all had to be bold; if one word was in 10-point New York, the next couldn't be in 12-point Geneva or 14-point Venice or 18-point London. The typeface, size, and style were properties of the text as a whole, and couldn't vary from one individual character to another.

The latest versions of the Toolbox remove this limitation. The new *styled* TextEdit routines maintain information not only about what characters to display, but also about each character's typeface, size, and other formatting characteristics. This means you can now change fonts in the middle of the text, display a single word in italic for emphasis, or display an isolated headline in a larger point size.

The styled TextEdit facilities are not limited to the Macintosh II; they're also included in ROM on the Macintosh SE, and can be used on earlier models beginning with version 4.1 of the `System` file.

Another capability the new Toolbox places at your disposal is that of displaying text in color. Character fonts for drawing text can now optionally be defined in color instead of monochrome. Even for monochrome fonts, the text style associated with each character can include an RGB color in which the character is to be drawn.

In this chapter, we'll learn how to put all this added formatting flexibility to work. By way of illustration, we'll sketch out how we might modify our old friend MiniEdit to handle multiple text styles. We won't bother with all the excruciating details here, just touch on a few example routines that shed light on the use of styled TextEdit. By learning the techniques presented here, you'll be ready to start doing your text editing with style.

Color Fonts

A color font is represented by the same *font record* [I:8.2.2] as the old monochrome kind. Just as in a monochrome font, the actual form of the characters is defined by a *font image* containing all the individual character images arranged consecutively in a horizontal row, commonly known as a *strike* of the font. The font image is still kept in the field of the font record named `bitImage` [I:8.2.2, I:8.2.3], but in a color font it's actually a pixel image instead.

Bits 2 and 3 of the `fontType` field [I:8.2.2, 7.1.1] now distinguish color from monochrome fonts by giving the pixel depth of the font image in the form of a binary exponent. (Recall that pixel depths are always restricted to powers of 2.) A monochrome font has a value of 0 in these two bits, representing a depth of 1 (2^0) bit per pixel; values of 1, 2, or 3 denote color fonts at pixel depths of 2 (2^1), 4 (2^2), and 8 (2^3) bits. At present, 8 bits is the maximum font depth the Toolbox supports.

The font image, already rather a sizable beast even in monochrome fonts, can grow to truly prodigious proportions as the pixel depth increases. This can cause problems for the font record's owTLoc field [I:8.2.2], which gives the distance in words from itself to the beginning of the font's offset/width table [I:8.2.3]. Since the offset/width table follows the font image within the font record, at high pixel depths this distance can exceed the mere 64K capacity of the 2-byte owTLoc field.

Luckily, the means are at hand to deal with this crisis. For reasons known only to the original programmer, the font record includes a redundant field, nDescent [I:8.2.2], which is simply the negative of another field, descent. Although the two are not contiguous in the font record, nDescent can nevertheless serve as a convenient parking place for the leftward extension of owTLoc when the latter overflows its allotted 2 bytes. A positive value in nDescent indicates that it has been appropriated for this new purpose; if it is less than 0, it is understood to contain the negative font descent, as originally intended.

An optional *font color table* defines the color values for the pixels in the font image. If present, the color table has the usual form for such creatures [4.4.1] and is read from a resource of type 'fctb' [7.4.1] with the same resource ID as the font itself. (For some reason, only fonts stored under resource type 'NFNT' [I:8.4.5] can have color tables; ordinary 'FONT' resources cannot.) A flag (bit 7) in the font record's fontType field [7.1.1] tells whether the font has a color table.

A font color table is only an amenity, however, not a necessity. For fonts that have no color table, the Toolbox uses a standard algorithm to assign color values by default, based on the foreground and background colors [5.4.1] of the port the characters are being drawn into. A pixel value of 0 is taken to refer to the port's background color; the maximum possible pixel value (15 in a 4-bit-deep font, for example) stands for the foreground color. All remaining color values are blended uniformly between the two extremes, using a weighted average of their RGB components, as in the Blend transfer mode [5.3.3].

Notice, in particular, that in the common case where the port's foreground and background colors are pure black and white, the intermediate pixel values stand for uniformly graded shades of gray. Such uniform gray tones also happen to be a built-in feature of the PostScript image-description language, meaning that they can be reproduced directly on the Laser-Writer or any other printer fluent in PostScript.

Gray-tone pixels are particularly useful for implementing a font-definition technique with the formidable-sounding name of *anti-aliasing*, in which the "jaggies" around the edges of the characters are smoothed out with suitably weighted gray pixels instead of stark black and white. Anti-aliased fonts aren't usable on a plain monochrome device, but on a monitor or printer with gray-scale capabilities, they can significantly improve the clarity and legibility of text, especially at small point sizes.

If a font's pixel depth doesn't match that of the graphics device on which it's being displayed, the Toolbox has to convert each character to the proper depth before drawing it. This can seriously degrade the system's performance, elevate the user's blood pressure, and lead to serious screen damage from shoes, paperweights, and other foreign objects. Just to keep things user-friendly, the Toolbox automatically expands each font to the current screen depth as soon as it's read in, then uses the expanded version to draw to the screen instead of the original. This temporary, expanded version of the font at the current screen depth is called a *synthetic font* [7.1.2].

All synthetic fonts currently in existence are kept in a single master list, the *synthetic-font list*, located via a handle in the low-memory global variable `SynListHandle` [7.1.2]. Bit 8 of the font record's `fontType` field [7.1.1] identifies a font as synthetic. However, some of the new international fonts for languages such as Chinese and Japanese contain so many characters that expansion to 4 or 8 bits per pixel would push their size beyond merely prodigious to downright gargantuan. In these cases, another `fontType` flag, bit 14, suppresses the expansion to a synthetic font and forces the Toolbox to use the original 1-bit version without modification.

Text Styles and Terminology

The term *text style* (or simply *style*) refers to the visual properties that determine the way a character appears on the screen or in print. These include its overall typeface design, its size, variations such as bold or italic, and (on the Macintosh II) its color. All of these properties are summarized in a *text style record* of type `TextStyle` [7.2.1].

Unfortunately, as we first pointed out in Volume One, Chapter 8, this whole subject of styles and style properties suffers from inconsistent, confusing, and often contradictory terminology. Consider the terms *font* and *typeface*, for instance. As we have been using the term since Volume One, *typeface* refers to the overall form or design of the text characters, independent of size or other variations. By Macintosh convention, typefaces are typically named after world cities, such as New York, Geneva, or Athens; those used on the LaserWriter and other PostScript printers use the more traditional names recognized by professional typographers, such as Helvetica, Garamond, or Palatino.

By contrast, a *font*, in the Macintosh Toolbox, is a specific, rather elaborate data structure [I:8.2.2] that defines the appearance of characters in a particular typeface and size, such as 12-point Monaco or 18-point Baskerville. Apple has belatedly recognized this distinction in its official terminology by introducing the term *font family* to refer to what we've been calling the typeface—the overall design of the characters, as distinct from any individual font. Yet the identifying number that designates a particular font family is called a *font number* [I:8.2.1], rather than a "family number," and is kept in the `txFont` field of the graphics port record [I:8.3.1] and set with the Toolbox routine `TextFont` [I:8.3.2].

A similar inconsistency surrounds the use of the word *style*. As originally defined by the Toolbox, the data type `Style` [I:8.3.1] is a Pascal set specifying variations on the form of a character, such as bold, italic, underline, outline, and shadow. In keeping with this usage, we adopted the term *type style* (or *character style*) for such variations when we first discussed this subject in Volume One. Regrettably, however, the field of the port record that holds the `Style` set is named `txFace` [I:8.3.1], and the Toolbox routine that sets it is `TextFace` [I:8.3.2].

Now, to compound the confusion still further, the term *text style* has been introduced to refer collectively to the whole combination of attributes that determine a character's appearance—its typeface, size, color, and variations like bold, italic, and underline. Moreover, the field names within a `TextStyle` record [7.2.1] continue to perpetuate the same inconsistencies as before, with `tsFont` holding the typeface and `tsFace` the `Style` set. When is a `Style` not a style?

For lack of a better solution, we will continue to use the term *type style* or *character style* for individual properties like bold and italic, which we will refer to individually as *style variations*. We will reserve *text style* for the more inclusive set of overall text characteristics (typeface, type size, type style, and text color), which we will individually call *style attributes*. Finally, when we say *type size*, we mean "type size."

If you're experiencing a feeling of confusion or disorientation at this point, please rest assured that it is a perfectly normal response to the foregoing discussion and no cause for undue alarm. If you aren't, it's probably because your eyes glazed over two paragraphs ago and you've been reading on autopilot ever since. Before proceeding to the next section, take a few minutes to go back and reread this one until you're feeling suitably bewildered. If this still doesn't work, put the book down and seek professional help.

Structure of Styled Text

The basic Toolbox data structure for text editing, as we learned in Volume Two, is the *edit record* [II:5.1.1]. This is a complete operating environment for the TextEdit routines, analogous to the graphics port for QuickDraw. The new version of TextEdit still uses this same structure, but when dealing with styled text, it changes the meaning of some of the record's fields. This modified form of the edit record structure is known as a *styled edit record* [7.2.2].

In the old, unstyled form of edit record, the `txFont`, `txFace`, and `txSize` fields hold the global style attributes that apply to all characters. In a styled edit record, where the style attributes can vary from one character to another, they're kept instead in a separate data structure, the *style record*, freeing the three original fields for other uses. The txSize field is set to -1 to identify the record as a styled edit record; txFont and txFace combine to hold a handle to the style record, which in turn contains the character styling information. There are also a couple of other fields with new meanings, which we'll get to later in the chapter.

The new TextEdit routine TEStylNew [7.3.1] creates a styled edit record, sets its txSize field to -1, creates its style record and other auxiliary data structures, and stores the style record's handle (the *style handle*) in the txFont and txFace fields where it belongs. (The old routine TENew [II:5.2.2] still creates an unstyled edit record, in which txSize is positive and all fields have their original meanings.) Another pair of new routines, GetStylHandle and SetStylHandle [7.3.1], access or change the style handle; always use these routines instead of reading or storing into the txFont and txFace fields directly. When the time comes to dispose of an edit record, the old TEDispose routine [II:5.2.2] now accepts both the styled and unstyled kinds, and disposes of the style record and other auxiliary structures in addition to the edit record itself.

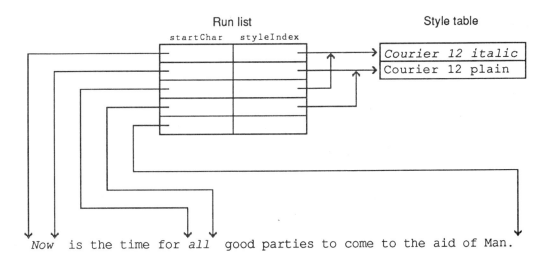

Figure 7-1 Run list and style table

Although in theory every character in an edit record's text could have a different style, in practice they tend to form long *runs* of consecutive characters in the same style. Thus, in general, the number of times the style changes is much smaller than the total number of characters in the text. For example, the text shown in Figure 7–1 is 63 characters long, but contains only four runs, all in the same typeface, size, and (presumably) color: 3 characters in italic, 17 (including spaces) in plain style, 3 more in italic, and another 40 in plain.

The structure of the *style record* [7.2.3], which holds the style information for an edit record's text, is based on this idea of uniform runs. At the heart of the style record are the *run list,* which gives the location and style of each run, and a handle to the *style table* [7.2.4], which holds the style definitions themselves. As the contents and style of the text change over time, the Toolbox automatically keeps the run list and style table up to date.

Each entry in the run list gives the starting character position for a run and the index of its style in the style table. Runs are listed in sequential order, so their lengths needn't be stored explicitly: the length of each run is found by subtracting its starting position from that of the next one following it. The list ends with a dummy entry to delimit the length of the last run, carrying a starting position beyond the last character of the text. The nRuns field of the style record [7.2.3] gives the index of this last entry in the run list; the first is at index 0.

Recall from Volume Two that TextEdit character positions refer to the points *between* the characters, not to the characters themselves. Thus, for example, the second run shown in Figure 7–1 extends from character position 3 (between the third and fourth characters in the text) to position 20 (between the twentieth and twenty-first). Position 0 lies at the start of the text, before the first character; the position at the end, following the last character, is equal to the total length of the text, given by the teLength field of the edit record [II:5.1.1].

The edit record's style table [7.2.4] holds the actual style definitions referred to in the run list. The table is simply a linear array of *style elements,* one for each distinct style occurring in the text. The array is indexed from 0 up to the value of the nStyles field in the style record [7.2.3]. No single style can occur more than once in the table: if two or more character runs are set in the same style, they both refer to the same entry in the style table. In addition to the fields defining its actual style attributes (typeface, size, type style, and color), each style element holds a reference count telling how many runs currently refer to it. The remaining two fields have to do with the style's vertical spacing properties, and are described in the next section.

Vertical Spacing

Since all characters in an unstyled edit record have the same style, every line of text is the same height. Two fields of the edit record [II:5.1.1] establish uniform vertical spacing for all lines: `fontAscent` defines the distance from the top of the destination rectangle to the first baseline, while `lineHeight` gives the distance thereafter from each baseline to the next (see Figure 7–2). The initial values of these fields are taken from the properties of the font in which the text is drawn [I:8.2.6], but you can change them, if necessary, to adjust the vertical spacing of the text in any way you wish.

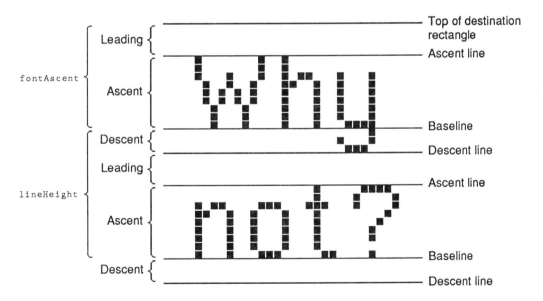

Figure 7–2 Vertical spacing parameters

Life is a bit more complicated in a styled edit record. Because the text style can vary from one character to another, the vertical spacing need not be the same from line to line. Instead, the `lhTab` field of the style record [7.2.3] holds a handle to a *line-height table*

[7.2.5] containing a separate line height and ascent value for each line of text. The entries in the line-height table parallel those of the edit record's own `lineStarts` table [II:5.1.1]; the `nLines` field in the edit record gives the index of the last entry in both tables.

Each separate text style has its own vertical spacing parameters, based on its individual font properties [I:8.2.6] and kept in the `stHeight` and `stAscent` fields of its style table entry [7.2.4]. The height and ascent for a given line are simply the maximum values for any single style occurring in the line. Whenever the line breaks change, whether implicitly (after editing operations, keyboard type-in, and so forth) or explicitly (through a direct call to the TextEdit routine `TECalText` [II:5.3.1]), the contents of the line-height table are automatically recalculated to match. Thus the vertical spacing is continually readjusted to accommodate the tallest text style in each line.

There are two ways to override these automatic calculations and exercise more control over the vertical spacing of your text. In the first place, the line-height table is honored only if the edit record's `lineHeight` and `fontAscent` fields are negative. `TE-StylNew` [7.3.1] initializes these fields to -1 when it creates a styled edit record, but you can change them if you wish. A positive value in either field will be used directly, bypassing the line-height table and resulting in uniform vertical spacing, as in the unstyled case.

Alternatively, you can leave `lineHeight` and `fontAscent` set to -1, but store your own values into the line-height table instead of letting the Toolbox calculate them automatically. For each entry in the table, the high-order bit of the `lhHeight` field [7.2.5] is a flag that optionally suppresses automatic calculation for that line and just uses the existing `lhHeight` and `lhAscent` values without change. (The flag bit itself is, of course, stripped from the `lhHeight` value first.) Notice that there is no equivalent flag in the `lhAscent` field: the one in `lhHeight` governs both fields together.

This technique allows you to control your vertical spacing on a line-by-line basis, rather than just setting a single, uniform value for the entire text, as in the first method described above. Notice also that you don't have to use it for every line in the table: it's possible to set the flag bit for some lines and leave the rest to be calculated automatically. The technique is very tricky to use, however, on text that keeps changing dynamically and having its line breaks recalculated; it's most useful for fixed text whose line breaks never change, such as in a static text box displayed with the `TextBox` routine [II:5.3.2].

Because of the mixed styles and variable line heights, the problem of finding the location of a given character or measuring the height of a sequence of lines can be a bit complicated. TextEdit provides a set of new utility routines [7.3.2] to help. `TEGetOffset` finds the character corresponding to a given point (such as, in particular, the mouse position); `TEGetPoint` finds the coordinates of a given character; `TEGetHeight` finds the total vertical extent of a sequence of lines. All coordinates are given in the local coordinate system of the edit record's port (normally a window on the screen), and those returned by `TEGetPoint` lie on the baseline at the bottom-left of the character. All these routines can be used equally well with both styled and unstyled edit records.

Manipulating Text Styles

The Toolbox routine `TEGetStyle` [7.3.3] returns style information for a single character in an edit record's text. Since character positions refer to the points between characters instead of the characters themselves, you have to identify the character you're interested in by the number of the position preceding it: 0 for the first character, 1 for the second, and so on up to (`teLength` - 1) for the last. The routine returns three variable parameters giving the character's style, height, and ascent. Another routine, `TENum-Styles` [7.3.3], returns the number of complete or partial style runs lying within a given range, specified by its starting and ending position. Notice that this routine counts *runs*, not *styles:* in Figure 7–1, for instance, it would return a result of 4, even though the text contains only two distinct styles (plain and italic), because each of them applies to two separate runs of characters.

The basic routine for setting text styles is `TESetStyle` [7.3.4]. You supply the new style in the form of a text style record [7.2.1]; the characters affected are those in the current selection range, defined by the edit record's `selStart` and `selEnd` fields [II:5.1.1]. Not every field of the record necessarily counts, however: the parameter `whichAttrs` contains flag bits telling which specific fields to apply, allowing you to set any desired combination of style attributes without affecting the rest.

The constants `DoFont`, `DoFace`, `DoSize`, and `DoColor` [7.3.4] denote the flag bits in the `whichAttrs` parameter corresponding to the four fields of the text style record [7.2.1]; you can add these arithmetically to produce any combination of style attributes you need. Thus, for example, setting `whichAttrs` to `DoSize` changes just the point size of the selected text while leaving all other attributes unaffected; setting it to (DoFont + DoSize) changes both the typeface and size, but not the type style and color. For convenience, the constant DoAll [7.3.4] represents the combination of all four style attributes together. There are also two more flag bits with special meanings, which we'll come to shortly.

Another routine closely related to TESetStyle is TEReplace-Style [7.3.4]. Instead of applying a new style to the current selection outright, TEReplaceStyle searches the selection for all occurrences of a specified style and replaces them with another. Again, you can use the whichAttrs parameter to operate selectively on some style attributes while ignoring the rest: for instance, you can change every character in 10-point Geneva to 12-point Helvetica or every occurrence of bold italic to bold underline.

As an example of style manipulation, suppose we decide to add three new menus to MiniEdit to control the typeface, size, and type style, respectively. (In keeping with established Macintosh convention, we'll title the typeface menu Font rather than Face; the other two will be called Size and Style.) Naturally, we'll have to include three new 'MENU' templates [II:4.8.1] in our application resource file and add the appropriate clauses to our SetUpMenus routine (Program II:4–2), to initialize the new menus, and to DoMenuChoice (Program II:4–5), to dispatch control after a mouse click (or an equivalent Command keystroke) in one of their items.

Program 7–1 (DoFontChoice) shows MiniEdit's routine for responding to a choice from the Font menu. This menu is built by calling AddResMenu [II:4.3.3] to find and list all available resources of type 'FONT' [I:8.4.5]. When the user chooses an item from the menu, our DoMenuChoice routine will pass control to the routine shown here.

The first thing DoFontChoice does is get the typeface name from the chosen menu item and convert it to an equivalent font number. After storing the font number into the appropriate field of our text style record, we call TESetStyle with a whichAttrs parameter of DoFont. This applies just the font number to the current selection without affecting any of the other existing style attributes. Finally, we call the MiniEdit routine FixStyleMenus (discussed later in this chapter) to check the chosen item on the Font menu and uncheck the one that was previously checked, if any.

Program 7-1 Handle choice from Font menu

```
{  Global variables  }

var
  FontMenu : MenuHandle;              {Handle to Font menu [II:4.1.1]}
  TheText  : TEHandle;                {Handle to active window's edit record [II:5.1.1]}


procedure DoFontChoice (theItem : INTEGER);

  {  Handle choice from Font menu. }

  var
    fontName : Str255;                {Name of selected typeface [I:2.1.1]}
    fontNum  : INTEGER;              {Font number of selected typeface [I:8.2.1]}
    newStyle : TextStyle;            {New text style for selected text [7.2.1]}

  begin {DoFontChoice}

    GetItem (FontMenu, theItem, fontName);   {Get typeface name from menu item [II:4.6.1]}
    GetFNum (fontName, fontNum);              {Convert to font number [I:8.2.5]}

    newStyle.tsFont := fontNum;              {Store font number in text style [7.2.1]}
    TESetStyle (DoFont, newStyle, TRUE, TheText); {Apply new style to selection [7.3.4]}

    FixStyleMenus                            {Mark menu item for new typeface [Prog. 7–3]}

  end;  {DoFontChoice}
```

We mentioned earlier that there are two more flag bits in the whichAttrs parameter with special meanings, in addition to the four denoting the fields of the text style record. The first of these, AddSize [7.3.4], causes the text style's tsSize field [7.2.1] to be interpreted as an incremental adjustment to the existing type size instead of an outright replacement. The adjustment can be either positive or negative: for example, a value of 2 for tsSize increases the size of every character in the current selection by two points, whereas - 1 reduces every character by one point. If both the DoSize and AddSize bits are set, AddSize takes precedence.

The last flag bit, DoToggle [7.3.4], modifies the meaning of the DoFace bit. To understand how it works, we have to introduce the concept of a *continuous* style. A style property (attribute or variation) is continuous over a range of text if every character within the range has the given property. For example, in the text

O *frabjous* day! Callooh! *Callay!*

the typeface, size, and bold style variation are continuous (every character is bold and in the same face and size), but italic is not (some characters are italic and others aren't) and neither is underline (none of the characters are underlined).

If both the DoFace and DoToggle bits of the whichAttrs parameter are on, TESetStyle tests each of the specified variations (bold, italic, and so forth) individually to see whether that variation is continuous over the selection range. If a variation is not continuous (that is, if one or more characters in the selection don't already have the variation), it is turned *on* for every character; if it is continuous (if every character already has the variation), it is turned *off* for every character. Thus, in the example above, if we call TESetStyle with the whichAttrs parameter set to (DoFace + DoToggle) and the tsFace field of newStyle equal to [Italic], every character will be made italic (since not all of them already are); if tsFace is equal to [Bold], the bold variation will be removed from all characters (since they all have it already).

Program 7-2 Handle choice from Style menu

```
{  Global declarations  }

const
    PlainItem       = 1;          {Item number for Plain command}
    BoldItem        = 2;          {Item number for Bold command}
    ItalicItem      = 3;          {Item number for Italic command}
    UnderlineItem   = 4;          {Item number for Underline command}
    OutlineItem     = 5;          {Item number for Outline command}
    ShadowItem      = 6;          {Item number for Shadow command}

var
    TheText : TEHandle;           {Handle to active window's edit record [II:5.1.1]}
```

Program 7–2 Handle choice from Style menu *(continued)*

```
procedure DoStyleChoice (theItem : INTEGER);

  {  Handle choice from Style menu. }

  var
     newStyle   : TextStyle;          {New text style for selected text [7.2.1]}
     whichAttrs : INTEGER;            {Style attributes to change [7.3.4]}

  begin {DoStyleChoice}

    case theItem of

      PlainItem:
        newStyle.tsFace := [];        {Set type style to empty set [7.2.1, I:8.3.1]}

      BoldItem:
        newStyle.tsFace := [Bold];    {Toggle bold style [7.2.1, I:8.3.1]}

      ItalicItem:
        newStyle.tsFace := [Italic];  {Toggle italic style [7.2.1, I:8.3.1]}

      UnderlineItem:
        newStyle.tsFace := [Underline]; {Toggle underline style [7.2.1, I:8.3.1]}

      OutlineItem:
        newStyle.tsFace := [Outline]; {Toggle outline style [7.2.1, I:8.3.1]}

      ShadowItem:
        newStyle.tsFace := [Shadow]   {Toggle shadow style [7.2.1, I:8.3.1]}

      end; {case theItem}

    if theItem = PlainItem then       {Plain style chosen?}
      whichAttrs := DoFace            {Set new style outright [7.3.4]}
    else
      whichAttrs := DoFace + DoToggle; {Toggle existing style [7.3.4]}

    TESetStyle (whichAttrs, newStyle, TRUE, TheText); {Apply new style to ]
                                                      { selection [7.3.4]}


    FixStyleMenus                     {Mark menu items for new style [Prog. 7–3]}

  end;  {DoStyleChoice}
```

Notice that this is exactly the proper behavior for implementing a menu command for a style variation: apply the variation to every character of the selected text unless they all have it already, in which case remove it. Program 7–2 (DoStyleChoice) shows the use of DoToggle in the MiniEdit routine for responding to a choice from the Style menu. First we dispatch on the item number to set the tsFace field of the text style to the requested variation (or to the empty set in the case of the Plain command). If Plain was chosen, we just set whichAttrs to DoFace, applying the empty style unconditionally to every character in the selection; for all other items, we set it to (DoFace + DoToggle), causing the given variation to be toggled on or off according to the existing properties of the selected text, as described in the preceding paragraph. After calling TESet-Style to apply the new style to the selection, we next call our MiniEdit routine FixStyleMenus to adjust the check marks on the menu to the new style.

Program 7–3 Mark menu items for style of current selection

```
{  Global declarations  }

const
   StyleID = 6;                       {Menu ID for Style menu}
      PlainItem = 1;                     {Item number for Plain command}
      ColorItem = 8;                     {Item number for Color... command}

var
   TheText    : TEHandle;             {Handle to active window's edit record [II:5.1.1]}
   FontMenu   : MenuHandle;           {Handle to Font menu [II:4.1.1]}
   SizeMenu   : MenuHandle;           {Handle to Size menu [II:4.1.1]}
   StyleMenu  : MenuHandle;           {Handle to Style menu [II:4.1.1]}


procedure FixStyleMenus;

   {  Mark menu items for style of current selection.  }

   var
      whichAttrs   : INTEGER;         {Which attributes are continuous?}
      styleValues  : TextStyle;       {Values of continuous attributes [7.2.1]}
      nItems       : INTEGER;         {Number of items in menu}
      thisItem     : INTEGER;         {Index variable for menu items}
      itemString   : Str255;          {Text of menu item [I:2.1.1]}
      isChecked    : BOOLEAN;         {Should menu item be checked?}
      fontName     : Str255;          {Name of typeface [I:2.1.1]}
      sizeString   : Str255;          {Type size in string form [I:2.1.1]}
      thisStyle    : StyleItem;       {Index variable for style variations [I:8.3.1]}
      itemColors   : MCEntryPtr;      {Pointer to menu color info entry [6.6.1]}
      ignore       : BOOLEAN;         {Dummy variable for function result}
```

Program 7-3 Mark menu items for style of current selection *(continued)*

```
begin {FixStyleMenus}

   whichAttrs := DoAll;                              {Examine all attributes [7.3.4]}
   ignore     := TEContinuousStyle (whichAttrs, styleValues, TheText);
                                                     {Find continuous attributes [7.3.3]}
   with styleValues do
      begin

         if BitAnd(whichAttrs, DoFont) <> 0 then    {Is typeface continuous? [7.3.4]}
            GetFontName (tsFont, fontName)           {Convert number to name [I:8.2.5, 7.2.1]}
         else
            fontName := '';                          {Use null font name}

         nItems := CountMItems (FontMenu);           {Get size of menu [II:4.3.5]}
         for thisItem := 1 to nItems do              {Loop through menu items}
            begin
               GetItem   (FontMenu, thisItem, itemString); {Get text of item [II:4.6.1]}
               isChecked := (itemString = fontName);      {Is this the one?}
               CheckItem (FontMenu, thisItem, isChecked)  {Mark or unmark item [II:4.6.4]}
            end; {for thisItem}

         if BitAnd(whichAttrs, DoSize) <> 0 then     {Is type size continuous? [7.3.4]}
            NumToString (tsSize, sizeString)         {Convert to string [I:2.3.7, 7.2.1]}
         else
            sizeString := '';                        {Use null size string}

         nItems := CountMItems (SizeMenu);           {Get size of menu [II:4.3.5]}
         for thisItem := 1 to nItems do              {Loop through menu items}
            begin
               GetItem   (SizeMenu, thisItem, itemString); {Get text of item [II:4.6.1]}
               isChecked := (itemString = sizeString);    {Is this the one?}
               CheckItem (SizeMenu, thisItem, isChecked)  {Mark or unmark item [II:4.6.4]}
            end; {for thisItem}

         if BitAnd(whichAttrs, DoFace) <> 0 then     {Is type style continuous? [7.3.4]}
            begin
               thisItem   := PlainItem;              {Start with Plain item}
               isChecked := (tsFace = []);           {Is plain style continuous? [7.2.1]}
               CheckItem (StyleMenu, thisItem, isChecked); {Mark or unmark item [II:4.6.4]}

               for thisStyle := Bold to Shadow do    {Loop through style variations [I:8.3.1]}
                  begin
                     thisItem   := thisItem + 1;     {Advance to next menu item}
                     isChecked := (thisStyle in tsFace); {Is this variation continuous? [7.2.1]}
                     CheckItem (StyleMenu, thisItem, isChecked) {Mark or unmark }
                                                                {  item [II:4.6.4]}

                  end {for thisStyle}
            end {then}
```

Program 7-3 Mark menu items for style of current selection *(continued)*

```
     else
        begin
          nItems := CountMItems (StyleMenu);          {Get size of menu [II:4.3.5]}
          for thisItem := 1 to nItems do             {Loop through menu items}
            CheckItem (StyleMenu, thisItem, FALSE);   {Unmark all items [II:4.6.4]}
        end; {else}



     itemColors := GetMCEntry (StyleID, ColorItem);   {Get item colors [6.6.3]}
     if BitAnd(whichAttrs, DoColor) <> 0 then         {Is text color continuous? }
                                                      {   [I:2.2.2, 7.3.4]}
        itemColors^.mctRGB2 := tsColor                {Set item's text color [6.6.1, 7.2.1]}
     else
        with itemColors^.mctRGB2 do
          begin
            red   := 0;                               {Set text color to black [4.2.1]}
            green := 0;
            blue  := 0
          end {with itemColors^.mctRGB2}

   end {with styleValues}

 end;   {FixStyleMenus}
```

FixStyleMenus is shown in Program 7-3. To find which style properties to mark on the menus, it uses the Toolbox routine TEContinuousStyle [7.3.3]. This routine accepts a whichAttrs parameter in the same form as the one for TESetStyle [7.3.4], except that it uses only the DoFont, DoFace, DoSize, and DoColor bits and ignores AddSize and DoToggle. On exit from the routine, this same whichAttrs parameter tells which of the requested attributes are continuous over the current selection; the actual values of the indicated attributes are returned in the variable parameter theStyle. The function result is TRUE if all of the originally requested attributes are continuous, FALSE if one or more of them are not.

TEContinuousStyle works straightforwardly for the DoFont, DoSize, and DoColor attributes, but its handling of DoFace needs some further explanation. If the DoFace bit in whichAttrs is set on return from the call, it can mean one of two things, depending on the contents of the Style set [I:8.3.1] returned in the tsFace field of parameter theStyle. If the set is not empty—that is, if it contains one or more style variations—then those specific variations are continuous over the selection range. Variations that are not included in the set are not continuous, but may still be present for some characters in the selection (though not for all of them). For example, the set [Bold, Underline] means that every character in the selection is bold and underlined; it does *not* necessarily mean that none of them are italic, outlined, or shadowed. If, on the other hand, tsFace is the empty set, then the entire selection is in plain style and none of its characters have any style variations at all.

Program 7–3 shows how to use this information to mark the items on our Font, Size, and Style menus according to the style of the current selection. We will call this routine after any operation that changes the style of the selection (as we've already seen in our DoFontChoice and DoStyleChoice routines, Programs 7–1 and 7–2), as well as when the selection itself is changed (DoSelect, Program II:5–4) or when a new window is activated (ActivateWindow, Program II:5–14). In each of these cases, we want to place a check mark in the menu beside just those items that are continuous over the selection and make sure all other items are unmarked.

Our first step is to call TEContinuousStyle with a which-Attrs parameter of DoAll, asking for all continuous style properties (typeface, size, variations, and color). On return from this call, the flag bits in whichAttrs tell which attributes are continuous over the selection, and the fields of the text style record styleValues give the corresponding attribute values. We then test each flag bit in turn and mark our menu items accordingly.

For the typeface and size attributes, we get the value from the style record and convert it to string form, using GetFontName [I:8.2.5] for the typeface and NumToString [I:2.3.7] for the size. Next we loop through the items of the corresponding menu, testing each in turn to see if it matches the attribute string. Using a Boolean variable, isChecked, to hold the result of the comparison, we then call CheckItem [II:4.6.4] to mark or unmark the item with a check mark. If the flag bit in whichAttrs tells us that the given attribute is not continuous (that is, that the selection contains mixed typefaces or sizes), we simply use the null string for our comparisons; this will not match any of the menu items, causing them all to be unmarked.

Handling type-style variations is a bit trickier. If the DoFace flag in whichAttrs is on, we know either that one or more style variations are continuous over the selection or else that the entire selection is in plain style. So we first check for an empty `Style` set and mark or unmark the menu item titled `Plain` accordingly. We then loop through all the individual style variations from `Bold` to `Shadow` [I:8.3.1], testing for each one separately and marking or unmarking it on the menu as needed. (Notice that the code here depends on the assumption that the items appear on the menu in the same order in which they're defined in the enumerated type `StyleItem` [I:8.3.1].) If the `DoFace` bit is not set in `whichAttrs`, then no single variation (including plain) is continuous, so we simply loop through all the items on the menu and unmark them all.

The last style attribute to account for is color. We'll assume that our `Style` menu ends with a command titled `Color...`, which brings up the Color Picker dialog [4.2.3] to allow the user to specify a color for the current selection. If the selection has a continuous color attribute, we will display this command on the menu in the same color as the text itself. To control the color of the menu item, we have to call `GetMCEntry` [6.6.3] to get a pointer to its entry in the menu color information table. If the selection's color is continuous, we store it into the appropriate field of the color info entry [6.6.1]; otherwise, we just set the field to plain black. (Notice that we will suffer an agonizing demise if `GetMCEntry` returns a `NIL` pointer, meaning that the `Color...` item on our `Style` menu has no explicit entry in the color information table. To elude the Grim Reaper, we must be sure to give the item an entry, either via an `'mctb'` resource [6.7.7] or with an explicit call to `SetMCEntries` [6.6.3] at initialization time.)

Editing Styled Text

One significant change in the new version of TextEdit is that it no longer maintains a separate Toolbox scrap [II:5.5.4] for cut-and-paste operations, but instead uses the main desk scrap [I:7.4.1] directly. Previously, the desk scrap was used only for cutting and pasting from one program or desk accessory to another; internal editing operations within a program used the Toolbox scrap instead. This meant you had to transfer text back and forth from one scrap to the other whenever control passed to or from another program: on entry and exit, when activating or deactivating a desk accessory window, or on receiving a suspend or resume event. To make matters worse, the flag bit in the event record [I:2.1.5] that notified you when control was passing to or from a desk accessory was not always set reliably, sometimes causing the contents of the scrap to fall through the crack between the accessory and your program.

Life is much simpler with the new TextEdit. All text cut and pasted in a styled edit record goes directly through the desk scrap and thus is available automatically, with no extra effort, when control transfers to or from another program. (For the sake of compatibility, cut or copied text is written to the internal Toolbox scrap as well, and unstyled edit records continue to use the Toolbox scrap as they always did.) The old transfer routines TEFromScrap and TEToScrap [II:5.5.5], which copy text from one scrap to the other, are still supported, but as long as you stick exclusively to styled edit records, you needn't ever bother with such scrap transfers.

The Style Scrap

As we learned in Volume One, the desk scrap consists of one or more separate items representing the same information in different forms, for use by different recipient programs. Each item is identified by a four-character type code similar to a resource type (though it may or may not actually be used as such in resource files). Every program that uses the scrap is expected to accept and to deliver at least one of the two standard types 'TEXT' [I:8.4.1] (unformatted ASCII text characters) and 'PICT' [I:5.5.5] (QuickDraw picture definitions), which serve as a uniform medium of data exchange between programs. In addition, a program may optionally add specialized item types for its own use, carrying further information beyond that conveyed by the two standard types. The scrap is supposed to contain no more than one item of any given type, though the Toolbox does not actively enforce this rule.

When operating in a styled edit record, the old TextEdit routines TECut and TECopy [II:5.5.2, 7.3.5] now write the characters of the current selection to the desk scrap as an item of the standard type 'TEXT'. A second item, under the new type 'styl', holds the accompanying style information in the form of a *style-scrap record* [7.2.7]. The new TextEdit routine TEStylPaste [7.3.5] pastes the contents of the scrap back into the document at the current selection or insertion point, using the styles defined by its matching 'styl' item. The old routine TEPaste [II:5.5.2, 7.3.5] continues to paste just the text without the accompanying style; instead, its style is determined according to the rules for unstyled text, which we'll come to in a minute.

The style-scrap record is simply a linear array of *scrap style elements* [7.2.7], one for each style run in the scrap's text, preceded by an integer length count giving the number of elements. Each element has essentially the same form as a style table element [7.2.4], except that instead of a reference count, the first field holds the starting character position of the run within the scrap's `'TEXT'` item. Unlike the style table, however, the style scrap may contain duplicate entries for the same style: its elements correspond one-to-one with the style runs in the cut or copied text.

The Null Style

Another important use for style-scrap records is in defining an edit record's *null style.* This is the style applied to new characters entered at an insertion point (that is, when the selection range, `selStart` to `selEnd`, is empty). The null style governs all characters that don't already have an explicit style of their own, whether typed from the keyboard via `TEKey` [II:5.5.1], pasted from the scrap with `TEPaste` [II:5.5.2, 7.3.5], or inserted directly into the document with the "scrapless" editing routine `TEInsert` [II:5.5.3].

The null style is defined by a *null-style record* [7.2.6], located via a handle in the `nullStyle` field of the style record [7.2.3]. The null-style record in turn holds a handle to a style-scrap record [7.2.7] giving the attributes of the current null style. This style-scrap record has the same form as the one used for the style scrap itself, but is limited to at most one element (since it's just defining a single style instead of an indefinite sequence of runs). Thus its `scrpNStyles` field, which gives the number of elements it contains, can never be greater than 1.

It's also possible (common, in fact) for `scrpNStyles` to be 0, meaning that no null style is currently defined. Every time the selection range is changed (by `TEClick` [II:5.4.1] or `TESetSelect` [II:5.4.2]), the null style is cleared by setting its `scrpNStyles` field to 0. Any unstyled text entered at such a time will take its style from the first character in the selection, if there is one, or (if the selection is empty) from the character preceding the insertion point. An explicit null style can be created, overriding this default behavior, in either of two ways. First, when the selection is empty, all calls to `TESetStyle` [7.3.4] apply to the null style instead. This allows styling commands like those on MiniEdit's `Font`, `Size`, and `Style` menus to control the style of text typed at an insertion point. Second, when `TEKey` [II:5.5.1] deletes the first character of a style run in response to a backspace character, the style of that run is copied to the null style to be remembered and applied to any subsequent type-in. Backspacing again, however, past the last character in the preceding run, clears the null style and reinstates the default styling behavior.

Scrapless Styling

Style-scrap records are also useful for styling operations that work with multiple text styles at once, since they can contain any number of runs in different styles. One such operation is `GetStylScrap` [7.3.6]. The name is misleading: rather than retrieving the contents of the global style scrap, as you might expect, this routine returns a scrap record describing the styles of the edit record's currently selected text. If the current selection is empty or the edit record is unstyled, it returns `NIL`.

Another routine with a misleading name is `SetStylScrap` [7.3.6], which has no effect on the style scrap itself. Rather, it uses a style-scrap record to set the styles for a range of characters within an edit record's text. This routine is similar in operation to `TESetStyle` [7.3.4], but with some important differences. First, instead of applying implicitly to the current selection range, it accepts a pair of explicit parameters, `startPos` and `endPos`, defining the range of characters affected. Second, the new styles are defined by a style-scrap record instead of a single text style, allowing a whole series of styles to be applied consecutively in one operation. And finally, all attributes of each style are used: there is no `whichAttrs` parameter to selectively choose some attributes and ignore others.

`TEStylInsert` [7.3.6] is the styled analog of the old "scrapless" insertion routine, `TEInsert` [II:5.5.3]. This routine inserts a specified sequence of characters at the beginning of the current selection without reference to the contents of the scrap and without disturbing the selected text. The text to be inserted is specified directly, via a pointer, and need not have been cut or copied from elsewhere in the document. A style-scrap record, `textStyles`, defines the styles for the inserted text. Both here and in `SetStylScrap`, it isn't necessary for the text and the scrap record to match in length. If the total length of all the runs in the scrap record exceeds the number of characters in the specified range or insertion, excess runs at the end will be ignored; if it falls short, the last run will be extended to cover all the remaining characters.

REFERENCE

7.1 Color Fonts

7.1.1 Font Type and Depth

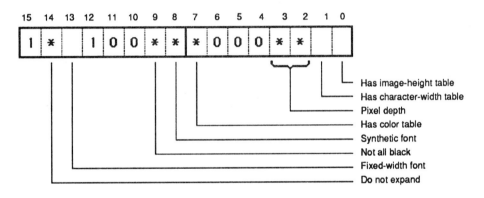

Font type flags

Notes

1. The figure shows the contents of the `fontType` field in a font record [I:8.2.2].

2. Bits marked with an asterisk (*) apply only to the Macintosh II and should be set to 0 on older models.

327

3. Bits 0 and 1 tell whether the font has an image-height table and a character-width table [I:8.2.3], respectively.

4. Bits 2 and 3 give the depth of the font's pixel image as an integer power of 2. For example, a value of 3 (binary 11) denotes a depth of 8 (2^3) bits per pixel. In a normal monochrome font, these bits are 0, indicating a pixel depth of 1 (2^0).

5. At high pixel depths, the font image can grow quite large, causing the font's owTLoc field (which holds the offset in words from itself to the beginning of the offset/width table [I:8.2.3]) to overflow its allotted 2 bytes. In this case, the nDescent field [I:8.2.2] (which is redundant anyway) is used as an additional 2-byte leftward extension to owTLoc. This usage is indicated by a positive value in nDescent; if this field is less than 0, it is understood to hold the negative font descent, as before.

6. Bit 7 tells whether the font has an associated color table of resource type 'fctb' [7.4.1]. This flag is applicable only for fonts stored as 'NFNT' resources [I:8.4.5].

7. Bit 9 should be set to 1 if the font's pixel image includes colors other than plain black and white.

8. Bits 8 and 13 identify the font as synthetic [7.1.2] and fixed-width [I:8.2.2], respectively.

9. If bit 14 is 1, the font must be used as is and must not be expanded into a synthetic font to match the screen depth. This flag is used mainly in fonts for large foreign character sets, such as Japanese or Chinese, that would require inordinate amounts of memory at high pixel depths.

10. All other bits in the flag word are reserved for future use and should be set to the constant values (0 or 1) shown in the figure.

7.1.2   Synthetic Fonts

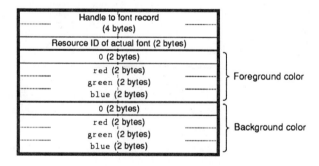

Synthetic-font list entry

Notes

1. A synthetic font is generated automatically by the Toolbox when a font read from a resource file doesn't match the pixel depth at which it is to be drawn.

2. A synthetic font is represented by an ordinary font record [I:8.2.2] with bit 8 set in its flag word [7.1.1] and its font image [I:8.2.3] expanded to the current screen depth.

3. The Toolbox maintains a list of all synthetic fonts currently in existence, located via a handle in the low-memory global variable SynListHandle.

4. Each entry in the synthetic-font list has the form shown in the figure.

Assembly Language Information

Assembly-language global variable:

Name	Address	Meaning
SynListHandle	$D32	Handle to first font in synthetic-font list

7.2 Styled Text

7.2.1   Text Styles

Definitions

```
type
   TextStyle = record
              tsFont  : INTEGER;      {Font number of typeface [I:8.2.1]}
              tsFace  : Style;        {Type style [I:8.3.1]}
              tsSize  : INTEGER;      {Type size in points}
              tsColor : RGBColor      {Text color [4.2.1]}
           end;
```

Notes

1. A text style defines the appearance of text characters when displayed or printed.

2. `tsFont` is a font number [I:8.2.1] identifying the typeface in which the text is to be drawn; `tsSize` is the type size in points.

3. `tsFace` is a `Style` set [I:8.3.1] defining the type style variations (such as bold or italic) to be applied.

4. `tsColor` is the text color in RGB form [4.2.1].

Assembly Language Information

Field offsets in a text style:

(Pascal) Field name	(Assembly) Offset name	Offset in bytes
tsFont	tsFont	0
tsFace	tsFace	2
tsSize	tsSize	4
tsColor	tsColor	6

Assembly-language constant:

Name	Value	Meaning
StyleSize	12	Size of a text style in bytes

7.2.2 Styled Edit Records

Definitions

```
type
   TEHandle = ^TEPtr;
   TEPtr    = ^TERec;
```

```
TERec    = record
             . . . ;
             lineHeight : INTEGER;      {Negative for variable line height [7.2.5]}
             fontAscent : INTEGER;      {Negative for variable line ascent [7.2.5]}
             txFont     : INTEGER;      {First half of style record handle [7.2.3]}
             txFace     : Style;        {Last half of style record handle [7.2.3]}
             . . . ;
             txSize     : INTEGER;      {-1 for styled text}
             . . .
           end;
```

Notes

1. These fields of an edit record [II:5.1.1] have new meanings in connection with styled text.

2. The Toolbox routine TEStylNew [7.3.1] creates a styled edit record and initializes its fields as described here; TENew [II:5.2.2] continues to create an unstyled edit record with all fields initialized as in the past.

3. A value of -1 in the txSize field identifies a styled edit record. If txSize ≥ 0, the edit record is unstyled and all fields have their original meanings [II:5.1.1].

4. The combined fields txFont and txFace hold a handle to a style record [7.2.3] defining the styles for the edit record's text.

5. In assembly language, the new offset constant teStylesH (see "Assembly Language Information" below) selects the style record handle within an edit record, replacing the old offsets teFont and teFace [II:5.1.1]. In Pascal, use the new Toolbox routines GetStylHandle and SetStylHandle [7.3.1] to access or set the style handle.

6. If the lineHeight and fontAscent fields are negative, the vertical spacing for each line of text can vary according to the text styles the line contains, and is defined by the style record's line-height table [7.2.5]. If these fields are positive, they specify fixed vertical spacing values for all text lines, as before [II:5.1.1].

7. The old Toolbox routine TEDispose [II:5.2.2] disposes of an edit record, whether styled or unstyled, along with all of its associated data structures (text [II:5.2.3], style record [7.2.3], style table [7.2.4], line-height table [7.2.5], and null-style record [7.2.6]).

Assembly Language Information

Field offset in an edit record:

(Pascal) Field name	(Assembly) Offset name	Offset in bytes
txFont	teStylesH	74

7.2.3   Style Records

Definitions

```
type
  TEStyleHandle = ^TEStylePtr;
  TEStylePtr    = ^TEStyleRec;

  TEStyleRec    = record
                  nRuns     : INTEGER;                    {Number of runs}
                  nStyles   : INTEGER;                    {Number of styles}
                  styleTab  : STHandle;                   {Style table [7.2.4]}
                  lhTab     : LHHandle;                   {Line-height table [7.2.5]}
                  teRefCon  : LONGINT;                    {Reference constant}
                  nullStyle : NullSTHandle;               {Null-style record [7.2.6]}
                  runs      : array [0..8000] of StyleRun {Array of style runs}
                end;

  StyleRun = record
             startChar   : INTEGER;                       {Starting character position}
             styleIndex  : INTEGER                        {Index in style table}
           end;
```

Notes

1. A style record defines the style attributes for an edit record's text.

2. The style record is located via a handle in the edit record's txFont and txFace fields [7.2.2] and accessed with GetStylHandle and SetStylHandle [7.3.1].

3. The *run list*, runs, divides the text into *style runs* of consecutive characters in the same style. The styles themselves are kept in a

separate *style table* [7.2.4], located via the handle in the style record's `styleTab` field.

4. Although the run list is nominally indexed from 0 to 8000, it may actually contain any number of runs. The nRuns field gives the index of its last element and determines the true length of the list.

5. Each element in the run list specifies the starting character position of a run and the index of its style within the style table.

6. The length of a run is the difference between its starting position and that of the next run following it in the run list.

7. The run list ends with a dummy entry at index nRuns, marking the character position beyond the end of the last run. The "starting position" for this dummy entry is equal to the overall length of the text in characters.

8. nStyles is the index of the last entry in the style table.

9. No single style occurs more than once in the style table. Runs with identical text styles share the same style entry in the table.

10. lhTab and nullStyle are handles to the edit record's line-height table [7.2.5] and null-style record [7.2.6], respectively.

11. teRefCon is a 4-byte reference "constant" that your program can use in any way you wish.

Assembly Language Information

Field offsets in a style record:

(Pascal) Field name	(Assembly) Offset name	Offset in bytes
nRuns	nRuns	0
nStyles	nStyles	2
styleTab	styleTab	4
lhTab	lhTab	8
teRefCon	teRefCon	12
nullStyle	nullStyle	16
runs	runs	20

Field offsets in a style run:

(Pascal) Field name	(Assembly) Offset name	Offset in bytes
startChar	startChar	0
styleIndex	styleIndex	4

Assembly-language constant:

Name	Value	Meaning
StStartSize	4	Size of a style run ("style start record") in bytes

7.2.4   Style Table

Definitions

```
type
  STHandle    = ^STPtr;
  STPtr       = ^TEStyleTable;
  TEStyleTable= array [0..1776] of STElement;

STElement = record
              stCount  : INTEGER;      {Number of runs in this style}
              stHeight : INTEGER;      {Line height}
              stAscent : INTEGER;      {Font ascent}
              stFont   : INTEGER;      {Font number of typeface [I:8.2.1]}
              stFace   : Style;        {Type style [I:8.3.1]}
              stSize   : INTEGER;      {Type size in points}
              stColor  : RGBColor      {Text color [4.2.1]}
            end;
```

Notes

1. A style table holds the style information for an edit record's style record [7.2.3].

2. The table's nominal capacity of 1776 red-white-and-blue elements is purely fictitious; it may actually contain any number of styles. The nStyles field in the style record [7.2.3] gives the index of its last element and determines the true length of the table.

3. No single style occurs more than once in the table. Character runs with identical text styles share the same table entry; the stCount field in each entry holds a reference count telling how many runs refer to it.

4. `stHeight` **and** `stAscent` **give the line height and ascent for a given text style, measured in points relative to the baseline.**

5. `stFont` **is a font number [I:8.2.1] identifying the typeface in which the text is to be drawn;** `stSize` **is the type size in points.**

6. `stFace` **is a** `Style` **set [I:8.3.1] defining the type style variations (such as bold or italic) to be applied.**

7. `stColor` **is the text color in RGB form [4.2.1].**

Assembly Language Information

Field offsets in a style element:

(Pascal) Field name	(Assembly) Offset name	Offset in bytes
stCount	stCount	0
stHeight	stHeight	2
stAscent	stAscent	4
stFont	stFont	6
stFace	stFace	8
stSize	stSize	10
stColor	stColor	12

Assembly-language constant:

Name	Value	Meaning
STRecSize	18	Size of a style element in bytes

7.2.5   Line-Height Table

Definitions

```
type
   LHHandle  = ^LHPtr;
   LHPtr     = ^LHTable;
   LHTable   = array [0..8000] of LHElement;

   LHElement = record
                  lhHeight : INTEGER;      {Line height in pixels}
                  lhAscent : INTEGER;      {Line ascent in pixels}
               end;
```

Notes

1. A line-height table defines the vertical spacing independently for each line of an edit record's text.

2. Entries in the table correspond one-to-one with those in the edit record's `lineStarts` array [II:5.1.1].

3. Each line's height and ascent are determined by the maximum values for any text style occurring within the line.

4. The information in the table applies only if the edit record's `lineHeight` or `fontAscent` field [7.2.2] is negative. If these fields are positive, they specify uniform vertical spacing for the text and the line-height table is ignored.

5. Although the line-height table is nominally indexed from 0 to 8000, it may actually contain any number of lines. The `nLines` field in the edit record [II:5.1.1] gives the index of its last element and determines the true length of the table.

6. Like the `lineStarts` array, the table ends with a dummy entry at index `nLines`, representing the end of the text beyond the last line.

7. Line heights and ascents are recalculated automatically whenever the line breaks themselves are changed, either as a result of an editing operation or through an explicit call to `TECalText` [II:5.3.1].

8. The high-order bit of each entry's `lhHeight` field is a flag that optionally suppresses automatic calculation for that line and uses the given line height and ascent values directly, without modification. (Naturally, the high-order flag bit is first stripped from `lhHeight`.) This allows you to control vertical spacing explicitly on a line-by-line basis, rather than uniformly for the entire text via the `lineHeight` and `fontAscent` fields of the edit record [7.2.2].

9. There is no equivalent flag bit in the `lhAscent` field; the one in `lhHeight` applies to both fields together.

10. This technique is most useful for fixed text whose line breaks will never change, such as in static text boxes displayed with the `TextBox` routine [II:5.3.2].

11. Through an oversight, the assembly-language interface does not define offset constants for the fields of a line-height element.

7.2.6   Null-Style Record

Definitions

```
type
  NullStHandle = ^NullStPtr;
  NullStPtr    = ^NullStRec;

  NullStRec    = record
                   teReserved : LONGINT;      {Reserved for future expansion}
                   nullScrap  : StScrpHandle  {Style scrap for null style [7.2.7]}
                 end;
```

Notes

1. A null-style record defines the style for text entered into an edit record at an insertion point (that is, when the selection range is empty).

2. `nullScrap` is a handle to a style-scrap record [7.2.7]. When a null style is in effect, this record's `scrpNStyles` field is set to 1 and its `scrpStyleTab` field holds a scrap style table [7.2.7] with a single entry defining the null style.

3. If the scrap record's `scrpNStyles` field [7.2.7] is 0, no null style is in effect. Entered text will then take its style from that of the character preceding the insertion point.

4. `teReserved` is a 4-byte utility field reserved for future use.

5. When text is entered at an insertion point with `TEKey` [II:5.5.1], `TEPaste` [II:5.5.2, 7.3.5], or `TEInsert` [II:5.5.3], the null style is copied into the main style table [7.2.4] (if it isn't already there) and then cleared to empty by setting its `scrpNStyles` field [7.2.7] to 0. The styled editing routine `TEStylPaste` [7.3.5] does the same if there is no style entry in the desk scrap, as does `TEStylInsert` [7.3.6] if its `textStyles` parameter is NIL.

6. The null style is set by `TESetStyle` [7.3.4] when the selection range is empty (`selStart = selEnd` [II:5.1.1]).

7. Changing the insertion point with `TESetSelect` [II:5.4.2] or `TEClick` [II:5.4.1] clears the null style to empty.

8. Backspacing to the beginning of a style run with `TEKey` [II:5.5.1] or clearing it with `TEDelete` [II:5.5.3] copies its style to the null style, to be applied to any text subsequently entered in its place. Backspacing further, beyond the beginning of the run, clears the null style to empty.

Assembly Language Information

Field offsets in a null-style record:

(Pascal) Field name	(Assembly) Offset name	Offset in bytes
teReserved	teReserved	0
nullScrap	nullScrap	4

Assembly-language constant:

Name	Value	Meaning
NullStSize	8	Size of a null-style record in bytes

7.2.7   Style Scrap

Definitions

```
type
  StScrpHandle  = ^StScrpPtr;
  StScrpPtr     = ^StScrpRec;
  StScrpRec     = record
                      scrpNStyles  : INTEGER;        {Number of styles}
                      scrpStyleTab : ScrpStTable     {Table of styles}
                  end;

  ScrpStTable   = array [0..1600] of ScrpStElement;
  ScrpStElement = record
                      scrpStartChar : LONGINT;       {Starting character position}
                      scrpHeight    : INTEGER;       {Line height}
                      scrpAscent    : INTEGER;       {Font ascent}
                      scrpFont      : INTEGER;       {Font number of typeface [I:8.2.1]}
                      scrpFace      : Style;         {Type style [I:8.3.1]}
                      scrpSize      : INTEGER;       {Type size in points}
                      scrpColor     : RGBColor       {Text color [4.2.1]}
                  end;
```

Notes

1. A style-scrap record holds the style information for text being cut and pasted via the desk scrap. Such records are also used to define an edit record's null style [7.2.6] and for passing style information to and from the scrapless styling routines `GetStylScrap`, `SetStylScrap`, and `TEStylInsert` [7.3.6].

2. When operating on a styled edit record [7.2.2], the TextEdit routines now use the main desk scrap [I:7.4] for all cut-and-paste editing. For backward compatibility, a duplicate handle to the same text is also stored in the internal Toolbox scrap [II:5.5.4]. Unstyled edit records [II:5.1.1] continue to use the Toolbox scrap only, as before.

3. The text itself is written to the desk scrap under type `'TEXT'` [I:8.4.1], with the associated style information stored separately as a style-scrap record (`StScrpRec`) under type `'styl'`.

4. Style information is written to the desk scrap only, never to the Toolbox scrap.

5. Although the scrap style table is nominally indexed from 0 to 1600, it may actually contain any number of entries. The `scrpNStyles` field gives the index of its last entry and determines the true length of the table.

6. Notice that the complete scrap style table, not just a handle, is embedded directly in the style-scrap record. Thus the record actually consists of a sequence of scrap style elements (`ScrpStElement`) preceded by a 2-byte length count telling how many.

7. Each scrap style element defines the style for a run of consecutive characters within the body of the text scrap. Its form is the same as that of a style table element [7.2.4], except that the first field is a 4-byte starting character position instead of a 2-byte reference count.

8. The length of each run is the difference between its starting position (`scrpStartChar`) and that of the next run following it in the table.

9. The table ends with a dummy entry at index `scrpNStyles`, marking the character position beyond the end of the last run. The "starting position" for this dummy entry is equal to the overall length of the scrap in characters.

10. Entries in the style scrap correspond one-to-one with consecutive runs of characters in the text scrap. This means that the identical style can occur more than once in the scrap—unlike the style table [7.2.4], which contains no duplicate entries.

Assembly Language Information

Field offsets in a style-scrap record:

(Pascal) Field name	(Assembly) Offset name	Offset in bytes
scrpNStyles	scrpNStyles	0
scrpStyleTab	scrpStyleTab	2

Field offsets in a scrap style element:

(Pascal) Field name	(Assembly) Offset name	Offset in bytes
scrpStartChar	scrpStartChar	0
scrpHeight	scrpHeight	4
scrpAscent	scrpAscent	6
scrpFont	scrpFont	8
scrpFace	scrpFace	10
scrpSize	scrpSize	12
scrpColor	scrpColor	14

Assembly-language constant:

Name	Value	Meaning
ScrpRecSize	20	Size of a scrap style element in bytes

7.3 Editing Styled Text

7.3.1 Preparation for Editing

Definitions

```
function  TEStylNew
          (destRect : Rect;          {Destination (wrapping) rectangle}
           viewRect : Rect)          {View (clipping) rectangle}
              : TEHandle;            {Handle to new edit record}
```

```
function  GetStylHandle
          (editRec : TEHandle)          {Handle to edit record}
              : TEStyleHandle;          {Handle to current style record}

procedure SetStylHandle
          (styleRec : TEStyleHandle;    {Handle to new style record}
           editRec  : TEHandle);        {Handle to edit record}
```

 Notes

1. TEStylNew creates a new styled edit record [7.2.2] and all of its associated data structures (style record [7.2.3], style table [7.2.4], line-height table [7.2.5], and null-style record [7.2.6]). The old TextEdit routine TENew [II:5.2.2] continues to create an unstyled edit record [II:5.1.1].

2. TEStylNew sets the new record's txSize field to -1, marking it as a styled record.

3. A handle to the new style record is stored in the edit record's txFont and txFace fields.

4. The edit record's lineHeight and fontAscent fields are both set to -1, placing vertical spacing under the control of the line-height table.

5. The destination and view rectangles are expressed in the local coordinates of the current port, normally a window in which text is to be edited. This port becomes the new edit record's graphics port.

6. The text of the new edit record is initially empty. You can give it text to edit with TESetText [II:5.2.3].

7. The style table [7.2.4] initially contains a single style with the text characteristics of the current port [I:8.3.1]. The line-height table is initialized to the height and ascent of this style.

8. All other fields of the new edit record are initialized to the same values as for an unstyled edit record [II:5.2.2].

9. The old Toolbox routine TEDispose [II:5.2.2] disposes of an edit record, whether styled or unstyled, along with its text and all other associated data structures.

10. GetStylHandle returns a styled edit record's style handle [7.2.4], taken from its txFont and txFace fields [7.2.2]. SetStylHandle assigns it a new style handle.

11. If editRec is an unstyled edit record, GetStylHandle returns NIL and SetStylHandle does nothing.

12. The trap macro for `TEStylNew` is spelled `_TEStyleNew`.

13. The trap macros for `GetStylHandle` and `SetStylHandle` expand to call the generic trap `_TEDispatch` with the routine selectors shown below.

Assembly Language Information

Trap macros and routine selectors:

(Pascal) Routine name	(Assembly) Trap macro	Trap word	Routine selector
TEStylNew	_TEStyleNew	$A83E	————
GetStylHandle	_GetStylHandle	$A83D	4
SetStylHandle	_SetStylHandle	$A83D	5

7.3.2   Character Location

Definitions

```
function   TEGetOffset
           (thePoint : Point;          {Point to be mapped, in window coordinates}
            editRec  : TEHandle)       {Handle to edit record}
              : INTEGER;               {Corresponding character index}

function   TEGetPoint
           (charIndex : INTEGER;       {Character index}
            editRec   : TEHandle)      {Handle to edit record}
              : Point;                 {Bottom-left of character in window coordinates}

function   TEGetHeight
           (lastLine  : LONGINT;       {Last line number}
            firstLine : LONGINT;       {First line number}
            editRec   : TEHandle)      {Handle to edit record}
              : LONGINT;               {Total height of lines in pixels}

procedure  CharExtra
           (extraWidth : Fixed);       {Extra character width in pixels}
```

Notes

1. `TEGetOffset` maps a given point (typically the mouse position) to the corresponding character position in an edit record's text; `TEGetPoint` maps a character position to the corresponding point.

2. TextEdit character positions fall *between* the text characters, not on them. These routines designate each character by the character position preceding it: for example, the first character in the text is at position 0. A character position equal to the length of the text is located at the very end, following the last character.

3. The point returned by `TEGetPoint` lies on the baseline at the given character position—that is, at the bottom-left of the corresponding character.

4. All points are expressed in local (window) coordinates.

5. `TEGetHeight` measures the total height of a sequence of text lines.

6. The measurement is based either on the edit record's line-height table [7.2.5] or on the uniform vertical spacing values in its `lineHeight` and `fontAscent` fields [7.2.2].

7. Line positions, like those for single characters, fall *between* the lines instead of coinciding with them. Line position 0 is at the beginning of the text; the line position at the end is equal to the edit record's `nLines` field [II:5.1.1].

8. Notice that the parameters are given in reverse order, with `lastLine` preceding `firstLine`.

9. All of these routines work for both styled and unstyled edit records.

10. `CharExtra` sets the value of the current port's `chExtra` field [5.1.3], which specifies the additional character width to be used in proportional spacing.

11. The extra character space is given in fixed-point form [I:2.3.1], with 16 bits before the binary point and 16 after it.

12. All text characters except spaces will be widened by the specified number of pixels; space characters are still governed by the `spExtra` field [I:8.3.1], as before.

13. Negative values for `extraWidth` are allowed, and will narrow all characters instead of widening them.

14. The port's `txSize` field [I:8.3.1] must already have been set to a valid value before the call to `CharExtra`.

15. `CharExtra` operates on color graphics ports [5.1.3] only; if a monochrome port [I:4.2.2] is current, it does nothing.

16. The trap macros for `TEGetPoint` and `TEGetHeight` expand to call the generic trap `_TEDispatch` with the routine selectors shown below.

Assembly Language Information

Trap macros and routine selectors:

(Pascal) Routine name	(Assembly) Trap macro	Trap word	Routine selector
TEGetOffset	_TEGetOffset	$A83C	————
TEGetPoint	_TEGetPoint	$A83D	8
TEGetHeight	_TEGetHeight	$A83D	9
CharExtra	_CharExtra	$AA23	————

7.3.3   Getting Style Information

Definitions

```
procedure TEGetStyle
            (charPos        : INTEGER;      {Character position of desired character}
             var theStyle   : TextStyle;    {Returns character's style attributes}
             var lineHeight  : INTEGER;      {Returns character's line height}
             var fontAscent  : INTEGER;      {Returns character's font ascent}
             editRec        : TEHandle);    {Handle to edit record}

function  TEContinuousStyle
            (var whichAttrs : INTEGER;      {Desired attributes; returns continuous attributes}
             var theStyle   : TextStyle;    {Values of continuous attributes}
             editRec        : TEHandle)     {Handle to edit record}
                 : BOOLEAN;                 {Are all requested attributes continuous?}

function  TENumStyles
            (startPos : LONGINT;            {Starting character position}
             endPos   : LONGINT;            {Ending character position}
             editRec  : TEHandle)           {Handle to edit record}
                 : LONGINT;                 {Number of style changes}
```

Notes

1. TEGetStyle returns the text style and vertical spacing for a single character in an edit record's text.

2. TextEdit character positions fall *between* the text characters, not on them. The desired character is designated by the character position preceding it: for example, a value of 0 for `charPos` requests the style of the first character in the text.

3. If `editRec` is an unstyled edit record [II:5.1.1], `TEGetStyle` returns its global text characteristics.

4. `TEContinuousStyle` examines selected style attributes of an edit record's text to see which of them are *continuous* (have the same uniform value) over the current selection range.

5. The edit record's `selStart` and `selEnd` fields [II:5.4.2] define the range of characters to be tested.

6. On entry, `whichAttrs` specifies which style attributes to test, using the same flag values as for `TESetStyle` or `TEReplaceStyle` [7.3.4].

7. On exit, `whichAttrs` identifies which of the requested attributes are continuous over the selection; `theStyle` contains the specific values of those attributes.

8. Only those fields of `theStyle` corresponding to continuous attributes are valid; the contents of other fields are meaningless and should be ignored.

9. The function result is `TRUE` if all of the requested attributes are continuous, `FALSE` if one or more of them are not.

10. In the case of the type-style attribute (`DoFace` [7.3.4]), the flag bit in `whichAttrs` is set if any one or more individual style variations (such as bold or italic) are continuous over the selection range, or if the entire selection is in plain style. Field `tsFace` [7.2.1] of `theStyle` returns a `Style` set [I:8.3.1] containing just those specific variations that apply to all characters in the selection. Variations not included in this set may still be present for one or more characters, but not for all of them. If the `DoFace` flag is set and `theStyle.tsFace` is empty, then the entire selection is in plain style.

11. If the current selection is an insertion point (`selStart = selEnd`), all style attributes are considered continuous. Attribute values returned in `theStyle` are those for the next character to be entered, taken from the null-style record [7.2.6] if there is one, otherwise from the style of the character preceding the insertion point.

12. `TENumStyles` returns the number of separate style runs in a specified range of characters.

13. `startPos` and `endPos` are character positions marking the beginning and end of the desired range.

14. The function result reports the number of separate *runs*, not the number of distinct *styles*. The same style may be counted more than once if it applies to two or more runs of characters separated by others in different styles.

15. The trap macros for these routines expand to call the generic trap _TEDispatch with the routine selectors shown below.

Assembly Language Information

Trap macros and routine selectors:

(Pascal) Routine name	(Assembly) Trap macro	Trap word	Routine selector
TEGetStyle	_TEGetStyle	$A83D	3
TEContinuousStyle	_TEContinuousStyle	$A83D	10
TENumStyles	_TENumStyles	$A83D	13

7.3.4 Styling Text

Definitions

```
procedure TESetStyle
          (whichAttrs : INTEGER;        {Style attributes to set}
           newStyle   : TextStyle;      {New attribute values}
           redraw     : BOOLEAN;        {Redraw after change?}
           editRec    : TEHandle);      {Handle to edit record}

procedure TEReplaceStyle
          (whichAttrs : INTEGER;        {Style attributes to replace}
           oldStyle   : TextStyle;      {Old attribute values to be replaced}
           newStyle   : TextStyle;      {New attribute values to replace them with}
           redraw     : BOOLEAN;        {Redraw after change?}
           editRec    : TEHandle);      {Handle to edit record}

const
   DoFont   =  1;                       {Set typeface}
   DoFace   =  2;                       {Set type style}
   DoSize   =  4;                       {Set type size}
   DoColor  =  8;                       {Set text color}
   DoAll    = 15;                       {All of the above}
   AddSize  = 16;                       {Adjust type size}
   DoToggle = 32;                       {Toggle existing attribute value}
```

Notes

1. TESetStyle sets the text style of an edit record's current selection; TEReplaceStyle searches the current selection for all occurrences of a given style and changes them to another.

2. whichAttrs is a word of flag bits specifying which style attributes to set or replace. The constants DoFont, DoFace, and so on represent the individual flags within this word.

3. newStyle is a text style record [7.2.1] containing the new values to be set for the designated attributes. Only those fields of this record corresponding to 1 bits in whichAttrs are used; the rest are ignored.

4. oldStyle is a text style record [7.2.1] defining the style to be replaced. Again, only those fields designated by 1 bits in whichAttrs are meaningful. All characters in the current selection whose values for these attributes match those in the oldStyle record will have them changed to the corresponding values from newStyle.

5. If the redraw parameter is TRUE, the text is redrawn in the new style.

6. If the current selection is an insertion point (selStart = selEnd), TESetStyle sets the null style [7.2.6] instead.

7. The flag constants DoFont, DoFace, DoSize, and DoColor refer to the corresponding fields of the text style record [7.2.1]. DoAll represents the combination of all four of these attributes.

8. AddSize changes the meaning of the text style's tsSize field [7.2.1]. Instead of an absolute type size, it is interpreted as an incremental adjustment (positive or negative) to be added to the existing type size of each character.

9. If both DoSize and AddSize are specified, AddSize takes precedence.

10. DoToggle modifies the operation of DoFace. For each type-style variation (bold, italic, and so on) specified by the tsFace field of newStyle, if the variation is continuous over the edit record's current selection (that is, if every character in the selection has the variation), then it is turned *off* for the entire selection. If the variation is not continuous (that is, if at least one character in the selection does not have the variation), then it is turned *on* for the entire selection.

11. If DoFace is not specified, DoToggle has no effect.

12. AddSize and DoToggle are meaningful only for TESetStyle, and are ignored by TEReplaceStyle.

13. The trap macros for these routines expand to call the generic trap _TEDispatch with the routine selectors shown below.

Assembly Language Information

Trap macros and routine selectors:

(Pascal) Routine name	(Assembly) Trap macro	Trap word	Routine selector
TESetStyle	_TESetStyle	$A83D	1
TEReplaceStyle	_TEReplaceStyle	$A83D	2

Bit numbers for style attributes:

Name	Value	Meaning
FontBit	0	Set typeface
FaceBit	1	Set type style
SizeBit	2	Set type size
ClrBit	3	Set text color
AddSizeBit	4	Adjust type size
ToglBit	5	Toggle existing attribute value

Constants for style attributes:

Name	Value	Meaning
DoFont	1	Set typeface
DoFace	2	Set type style
DoSize	4	Set type size
DoColor	8	Set text color
DoAll	15	All of the above
AddSize	16	Adjust type size
DoToggle	32	Toggle existing attribute value

7.3.5   Cutting and Pasting Styled Text

Definitions

```
procedure TECut
        (editRec : TEHandle);          {Handle to edit record}
```

```
procedure TECopy
          (editRec : TEHandle);          {Handle to edit record}

procedure TEPaste
          (editRec : TEHandle);          {Handle to edit record}

procedure TEStylPaste
          (editRec : TEHandle);          {Handle to edit record}
```

 Notes

1. In a styled edit record, the old editing routines TECut, TECopy, and TEPaste [II:5.5.2] now operate directly via the global desk scrap [I:7.4] instead of the internal Toolbox text scrap.

2. Text cut or copied to the scrap is stored under type 'TEXT' [I:8.4.1], accompanied by a style-scrap record [7.2.7] under type 'styl'.

3. TEStylPaste pastes the styled contents of the scrap into the edit record's text at the current selection range or insertion point.

4. The old routine TEPaste [II:5.5.2] pastes just the text from the scrap but ignores the style, using instead the style of the first character being replaced. If the selection is empty (an insertion point), it uses the edit record's current null style [7.2.6], if any, or the style of the character preceding the insertion point.

5. If the desk scrap does not contain a 'styl' entry, TEStylPaste is equivalent to TEPaste.

6. For backward compatibility, all text cut or copied in a styled edit record is also written to the Toolbox scrap, but without its accompanying style information.

7. Although the Toolbox and desk scraps are always in agreement for styled edit records, the old transfer routines TEFromScrap and TEToScrap [II:5.5.5] are still supported for compatibility.

8. In unstyled edit records, cutting and pasting take place via the Toolbox scrap only, as before [II:5.5.2], and TEStylPaste is equivalent to TEPaste.

9. The trap macro for TEStylPaste expands to call the generic trap _TEDispatch with the routine selectors shown below.

Assembly Language Information

Trap macros and routine selector:

(Pascal) Routine name	(Assembly) Trap macro	Trap word	Routine selector
TECut	_TECut	$A9D6	————
TECopy	_TECopy	$A9D5	————
TEPaste	_TEPaste	$A9DB	————
TEStylPaste	_TEStylPaste	$A83D	0

7.3.6   Scrapless Styling

Definitions

```
function  GetStylScrap
            (editRec : TEHandle)        {Handle to edit record}
              : StScrpHandle;           {Styles for current selection}

procedure SetStylScrap
            (startPos  : LONGINT;       {Starting character position}
             endPos    : LONGINT;       {Ending character position}
             newStyles : StScrpHandle;  {Styles to apply}
             redraw    : BOOLEAN;       {Redraw after change?}
             editRec   : TEHandle);     {Handle to edit record}

procedure TEStylInsert
            (textPtr    : Ptr;          {Pointer to insertion text}
             textLength : LONGINT;      {Length of insertion text in characters}
             textStyles : StScrpHandle; {Styles for insertion text}
             editRec    : TEHandle);    {Handle to edit record}
```

Notes

1. These routines manipulate an edit record's style information without using or affecting the contents of the scrap.

2. GetStylScrap returns a style-scrap record [7.2.7] describing the styles of the currently selected text.

3. If the current selection is empty (selStart = selEnd [II:5.1.1]) or if editRec is an unstyled edit record, the function result is NIL.

4. SetStylScrap applies the styles defined by a style-scrap record [7.2.7] to a specified range of characters.

5. If the character range from startPos to endPos is shorter than the total number of characters covered by newStyles, unused styles at the end of newStyles are ignored; if longer, the last style defined is applied to all excess characters in the range.

6. The current selection range is not affected.

7. If the redraw parameter is TRUE, the text is redrawn in the new styles.

8. If newStyles = NIL or if editRec is an unstyled edit record, SetStylScrap has no effect.

9. TEStylInsert inserts styled text at the beginning of the current selection, but without replacing the selected text. If the selection is an insertion point, the new text is inserted at that point.

10. The selection range is adjusted by the length of the insertion, so that the same characters remain selected after the operation as before.

11. textPtr is a pointer to the text to be inserted; textLength is its length in characters.

12. textStyles is a handle to a style-scrap record [7.2.7] defining the styles for the inserted text.

13. The edit record's text is automatically rewrapped to the destination rectangle and redisplayed within the view rectangle.

14. If textStyles = NIL or if editRec is an unstyled edit record, TEStylInsert is equivalent to TEInsert [II:5.5.3].

15. The trap macros for these routines expand to call the generic trap _TEDispatch with the routine selectors shown below.

Assembly Language Information

Trap macros and routine selectors:

(Pascal) Routine name	(Assembly) Trap macro	Trap word	Routine selector
GetStylScrap	_GetStylScrap	$A83D	6
SetStylScrap	_SetStylScrap	$A83D	11
TEStylInsert	_TEStylInsert	$A83D	7

7.4 Text-Related Resources

7.4.1   Resource Type 'fctb'

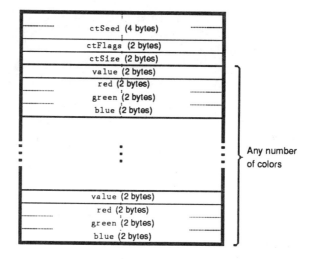

Structure of an 'fctb' resource

Notes

1. A resource of type 'fctb' defines the color table for a color font.

2. Only font resources of type 'NFNT' [I:8.4.5] can have a color table; ordinary 'FONT' resources cannot.

3. The color table ('fctb') must have the same resource ID as the font ('NFNT') itself.

4. The structure of the resource is the same as that of an ordinary color table resource of type 'clut'. All fields have the same form and meaning described in [4.4.1] and [4.7.1].

5. Fields ctSeed and ctFlags should both be 0.

6. The fontType field in the font record itself [7.1.1] defines the font's pixel depth.

7. Any color indices not explicitly defined in the 'fctb' resource are automatically assigned color values based on the foreground and background colors of the current port. The lowest-numbered missing color index is assigned to the port's background color, the highest-numbered to the foreground color, and all others to intermediate colors spaced uniformly between the two. If only one color index is missing, it is assigned to the background color.

8. For fonts that have no 'fctb' resource, all color values are assigned automatically, as described in the preceding note.

APPENDIX

A

Toolbox Summary

Chapter 2 General Utilities

2.1 System Configuration

2.1.1 Operating Environment

```
function SysEnvirons
          (whichVersion    : INTEGER;          {Desired version of environment record}
       var theEnvirons : SysEnvRec)            {Description of operating environment}
             : OSErr;                          {Result code}

type
  SysEnvRec = record
                environsVersion : INTEGER;     {Version number of environment record}
                machineType     : INTEGER;     {Model of Macintosh hardware}
                systemVersion   : INTEGER;     {Version number of System file}
                processor       : INTEGER;     {CPU type}
                hasFPU          : BOOLEAN;      {Floating-point coprocessor present?}
                hasColorQD      : BOOLEAN;      {Color QuickDraw available?}
                keyboardType    : INTEGER;     {Type of keyboard}
                atDrvrVersNum   : INTEGER;     {Version number of AppleTalk driver}
                sysVRefNum      : INTEGER      {Volume or directory containing System file}
              end;
```

```
const
   CurSysEnvVers   =  1;                  {Current version of SysEnvirons}

                                              {Machine codes: }
   EnvMachUnknown  =  0;                   {Unrecognized hardware model}
   EnvXL           = -2;                   {Macintosh XL (Lisa)}
   EnvMac          = -1;                   {Original Skinny or Fat Mac}
   Env512Ke        =  1;                   {Macintosh 512K enhanced}
   EnvMacPlus      =  2;                   {Macintosh Plus}
   EnvSE           =  3;                   {Macintosh SE}
   EnvMacII        =  4;                   {Macintosh II}
   EnvMacIIx       =  5;                   {Macintosh IIx}
   EnvMacIIcx      =  6;                   {Macintosh IIcx}
   EnvSE30         =  7;                   {Macintosh SE/30}
```

{CPU codes: }
```
   EnvCPUUnknown   =  0;                   {Unrecognized processor}
   Env68000        =  1;                   {MC68000 processor}
   Env68010        =  2;                   {MC68010 processor}
   Env68020        =  3;                   {MC68020 processor}
   Env68030        =  4;                   {MC68030 processor}
```

{Keyboard codes: }
```
   EnvUnknownKbd   =  0;                   {Unrecognized keyboard type}
   EnvMacKbd       =  1;                   {Original Macintosh keyboard}
   EnvMacAndPad    =  2;                   {Original keyboard with optional keypad}
   EnvMacPlusKbd   =  3;                   {Macintosh Plus keyboard}
   EnvAExtendKbd   =  4;                   {Apple Extended Keyboard}
   EnvStandADBKbd  =  5;                   {Standard Apple Desktop Bus keyboard}
```

{Result codes: }
```
   EnvNotPresent   = -5500;                {SysEnvirons not implemented}
   EnvBadVers      = -5501;                {Invalid version number requested}
   EnvVersTooBig   = -5502;                {Requested version not available}
```

2.1.2 DispatchTable

```
function   GetTrapAddress
              (trapNum : INTEGER)          {Trap number of desired Toolbox routine}
              : LONGINT;                   {Address of existing routine in memory}

procedure  SetTrapAddress
              (newAddr : LONGINT;          {Address of replacement routine}
               trapNum : INTEGER);         {Trap number of Toolbox routine to be replaced}

function   NGetTrapAddress
              (trapNum   : INTEGER;        {Trap number of desired Toolbox routine}
               whichType : TrapType)       {OS or Toolbox trap?}
              : LONGINT;                   {Address of existing routine in memory}

procedure  NSetTrapAddress
              (newAddr   : LONGINT;        {Address of replacement routine}
               trapNum   : INTEGER;        {Trap number of Toolbox routine to be replaced}
               whichType : TrapType);      {OS or Toolbox trap?}
```

```
type
   TrapType = (OSTrap,                          {Routine resides in OS dispatch table}
               ToolTrap);                        {Routine resides in Toolbox dispatch table}
const
   UnimplTrapNum = $9F;                          {Trap number of unimplemented Toolbox trap}
```

2.1.3 Memory Address Mode

```
function   GetMMUMode
               : SignedByte;                     {Current address mode}

procedure  SwapMMUMode
               (var addrMode : SignedByte);      {New address mode; returns previous mode}

function   StripAddress
               (longAddr : Ptr)                  {32-bit address}
               : Ptr;                            {24-bit address}
const
   False32B = 0;                                 {24-bit address mode}
   True32B  = 1;                                 {32-bit address mode}
```

2.1.4 Global Variable Access

```
procedure  SetUpA5;

procedure  RestoreA5;

function   SetA5
               (newA5 : LONGINT)                 {New value to be stored in A5}
               : LONGINT;                        {Previous contents of A5}

function   SetCurrentA5
               : LONGINT;                        {Previous contents of A5}
```

2.1.5 Shutdown and Restart

```
procedure  ShutDwnPower;

procedure  ShutDwnStart;

const
   ShutDownAlert = 42;                           {System error number of shutdown alert}
```

2.1.6 Shutdown Procedures

```
procedure  ShutDwnInstall
               (shutDownProc : ProcPtr;          {Shutdown procedure to install}
                whenToCall   : INTEGER);         {When should procedure be called?}
```

```
procedure ShutDwnRemove
          (shutDownProc : ProcPtr);        {Shutdown procedure to remove}
const
   SDOnPowerOff      = 1;                   {Call procedure before power-off}
   SDOnRestart       = 2;                   {Call procedure before restart}
   SDRestartOrPower  = 3;                   {Call procedure before power-off or restart}
   SDOnUnmount       = 4;                   {Call procedure before unmounting volumes}
   SDOnDrivers       = 8;                   {Call procedure before closing drivers}
```

2.2 Memory

2.2.2 Memory Allocation

```
function  NewHandleClear
          (blockSize : Size)               {Size of needed block in bytes}
              : Handle;                     {Handle to new relocatable block}
function  NewHandleSys
          (blockSize : Size)               {Size of needed block in bytes}
              : Handle;                     {Handle to new relocatable block}
function  NewHandleSysClear
          (blockSize : Size)               {Size of needed block in bytes}
              : Handle;                     {Handle to new relocatable block}
function  NewPtrClear
          (blockSize : Size)               {Size of needed block in bytes}
              : Ptr;                        {Pointer to new nonrelocatable block}
function  NewPtrSys
          (blockSize : Size)               {Size of needed block in bytes}
              : Ptr;                        {Pointer to new nonrelocatable block}
function  NewPtrSysClear
          (blockSize : Size)               {Size of needed block in bytes}
              : Ptr;                        {Pointer to new nonrelocatable block}
```

2.2.3 Temporary Allocation

```
function  MFTempNewHandle
          (blockSize      : Size;          {Size of needed block in bytes}
           var resultCode : OSErr)         {Result code}
              : Handle;                     {Handle to temporary relocatable block}
procedure MFTempDisposHandle
          (theHandle      : Handle;        {Handle to temporary block to be deallocated}
           var resultCode : OSErr);        {Result code}
procedure MFTempHLock
          (theHandle      : Handle;        {Handle to temporary block to be locked}
           var resultCode : OSErr);        {Result code}
```

```
procedure MFTempHUnlock
            (theHandle      : Handle;         {Handle to temporary block to be unlocked}
             var resultCode : OSErr);         {Result code}
```

2.2.4 Available Temporary Space

```
function MFFreeMem
              : LONGINT;                      {Total bytes available for temporary allocation}

function MFMaxMem
           (var growBytes : Size)             {Returns maximum bytes for temporary expansion}
              : Size;                         {Size of largest available temporary block}

function MFTopMem
              : Ptr;                          {Pointer to end of memory}
```

2.3 Resources

2.3.2 ROM-Based Resources

```
function RGetResource
            (rsrcType : ResType;              {Resource type}
             rsrcID   : INTEGER)              {Resource ID}
              : Handle;                       {Handle to resource}
```

2.4 Arithmetic

2.4.1 Small Fractions

```
type
   SmallFract = INTEGER;

const
   MaxSmallFract = $0000FFFF;                 {Largest possible small fraction}

function Fix2SmallFract
            (theNumber : Fixed)               {Fixed-point number to be converted}
              : SmallFract;                   {Equivalent small fraction}

function SmallFract2Fix
            (theNumber : SmallFract)          {Small fraction to be converted}
              : Fixed;                        {Equivalent fixed-point number}
```

Chapter 3 Events

3.1 Events

3.1.1 Event Messages

```
const
  ADBAddrMask   = $00FF0000;          {Mask for ADB address}
  KeyCodeMask   = $0000FF00;          {Mask for key code}
  CharCodeMask  = $000000FF;          {Mask for character code}
```

3.1.2 Event Modifiers

```
const
  ControlKey = $1000;          {Control key}
  OptionKey  = $0800;          {Option key}
  AlphaLock  = $0400;          {Caps Lock key}
  ShiftKey   = $0200;          {Shift key}
  CmdKey     = $0100;          {Command key}

  BtnState   = $0080;          {Mouse button}

  ActiveFlag = $0001;          {Activate or deactivate event?}
```

3.1.3 Retrieving Events

```
function WaitNextEvent
            (mask         : INTEGER;       {Mask designating event types of interest}
         var theEvent : EventRecord;       {Returns information about event}
             sleepTicks   : LONGINT;       {Length of time to suspend program, in ticks}
             mouseRgn     : RgnHandle)     {Mouse-tracking region in global coordinates}
                 : BOOLEAN;                {Should application respond to event?}
```

3.2 Notifications

3.2.1 Notification Records

```
type
  NMRec = record
            qLink      : QElemPtr;        {Pointer to next queue element}
            qType      : INTEGER;         {Queue type (= NMType)}
            nmFlags    : INTEGER;         {Private}
            nmPrivate  : LONGINT;         {Private}
            nmReserved : INTEGER;         {Private}
            nmMark     : INTEGER;         {Item to mark on Apple menu}
            nmSIcon    : Handle;          {Handle to small icon to display in menu bar}
            nmSound    : Handle;          {Handle to sound to be played}
            nmStr      : StringPtr;       {Pointer to text to display in alert box}
            nmResp     : ProcPtr;         {Pointer to response procedure}
            nmRefCon   : LONGINT          {Reference constant for application use}
          end;

const
  NMType = 8;                            {Queue type for a notification queue}
```

3.2.2 Posting Notifications

```
function NMInstall
         (theRequest : QElemPtr)         {Pointer to notification request}
             : OSErr;                    {Result code}

function NMRemove
         (theRequest : QElemPtr)         {Pointer to notification request}
             : OSErr;                    {Result code}

const
  NMTypeErr = -299;                      {Wrong queue type}
  QErr      =   -1;                      {Element not found in queue}
```

3.2.3 Response Procedures

```
procedure YourResponse
         (theRequest : QElemPtr);        {Pointer to notification request}
```

Chapter 4 Color Fundamentals

4.1 Classic Color Model

4.1.1 Color Values

```
const
                                    {Bit numbers for color planes: }
    NormalBit  = 0;                     {Normal monochrome (black-on-white)}
    InverseBit = 1;                     {Inverse monochrome (white-on-black)}

    BlueBit    = 2;                 {Blue}
    GreenBit   = 3;                 {Green}
    RedBit     = 4;                 {Red}

    BlackBit   = 5;                 {Black}
    YellowBit  = 6;                 {Yellow}
    MagentaBit = 7;                 {Magenta}
    CyanBit    = 8;                 {Cyan}

                                    {Color values for drawing operations: }
    BlackColor    = $0021;          {Black}
    WhiteColor    = $001E;          {White}

    RedColor      = $00CD;          {Red}
    GreenColor    = $0155;          {Green}
    BlueColor     = $0199;          {Blue}

    CyanColor     = $0111;          {Cyan}
    MagentaColor  = $0089;          {Magenta}
    YellowColor   = $0045;          {Yellow}
```

4.1.2 Foreground and Background Colors

```
type
    GrafPort = record
                . . . ;
                fgColor : LONGINT;      {Current foreground color}
                bkColor : LONGINT;      {Current background color}
                . . .
            end;
procedure ForeColor
            (newColor : LONGINT);       {New foreground color}

procedure BackColor
            (newColor : LONGINT);       {New background color}
```

4.1.3 Color Planes

```
type
  GrafPort = record
                . . . ;
                colrBit : INTEGER;          {Current color plane}
                . . .
            end;

procedure ColorBit
          (whichPlane : INTEGER);           {New color plane}
```

4.2   Color Representation

4.2.1 Color Formats

```
type
  RGBColor = record
                red   : INTEGER;            {Level of red component}
                green : INTEGER;            {Level of green component}
                blue  : INTEGER             {Level of blue component}
            end;

  CMYColor = record
                cyan    : SmallFract;       {Level of cyan component}
                magenta : SmallFract;       {Level of magenta component}
                yellow  : SmallFract        {Level of yellow component}
            end;

  HSVColor = record
                hue        : SmallFract;    {Hue}
                saturation : SmallFract;    {Saturation}
                value      : SmallFract     {Value (brightness)}
            end;

  HSLColor = record
                hue        : SmallFract;    {Hue}
                saturation : SmallFract;    {Saturation}
                lightness  : SmallFract     {Lightness}
            end;
```

4.2.2 Color Conversion

```
procedure RGB2CMY
          (fromColor   : RGBColor;          {Color to be converted, in RGB format}
       var toColor     : CMYColor);         {Equivalent color in CMY format}

procedure CMY2RGB
          (fromColor   : CMYColor;          {Color to be converted, in CMY format}
       var toColor     : RGBColor);         {Equivalent color in RGB format}
```

```
procedure RGB2HSV
            (fromColor    : RGBColor;          {Color to be converted, in RGB format}
         var toColor : HSVColor);              {Equivalent color in HSV format}
procedure HSV2RGB
            (fromColor    : HSVColor;          {Color to be converted, in HSV format}
         var toColor : RGBColor);              {Equivalent color in RGB format}
procedure RGB2HSL
            (fromColor    : RGBColor;          {Color to be converted, in RGB format}
         var toColor : HSLColor);              {Equivalent color in HSL format}
procedure HSL2RGB
            (fromColor    : HSLColor;          {Color to be converted, in HSL format}
         var toColor : RGBColor);              {Equivalent color in RGB format}
```

4.2.3 The Color Picker

```
function GetColor
            (topLeft          : Point;         {Top-left corner of dialog in screen coordinates}
            promptString     : Str255;         {Prompting string}
            startColor       : RGBColor;       {Initial color to propose in dialog box}
         var pickedColor : RGBColor)           {Returns color selected by user}
                          : BOOLEAN;           {Did user confirm color selection?}
```

4.3 Graphics Devices

4.3.1 Device Records

```
type
   GDHandle = ^GDPtr;
   GDPtr    = ^GDevice;

   GDevice = record
            gdRefNum     : INTEGER;        {Driver reference number}
            gdID         : INTEGER;        {Client ID for matching routines [4.6.2]}
            gdType       : INTEGER;        {Device type}
            gdITable     : ITabHandle;     {Inverse table [4.4.2]}
            gdResPref    : INTEGER;        {Preferred inverse table resolution [4.4.2]}
            gdSearchProc : SProcHndl;      {List of custom search functions [4.6.1]}
            gdCompProc   : CProcHndl;      {List of custom complement procedures [4.6.1]}
            gdFlags      : INTEGER;        {Attribute flags [4.3.5]}
            gdPMap       : PixMapHandle;   {Pixel map to hold displayed image}
            gdRefCon     : LONGINT;        {CalcCMask and SeedCFill parameters [5.4.5]}
            gdNextGD     : GDHandle;       {Next device in device list}
            gdRect       : Rect;           {Boundary rectangle}
            gdMode       : LONGINT;        {Current display mode}
```

```
            gdCCBytes    : INTEGER;        {Private}
            gdCCDepth    : INTEGER;        {Private}
            gdCCXData    : Handle;         {Private}
            gdCCXMask    : Handle;         {Private}
            gdReserved   : LONGINT         {Reserved for future expansion}
        end;
const
  CLUTType    = 0;                         {Mapped device with color lookup table}
  FixedType   = 1;                         {Fixed device, no lookup table}
  DirectType  = 2;                         {Direct RGB device}
```

4.3.2 Creating and Destroying Devices

```
function  NewGDevice
            (dRefNum  : INTEGER;           {Driver reference number}
             initMode : LONGINT)           {Initial display mode}
               : GDHandle;                 {Handle to device record}

procedure InitGDevice
            (dRefNum    : INTEGER;         {Driver reference number}
             newMode    : LONGINT;         {New display mode}
             theDevice  : GDHandle);       {Handle to device record}

procedure DisposGDevice
            (theDevice  : GDHandle);       {Handle to device record}
```

4.3.3 Device List

```
function GetDeviceList
               : GDHandle;                 {First device in list}

function GetNextDevice
            (thisDevice : GDHandle)        {Handle to a device}
               : GDHandle;                 {Next device in list}
```

4.3.4 Current Device

```
procedure SetGDevice
            (newDevice : GDHandle);        {Handle to device to be made current}

function  GetGDevice
               : GDHandle;                 {Handle to current device}

function  GetMaxDevice
            (globalRect : Rect)            {Rectangle to intersect with, in global coordinates}
               : GDHandle;                 {Deepest device that intersects with this rectangle}

function  GetMainDevice
               : GDHandle;                 {Handle to main device}
```

4.3.5 Device Attributes

```
function  TestDeviceAttribute
            (theDevice : GDHandle;        {Handle to device record}
             whichAttr : INTEGER)         {Bit number of desired attribute}
            : BOOLEAN;                    {Current value of attribute}

procedure SetDeviceAttribute
            (theDevice : GDHandle;        {Handle to device record}
             whichAttr : INTEGER;         {Bit number of desired attribute}
             newValue  : BOOLEAN);        {New value of attribute}

const
  GDDevType    =  0;                      {Supports color}
  RAMInit      = 10;                      {Initialized from RAM}
  MainScreen   = 11;                      {Is main device (contains menu bar)}
  AllInit      = 12;                      {Initialized from a 'scrn' resource}
  ScreenDevice = 13;                      {Is a screen device}
  NoDriver     = 14;                      {Has no driver}
  ScreenActive = 15;                      {Available for drawing}
```

4.4   Color Tables

4.4.1 Color Table Structure

```
type
  CTabHandle = ^CTabPtr;
  CTabPtr    = ^ColorTable;
  ColorTable = record
                 ctSeed  : LONGINT;       {Seed value for coordinating inverse table}
                 ctFlags : INTEGER;       {Attribute flags}
                 ctSize  : INTEGER;       {Number of entries minus 1}
                 ctTable : CSpecArray     {Array of color specifications}
               end;

  CSpecArray = array [0..0] of ColorSpec;
  ColorSpec  = record
                 value : INTEGER;         {Color index}
                 rgb   : RGBColor         {True color value}
               end;
```

4.4.2 Inverse Tables

```
type
  ITabHandle = ^ITabPtr;
  ITabPtr    = ^ITab;
  ITab       = record
                   iTabSeed : LONGINT;          {Seed value}
                   iTabRes  : INTEGER;          {Bit resolution}
                   itTable  : array [0..0] of SignedByte  {Array of color indices}
               end;

procedure MakeITable
            (colorTab   : CTabHandle;       {Handle to color table}
             inverseTab : ITabHandle;       {Handle to inverse table}
             bitRes     : INTEGER);         {Desired bit resolution}
```

4.4.3 Creating and Destroying Color Tables

```
function  GetCTable
            (cTabID : INTEGER)              {Resource ID of color table resource}
               : CTabHandle;                {Handle to new color table}

function  GetCTSeed
               : LONGINT;                   {Seed value for color table}

procedure DisposCTable
            (theTable : CTabHandle);        {Handle to color table to destroy}
```

4.4.4 Color Mapping

```
procedure Index2Color
            (theIndex     : LONGINT;        {Color index}
             var theColor : RGBColor);      {Returns corresponding color value}

function  Color2Index
            (theColor : RGBColor)           {Color value}
               : LONGINT;                   {Corresponding color index}

function  RealColor
            (theColor : RGBColor)           {Color value}
               : BOOLEAN;                   {Exact match available?}

procedure InvertColor
            (var theColor : RGBColor);      {Color to be inverted; returns complement}

procedure GetSubtable
            (theSubtable : CTabHandle;      {Subtable of matched colors}
             iTabRes     : INTEGER;         {Bit resolution for matching}
             sourceTable : CTabHandle);     {Color table to be searched}
```

4.4.5 Color Table Management

```
procedure SetEntries
          (startIndex : INTEGER;          {First color index to be set}
           nEntries   : INTEGER;          {Number of colors minus 1}
           newColors  : CSpecArray);      {Array of color specifications}
procedure SaveEntries
          (mainTable         : CTabHandle; {Color table to copy from}
           saveTable         : CTabHandle; {Color table to copy to}
           var whichEntries  : ReqListRec); {List of entries to copy}
procedure RestoreEntries
          (saveTable         : CTabHandle; {Color table to copy from}
           mainTable         : CTabHandle; {Color table to copy to}
           var whichEntries  : ReqListRec); {List of entries to copy}
type
  ReqListRec = record
                 reqLSize : INTEGER;                  {Number of entries to copy}
                 reqLData : array [0..0] of INTEGER   {Array of index numbers}
               end;
```

4.4.6 Protecting and Reserving Entries

```
procedure ProtectEntry
          (colorIndex : INTEGER;          {Color index}
           onOrOff    : BOOLEAN);         {Protect or release?}
procedure ReserveEntry
          (colorIndex : INTEGER;          {Color index}
           onOrOff    : BOOLEAN);         {Reserve or relinquish?}
```

4.5   Color Palettes

4.5.1 Palette Records

```
type
  PaletteHandle = ^PalettePtr;
  PalettePtr    = ^Palette;
  Palette       = record
                    pmEntries   : INTEGER;                     {Number of colors}
                    pmDataFields : array [0..6] of INTEGER;    {Private}
                    pmInfo      : array [0..0] of ColorInfo    {Array of colors}
                  end;
```

```
ColorInfo = record
                ciRGB        : RGBColor;              {RGB color value}
                ciUsage      : INTEGER;               {Usage level}
                ciTolerance  : INTEGER;               {Color tolerance}
                ciDataFields : array [0..2] of INTEGER {Private}
            end;
const
    PMCourteous = 0;                      {Courteous color}
    PMDithered  = 1;                      {Dithered color (not yet implemented)}
    PMTolerant  = 2;                      {Tolerant color}
    PMAnimated  = 4;                      {Animated color}
    PMExplicit  = 8;                      {Explicit color}
```

4.5.2 Initializing the Toolbox for Palettes

```
procedure InitPalettes;
```

4.5.3 Creating and Destroying Palettes

```
function  NewPalette
                (nEntries        : INTEGER;       {Number of colors in palette}
                 entryColors     : CTabHandle;    {Table of colors}
                 entryUsage      : INTEGER;       {Usage level for all entries}
                 entryTolerance : INTEGER)        {Tolerance value for all entries}
                    : PaletteHandle;              {Handle to new palette}

function  GetNewPalette
                (paletteID : INTEGER)             {Resource ID of palette}
                    : PaletteHandle;              {Handle to new palette}

procedure DisposePalette
                (thePalette : PaletteHandle);     {Handle to palette to be destroyed}
```

4.5.4 Setting Palette Colors

```
procedure GetEntryColor
                (thePalette    : PaletteHandle;    {Handle to palette}
                 entryIndex    : INTEGER;          {Palette index of desired entry}
                 var entryColor : RGBColor);       {Returns current color value}

procedure SetEntryColor
                (thePalette : PaletteHandle;       {Handle to palette}
                 entryIndex : INTEGER;             {Palette index of desired entry}
                 newColor   : RGBColor);           {New color value}

procedure GetEntryUsage
                (thePalette          : PaletteHandle; {Handle to palette}
                 entryIndex          : INTEGER;       {Palette index of desired entry}
                 var entryUsage      : INTEGER;       {Returns current usage level}
                 var entryTolerance : INTEGER);      {Returns current tolerance value}
```

```
procedure  SetEntryUsage
            (thePalette   : PaletteHandle;    {Handle to palette}
             entryIndex   : INTEGER;          {Palette index of desired entry}
             newUsage     : INTEGER;          {New usage level}
             newTolerance : INTEGER);         {New tolerance value}
```

4.5.5 Palette Conversion

```
procedure  CTab2Palette
            (fromCTab       : CTabHandle;      {Color table to convert from}
             toPalette      : PaletteHandle;   {Palette to convert to}
             entryUsage     : INTEGER;         {Usage level for all entries}
             entryTolerance : INTEGER);        {Tolerance value for all entries}
procedure  Palette2CTab
            (fromPalette : PaletteHandle;      {Palette to convert from}
             toCTab      : CTabHandle);        {Color table to convert to}
procedure  CopyPalette
            (fromPalette : PaletteHandle;      {Palette to copy from}
             toPalette   : PaletteHandle;      {Palette to copy to}
             fromEntry   : INTEGER;            {Index of first entry to copy from}
             toEntry     : INTEGER;            {Index of first entry to copy to}
             nEntries    : INTEGER);           {Number of entries to copy}
```

4.6   Nuts and Bolts

4.6.1 Custom Matching Routines

```
type
  SProcHndl = ^SProcPtr;
  SProcPtr  = ^SProcRec;
  SProcRec  = record
                nxtSrch  : Handle;     {Handle to next list element}
                srchProc : ProcPtr     {Pointer to search function}
              end;

  CProcHndl = ^CProcPtr;
  CProcPtr  = ^CProcRec;
  CProcRec  = record
                nxtComp  : CProcHndl;  {Handle to next list element}
                compProc : ProcPtr     {Pointer to complement procedure}
              end;
function   YourSearchProc
            (colorValue     : RGBColor;   {Color to be matched}
         var colorIndex : LONGINT)        {Returns corresponding color index}
               : BOOLEAN;                 {Was color matched?}
```

```
procedure YourCompProc
            (var colorValue : RGBColor);    {Color to be inverted; returns complement}
```

4.6.2 Installing Matching Routines

```
procedure AddSearch
            (searchFunc : ProcPtr);         {Search function to be added}
procedure AddComp
            (compProc : ProcPtr);           {Complement procedure to be added}
procedure DelSearch
            (searchFunc : ProcPtr);         {Search function to be deleted}
procedure DelComp
            (compProc : ProcPtr);           {Complement procedure to be deleted}
procedure SetClientID
            (clientID : INTEGER);           {Client ID to be set}
```

4.7 Color-Related Resources

4.7.1 Resource type 'clut'

```
const
   DefQDColors = 127;                       {Resource ID of "classic QuickDraw" color table}
```

Chapter 5 Color Drawing

5.1 Graphical Foundations

5.1.1 Pixel Maps

```
type
   PixMapHandle = ^PixMapPtr;
   PixMapPtr    = ^PixMap;

   PixMap       = record
                     baseAddr   : Ptr;       {Pointer to pixel image}
                     rowBytes   : INTEGER;   {Row width in bytes}
                     bounds     : Rect;      {Boundary rectangle}
                     pmVersion  : INTEGER;   {Color QuickDraw version number}
                     packType   : INTEGER;   {Format of packed image}
                     packSize   : LONGINT;   {Size of packed image in bytes}
                     hRes       : Fixed;     {Horizontal resolution in pixels per inch}
                     vRes       : Fixed;     {Vertical resolution in pixels per inch}
```

```
           pixelType   : INTEGER;        {Storage format}
           pixelSize   : INTEGER;        {Physical pixel size in bits}
           cmpCount    : INTEGER;        {Number of color planes}
           cmpSize     : INTEGER;        {Logical pixel size per plane, in bits}
           planeBytes  : LONGINT;        {Plane offset in bytes}
           pmTable     : CTabHandle;     {Handle to color table}
           pmReserved  : LONGINT         {Reserved for future expansion}
       end;
```

5.1.2 Creating and Destroying Pixel Maps

```
function   NewPixMap
             : PixMapHandle;             {Handle to new pixel map}

procedure CopyPixMap
         (fromPix : PixMapHandle;        {Pixel map to be copied}
          toPix   : PixMapHandle);       {Pixel map to copy it to}

procedure SetPortPix
         (thePix : PixMapHandle);        {New pixel map for current port}

procedure DisposPixMap
         (thePix : PixMapHandle);        {Pixel map to be destroyed}
```

5.1.3 Color Graphics Ports

```
type
   CGrafPtr  = ^CGrafPort;

   CGrafPort = record
             device      : INTEGER;       {Device code for font selection [I:8.3.1]}
             portPixMap  : PixMapHandle;  {Pixel map for this port [5.1.1]}
             portVersion : INTEGER;       {Color QuickDraw version number}
             grafVars    : Handle;        {Handle to auxiliary port record [5.1.4]}
             chExtra     : INTEGER;       {Extra character width}
             pnLocHFrac  : INTEGER;       {Fractional pen location}
             portRect    : Rect;          {Port rectangle}
             visRgn      : RgnHandle;     {Visible region}
             clipRgn     : RgnHandle;     {Clipping region}
             bkPixPat    : PixPatHandle;  {Background pixel pattern [5.2.1]}
             rgbFgColor  : RGBColor;      {RGB value of foreground color [5.4.1]}
             rgbBkColor  : RGBColor;      {RGB value of background color [5.4.1]}
             pnLoc       : Point;         {Current pen location [I:5.2.1]}
             pnSize      : Point;         {Dimensions of graphics pen [I:5.2.1]}
             pnMode      : INTEGER;       {Transfer mode for graphics pen [5.3.1]}
             pnPixPat    : PixPatHandle;  {Pixel pattern for line drawing [5.2.1]}
             fillPixPat  : PixPatHandle;  {Pixel pattern for area fill [5.2.1]}
             pnVis       : INTEGER;       {Pen visibility level [I:5.2.3]}
             txFont      : INTEGER;       {Font number for text [I:8.2.1, I:8.3.1]}
             txFace      : Style;         {Type style for text [I:8.3.1]}
             txMode      : INTEGER;       {Transfer mode for text [5.3.1, I:8.3.1]}
             txSize      : INTEGER;       {Type size for text [I:8.3.1]}
```

```
            spExtra     : Fixed;           {Extra space between words [I:8.3.1]}
            fgColor     : LONGINT;         {Color index of foreground color [5.4.1]}
            bkColor     : LONGINT;         {Color index of background color [5.4.1]}
            colrBit     : INTEGER;         {Current color plane [4.1.3]}
            patStretch  : INTEGER;         {Private}
            picSave     : Handle;          {Private}
            rgnSave     : Handle;          {Private}
            polySave    : Handle;          {Private}
            grafProcs   : QDProcsPtr       {Pointer to bottleneck procedures [5.5.1]}
        end;
```

5.1.4 Auxiliary Port Record

```
type
  GVarHandle = ^GVarPtr;
  GVarPtr    = ^GrafVars;

  GrafVars   = record
            rgbOpColor     : RGBColor;     {Reference color for transfer modes}
            rgbHiliteColor : RGBColor;     {Highlighting color}
            pmFgColor      : Handle;       {Palette containing foreground color}
            pmFgIndex      : INTEGER;      {Palette index of foreground color}
            pmBkColor      : Handle;       {Palette containing background color}
            pmBkIndex      : INTEGER;      {Palette index of background color}
            pmFlags        : INTEGER       {Private flags for palette usage}
        end;
```

5.1.5 Creating and Destroying Color Ports

```
procedure OpenCPort
        (whichPort : CGrafPtr);           {Pointer to port to open}

procedure InitCPort
        (whichPort : CGrafPtr);           {Pointer to port to initialize}

procedure CloseCPort
        (whichPort : CGrafPtr);           {Pointer to port to close}
```

5.1.6 Pixel Access

```
procedure GetCPixel
        (hCoord         : INTEGER;        {Horizontal coordinate of pixel}
         vCoord         : INTEGER;        {Vertical coordinate of pixel}
         var pixelColor : RGBColor);      {Returns current color of pixel}

procedure SetCPixel
        (hCoord     : INTEGER;            {Horizontal coordinate of pixel}
         vCoord     : INTEGER;            {Vertical coordinate of pixel}
         pixelColor : RGBColor);          {Desired new color of pixel}
```

5.1.7 Error Reporting

```
function QDError
            : INTEGER;                          {Result code of last QuickDraw or color operation}
const
    NoErr      =     0;                         {No error; all is well}
    CMatchErr  = -150;                          {Unable to match requested color}
    CTempMemErr = -151;                         {Unable to allocate temporary memory}
    CNoMemErr  = -152;                          {Unable to allocate memory}
    CRangeErr  = -153;                          {Color index out of range}
    CProtectErr = -154;                         {Color table protection violation}
    CDevErr    = -155;                          {Invalid type for graphics device}
    CResErr    = -156;                          {Invalid resolution for inverse table}
```

5.2   Pixel Patterns

5.2.1 Pixel Pattern Structure

```
type
    PixPatHandle = ^PixPatPtr;
    PixPatPtr    = ^PixPat;
    PixPat       = record
                      patType   : INTEGER;        {Pattern type}
                      patMap    : PixMapHandle;   {Characteristics of pixel image}
                      patData   : Handle;         {Pixel image}
                      patXData  : Handle;         {Expanded pixel image}
                      patXValid : INTEGER;        {Is expanded image valid?}
                      patXMap   : Handle;         {Characteristics of expanded image}
                      pat1Data  : Pattern         {Bit pattern for old-style ports}
                   end;
```

5.2.2 Creating and Destroying Pixel Patterns

```
function   NewPixPat
             : PixPatHandle;                      {Handle to new pixel pattern}
function   GetPixPat
           (patternID : INTEGER)                  {Resource ID of desired pixel pattern}
             : PixPatHandle;                      {Handle to pattern in memory}
procedure  DisposPixPat
           (thePixPat : PixPatHandle);            {Pixel pattern to be destroyed}
```

5.2.3 Filling Pixel Patterns

```
procedure MakeRGBPat
         (toPixPat  : PixPatHandle;      {Pixel pattern to be filled}
          fromColor : RGBColor);         {Color value to be approximated}
procedure CopyPixPat
         (fromPixPat : PixPatHandle;     {Pixel pattern to be copied}
          toPixPat   : PixPatHandle);    {Pixel pattern to copy it to}
```

5.2.4 Using Pixel Patterns

```
procedure PenPixPat
         (newPenPat : PixPatHandle);     {New pen pattern}
procedure BackPixPat
         (newBackPat : PixPatHandle);    {New background pattern}
procedure SetDeskCPat
         (newDeskPat : PixPatHandle);    {New desk pattern}
```

5.3   Color Transfer Modes

5.3.1 Mode Constants

```
const
  Blend        = 32;       {Blend colors [5.3.3]}
  AddPin       = 33;       {Add with maximum [5.3.2]}
  AddOver      = 34;       {Add with wraparound [5.3.2]}
  SubPin       = 35;       {Subtract with minimum [5.3.2]}
  Transparent  = 36;       {Copy with transparency [5.3.4]}
  ADMax        = 37;       {Arithmetic maximum [5.3.3]}
  SubOver      = 38;       {Subtract with wraparound [5.3.2]}
  ADMin        = 39;       {Arithmetic minimum [5.3.3]}
  Hilite       = 50;       {Highlight background [5.3.4]}
```

5.3.2 Additive and Subtractive Modes

```
const
  AddOver = 34;            {Add with wraparound}
  AddPin  = 33;            {Add with maximum}
  SubOver = 38;            {Subtract with wraparound}
  SubPin  = 35;            {Subtract with minimum}
procedure OpColor
         (newColor : RGBColor);      {Color to pin to}
```

5.3.3 Comparative and Combinative Modes

```
const
  ADMax = 37;                        {Arithmetic maximum}
  ADMin = 39;                        {Arithmetic minimum}
  Blend = 32;                        {Blend colors}
```

5.3.4 Transparency and Highlighting

```
const
  Transparent = 36;                  {Copy with transparency}
  Hilite    = 50;                    {Highlight background}

  HiliteMode  = $938;                {Address of highlighting flag}
  PHiliteBit  =    0;                {Bit number of highlight bit for BitClr [I:2.2.1]}

procedure HiliteColor
        (newColor : RGBColor);       {New highlight color}
```

5.4   Color Drawing Operations

5.4.1 Foreground and Background Colors

```
procedure GetForeColor
        (var theColor : RGBColor);     {Current foreground color}
procedure GetBackColor
        (var theColor : RGBColor);     {Current background color}
procedure RGBForeColor
        (newColor : RGBColor);         {New foreground color}
procedure RGBBackColor
        (newColor : RGBColor);         {New background color}
procedure PMForeColor
        (paletteEntry : INTEGER);      {Palette index of new foreground color}
procedure PMBackColor
        (paletteEntry : INTEGER);      {Palette index of new background color}
```

5.4.2 Shape Drawing

```
procedure FillCRect
        (theRect : Rect;               {Rectangle to be filled}
         fillPat : PixPatHandle);      {Pixel pattern to fill with}
procedure FillCRoundRect
        (theRect      : Rect;          {Body of rectangle}
         cornerWidth  : INTEGER;       {Width of corner oval}
         cornerHeight : INTEGER;       {Height of corner oval}
         fillPat      : PixPatHandle); {Pixel pattern to fill with}
```

```
procedure FillCOval
          (inRect  : Rect;                    {Rectangle defining oval}
           fillPat : PixPatHandle);           {Pixel pattern to fill with}
procedure FillCArc
          (inRect     : Rect;                 {Rectangle defining oval}
           startAngle : INTEGER;              {Starting angle}
           arcAngle   : INTEGER;              {Extent of arc}
           fillPat    : PixPatHandle);        {Pixel pattern to fill with}
procedure FillCPoly
          (thePolygon : PolyHandle;           {Handle to polygon to be filled}
           fillPat    : PixPatHandle);        {Pixel pattern to fill with}
procedure FillCRgn
          (theRegion : RgnHandle;             {Handle to region to be filled}
           fillPat   : PixPatHandle);         {Pixel pattern to fill with}
```

5.4.3 Color Table Animation

```
procedure AnimateEntry
          (inWindow     : WindowPtr;          {Window the palette belongs to}
           paletteIndex : INTEGER;            {Palette index of entry to be set}
           newColor     : RGBColor);          {Color to set it to}
procedure AnimatePalette
          (inWindow   : WindowPtr;            {Window the palette belongs to}
           newColors  : CTabHandle;           {Color table containing new color values}
           firstColor : INTEGER;              {Color table index of first new color}
           firstEntry : INTEGER;              {Palette index of first entry to be set}
           nColors    : INTEGER);             {Number of entries to be set}
```

5.4.4 Low-Level Pixel Transfer

```
procedure CopyBits
          (sourceMap  : BitMap;               {Bit or pixel map to copy from}
           destMap    : BitMap;               {Bit or pixel map to copy to}
           sourceRect : Rect;                 {Rectangle to copy from}
           destRect   : Rect;                 {Rectangle to copy to}
           transMode  : INTEGER;              {Transfer mode}
           clipTo     : RgnHandle);           {Region to clip to}
procedure CopyMask
          (sourceMap  : BitMap;               {Bit or pixel map to copy from}
           maskMap    : BitMap;               {Bit map containing mask}
           destMap    : BitMap;               {Bit or pixel map to copy to}
           sourceRect : Rect;                 {Rectangle to copy from}
           maskRect   : Rect;                 {Rectangle containing mask}
           destRect   : Rect);                {Rectangle to copy to}
```

5.4.5 Special Operations

```
procedure CalcCMask
         (sourceMap   : BitMap;        {Bit or pixel map to operate on}
          maskMap     : BitMap;        {Bit map to hold result mask}
          sourceRect  : Rect;          {Rectangle to operate on}
          maskRect    : Rect;          {Rectangle to hold result mask}
          edgeColor   : RGBColor;      {Color defining edge of masked region}
          searchFunc  : ProcPtr;       {Pointer to custom search function}
          searchParam : LONGINT);      {Parameter for custom search function}

procedure SeedCFill
         (sourceBits  : BitMap;        {Bit or pixel map to operate on}
          maskBits    : BitMap;        {Bit map to hold result mask}
          sourceRect  : Rect;          {Rectangle to operate on}
          maskRect    : Rect;          {Rectangle to hold result mask}
          seedHoriz   : INTEGER;       {Horizontal coordinate of starting point}
          seedVert    : INTEGER;       {Vertical coordinate of starting point}
          searchFunc  : ProcPtr;       {Pointer to custom search function}
          searchParam : LONGINT);      {Parameter for custom search function}

type
  MatchRec = record
               red       : INTEGER;    {Red component of seed or edge color}
               green     : INTEGER;    {Green component of seed or edge color}
               blue      : INTEGER;    {Blue component of seed or edge color}
               matchData : LONGINT     {Value passed for searchParam}
             end;
```

5.5 Nuts and Bolts

5.5.1 Color Bottleneck

```
type
  CQDProcsPtr = ^CQDProcs;

  CQDProcs    = record
                  textProc    : Ptr;   {Draw text}
                  lineProc    : Ptr;   {Draw lines}
                  rectProc    : Ptr;   {Draw rectangles}
                  rRectProc   : Ptr;   {Draw rounded rectangles}
                  ovalProc    : Ptr;   {Draw ovals}
                  arcProc     : Ptr;   {Draw arcs and wedges}
                  polyProc    : Ptr;   {Draw polygons}
                  rgnProc     : Ptr;   {Draw regions}
                  bitsProc    : Ptr;   {Copy bit images}
                  commentProc : Ptr;   {Process picture comments}
                  txMeasProc  : Ptr;   {Measure text}
                  getPicProc  : Ptr;   {Retrieve picture definitions}
                  putPicProc  : Ptr;   {Save picture definitions}
```

```
            opCodeProc   : Ptr;      {Process unknown picture operation}
            newProc1     : Ptr;      {Reserved for future expansion}
            newProc2     : Ptr;      {Reserved for future expansion}
            newProc3     : Ptr;      {Reserved for future expansion}
            newProc4     : Ptr;      {Reserved for future expansion}
            newProc5     : Ptr;      {Reserved for future expansion}
            newProc6     : Ptr       {Reserved for future expansion}
        end;
procedure SetStdCProcs
        (var theProcs : CQDProcs);   {Color bottleneck record to initialize}
```

Chapter 6 Color and the Toolbox

6.1 Color Icons

6.1.1 Color Icon Structure

```
type
    CIconHandle = ^CIconPtr;
    CIconPtr    = ^CIcon;

    CIcon       = record
                    iconPMap     : PixMap;             {Full pixel map}
                    iconMask     : BitMap;             {Bit mask}
                    iconBMap     : BitMap;             {Substitute bit map}
                    iconData     : Handle;             {Handle to pixel image}
                    iconMaskData : array [0..0] of INTEGER  {Private}
                end;
```

6.1.2 Using Color Icons

```
function GetCIcon
        (iconID : INTEGER)           {Resource ID of desired icon}
            : CIconHandle;           {Handle to icon in memory}

procedure PlotCIcon
        (inRect  : Rect;             {Rectangle to plot in}
          theIcon : CIconHandle);    {Handle to icon}

procedure DisposCIcon
        (theIcon : CIconHandle);     {Handle to icon to be destroyed}
```

6.2   Color Cursors

6.2.1 Color Cursor Structure

```
type
  CCrsrHandle = ^CCrsrPtr;
  CCrsrPtr    = ^CCrsr;

  CCrsr       = record
                  crsrType   : INTEGER;        {Cursor type}
                  crsrMap    : PixMapHandle;    {Characteristics of pixel image}
                  crsrData   : Handle;          {Pixel image}
                  crsrXData  : Handle;          {Expanded pixel image}
                  crsrXValid : INTEGER;         {Depth of expanded image}
                  crsrXHandle : Handle;         {Reserved for future use}
                  crsr1Data  : Bits16;          {Bit image for old-style ports}
                  crsrMask   : Bits16;          {Transfer mask}
                  crsrHotSpot : Point;          {Point coinciding with mouse}
                  crsrXTable : LONGINT;         {Reserved for future use}
                  crsrID     : LONGINT          {Seed value for color table}
                end;
  Bits16      = array [0..15] of INTEGER;       {16 rows of 16 bits each}
```

6.2.2 Using Color Cursors

```
function  GetCCursor
            (cursorID : INTEGER)               {Resource ID of desired color cursor}
              : CCrsrHandle;                    {Handle to cursor in memory}
procedure SetCCursor
            (newCursor : CCrsrHandle);          {Color cursor to be made current}
procedure DisposCCursor
            (oldCursor : CCrsrHandle);          {Color cursor to be destroyed}
```

6.3   Color Windows

6.3.1 Color Window Records

```
type
  CWindowPtr  = CGrafPtr;
  CWindowPeek = ^CWindowRecord;
```

```
CWindowRecord = record
                 port          : CGrafPort;      {Color graphics port for this window}
                 windowKind    : INTEGER;        {Window class}
                 visible       : BOOLEAN;        {Is window visible?}
                 hilited       : BOOLEAN;        {Is window highlighted?}
                 goAwayFlag    : BOOLEAN;        {Does window have close region?}
                 spareFlag     : BOOLEAN;        {Is zooming enabled?}
                 strucRgn      : RgnHandle;      {Handle to structure region}
                 contRgn       : RgnHandle;      {Handle to content region}
                 updateRgn     : RgnHandle;      {Handle to update region}
                 windowDefProc : Handle;         {Handle to window definition function}
                 dataHandle    : Handle;         {Handle to definition function's data}
                 titleHandle   : StringHandle;   {Handle to window's title}
                 titleWidth    : INTEGER;        {Private}
                 controlList   : ControlHandle;  {Handle to start of control list}
                 nextWindow    : CWindowPeek;    {Pointer to next window in window list}
                 windowPic     : PicHandle;      {Picture for drawing window's contents}
                 refCon        : LONGINT         {Reference constant}
               end;
```

6.3.2 Auxiliary Window Records

```
type
   AuxWinHndl = ^AuxWinPtr;
   AuxWinPtr  = ^AuxWinRec;

   AuxWinRec  = record
                  awNext      : AuxWinHndl;   {Next record in auxiliary window list}
                  awOwner     : WindowPtr;    {Window this record belongs to}
                  awCTable    : CTabHandle;   {Window color table}
                  dialogCItem : Handle;       {Dialog item color list}
                  awFlags     : LONGINT;      {Private}
                  awReserved  : CTabHandle;   {Reserved for future use}
                  awRefCon    : LONGINT       {Reference constant for application use}
                end;
```

6.3.3 Window Color Tables

```
type
   WCTabHandle = ^WCTabPtr;
   WCTabPtr    = ^WinCTab;

   WinCTab     = record
                   wcSeed     : LONGINT;              {Reserved for future use}
                   wcReserved : INTEGER;              {Reserved for future use}
                   ctSize     : INTEGER;              {Number of entries minus 1}
                   ctTable    : array [0..4] of ColorSpec   {Array of color specifications}
                 end;
```

```
const
   WContentColor  = 0;                        {Background fill color for content region}
   WFrameColor    = 1;                        {Frame and border color}
   WTextColor     = 2;                        {Text color for window title}
   WHiliteColor   = 3;                        {Background color for close and zoom boxes}
   WTitleBarColor = 4;                        {Background color for title bar}
```

6.3.4 Creating Color Windows

```
function NewCWindow
              (wStorage      : Ptr;           {Storage for window record}
               windowRect    : Rect;          {Window's port rectangle in screen coordinates}
               title         : Str255;        {Window's title}
               visible       : BOOLEAN;       {Is window initially visible?}
               windowType    : INTEGER;       {Window definition ID}
               behindWindow  : WindowPtr;     {Window in front of this one}
               hasClose      : BOOLEAN;       {Does window have a close region?}
               refCon        : LONGINT)       {Window's reference constant}
                  : WindowPtr;                {Pointer to new window}

function GetNewCWindow
              (templateID    : INTEGER;       {Resource ID of window template}
               wStorage      : Ptr;           {Storage for window record}
               behindWindow  : WindowPtr)     {Window in front of this one}
                  : WindowPtr;                {Pointer to new window}
```

6.3.5 Color Window Properties

```
procedure SetWinColor
              (theWindow : WindowPtr;         {Pointer to the window}
               newCTab   : WCTabHandle);      {New color table}

function  GetAuxWin
              (theWindow      : WindowPtr;    {Pointer to the window}
               var theAuxRec  : AuxWinHndl)   {Returns handle to auxiliary window record}
                  : BOOLEAN;                  {Does window have an auxiliary record?}

function  GetWVariant
              (theWindow : WindowPtr)         {Pointer to the window}
                  : INTEGER;                  {Window's variation code}
```

6.3.6 Window Palettes

```
procedure SetPalette
              (theWindow  : WindowPtr;        {Pointer to the window}
               thePalette : PaletteHandle;    {Handle to new palette}
               doUpdates  : BOOLEAN);         {Automatic updates?}
```

```
function  GetPalette
            (theWindow : WindowPtr)        {Pointer to the window}
                : PaletteHandle;           {Handle to current palette}
procedure ActivatePalette
            (theWindow : WindowPtr);       {Pointer to the window}
```

6.3.7 Screen Properties

```
procedure GetCWMgrPort
            (var cwMgrPort : CGrafPtr);    {Returns pointer to Color Window Manager port}
function  GetGrayRgn
                : RgnHandle;               {Handle to desktop region}
```

6.4   Color Controls

6.4.1 Auxiliary Control Records

```
type
  AuxCtlHndl = ^AuxCtlPtr;
  AuxCtlPtr  = ^AuxCtlRec;

  AuxCtlRec = record
                acNext     : AuxCtlHndl;     {Next record in auxiliary control list}
                acOwner    : ControlHandle;  {Control this record belongs to}
                acCTable   : CCTabHandle;    {Control color table}
                acFlags    : INTEGER;        {Private}
                acReserved : LONGINT;        {Reserved for future use}
                acRefCon   : LONGINT         {Reference constant for application use}
              end;
```

6.4.2 Control Color Tables

```
type
  CCTabHandle = ^CCTabPtr;
  CCTabPtr    = ^CtlCTab;

  CtlCTab     = record
                  ccSeed  : LONGINT;                {Reserved for future use}
                  ccRider : INTEGER;                {Reserved for future use}
                  ctSize  : INTEGER;                {Number of entries minus 1}
                  ctTable : array [0..3] of ColorSpec {Array of color specifications}
                end;
```

```
const
  CFrameColor = 0;                              {Frame and border color}
  CBodyColor  = 1;                              {Background fill color}
  CTextColor  = 2;                              {Text color for control title}
  CThumbColor = 3;                              {Fill color for scroll box}
```

6.4.3 Color Control Properties

```
procedure SetCtlColor
          (theControl : ControlHandle;         {Handle to the control}
           newCTab     : CCTabHandle);          {New color table}

function  GetAuxCtl
          (theControl    : ControlHandle;       {Handle to the control}
           var theAuxRec : AuxCtlHndl)          {Returns handle to auxiliary control record}
              : BOOLEAN;                         {Does control have an auxiliary record?}

function  GetCVariant
          (theControl : ControlHandle)          {Handle to the control}
              : INTEGER;                         {Control's variation code}
```

6.5   Color Dialogs

6.5.1 Creating Color Dialogs

```
function NewCDialog
          (dStorage     : Ptr;                  {Storage for dialog record}
           windowRect   : Rect;                 {Dialog window's port rectangle}
           title        : Str255;               {Title of dialog window}
           visible      : BOOLEAN;              {Is dialog window initially visible?}
           windowType   : INTEGER;              {Dialog window's definition ID}
           behindWindow : WindowPtr;            {Window in front of this one}
           hasClose     : BOOLEAN;              {Does dialog window have a close box?}
           refCon       : LONGINT;              {Dialog window's reference constant}
           itemList     : Handle)               {Handle to item list}
              : DialogPtr;                       {Pointer to new dialog record}
```

6.6   Color Menus

6.6.1 Menu Color Information Tables

```
type
  MCTableHandle = ^MCTablePtr;
  MCTablePtr    = ^MCTable;
  MCTable       = array [0..0] of MCEntry; {Any number of entries}
```

```
MCEntryPtr    = ^MCEntry;
MCEntry       = record
                    mctID       : INTEGER;    {Menu ID number}
                    mctItem     : INTEGER;    {Item number within the menu}
                    mctRGB1     : RGBColor;   {Color information (see table, [6.6.1])}
                    mctRGB2     : RGBColor;   {Color information (see table, [6.6.1])}
                    mctRGB3     : RGBColor;   {Color information (see table, [6.6.1])}
                    mctRGB4     : RGBColor;   {Color information (see table, [6.6.1])}
                    mctReserved : INTEGER     {Private}
               end;
const
  MCTLastIDIndic = -99;                       {Dummy menu ID for last entry in table}
```

6.6.2 Access to Menu Colors

```
function   GetMCInfo
              : MCTableHandle;                {Copy of current menu color info table}

procedure  SetMCInfo
              (newMCTab : MCTableHandle);     {New menu color info table}

procedure  DispMCInfo
              (oldMCTab : MCTableHandle);     {Menu color info table to be destroyed}
```

6.6.3 Managing Menu Colors

```
function   GetMCEntry
              (menuID  : INTEGER;             {Menu ID of desired menu}
               theItem : INTEGER)             {Item number within the menu}
                 : MCEntryPtr;                {Pointer to item's color information entry}

procedure  SetMCEntries
              (nEntries  : INTEGER;           {Number of entries in table}
               newColors : MCTablePtr);       {Table of new menu colors}

procedure  DelMCEntries
              (menuID  : INTEGER;             {Menu ID of desired menu}
               theItem : INTEGER);            {Item number within the menu}

const
  MCTAllItems = -98;                          {Delete all items in menu}
```

Chapter 7 Styled Text

7.2 Styled Text

7.2.1 Text Styles

```
type
   TextStyle = record
                 tsFont  : INTEGER;         {Font number of typeface [I:8.2.1]}
                 tsFace  : Style;           {Type style [I:8.3.1]}
                 tsSize  : INTEGER;         {Type size in points}
                 tsColor : RGBColor         {Text color [4.2.1]}
               end;
```

7.2.2 Styled Edit Records

```
type
   TEHandle = ^TEPtr;
   TEPtr    = ^TERec;

   TERec    = record
                . . . ;
                lineHeight : INTEGER;       {Negative for variable line height [7.2.5]}
                fontAscent : INTEGER;       {Negative for variable line ascent [7.2.5]}
                . . . ;
                txFont     : INTEGER;       {First half of style record handle [7.2.3]}
                txFace     : Style;         {Last half of style record handle [7.2.3]}
                . . . ;
                txSize     : INTEGER;       {-1 for styled text}
                . . .
              end;
```

7.2.3 Style Records

```
type
   TEStyleHandle = ^TEStylePtr;
   TEStylePtr    = ^TEStyleRec;

   TEStyleRec    = record
                     nRuns     : INTEGER;                      {Number of runs}
                     nStyles   : INTEGER;                      {Number of styles}
                     styleTab  : STHandle;                     {Style table [7.2.4]}
                     lhTab     : LHHandle;                     {Line-height table [7.2.5]}
                     teRefCon  : LONGINT;                      {Reference constant}
                     nullStyle : NullSTHandle;                 {Null-style record [7.2.6]}
                     runs      : array [0..8000] of StyleRun   {Array of style runs}
                   end;
```

```
StyleRun = record
               startChar  : INTEGER;        {Starting character position}
               styleIndex : INTEGER         {Index in style table}
           end;
```

7.2.4 Style Table

```
type
   STHandle      = ^STPtr;
   STPtr         = ^TEStyleTable;
   TEStyleTable = array [0..1776] of STElement;

   STElement = record
                   stCount  : INTEGER;        {Number of runs in this style}
                   stHeight : INTEGER;        {Line height}
                   stAscent : INTEGER;        {Font ascent}
                   stFont   : INTEGER;        {Font number of typeface [I:8.2.1]}
                   stFace   : Style;          {Type style [I:8.3.1]}
                   stSize   : INTEGER;        {Type size in points}
                   stColor  : RGBColor        {Text color [4.2.1]}
               end;
```

7.2.5 Line-Height Table

```
type
   LHHandle  = ^LHPtr;
   LHPtr     = ^LHTable;
   LHTable   = array [0..8000] of LHElement;

   LHElement = record
                   lhHeight : INTEGER;        {Line height in pixels}
                   lhAscent : INTEGER         {Line ascent in pixels}
               end;
```

7.2.6 Null-Style Record

```
type
   NullStHandle = ^NullStPtr;
   NullStPtr    = ^NullStRec;

   NullStRec    = record
                      teReserved : LONGINT;        {Reserved for future expansion}
                      nullScrap  : StScrpHandle     {Style scrap for null style [7.2.7]}
                  end;
```

7.2.7 Style Scrap

```
type
  StScrpHandle  = ^StScrpPtr;
  StScrpPtr     = ^StScrpRec;
  StScrpRec     = record
                      scrpNStyles  : INTEGER;        {Number of styles}
                      scrpStyleTab : ScrpStTable     {Table of styles}
                  end;

  ScrpStTable   = array [0..1600] of ScrpStElement;
  ScrpStElement = record
                      scrpStartChar : LONGINT;       {Starting character position}
                      scrpHeight    : INTEGER;       {Line height}
                      scrpAscent    : INTEGER;       {Font ascent}
                      scrpFont      : INTEGER;       {Font number of typeface [I:8.2.1]}
                      scrpFace      : Style;         {Type style [I:8.3.1]}
                      scrpSize      : INTEGER;       {Type size in points}
                      scrpColor     : RGBColor       {Text color [4.2.1]}
                  end;
```

7.3   Editing Styled Text

7.3.1 Preparation for Editing

```
function   TEStylNew
              (destRect : Rect;           {Destination (wrapping) rectangle}
               viewRect : Rect)           {View (clipping) rectangle}
                : TEHandle;               {Handle to new edit record}

function   GetStylHandle
              (editRec : TEHandle)        {Handle to edit record}
                : TEStyleHandle;          {Handle to current style record}

procedure  SetStylHandle
              (styleRec : TEStyleHandle;  {Handle to new style record}
               editRec  : TEHandle);      {Handle to edit record}
```

7.3.2 Character Location

```
function   TEGetOffset
              (thePoint : Point;          {Point to be mapped, in window coordinates}
               editRec  : TEHandle)       {Handle to edit record}
                : INTEGER;                {Corresponding character index}

function   TEGetPoint
              (charIndex : INTEGER;       {Character index}
               editRec   : TEHandle)      {Handle to edit record}
                : Point;                  {Bottom-left of character in window coordinates}
```

```
function   TEGetHeight
              (lastLine  : LONGINT;            {Last line number}
               firstLine : LONGINT;            {First line number}
               editRec   : TEHandle)           {Handle to edit record}
                 : LONGINT;                    {Total height of lines in pixels}

procedure  CharExtra
              (extraWidth : Fixed);            {Extra character width in pixels}
```

7.3.3 Getting Style Information

```
procedure  TEGetStyle
              (charPos         : INTEGER;      {Character position of desired character}
               var theStyle    : TextStyle;    {Returns character's style attributes}
               var lineHeight  : INTEGER;      {Returns character's line height}
               var fontAscent  : INTEGER;      {Returns character's font ascent}
               editRec         : TEHandle);    {Handle to edit record}

function   TEContinuousStyle
              (var whichAttrs  : INTEGER;      {Desired attributes; returns continuous attributes}
               var theStyle    : TextStyle;    {Values of continuous attributes}
               editRec         : TEHandle)     {Handle to edit record}
                 : BOOLEAN;                    {Are all requested attributes continuous?}

function   TENumStyles
              (startPos : LONGINT;             {Starting character position}
               endPos   : LONGINT;             {Ending character position}
               editRec  : TEHandle)            {Handle to edit record}
                 : LONGINT;                    {Number of style changes}
```

7.3.4 Styling Text

```
procedure  TESetStyle
              (whichAttrs : INTEGER;           {Style attributes to set}
               newStyle   : TextStyle;         {New attribute values}
               redraw     : BOOLEAN;           {Redraw after change?}
               editRec    : TEHandle);         {Handle to edit record}

procedure  TEReplaceStyle
              (whichAttrs : INTEGER;           {Style attributes to replace}
               oldStyle   : TextStyle;         {Old attribute values to be replaced}
               newStyle   : TextStyle;         {New attribute values to replace them with}
               redraw     : BOOLEAN;           {Redraw after change?}
               editRec    : TEHandle);         {Handle to edit record}
```

```
const
  DoFont   =  1;                          {Set typeface}
  DoFace   =  2;                          {Set type style}
  DoSize   =  4;                          {Set type size}
  DoColor  =  8;                          {Set text color}
  DoAll    = 15;                          {All of the above}
  AddSize  = 16;                          {Adjust type size}
  DoToggle = 32;                          {Toggle existing attribute value}
```

7.3.5 Cutting and Pasting Styled Text

```
procedure TECut
          (editRec : TEHandle);           {Handle to edit record}

procedure TECopy
          (editRec : TEHandle);           {Handle to edit record}

procedure TEPaste
          (editRec : TEHandle);           {Handle to edit record}

procedure TEStylPaste
          (editRec : TEHandle);           {Handle to edit record}
```

7.3.6 Scrapless Styling

```
function  GetStylScrap
          (editRec : TEHandle)            {Handle to edit record}
              : StScrpHandle;             {Styles for current selection}

procedure SetStylScrap
          (startPos  : LONGINT;           {Starting character position}
           endPos    : LONGINT;           {Ending character position}
           newStyles : StScrpHandle;      {Styles to apply}
           redraw    : BOOLEAN;           {Redraw after change?}
           editRec   : TEHandle);         {Handle to edit record}

procedure TEStylInsert
          (textPtr    : Ptr;             {Pointer to insertion text}
           textLength : LONGINT;          {Length of insertion text in characters}
           textStyles : StScrpHandle;     {Styles for insertion text}
           editRec    : TEHandle);        {Handle to edit record}
```

Resource Formats

Resource Type `'actb'` [6.7.3]

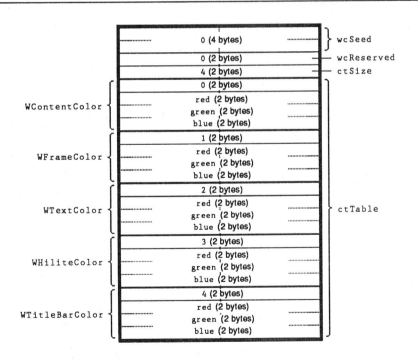

Resource Type `'cctb'` [6.7.4]

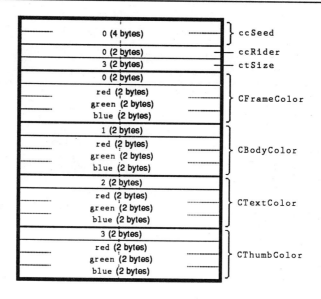

Resource Type `'cicn'` [6.7.1]

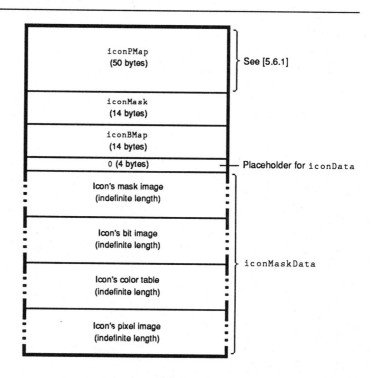

Resource Type 'clut' [4.7.1]

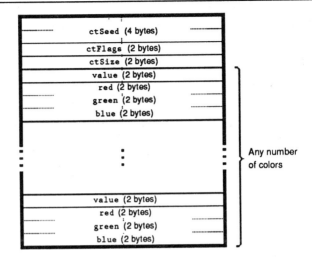

Resource Type 'crsr' [6.7.2]

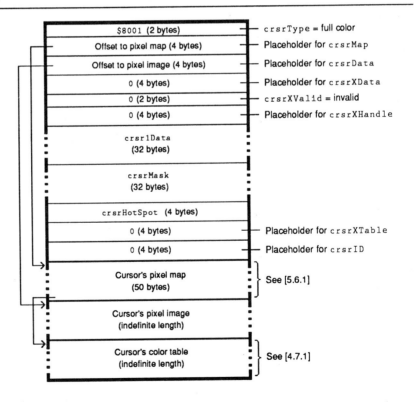

Resource Type 'dctb' [6.7.3]

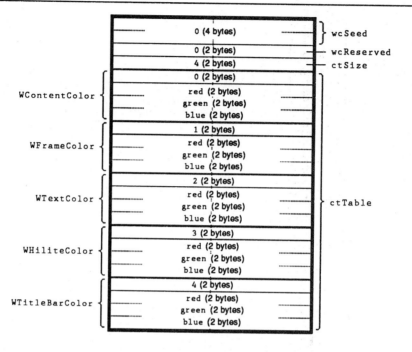

Resource Type 'fctb' [7.4.1]

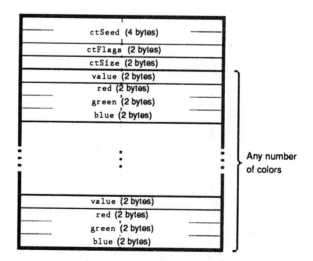

Resource Type `'ictb'` [6.7.5]

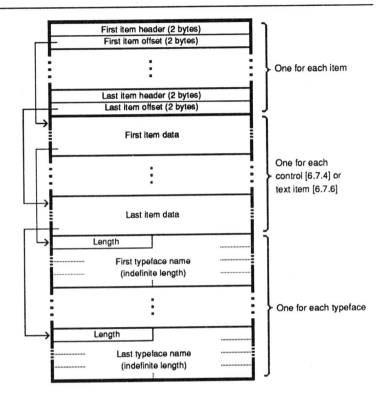

Text Item Data in an `'ictb'` Resource [6.7.6]

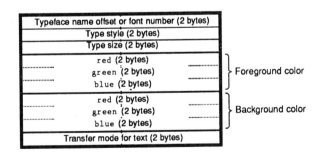

Resource Type `'mctb'` [6.7.7]

Number of entries (2 bytes)
First table entry (30 bytes; see next figure)
⋮
Last table entry (30 bytes; see next figure)

Any number of entries

Table Entry in an `'mctb'` Resource   [6.7.7]

mctID (2 bytes)
mctItem (2 bytes)
mctRGB1 (6 bytes)
mctRGB2 (6 bytes)
mctRGB3 (6 bytes)
mctRGB4 (6 bytes)
mctReserved (2 bytes)

Resource Type 'pltt' [4.7.2]

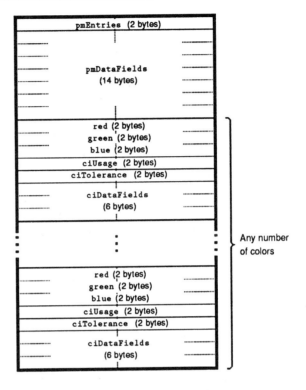

Resource Type 'ppat' [5.6.1]

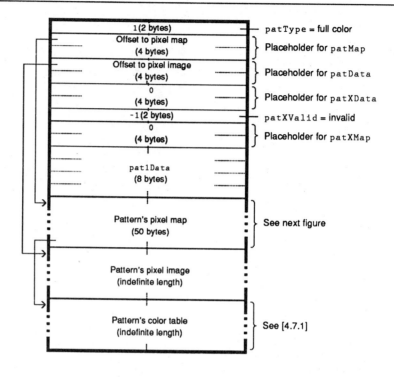

Detail of a Pixel Map in a `'ppat'` Resource [5.6.1]

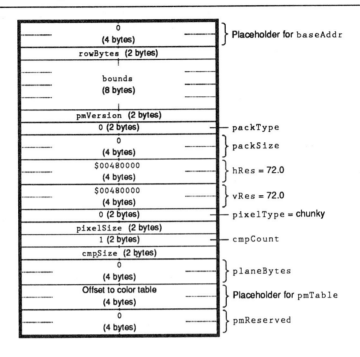

Resource Type `'SICN'` [3.3.1]

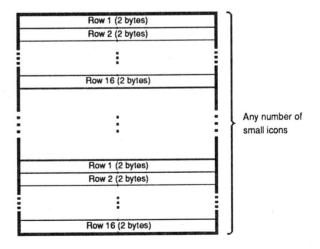

Resource Type 'SIZE' [3.3.2]

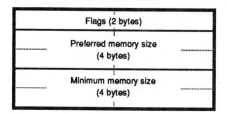

Resource Type 'wctb' [6.7.3]

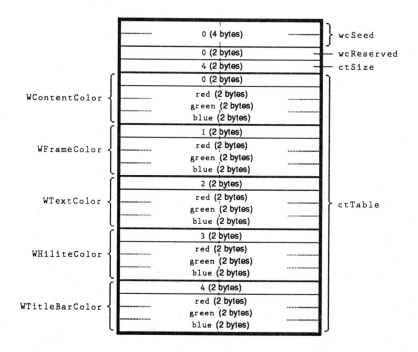

APPENDIX C

Reference Figures

Trap Word Formats [Figure 2-1]

a. Operating System trap

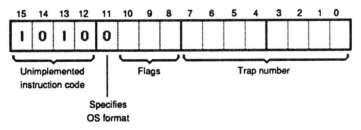

b. Toolbox trap

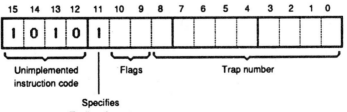

Macintosh II 24-Bit Memory Layout [2.2.1]

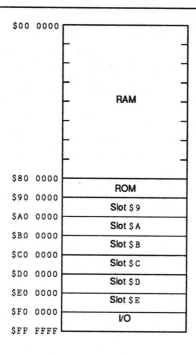

$00 0000	RAM
$80 0000	ROM
$90 0000	Slot $9
$A0 0000	Slot $A
$B0 0000	Slot $B
$C0 0000	Slot $C
$D0 0000	Slot $D
$E0 0000	Slot $E
$F0 0000	I/O
$FF FFFF	

Macintosh II 32-Bit Memory Layout [2.2.1]

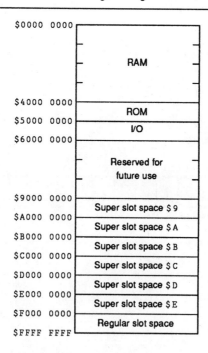

$0000 0000	RAM
$4000 0000	ROM
$5000 0000	I/O
$6000 0000	Reserved for future use
$9000 0000	Super slot space $9
$A000 0000	Super slot space $A
$B000 0000	Super slot space $B
$C000 0000	Super slot space $C
$D000 0000	Super slot space $D
$E000 0000	Super slot space $E
$F000 0000	Regular slot space
$FFFF FFFF	

Macintosh II 32-Bit Regular Slot Space [2.2.1]

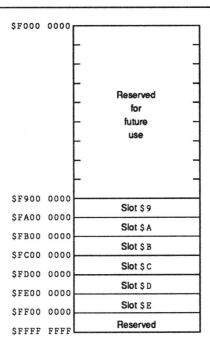

Event Message for Suspend/Resume Events [3.1.1]

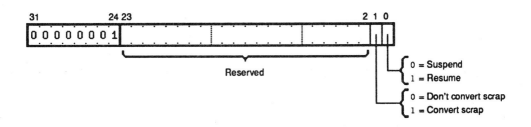

Event Message for Mouse-Moved Events [3.1.1]

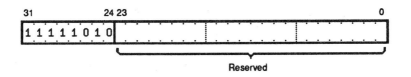

Event Message for Keyboard Events [3.1.1]

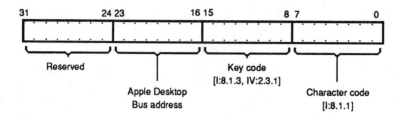

Event Modifiers [3.1.2]

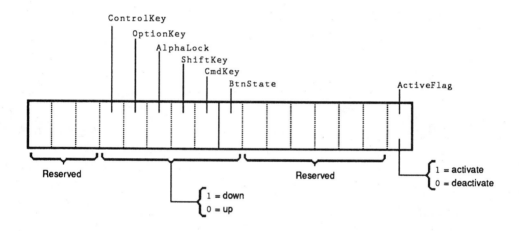

MultiFinder Flags [3.3.3]

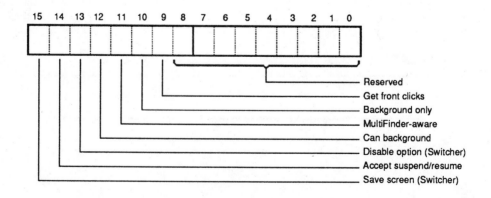

Classic QuickDraw Color Bits [4.1.1]

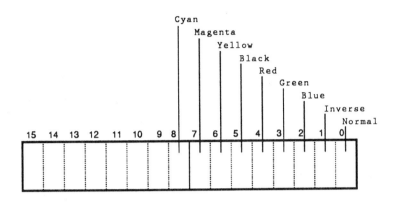

Graphics Device Attribute Flags [4.3.5]

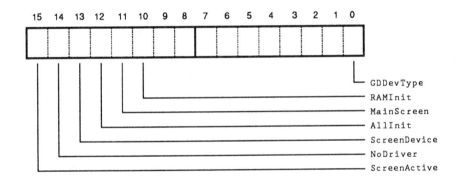

Flag Bits for Dialog Text Styles [6.7.6]

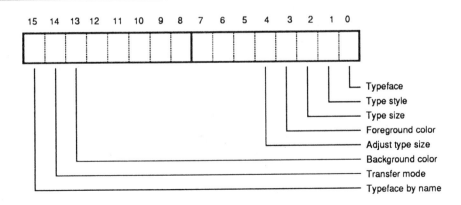

Font Type Flags [7.1.1]

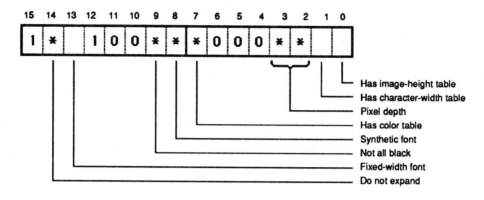

* Macintosh II only

Synthetic-Font List Entry [7.1.2]

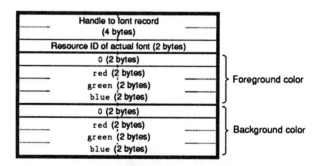

A P P E N D I X

D

Reference Tables

Standard Resource Types [2.3.1]

Resource Type	Description	See Section
'PAT '	Bit pattern	[I:5.5.1]
'PAT#'	Bit pattern list	[I:5.5.2]
'ppat'	Pixel pattern	[IV:5.6.1]
'ppt#'	Pixel pattern list	
'bmap'	Bit map	
'PICT'	QuickDraw picture	[I:5.5.5]
'ICON'	Icon	[I:5.5.3]
'ICN#'	Icon list	[I:5.5.4]
'SICN'	Small icon	[IV:3.3.1]
'cicn'	Color icon	[IV:6.7.1]
'TEXT'	Any text	[I:8.4.1]
'STR '	Pascal-format string	[I:8.4.2]
'STR#'	String list	[I:8.4.3]
'FONT'	Font	[I:8.4.5]
'NFNT'	Non-menu font	[I:8.4.5]
'FWID'	Font width table	[I:8.4.6]
'FRSV'	Reserved font list	[I:8.4.7]
'FOND'	Font family definition	

407

Resource Type	Description	See Section
'CURS'	Cursor	[II:2.9.1]
'crsr'	Color cursor	[IV:6.7.2]
'KMAP'	Key code map	
'KCHR'	Character code map	
'KSWP'	Keyboard script table	
'FKEY'	Low-level keyboard routine	[II:2.9.2, III:6.3.1]
'WIND'	Window template	[II:3.7.1]
'MENU'	Menu	[II:4.8.1]
'MBAR'	Menu bar	[II:4.8.2]
'CNTL'	Control template	[II:6.6.1]
'ALRT'	Alert template	[II:7.6.1]
'DLOG'	Dialog template	[II:7.6.2]
'DITL'	Dialog or alert item list	[II:7.6.3]
'WDEF'	Window definition function	[III:2.5.1]
'CDEF'	Control definition function	[III:2.5.2]
'MDEF'	Menu definition procedure	[III:2.5.3]
'MBDF'	Menu bar definition function	
'LDEF'	List definition procedure	
'CODE'	Code segment	[I:7.5.1]
'PACK'	Package	[I:7.5.2]
'DRVR'	Device driver (including desk accessories)	[III:3.3.1, I:7.5.5]
'SERD'	Serial driver	
'FMTR'	Disk formatting code	
'PREC'	Print record	[III:4.6.1]
'PDEF'	Printing code	[III:4.6.2]
'FREF'	Finder file reference	[I:7.5.3]
'BNDL'	Finder bundle	[I:7.5.4]
'SIZE'	Partition size (MultiFinder)	[IV:3.3.2]
'mstr'	MultiFinder string	[IV:3.3.4]
'mst#'	MultiFinder string list	[IV:3.3.4]
'MACS'	Macintosh system autograph	
'vers'	Software version ID	
'scrn'	Screen configuration	

Resource Type	Description	See Section
'clut'	Color lookup table	[IV:4.7.1]
'pltt'	Color palette	[IV:4.7.2]
'gama'	Color correction table	
'mitq'	Color inverse table, memory requirements	
'fctb'	Font color table	
'wctb'	Window color table	[IV:6.7.3]
'cctb'	Control color table	[IV:6.7.4]
'mctb'	Menu color table	[IV:6.7.7]
'actb'	Alert color table	[IV:6.7.3]
'dctb'	Dialog color table	[IV:6.7.3]
'ictb'	Dialog item color table	[IV:6.7.5]
'snth'	Sound synthesizer	
'snd '	Sound definition	
'INIT'	Initialization resource	[I:8.4.4]
'DSAT'	"Dire straits" alert table	
'PTCH'	System patch code	
'ptch'	System patch	
'boot'	Boot blocks	
'lmem'	Low-memory globals	
'ROvr'	ROM override code	
'ROv#'	ROM override list	
'CACH'	RAM cache code	
'ADBS'	Apple Desktop Bus service routine	
'MMAP'	Mouse tracking code	
'mcky'	Mouse tracking data	
'INTL'	International localization resource	
'itl0'	International localization, date and time formats	
'itl1'	International localization, day and month names	
'itl2'	International localization, sort hooks	
'itlb'	International localization, script bundles	
'itlc'	International localization, script configuration	
'NBPC'	Name-Binding Protocol code (AppleTalk)	
'PAPA'	Printer Access Protocol address (AppleTalk)	
'mppc'	Macintosh Packet Protocol configuration (AppleTalk)	
'atpl'	AppleTalk private resource	

Resource Type	Description	See Section
'PRES'	Printer resource (Chooser)	
'PRER'	Printer resource, remote (Chooser)	
'RDEV'	Remote device (Chooser)	
'clst'	Cached icon list (Chooser, Control Panel)	
'cdev'	Control Panel device	
'ctab'	Control Panel device table	
'mach'	Machine compatibility list (Control Panel)	
'nrct'	Rectangle list (Control Panel)	
'KCAP'	Keyboard layout (Key Caps)	
'INT#'	Integer list (Find File)	
'APPL'	Application table (Finder)	
'FDIR'	Finder directory	
'FOBJ'	Finder object	
'FCMT'	Finder comment	
'LAYO'	Folder layout (Finder)	
'MINI'	MiniFinder resource	
'FBTN'	File button (MiniFinder)	
'insc'	Installer script	
'TMPL'	Resource type template (ResEdit)	

Macintosh II ROM-Based Resources [2.3.2]

Resource Type	Resource ID	Description
'CURS'	1*	I-beam cursor [II:2.5.2, II:2.9.1]
	2*	Cross cursor [II:2.5.2, II:2.9.1]
	3*	Plus-sign cursor [II:2.5.2, II:2.9.1]
	4*	Wristwatch cursor [II:2.5.2, II:2.9.1]
'KMAP'	0*	Standard key code map
'KCHR'	0	Standard character code map

*Also included in Macintosh SE ROM

Resource Type	Resource ID	Description
'FONT'	0*	Name of system font [I:8.2.1, I:8.4.5]
	12*	System font (12-point Chicago) [I:8.2.1, I:8.4.5]
	384	Name of Geneva font [I:8.2.1, I:8.4.5]
	393*	9-point Geneva font [I:8.2.1, I:8.4.5]
	396*	12-point Geneva font [I:8.2.1, I:8.4.5]
	512	Name of Monaco font [I:8.2.1, I:8.4.5]
	521*	12-point Monaco font [I:8.2.1, I:8.4.5]
'NFNT'	2	System font (12-point Chicago), 4 bits deep
	3	System font (12-point Chicago), 8 bits deep
	34	9-point Geneva font, 4 bits deep
'PACK'	4*	Floating-Point Arithmetic Package [I:7.2.1, I:7.5.2]
	5*	Transcendental Functions Package [I:7.2.1, I:7.5.2]
	7*	Binary/Decimal Conversion Package [I:7.2.1, I:7.5.2]
'DRVR'	3*	Sound driver (.Sound) [III:3.3.1, I:7.5.5]
	4*	Disk driver (.Sony) [III:3.3.1, I:7.5.5]
	9*	AppleTalk driver, Macintosh Packet Protocol (.MPP) [III:3.3.1, I:7.5.5]
	10*	AppleTalk driver, AppleTalk Transaction Protocol (.ATP) [III:3.3.1, I:7.5.5]
	40*	AppleTalk driver, Extended Protocol Package (.XPP) [III:3.3.1, I:7.5.5]
'SERD'	0*	Serial drivers (.AIn, .AOut, .BIn, .BOut) [III:3.3.1, I:7.5.5]
'WDEF'	0*	Definition function for document windows [III:2.5.1]
	1*	Definition function for accessory windows [III:2.5.1]
'CDEF'	0*	Definition function for standard buttons [III:2.5.2]
	1*	Definition function for scroll bars [III:2.5.2]
'MDEF'	0*	Definition procedure for text menus [III:2.5.3]
'MBDF'	0*	Standard menu bar definition procedure

*Also included in Macintosh SE ROM

Resource Type	Resource ID	Description
'clut'	1	Standard color table, 1 bit deep [IV:4.7.1]
	2	Standard color table, 2 bits deep [IV:4.7.1]
	4	Standard color table, 4 bits deep [IV:4.7.1]
	8	Standard color table, 8 bits deep [IV:4.7.1]
	127	Standard color table, classic color model [IV:4.7.1]
'gama'	0	Standard color correction table
'mitq'	0	Standard color inverse table memory requirements
'wctb'	0	Color table for standard windows [IV:6.7.3]
'cctb'	0	Color table for standard controls [IV:6.7.4]
'snd '	1	Standard system beep

Resource IDs for Types 'mstr' and 'mst#' [3.3.4]

Resource ID	Meaning
100	Name of menu containing Quit command
101	Name of Quit command
102	Name of menu containing Open command
103	Name of Open command

RGB Values of Standard Primary Colors [4.2.2]

Table Index	Color	Red Dec.	Red Hex.	Green Dec.	Green Hex.	Blue Dec.	Blue Hex.
0	Black	0	$0000	0	$0000	0	$0000
1	Yellow	64512	$FC00	62333	$F37D	1327	$052F
2	Magenta	62167	$F2D7	2134	$0856	34028	$84EC
3	Red	56683	$DD6B	2242	$08C2	1698	$06A2
4	Cyan	577	$0241	43860	$AB54	60159	$EAFF
5	Green	0	$0000	32768	$8000	4528	$11B0
6	Blue	0	$0000	0	$0000	54272	$D400
7	White	65535	$FFFF	65535	$FFFF	65535	$FFFF

Standard System Palette [4.7.2]

Palette Index	Color	Red Dec.	Red Hex.	Green Dec.	Green Hex.	Blue Dec.	Blue Hex.
0	White	65535	$FFFF	65535	$FFFF	65535	$FFFF
1	Black	0	$0000	0	$0000	0	$0000
2	Yellow	64512	$FC00	62333	$F37D	1327	$052F
3	Orange	65535	$FFFF	25738	$648A	652	$028C
4	Blue-green	881	$0371	50943	$C6FF	40649	$9EC9
5	Green	0	$0000	40960	$A000	0	$0000
6	Blue	0	$0000	0	$0000	54272	$D400
7	Red	56683	$DD6B	2242	$08C2	1698	$06A2
8	Light gray	49152	$C000	49152	$C000	49152	$C000
9	Medium gray	32768	$8000	32768	$8000	32768	$8000
10	Beige	65535	$FFFF	50140	$C3DC	33120	$8160
11	Brown	37887	$93FF	10266	$281A	4812	$12CC
12	Olive green	25892	$6524	49919	$C2FF	0	$0000
13	Bright green	0	$0000	65535	$FFFF	1265	$04F1
14	Sky blue	26078	$65DE	44421	$AD85	65535	$FFFF
15	Violet	32768	$8000	0	$0000	65535	$FFFF

Monochrome Modes in a Color Port [Table 5–1]

Mode	Effect of Black Source Pixels	Effect of White Source Pixels
Copy	Foreground color	Background color
NotCopy	Background color	Foreground color
Or	Foreground color	No change
NotOr	No change	Foreground color
Bic	Background color	No change
NotBic	No change	Background color
XOr	Invert bits	No change
NotXOr	No change	Invert bits

Color Modes in a Monochrome Port [Table 5–2]

Color Mode	Equivalent Monochrome Mode
AddOver	XOr
AddPin	Bic
SubOver	XOr
SubPin	Or
ADMax	Bic
ADMin	Or
Blend	Copy
Transparent	Or
Hilite	XOr

Initial Values of `CGrafPort` Fields [5.1.5]

Field	Initial Value
device	0 (screen)
portPixMap	Copy of current device's pixel map
portVersion	$C000
chExtra	0
pnLocHFrac	0.5
portRect	portPixMap^^.bounds
visRgn	Rectangular region equal to portRect
clipRgn	Rectangular region (-32768, -32768) to (+32767, +32767)
bkPixPat	Solid white
rgbFgColor	Black
rgbBkColor	White
pnLoc	(0, 0)
pnSize	(1, 1)
pnMode	PatCopy [I:5.1.3]
pnPixPat	Solid black
fillPixPat	Solid black
pnVis	0 (visible) [I:5.2.3]
txFont	0 (system font) [I:8.2.1]

Field	Initial Value
txFace	Plain [I:8.3.1]
txMode	SrcOr [I:5.1.3]
txSize	0 (standard size) [I:8.3.1]
spExtra	0
fgColor	Black
bkColor	White
colrBit	0
patStretch	0
picSave	NIL
rgnSave	NIL
polySave	NIL
grafProcs	NIL (standard bottlenecks) [III:2.1, 5.5.1]

Menu Color Information [6.6.1]

Field Name	Menu Bar	Menu Title	Menu Item
mctID	0	Menu ID	Menu ID
mctItem	0	0	Item number
mctRGB1	Default text color for menu titles	Text color for menu title	Text color for mark character
mctRGB2	Default background color for menus	Background color for menu title	Text color for item text
mctRGB3	Default text color for menu items	Default text color for menu items	Text color for keyboard alias
mctRGB4	Background color for menu bar	Background color for menu	Background color for item

APPENDIX E

Error Codes

Operating System Errors

The following is a complete list of Operating System error codes. Not all are covered in these books, and some of the meanings may be obscure. (I don't know what a bit-slip nybble is either.) For the errors you're most likely to encounter, see reference sections [I:3.1.2, I:6.6.1, II:8.2.8, III:4.2.4, IV:5.1.7].

Number	Name	Meaning
0	NoErr	No error; all is well
-1	IPrSavPFil	Error saving print file
-1	QErr	Queue element not found during deletion
-2	VTypErr	Invalid queue element
-3	CorErr	Trap ("core routine") number out of range
-4	UnimpErr	Unimplemented trap
-8	SENoDB	No debugger installed
-17	ControlErr	Driver error during Control operation

Number	Name	Meaning
-18	StatusErr	Driver error during Status operation
-19	ReadErr	Driver error during Read operation
-20	WritErr	Driver error during Write operation
-21	BadUnitErr	Bad unit number
-22	UnitEmptyErr	No such entry in unit table
-23	OpenErr	Driver error during Open operation
-24	CloseErr	Driver error during Close operation
-25	DRemovErr	Attempt to remove an open driver
-26	DInstErr	Attempt to install nonexistent driver
-27	AbortErr	Driver operation canceled
-28	NotOpenErr	Driver not open
-29	UnitTblFullErr	Unit table full
-30	DCEExtErr	DCE extension error
-33	DirFulErr	Directory full
-34	DskFulErr	Disk full
-35	NSVErr	No such volume
-36	IOErr	Disk I/O error
-37	BdNamErr	Bad name
-38	FNOpenErr	File not open
-39	EOFErr	Attempt to read past end-of-file
-40	PosErr	Attempt to position before start of file
-41	MFulErr	Memory (system heap) full
-42	TMFOErr	Too many files open (more than 12)
-43	FNFErr	File not found
-44	WPrErr	Disk is write-protected
-45	FLckdErr	File locked
-46	VLckdErr	Volume locked
-47	FBsyErr	File busy
-48	DupFNErr	Duplicate file name
-49	OpWrErr	File already open for writing
-50	ParamErr	Invalid parameter list
-51	RfNumErr	Invalid reference number
-52	GFPErr	Error during GetFPos
-53	VolOffLinErr	Volume off-line

Number	Name	Meaning
-54	PermErr	Permission violation
-55	VolOnLinErr	Volume already on-line
-56	NSDrvErr	No such drive
-57	NoMacDskErr	Non-Macintosh disk
-58	ExtFSErr	External file system
-59	FSRnErr	Unable to rename file
-60	BadMDBErr	Bad master directory block
-61	WrPermErr	No write permission
-64	FontDecError	Error during font declaration
-65	FontNotDeclared	Font not declared
-66	FontSubErr	Font substitution occurred
-64	NoDriveErr	No such drive
-65	OffLinErr	Drive off-line
-66	NoNybErr	Can't find 5 nybbles
-67	NoAdrMkErr	No address mark
-68	DataVerErr	Data read doesn't verify
-69	BadCksmErr	Bad checksum (address mark)
-70	BadBtSlpErr	Bad bit-slip nybbles (address mark)
-71	NoDtaMkErr	No data mark
-72	BadDCksum	Bad checksum (data mark)
-73	BadDBtSlp	Bad bit-slip nybbles (data mark)
-74	WrUnderrun	Write underrun
-75	CantStepErr	Can't step disk drive
-76	Tk0BadErr	Track 0 bad
-77	InitIWMErr	Can't initialize disk chip ("Integrated Wozniak Machine")
-78	TwoSideErr	Two-sided operation on one-sided drive
-79	SpdAdjErr	Can't adjust disk speed
-80	SeekErr	Seek to wrong track
-81	SectNFErr	Sector not found
-82	Fmt1Err	Can't find sector 0 after track format
-83	Fmt2Err	Can't get enough sync
-84	VerErr	Track failed to verify
-85	ClkRdErr	Error reading clock
-86	ClkWrErr	Error writing clock

Number	Name	Meaning
-87	PRWrErr	Error writing parameter RAM
-88	PRInitErr	Parameter RAM uninitialized
-89	RcvrErr	Receiver error (serial communications)
-90	BreakRecd	Break received (serial communications)
-91	DDPSktErr	Socket error (AppleTalk, Datagram Delivery Protocol)
-92	DDPLenErr	Packet too long (AppleTalk, Datagram Delivery Protocol)
-93	NoBridgeErr	No bridge found (AppleTalk)
-94	LAPProtErr	Protocol error (AppleTalk, Link Access Protocol)
-95	ExcessCollsns	Excessive collisions (AppleTalk)
-97	PortInUse	Port already in use (AppleTalk)
-98	PortNotCf	Port not configured for this connection (AppleTalk)
-99	MemROZError	Error in read-only zone
-100	NoScrapErr	No desk scrap
-102	NoTypeErr	No item in scrap of requested type
-108	MemFullErr	No room; heap is full
-109	NilHandleErr	Illegal operation on empty handle
-110	MemAdrErr	Bad memory address
-111	MemWZErr	Illegal operation on free block
-112	MemPurErr	Illegal operation on locked block
-113	MemAZErr	Address not in heap zone
-114	MemPCErr	Pointer check failed
-115	MemBCErr	Block check failed
-116	MemSCErr	Size check failed
-117	MemLockedErr	Attempt to move a locked block
-120	DirNFErr	Directory not found
-121	TMWDOErr	Too many working directories open
-122	BadMovErr	Invalid move operation
-123	WrgVolTypErr	Wrong volume type (not HFS)
-124	VolGoneErr	Server volume disconnected
-125	UpdPixMemErr	Not enough memory to update pixel map
-126	MBarNFnd	Menu bar definition function not found

Number	Name	Meaning
-127	HMenuFindErr	Can't find parent of hierarchical menu
-127	FSDSIntErr	Internal file system error
-150	CMatchErr	Unable to match requested color
-151	CTempMemErr	Unable to allocate temporary memory
-152	CNoMemErr	Unable to allocate memory
-153	CRangeErr	Color index out of range
-154	CProtectErr	Color table protection violation
-155	CDevErr	Invalid type for graphics device
-156	CResErr	Invalid resolution for inverse table
-192	ResNotFound	Resource not found
-193	ResFNotFound	Resource file not found
-194	AddResFailed	AddResource failed
-196	RmvResFailed	RmveResource failed
-198	ResErrAttr	Operation prohibited by resource attribute
-199	MapReadErr	Error reading resource map
-200	NoHardware	No sound hardware
-201	NotEnoughHardware	Not enough sound channels
-203	QueueFull	Sound queue full
-204	ResProblem	Problem loading sound resource
-205	BadChannel	Invalid queue length for sound channel
-206	BadFormat	Invalid sound resource
-290	SMSDMInitErr	Error initializing slot devices
-291	SMSRTInitErr	Error initializing Slot Resource Table
-292	SMPRAMInitErr	Error initializing PRAM
-293	SMPriInitErr	Error initializing card
-299	NMTypErr	Wrong queue type for notification
-300	SMEmptySlot	No card in slot
-301	SMCRCFail	Bad checksum in declaration data
-302	SMFormatErr	Invalid format block
-303	SMRevisionErr	Wrong revision level
-304	SMNoDir	Invalid directory offset
-305	SMLWTstBad	Bad test pattern
-306	SMNoSInfoArray	Error allocating slot info array

Number	Name	Meaning
-307	SMResrvErr	Reserved field nonzero
-308	SMSMUnExBusErr	Unexpected bus error
-309	SMBLFieldBad	Bad byte lanes
-310	SMFHBlockRdErr	Error reading format header
-312	SMDisposePErr	Error disposing of format header
-313	SMNoBoardSRsrc	No board slot resource list
-314	SMGetPRErr	Error reading PRAM init data
-315	SMNoBoardID	No board ID
-316	SMInitStatVErr	Error in vendor init status
-317	SMInitTblErr	Error initializing Slot Resource Table
-318	SMNoJmpTbl	Error creating jump table
-319	SMBadBoardID	Invalid board ID
-320	SMBusErrTO	Bus error timeout
-330	SMBadRefID	Invalid reference ID
-331	SMBadSList	Slot resources out of order
-332	SMReservedErr	Reserved field nonzero
-333	SMCodeRevErr	Invalid code revision
-334	SMCPUErr	Invalid CPU field
-335	SMSPointerNil	No slot resource list
-336	SMNilSBlockErr	Bad block size
-337	SMSlotOOBErr	Slot out of bounds
-338	SMSelOOBErr	Selector out of bounds
-339	SMNewPErr	Error allocating block
-340	SMBlkMoveErr	Error moving block
-341	SMCkStatusErr	Bad slot status
-342	SMGetDrvrNamErr	Error getting driver name
-343	SMDisDrvrNamErr	Error disposing of driver name
-344	SMNoMoreSRsrcs	No more slot resources
-345	SMSGetDrvrErr	Error loading driver
-346	SMBadSPtrErr	Bad slot pointer
-347	SMByteLanesErr	Bad byte lanes
-348	SMOffsetErr	Invalid offset
-349	SMNoGoodOpens	No successful opens
-350	SMSRTOvrflErr	Slot Resource Table overflow
-351	SMRecNotFnd	Record not found in Slot Resource Table
-360	SlotNumErr	Invalid slot number
-500	RgnTooBigErr	Region too big
-501	TEScrapSizeErr	Scrap item too big for edit record

Number	Name	Meaning
-502	HWParamrErr	Hardware parameter error
-1024	NBPBuffOvr	Buffer overflow (AppleTalk, Name Binding Protocol)
-1025	NBPNoConfirm	Name not confirmed (AppleTalk, Name Binding Protocol)
-1026	NBPConfDiff	Name confirmed for different socket (AppleTalk, Name Binding Protocol)
-1027	NBPDuplicate	Name already exists (AppleTalk, Name Binding Protocol)
-1028	NBPNotFound	Name not found (AppleTalk, Name Binding Protocol)
-1029	NBPNISErr	Names information socket error (AppleTalk, Name Binding Protocol)
-1066	ASPBadVersNum	Version not supported (AppleTalk Session Protocol)
-1067	ASPBufTooSmall	Buffer too small (AppleTalk Session Protocol)
-1068	ASPNoMoreSess	No more sessions available (AppleTalk Session Protocol)
-1069	ASPNoServers	No servers at this address (AppleTalk Session Protocol)
-1070	ASPParamErr	Parameter error (AppleTalk Session Protocol)
-1071	ASPServerBusy	Server busy (AppleTalk Session Protocol)
-1072	ASPSessClosed	Session closed (AppleTalk Session Protocol)
-1073	ASPSizeErr	Command block too big (AppleTalk Session Protocol)
-1074	ASPTooMany	Too many clients (AppleTalk Session Protocol)
-1075	ASPNoAck	Server not responding (AppleTalk Session Protocol)
-1096	ReqFailed	Request failed (AppleTalk)
-1097	TooManyReqs	Too many concurrent requests (AppleTalk)
-1098	TooManySkts	Too many responding sockets (AppleTalk)
-1099	BadATPSkt	Bad responding socket (AppleTalk Transaction Protocol)
-1100	BadBuffNum	Bad buffer number (AppleTalk)
-1101	NoRelErr	No release received (AppleTalk)

Number	Name	Meaning
-1102	CBNotFound	Control block not found (AppleTalk)
-1103	NoSendResp	AddResponse before SendResponse (AppleTalk)
-1104	NoDataArea	Too many outstanding calls (AppleTalk)
-1105	ReqAborted	Request canceled (AppleTalk)
-3101	Buf2SmallErr	Buffer too small (AppleTalk)
-3102	NoMPPError	Driver not installed (AppleTalk, Macintosh Packet Protocol)
-3103	CkSumErr	Bad checksum (AppleTalk)
-3104	ExtractErr	No tuple in buffer (AppleTalk)
-3105	ReadQErr	Invalid socket or protocol type (AppleTalk)
-3106	ATPLenErr	Packet too long (AppleTalk Transaction Protocol)
-3107	ATPBadRsp	Bad response (AppleTalk Transaction Protocol)
-3108	RecNotFnd	No AppleBus record (AppleTalk)
-3109	SktClosedErr	Socket closed (AppleTalk)
-5000	AFPAccessDenied	Access denied (AppleTalk Filing Protocol)
-5001	AFPAuthContinue	Authorization continue (AppleTalk Filing Protocol)
-5002	AFPBadUAM	Bad UAM (AppleTalk Filing Protocol)
-5003	AFPBadVersNum	Bad version number (AppleTalk Filing Protocol)
-5004	AFPBitMapErr	Bit map error (AppleTalk Filing Protocol)
-5005	AFPCantMove	Can't move (AppleTalk Filing Protocol)
-5006	AFPDenyConflict	Deny conflict (AppleTalk Filing Protocol)
-5007	AFPDirNotEmpty	Directory not empty (AppleTalk Filing Protocol)
-5008	AFPDiskFull	Disk full (AppleTalk Filing Protocol)
-5009	AFPEOFError	End-of-file error (AppleTalk Filing Protocol)
-5010	AFPFileBusy	File busy (AppleTalk Filing Protocol)

Number	Name	Meaning
-5011	AFPFlatVol	Flat volume (AppleTalk Filing Protocol)
-5012	AFPItemNotFound	Item not found (AppleTalk Filing Protocol)
-5013	AFPLockErr	Lock error (AppleTalk Filing Protocol)
-5014	AFPMiscErr	Miscellaneous error (AppleTalk Filing Protocol)
-5015	AFPNoMoreLocks	No more locks (AppleTalk Filing Protocol)
-5016	AFPNoServer	No server (AppleTalk Filing Protocol)
-5017	AFPObjectExists	Object already exists (AppleTalk Filing Protocol)
-5018	AFPObjectNotFound	Object not found (AppleTalk Filing Protocol)
-5019	AFPParmErr	Parameter error (AppleTalk Filing Protocol)
-5020	AFPRangeNotLocked	Range not locked (AppleTalk Filing Protocol)
-5021	AFPRangeOverlap	Range overlap (AppleTalk Filing Protocol)
-5022	AFPSessClosed	Session closed (AppleTalk Filing Protocol)
-5023	AFPUserNotAuth	User not authorized (AppleTalk Filing Protocol)
-5024	AFPCallNotSupported	Call not supported (AppleTalk Filing Protocol)
-5025	AFPObjectTypeErr	Object type error (AppleTalk Filing Protocol)
-5026	AFPTooManyFilesOpen	Too many files open (AppleTalk Filing Protocol)
-5027	AFPServerGoingDown	Server going down (AppleTalk Filing Protocol)
-5028	AFPCantRename	Can't rename (AppleTalk Filing Protocol)
-5029	AFPDirNotFound	Directory not found (AppleTalk Filing Protocol)
-5030	AFPIconTypeErr	Icon type error (AppleTalk Filing Protocol)
-5031	AFPVolLocked	Volume is read-only (AppleTalk Filing Protocol)
-5032	AFPObjectLocked	Object locked for this operation (AppleTalk Filing Protocol)
-5500	EnvNotPresent	SysEnvirons not implemented

Number	Name	Meaning
-5501	EnvBadVers	Invalid version number requested (SysEnvirons)
-5502	EnvVersTooBig	Requested version not available (SysEnvirons)
1	EvtNotEnb	Event type not enabled (PostEvent)
1	SWOverrunErr	Software overrun (serial driver)
16	ParityErr	Parity error (serial driver)
32	HWOverrunErr	Hardware overrun (serial driver)
64	FramingErr	Framing error (serial driver)
128	IPrAbort	Printing canceled in progress

"Dire Straits" Errors

The following errors are reported directly to the user—not to the running program—by the "Dire Straits" Manager (officially called the System Error Handler). Errors in this category are considered so serious that recovery is impossible: the Toolbox simply displays a "dire straits" alert box (the one with the bomb icon) on the screen, forcing the user to restart the system. Some people insist that DS really stands for "deep spaghetti," but most Macintosh programmers prefer a more colorful term.

Number	Name	Meaning
1	DSBusErr	Bus error
2	DSAddressErr	Address error
3	DSIllInstErr	Illegal instruction
4	DSZeroDivErr	Attempt to divide by zero
5	DSChkErr	Check trap
6	DSOvflowErr	Overflow trap
7	DSPrivErr	Privilege violation
8	DSTraceErr	Trace trap
9	DSLineAErr	"A emulator" trap
10	DSLineFErr	"F emulator" trap
11	DSMiscErr	Miscellaneous hardware exception
12	DSCoreErr	Unimplemented core routine
13	DSIRQErr	Uninstalled interrupt
14	DSIOCoreErr	I/O core error
15	DSLoadErr	Segment Loader error
16	DSFPErr	Floating-point error
17	DSNoPackErr	Package 0 not present
18	DSNoPk1	Package 1 not present
19	DSNoPk2	Package 2 not present
20	DSNoPk3	Package 3 not present
21	DSNoPk4	Package 4 not present
22	DSNoPk5	Package 5 not present
23	DSNoPk6	Package 6 not present
24	DSNoPk7	Package 7 not present

Number	Name	Meaning
25	DSMemFullErr	Out of memory
26	DSBadLaunch	Can't launch program
27	DSFSErr	File system error
28	DSStkNHeap	Stack/heap collision
30	DSReinsert	Ask user to reinsert disk
31	DSNotTheOne	Wrong disk inserted
33	NegZCBFreeErr	Negative heap space available
40	DSGreeting	"Welcome to Macintosh"
41	DSFinderErr	Can't load Finder
42	ShutDownAlert	System shutdown alert
51	DSBadSlotInt	Unserviceable slot interrupt
81	DSBadSANEOpcode	Bad SANE opcode (Standard Apple Numeric Environment)
84	MenuPrgErr	Menu purged from heap
87	WDEFNFnd	Window definition function not found
88	CDEFNFnd	Control definition function not found
98	DSNoPatch	Can't patch for this model
99	DSBadPatch	Can't load patch resource
32767	DSSysErr	General system error

Summary of Trap Macros and Trap Words

Trap Macros

The following is an alphabetical list of assembly-language trap macros covered in the four volumes of this book, with their corresponding trap words. For routines belonging to the standard packages, the trap word shown is one of the eight package traps (_Pack0 to _Pack7) and is followed by a routine selector in parentheses; similarly, routines called via "universal" traps such as _OSDispatch, _TEDispatch, or _PrGlue list the appropriate trap word along with a specific routine selector. Routines marked with an asterisk (*) were introduced in the 128K Macintosh Plus ROM (version $75); those with a dagger (†) are new in the 256K ROMs for the Macintosh SE (version $76) or Macintosh II (version $78).

Trap Macro Name	Trap Word	Reference Section
†_ActivatePalette	$AA94	[IV:6.3.6]
†_AddComp	$AA3B	[IV:4.6.2]
_AddPt	$A87E	[I:4.4.1]
_AddResMenu	$A94D	[II:4.3.3]
_AddResource	$A9AB	[I:6.5.3]
†_AddSearch	$AA3A	[IV:4.6.2]
_Alert	$A985	[II:7.4.2]

Trap Macro Name	Trap Word	Reference Section
_Allocate	$A010	[II:8.2.5]
†_AnimateEntry	$AA99	[IV:5.4.3]
†_AnimatePalette	$AA9A	[IV:5.4.3]
_AppendMenu	$A933	[II:4.3.1]
_BackColor	$A863	[IV:4.1.2]
_BackPat	$A87C	[I:5.1.1]
†_BackPixPat	$AA0B	[IV:5.2.4]
_BeginUpdate	$A922	[II:3.4.1]
_BitAnd	$A858	[I:2.2.2]
_BitClr	$A85F	[I:2.2.1]
_BitNot	$A85A	[I:2.2.2]
_BitOr	$A85B	[I:2.2.2]
_BitSet	$A85E	[I:2.2.1]
_BitShift	$A85C	[I:2.2.2]
_BitTst	$A85D	[I:2.2.1]
_BitXOr	$A859	[I:2.2.2]
_BlockMove	$A02E	[I:3.2.5]
_BringToFront	$A920	[II:3.3.3]
_Button	$A974	[II:2.4.2]
†_CalcCMask	$AA4F	[IV:5.4.5]
*_CalcMask	$A838	[I:5.1.6]
_CalcMenuSize	$A948	[II:4.7.1]
_CautionAlert	$A988	[II:7.4.2]
_Chain	$A9F3	[I:7.1.1]
_ChangedResource	$A9AA	[I:6.5.2]
†_CharExtra	$AA23	[IV:7.3.2]
_CharWidth	$A88D	[I:8.3.4]
_CheckItem	$A945	[II:4.6.4]
_ClearMenuBar	$A934	[II:4.4.1]
_ClipRect	$A87B	[I:4.3.6]
_Close	$A001	[II:8.2.2, III:3.2.1]
_CloseCPort	$A87D	[IV:5.1.5]
_CloseDeskAcc	$A9B7	[II:4.5.2, III:6.2.1]
_CloseDialog	$A982	[II:7.2.3]
_ClosePgon	$A8CC	[I:4.1.4]
_ClosePicture	$A8F4	[I:5.4.2]
_ClosePort	$A87D	[I:4.3.2]
_CloseResFile	$A99A	[I:6.2.1]

Trap Macro Name	Trap Word	Reference Section
_CloseRgn	$A8DB	[I:4.1.6]
_CloseWindow	$A92D	[II:3.2.3]
_CmpString	$A03C	[I:2.1.2]
†_CMY2RGB	$A82E (3)	[IV:4.2.2]
_ColorBit	$A864	[IV:4.1.3]
†_Color2Index	$AA33	[IV:4.4.4]
_CompactMem	$A04C	[I:3.3.2]
_Control	$A004	[III:3.2.3]
_CopyBits	$A8EC	[I:5.1.2, IV:5.4.4]
*_CopyMask	$A817	[I:5.1.4, IV:5.4.4]
†_CopyPalette	$AAA1	[IV:4.5.5]
†_CopyPixMap	$AA05	[IV:5.1.2]
†_CopyPixPat	$AA09	[IV:5.2.3]
_CopyRgn	$A8DC	[I:4.1.7]
_CouldAlert	$A989	[II:7.5.3]
_CouldDialog	$A979	[II:7.5.3]
_CountMItems	$A950	[II:4.3.4]
_CountResources	$A99C	[I:6.3.3]
_CountTypes	$A99E	[I:6.3.3]
*_Count1Resources	$A80D	[I:6.3.3]
*_Count1Types	$A81C	[I:6.3.3]
_Create	$A008	[II:8.2.1]
_CreateResFile	$A9B1	[I:6.5.1]
†_CTab2Palette	$AA9F	[IV:4.5.5]
_CurResFile	$A994	[I:6.2.2]
_Date2Secs	$A9C7	[I:2.4.3]
_Delay	$A03B	[II:2.7.1]
†_DelComp	$AA4D	[IV:4.6.2]
_Delete	$A009	[II:8.2.7]
_DeleteMenu	$A936	[II:4.4.1]
†_DelMCEntries	$AA60	[IV:6.6.3]
*_DelMenuItem	$A952	[II:4.3.4]
†_DelSearch	$AA4C	[IV:4.6.2]
_DeltaPoint	$A94F	[I:4.4.1]
_Dequeue	$A96E	[III:3.1.7]
_DetachResource	$A992	[I:6.3.2]
_DialogSelect	$A980	[II:7.4.4]
_DIBadMount	$A9E9 (0)	[II:8.4.1]
_DiffRgn	$A8E6	[I:4.4.8]

Trap Macro Name	Trap Word	Reference Section
_DIFormat	$A9E9 (6)	[II:8.4.2]
_DILoad	$A9E9 (2)	[II:8.4.3]
_DisableItem	$A93A	[II:4.6.2]
†_DispMCInfo	$AA63	[IV:6.6.2]
†_DisposCCursor	$AA26	[IV:6.2.2]
†_DisposCIcon	$AA25	[IV:6.1.2]
_DisposControl	$A955	[II:6.2.2]
†_DisposCTable	$AA24	[IV:4.4.3]
_DisposDialog	$A983	[II:7.2.3]
†_DisposePalette	$AA93	[IV:4.5.3]
†_DisposGDevice	$AA30	[IV:4.3.2]
_DisposHandle	$A023	[I:3.2.2]
_DisposMenu	$A932	[II:4.2.3]
†_DisposPixMap	$AA04	[IV:5.1.2]
†_DisposPixPat	$AA08	[IV:5.2.2]
_DisposPtr	$A01F	[I:3.2.2]
_DisposRgn	$A8D9	[I:4.1.6]
_DisposWindow	$A914	[II:3.2.3]
_DIUnload	$A9E9 (4)	[II:8.4.3]
_DIVerify	$A9E9 (8)	[II:8.4.2]
_DIZero	$A9E9 (10)	[II:8.4.2]
_DragControl	$A967	[II:6.4.3]
_DragWindow	$A925	[II:3.5.4]
_DrawChar	$A883	[I:8.3.3]
_DrawControls	$A969	[II:6.3.1]
_DrawDialog	$A981	[II:7.4.1]
_DrawGrowIcon	$A904	[II:3.3.4]
_DrawMenuBar	$A937	[II:4.4.3]
_DrawPicture	$A8F6	[I:5.4.3]
_DrawString	$A884	[I:8.3.3]
_DrawText	$A885	[I:8.3.3]
_Eject	$A017	[II:8.1.3]
_EmptyHandle	$A02B	[I:3.3.3]
_EmptyRect	$A8AE	[I:4.4.4]
_EmptyRgn	$A8E2	[I:4.4.7]
_EnableItem	$A939	[II:4.6.2]
_EndUpdate	$A923	[II:3.4.1]
_Enqueue	$A96F	[III:3.1.7]
_EqualPt	$A881	[I:4.4.1]

Trap Macro Name	Trap Word	Reference Section
_EqualRect	$A8A6	[I:4.4.5]
_EqualRgn	$A8E3	[I:4.4.8]
_EraseArc	$A8C0	[I:5.3.5]
_EraseOval	$A8B9	[I:5.3.4]
_ErasePoly	$A8C8	[I:5.3.6]
_EraseRect	$A8A3	[I:5.3.2]
_EraseRgn	$A8D4	[I:5.3.7]
_EraseRoundRect	$A8B2	[I:5.3.3]
_ErrorSound	$A98C	[II:7.5.1]
_EventAvail	$A971	[II:2.2.1]
_ExitToShell	$A9F4	[I:7.1.3]
_FillArc	$A8C2	[I:5.3.5]
†_FillCArc	$AA11	[IV:5.4.2]
†_FillCOval	$AA0F	[IV:5.4.2]
†_FillCPoly	$AA13	[IV:5.4.2]
†_FillCRect	$AA0E	[IV:5.4.2]
†_FillCRgn	$AA12	[IV:5.4.2]
†_FillCRoundRect	$AA10	[IV:5.4.2]
_FillOval	$A8BB	[I:5.3.4]
_FillPoly	$A8CA	[I:5.3.6]
_FillRect	$A8A5	[I:5.3.2]
_FillRgn	$A8D6	[I:5.3.7]
_FillRoundRect	$A8B4	[I:5.3.3]
_FindControl	$A96C	[II:6.4.1]
*_FindDItem	$A984	[II:7.3.4]
_FindWindow	$A92C	[II:3.5.1]
*_FixATan2	$A818	[I:2.3.6]
*_FixDiv	$A84D	[I:2.3.2]
_FixMul	$A868	[I:2.3.2]
_FixRatio	$A869	[I:2.3.2]
_FixRound	$A86C	[I:2.3.1]
*_Fix2Frac	$A841	[I:2.3.3]
*_Fix2Long	$A840	[I:2.3.1]
†_Fix2SmallFract	$A82E (1)	[IV:2.4.1]
_FlashMenuBar	$A94C	[II:4.7.2]
_FlushEvents	$A032	[II:2.3.1]
_FlushVol	$A013	[II:8.1.3]
*_FontMetrics	$A835	[I:8.2.6]
_ForeColor	$A862	[IV:4.1.2]

Trap Macro Name	Trap Word	Reference Section
*_FracCos	$A847	[I:2.3.6]
*_FracDiv	$A84B	[I:2.3.4]
*_FracMul	$A84A	[I:2.3.4]
*_FracSin	$A848	[I:2.3.6]
*_FracSqrt	$A849	[I:2.3.4]
*_Frac2Fix	$A842	[I:2.3.3]
_FrameArc	$A8BE	[I:5.3.5]
_FrameOval	$A8B7	[I:5.3.4]
_FramePoly	$A8C6	[I:5.3.6]
_FrameRect	$A8A1	[I:5.3.2]
_FrameRgn	$A8D2	[I:5.3.7]
_FrameRoundRect	$A8B0	[I:5.3.3]
_FreeAlert	$A98A	[II:7.5.3]
_FreeDialog	$A97A	[II:7.5.3]
_FreeMem	$A01C	[I:3.3.1]
_FrontWindow	$A924	[II:3.3.3]
_GetAppParms	$A9F5	[I:7.3.4]
†_GetAuxCtl	$AA44	[IV:6.4.3]
†_GetAuxWin	$AA42	[IV:6.3.5]
†_GetBackColor	$AA1A	[IV:5.4.1]
†_GetCCursor	$AA1B	[IV:6.2.2]
†_GetCIcon	$AA1E	[IV:6.1.2]
_GetClip	$A87A	[I:4.3.6]
†_GetColor	$A82E (9)	[IV:4.2.3]
†_GetCPixel	$AA17	[IV:5.1.6]
_GetCRefCon	$A95A	[II:6.2.3]
†_GetCTable	$AA18	[IV:4.4.3]
_GetCTitle	$A95E	[II:6.2.3]
_GetCtlAction	$A96A	[II:6.4.2]
_GetCtlValue	$A960	[II:6.2.4]
†_GetCTSeed	$AA28	[IV:4.4.3]
_GetCursor	$A9B9	[II:2.5.2]
†_GetCVariant	$A809	[IV:6.4.3]
†_GetCWMgrPort	$AA48	[IV:6.3.7]
†_GetDeviceList	$AA29	[IV:4.3.3]
_GetDItem	$A98D	[II:7.3.1]
†_GetEntryColor	$AA9B	[IV:4.5.4]
†_GetEntryUsage	$AA9D	[IV:4.5.4]
_GetEOF	$A011	[II:8.2.5]

Trap Macro Name	Trap Word	Reference Section
_GetFileInfo	$A00C	[I:7.3.3]
_GetFName	$A8FF	[I:8.2.5]
_GetFNum	$A900	[I:8.2.5]
_GetFontInfo	$A88B	[I:8.2.6]
†_GetForeColor	$AA19	[IV:5.4.1]
_GetFPos	$A018	[II:8.2.4]
†_GetGDevice	$AA32	[IV:4.3.4]
_GetHandleSize	$A025	[I:3.2.3]
_GetIndResource	$A99D	[I:6.3.3]
_GetIndType	$A99F	[I:6.3.3]
_GetItem	$A946	[II:4.6.1]
_GetIText	$A990	[II:7.3.2]
_GetItmIcon	$A93F	[II:4.6.5]
_GetItmMark	$A943	[II:4.6.4]
_GetItmStyle	$A941	[II:4.6.3]
_GetKeys	$A976	[II:2.6.1]
†_GetMainDevice	$AA2A	[IV:4.3.4]
_GetMaxCtl	$A962	[II:6.2.4]
†_GetMaxDevice	$AA27	[IV:4.3.4]
†_GetMCEntry	$AA64	[IV:6.6.3]
†_GetMCInfo	$AA61	[IV:6.6.2]
_GetMenuBar	$A93B	[II:4.4.4]
_GetMHandle	$A949	[II:4.4.5]
_GetMinCtl	$A961	[II:6.2.4]
_GetMouse	$A972	[II:2.4.1]
_GetNamedResource	$A9A1	[I:6.3.1]
_GetNewControl	$A9BE	[II:6.2.1]
†_GetNewCWindow	$AA46	[IV:6.3.4]
_GetNewDialog	$A97C	[II:7.2.2]
_GetNewMBar	$A9C0	[II:4.4.2]
†_GetNewPalette	$AA92	[IV:4.5.3]
_GetNewWindow	$A9BD	[II:3.2.2]
†_GetNextDevice	$AA2B	[IV:4.3.3]
_GetNextEvent	$A970	[II:2.2.1]
†_GetPalette	$AA96	[IV:6.3.6]
_GetPattern	$A9B8	[I:5.1.1]
_GetPen	$A89A	[I:5.2.4]
_GetPenState	$A898	[I:5.2.1]
_GetPicture	$A9BC	[I:5.4.2]

Trap Macro Name	Trap Word	Reference Section
_GetPixel	$A865	[I:4.2.3]
†_GetPixPat	$AA0C	[IV:5.2.2]
_GetPort	$A874	[I:4.3.3]
_GetPtrSize	$A021	[I:3.2.3]
_GetResAttrs	$A9A6	[I:6.4.2]
_GetResFileAttrs	$A9F6	[I:6.6.2]
_GetResInfo	$A9A8	[I:6.4.1]
_GetResource	$A9A0	[I:6.3.1]
_GetRMenu	$A9BF	[II:4.2.2]
_GetScrap	$A9FD	[I:7.4.3]
_GetString	$A9BA	[I:8.1.2]
†_GetStylHandle	$A83D (4)	[IV:7.3.1]
†_GetStylScrap	$A83D (6)	[IV:7.3.6]
†_GetSubtable	$AA37	[IV:4.4.4]
_GetTrapAddress	$A146	[IV:2.1.2]
_GetVol	$A014	[II:8.1.2]
_GetVolInfo	$A007	[II:8.1.1]
_GetWindowPic	$A92F	[II:3.4.3]
_GetWMgrPort	$A910	[II:3.6.1]
_GetWRefCon	$A917	[II:3.2.4]
_GetWTitle	$A919	[II:3.2.4]
†_GetWVariant	$A80A	[IV:6.3.5]
*_Get1IxResource	$A80E	[I:6.3.3]
*_Get1IxType	$A80F	[I:6.3.3]
*_Get1NamedResource	$A820	[I:6.3.1]
*_Get1Resource	$A81F	[I:6.3.1]
_GlobalToLocal	$A871	[I:4.4.2]
_GrafDevice	$A872	[I:8.3.2]
_GrowWindow	$A92B	[II:3.5.4]
_HandAndHand	$A9E4	[I:3.2.6]
_HandToHand	$A9E1	[I:3.2.5]
*_HClrRBit	$A068	[I:3.2.4]
*_HGetState	$A069	[I:3.2.4]
_HideControl	$A958	[II:6.3.1]
_HideCursor	$A852	[II:2.5.3]
*_HideDItem	$A827	[II:7.3.3]
_HidePen	$A896	[I:5.2.3]
_HideWindow	$A916	[II:3.3.1]
†_HiliteColor	$AA22	[IV:5.3.4]

Trap Macro Name	Trap Word	Reference Section
_HiliteControl	$A95D	[II:6.3.3]
_HiliteMenu	$A938	[II:4.5.4]
_HiliteWindow	$A91C	[II:3.3.4]
_HiWord	$A86A	[I:2.2.3]
_HLock	$A029	[I:3.2.4]
_HNoPurge	$A04A	[I:3.2.4]
_HomeResFile	$A9A4	[I:6.4.3]
_HPurge	$A049	[I:3.2.4]
*_HSetRBit	$A067	[I:3.2.4]
*_HSetState	$A06A	[I:3.2.4]
†_HSL2RGB	$A82E (5)	[IV:4.2.2]
†_HSV2RGB	$A82E (7)	[IV:4.2.2]
_HUnlock	$A02A	[I:3.2.4]
†_Index2Color	$AA34	[IV:4.4.4]
_InfoScrap	$A9F9	[I:7.4.2]
_InitAllPacks	$A9E6	[I:7.2.2]
†_InitCPort	$AA01	[IV:5.1.5]
_InitCursor	$A850	[II:2.5.2]
_InitDialogs	$A97B	[II:7.2.1]
_InitFonts	$A8FE	[I:8.2.4]
†_InitGDevice	$AA2E	[IV:4.3.2]
_InitGraf	$A86E	[I:4.3.1]
_InitMenus	$A930	[II:4.2.1]
_InitPack	$A9E5	[I:7.2.2]
†_InitPalettes	$AA90	[IV:4.5.2]
_InitPort	$A86D	[I:4.3.2]
_InitWindows	$A912	[II:3.2.1]
_InsertMenu	$A935	[II:4.4.1]
_InsertResMenu	$A951	[II:4.3.3]
_InsetRect	$A8A9	[I:4.4.4]
_InsetRgn	$A8E1	[I:4.4.7]
*_InsMenuItem	$A826	[II:4.3.1]
_InvalRect	$A928	[II:3.4.2]
_InvalRgn	$A927	[II:3.4.2]
_InverRect	$A8A4	[I:5.3.2]
_InverRgn	$A8D5	[I:5.3.7]
_InverRoundRect	$A8B3	[I:5.3.3]
_InvertArc	$A8C1	[I:5.3.5]
†_InvertColor	$AA35	[IV:4.4.4]

Trap Macro Name	Trap Word	Reference Section
_InvertOval	$A8BA	[I:5.3.4]
_InvertPoly	$A8C9	[I:5.3.6]
_IsDialogEvent	$A97F	[II:7.4.4]
_IUDateString	$A9ED (0)	[I:2.4.4]
_IUTimeString	$A9ED (2)	[I:2.4.4]
_KillControls	$A956	[II:6.2.2]
_KillIO	$A006	[III:3.2.3]
_KillPicture	$A8F5	[I:5.4.2]
_KillPoly	$A8CD	[I:4.1.4]
_Launch	$A9F2	[I:7.1.1]
_Line	$A892	[I:5.2.4]
_LineTo	$A891	[I:5.2.4]
_LoadSeg	$A9F0	[I:7.1.2]
_LocalToGlobal	$A870	[I:4.4.2]
_LodeScrap	$A9FB	[I:7.4.4]
_LongMul	$A867	[I:2.3.3]
*_Long2Fix	$A83F	[I:2.3.1]
_LoWord	$A86B	[I:2.2.3]
†_MakeITable	$AA39	[IV:4.4.2]
†_MakeRGBPat	$AA0D	[IV:5.2.3]
_MapPoly	$A8FC	[I:4.4.9]
_MapPt	$A8F9	[I:4.4.9]
_MapRect	$A8FA	[I:4.4.9]
_MapRgn	$A8FB	[I:4.4.9]
*_MaxApplZone	$A063	[I:3.3.4]
*_MaxBlock	$A061	[I:3.3.1]
_MaxMem	$A11D	[I:3.3.1]
*_MaxSizeRsrc	$A821	[I:6.4.3]
*_MeasureText	$A837	[I:8.3.4]
_MenuKey	$A93E	[II:4.5.1]
_MenuSelect	$A93D	[II:4.5.1]
†_MFFreeMem	$A88F (24)	[IV:2.2.4]
†_MFMaxMem	$A88F (21)	[IV:2.2.4]
†_MFTempDisposHandle	$A88F (32)	[IV:2.2.3]
†_MFTempHLock	$A88F (30)	[IV:2.2.3]
†_MFTempHUnlock	$A88F (31)	[IV:2.2.3]
†_MFTempNewHandle	$A88F (29)	[IV:2.2.3]
†_MFTopMem	$A88F (22)	[IV:2.2.4]

Trap Macro Name	Trap Word	Reference Section
_ModalDialog	$A991	[II:7.4.3]
_MoreMasters	$A036	[I:3.2.5]
_MountVol	$A00F	[II:8.1.3]
_Move	$A894	[I:5.2.4]
_MoveControl	$A959	[II:6.3.2]
*_MoveHHi	$A064	[I:3.2.5]
_MovePortTo	$A877	[I:4.3.5]
_MoveTo	$A893	[I:5.2.4]
_MoveWindow	$A91B	[II:3.3.2]
_Munger	$A9E0	[II:5.5.6]
†_NewCDialog	$AA4B	[IV:6.5.1]
_NewControl	$A954	[II:6.2.1]
†_NewCWindow	$AA45	[IV:6.3.4]
_NewDialog	$A97D	[II:7.2.2]
*_NewEmptyHandle	$A166	[I:3.2.1]
†_NewGDevice	$AA2F	[IV:4.3.2]
_NewHandle	$A122	[I:3.2.1]
_NewHandleClear	$A322	[IV:2.2.2]
_NewHandleSys	$A522	[IV:2.2.2]
_NewHandleSysClear	$A722	[IV:2.2.2]
_NewMenu	$A931	[II:4.2.2]
†_NewPalette	$AA91	[IV:4.5.3]
†_NewPixMap	$AA03	[IV:5.1.2]
†_NewPixPat	$AA07	[IV:5.2.2]
_NewPtr	$A11E	[I:3.2.1]
_NewPtrClear	$A31E	[IV:2.2.2]
_NewPtrSys	$A51E	[IV:2.2.2]
_NewPtrSysClear	$A71E	[IV:2.2.2]
_NewRgn	$A8D8	[I:4.1.6]
_NewString	$A906	[I:8.1.2]
_NewWindow	$A913	[II:3.2.2]
†_NMInstall	$A05E	[IV:3.2.2]
†_NMRemove	$A05F	[IV:3.2.2]
_NoteAlert	$A987	[II:7.4.2]
_NumToString	$A9EE (0)	[I:2.3.4]
_ObscureCursor	$A856	[II:2.5.4]
_OffLine	$A035	[II:8.1.3]
_OffsetPoly	$A8CE	[I:4.4.6]

Trap Macro Name	Trap Word	Reference Section
_OffsetRect	$A8A8	[I:4.4.4]
_OfsetRgn	$A8E0	[I:4.4.7]
†_OpColor	$AA21	[IV:5.3.2]
_Open	$A000	[II:8.2.2, III:3.2.1]
†_OpenCPort	$AA00	[IV:5.1.5]
_OpenDeskAcc	$A9B6	[II:4.5.2, III:6.2.1]
_OpenPicture	$A8F3	[I:5.4.2]
_OpenPoly	$A8CB	[I:4.1.4]
_OpenPort	$A86F	[I:4.3.2]
_OpenResFile	$A997	[I:6.2.1]
_OpenRF	$A00A	[II:8.2.2]
_OpenRgn	$A8DA	[I:4.1.6]
†_OSDispatch	$A88F	[IV:2.2.3–2.2.4]
_Pack0	$A9E7	[I:7.2.1]
_Pack1	$A9E8	[I:7.2.1]
_Pack2	$A9E9	[I:7.2.1]
_Pack3	$A9EA	[I:7.2.1]
_Pack4	$A9EB	[I:7.2.1]
_Pack5	$A9EC	[I:7.2.1]
_Pack6	$A9ED	[I:7.2.1]
_Pack7	$A9EE	[I:7.2.1]
*_Pack8	$A816	[I:7.2.1]
*_Pack9	$A82B	[I:7.2.1]
*_Pack10	$A82C	[I:7.2.1]
*_Pack11	$A82D	[I:7.2.1]
*_Pack12	$A82E	[I:7.2.1]
*_Pack13	$A82F	[I:7.2.1]
*_Pack14	$A830	[I:7.2.1]
*_Pack15	$A831	[I:7.2.1]
_PaintArc	$A8BF	[I:5.3.5]
_PaintOval	$A8B8	[I:5.3.4]
_PaintPoly	$A8C7	[I:5.3.6]
_PaintRect	$A8A2	[I:5.3.2]
_PaintRgn	$A8D3	[I:5.3.7]
_PaintRoundRect	$A8B1	[I:5.3.3]
†_Palette2CTab	$AAA0	[IV:4.5.5]
_ParamText	$A98B	[II:7.4.6]
_PenMode	$A89C	[I:5.2.2]
_PenNormal	$A89E	[I:5.2.2]

Trap Macro Name	Trap Word	Reference Section
_PenPat	$A89D	[I:5.2.2]
†_PenPixPat	$AA0A	[IV:5.2.4]
_PenSize	$A89B	[I:5.2.2]
_PicComment	$A8F2	[III:2.1.7]
_PinRect	$A94E	[I:4.4.3]
†_PlotCIcon	$AA1F	[IV:6.1.2]
†_PMBackColor	$AA98	[IV:5.4.1]
†_PMForeColor	$AA97	[IV:5.4.1]
_PortSize	$A876	[I:4.3.5]
_PostEvent	$A02F	[II:2.3.2]
*_PrClosDoc	$A8FD ($08000484)	[III:4.3.1]
*_PrClose	$A8FD ($D0000000)	[III:4.2.1]
*_PrClosPage	$A8FD ($1800040C)	[III:4.3.2]
*_PrCtlCall	$A8FD ($A0000E00)	[III:4.4.3]
*_PrDlgMain	$A8FD ($4A040894)	[III:4.5.1]
*_PrDrvrClose	$A8FD ($88000000)	[III:4.4.1]
*_PrDrvrDCE	$A8FD ($94000000)	[III:4.4.2]
*_PrDrvrOpen	$A8FD ($80000000)	[III:4.4.1]
*_PrDrvrVers	$A8FD ($9A000000)	[III:4.4.2]
*_PrError	$A8FD ($BA000000)	[III:4.2.4]
*_PrGlue	$A8FD	[III:4.2–4.5]
*_PrintDefault	$A8FD ($20040480)	[III:4.2.2]
*_PrJobDialog	$A8FD ($32040488)	[III:4.2.3]
*_PrJobInit	$A8FD ($44040410)	[III:4.5.1]
*_PrJobMerge	$A8FD ($5804089C)	[III:4.2.3]
*_PrNoPurge	$A8FD ($B0000000)	[III:4.4.2]
*_PrOpen	$A8FD ($C8000000)	[III:4.2.1]
*_PrOpenDoc	$A8FD ($04000C00)	[III:4.3.1]
*_PrOpenPage	$A8FD ($10000808)	[III:4.3.2]
†_ProtectEntry	$AA3D	[IV:4.4.6]
*_PrPicFile	$A8FD ($60051480)	[III:4.3.3]
*_PrPurge	$A8FD ($A8000000)	[III:4.4.2]
*_PrSetError	$A8FD ($C0000200)	[III:4.2.4]
*_PrStlDialog	$A8FD ($2A040484)	[III:4.2.3]
*_PrStlInit	$A8FD ($3C04040C)	[III:4.5.1]
*_PrValidate	$A8FD ($52040498)	[III:4.2.2]
_Pt2Rect	$A8AC	[I:4.1.2]
_PtInRect	$A8AD	[I:4.4.3]
_PtInRgn	$A8E8	[I:4.4.3]

Trap Macro Name	Trap Word	Reference Section
_PtrAndHand	$A9EF	[I:3.2.6]
_PtrToHand	$A9E3	[I:3.2.5]
_PtrToXHand	$A9E2	[I:3.2.5]
_PtToAngle	$A8C3	[I:5.3.5]
_PurgeMem	$A04D	[I:3.3.3]
*_PurgeSpace	$A162	[I:3.3.1]
_PutScrap	$A9FE	[I:7.4.3]
†_QDError	$AA40	[IV:5.1.7]
_Random	$A861	[I:2.3.5]
_Read	$A002	[II:8.2.3, III:3.2.2]
†_RealColor	$AA36	[IV:4.4.4]
_RealFont	$A902	[I:8.2.5]
_ReallocHandle	$A027	[I:3.3.3]
_RecoverHandle	$A128	[I:3.2.1]
_RectInRgn	$A8E9	[I:4.4.3]
_RectRgn	$A8DF	[I:4.1.7]
_ReleaseResource	$A9A3	[I:6.3.2]
*_RelString	$A050	[I:2.1.2]
_Rename	$A00B	[II:8.2.7]
_ResError	$A9AF	[I:6.6.1]
†_ReserveEntry	$AA3E	[IV:4.4.6]
_ResrvMem	$A040	[I:3.2.1]
†_RestoreEntries	$AA4A	[IV:4.4.5]
†_RGBBackColor	$AA15	[IV:5.4.1]
†_RGBForeColor	$AA14	[IV:5.4.1]
†_RGB2CMY	$A82E (4)	[IV:4.2.2]
†_RGB2HSL	$A82E (6)	[IV:4.2.2]
†_RGB2HSV	$A82E (8)	[IV:4.2.2]
†_RGetResource	$A80C	[IV:2.3.2]
_RmveResource	$A9AD	[I:6.5.3]
_RstFilLock	$A042	[II:8.2.6]
†_SaveEntries	$AA49	[IV:4.4.5]
_ScalePt	$A8F8	[I:4.4.9]
_ScrollRect	$A8EF	[I:5.1.5]
†_SDInstall	$A895 (3)	[IV:2.1.6]
†_SDPowerOff	$A895 (1)	[IV:2.1.5]
†_SDRemove	$A895 (4)	[IV:2.1.6]
†_SDRestart	$A895 (2)	[IV:2.1.5]

Trap Macro Name	Trap Word	Reference Section
_Secs2Date	$A9C6	[I:2.4.3]
_SectRect	$A8AA	[I:4.4.5]
_SectRgn	$A8E4	[I:4.4.8]
†_SeedCFill	$AA50	[IV:5.4.5]
*_SeedFill	$A839	[I:5.1.6]
_SelectWindow	$A91F	[II:3.5.2]
_SelIText	$A97E	[II:7.3.2]
_SendBehind	$A921	[II:3.3.3]
_SetApplLimit	$A02D	[I:3.3.4]
†_SetCCursor	$AA1C	[IV:6.2.2]
†_SetClientID	$AA3C	[IV:4.6.2]
_SetClip	$A879	[I:4.3.6]
†_SetCPixel	$AA16	[IV:5.1.6]
_SetCRefCon	$A95B	[II:6.2.3]
_SetCTitle	$A95F	[II:6.2.3]
_SetCtlAction	$A96B	[II:6.4.2]
†_SetCtlColor	$AA43	[IV:6.4.3]
_SetCtlValue	$A963	[II:6.2.4]
_SetCursor	$A851	[II:2.5.2]
_SetDateTime	$A03A	[I:2.4.1]
†_SetDeskCPat	$AA47	[IV:5.2.4]
†_SetDeviceAttribute	$AA2D	[IV:4.3.5]
_SetDItem	$A98E	[II:7.3.1]
_SetEmptyRgn	$A8DD	[I:4.1.7]
†_SetEntries	$AA3F	[IV:4.4.5]
†_SetEntryColor	$AA9C	[IV:4.5.4]
†_SetEntryUsage	$AA9E	[IV:4.5.4]
_SetEOF	$A012	[II:8.2.5]
_SetFileInfo	$A00D	[I:7.3.3]
_SetFilLock	$A041	[II:8.2.6]
_SetFontLock	$A903	[I:8.2.7]
_SetFPos	$A044	[II:8.2.4]
*_SetFScaleDisable	$A834	[I:8.2.8]
†_SetGDevice	$AA31	[IV:4.3.4]
_SetHandleSize	$A024	[I:3.2.3]
_SetItem	$A947	[II:4.6.1]
_SetIText	$A98F	[II:7.3.2]
_SetItmIcon	$A940	[II:4.6.5]
_SetItmMark	$A944	[II:4.6.4]

Trap Macro Name	Trap Word	Reference Section
_SetItmStyle	$A942	[II:4.6.3]
_SetMaxCtl	$A965	[II:6.2.4]
†_SetMCEntries	$AA65	[IV:6.6.3]
†_SetMCInfo	$AA62	[IV:6.6.2]
_SetMenuBar	$A93C	[II:4.4.4]
_SetMFlash	$A94A	[II:4.7.2]
_SetMinCtl	$A964	[II:6.2.4]
_SetOrigin	$A878	[I:4.3.4]
†_SetPalette	$AA95	[IV:6.3.6]
_SetPBits	$A875	[I:4.3.4]
_SetPenState	$A899	[I:5.2.1]
_SetPort	$A873	[I:4.3.3]
†_SetPortPix	$AA06	[IV:5.1.2]
_SetPt	$A880	[I:4.1.1]
_SetPtrSize	$A020	[I:3.2.3]
_SetRecRgn	$A8DE	[I:4.1.7]
_SetRect	$A8A7	[I:4.1.2]
_SetResAttrs	$A9A7	[I:6.4.2]
_SetResFileAttrs	$A9F7	[I:6.6.2]
_SetResInfo	$A9A9	[I:6.4.1]
_SetResPurge	$A993	[I:6.5.5]
†_SetStdCProcs	$AA4E	[IV:5.5.1]
_SetStdProcs	$A8EA	[III:2.1.1]
_SetString	$A907	[I:8.1.2]
†_SetStylHandle	$A83D (5)	[IV:7.3.1]
†_SetStylScrap	$A83D (11)	[IV:7.3.6]
_SetTrapAddress	$A047	[IV:2.1.2]
_SetVol	$A015	[II:8.1.2]
†_SetWinColor	$AA41	[IV:6.3.5]
_SetWindowPic	$A92E	[II:3.4.3]
_SetWRefCon	$A918	[II:3.2.4]
_SetWTitle	$A91A	[II:3.2.4]
_SFGetFile	$A9EA (2)	[II:8.3.2]
_SFPutFile	$A9EA (1)	[II:8.3.3]
_ShieldCursor	$A855	[II:2.5.4]
_ShowControl	$A957	[II:6.3.1]
_ShowCursor	$A853	[II:2.5.3]
*_ShowDItem	$A828	[II:7.3.3]
_ShowHide	$A908	[II:3.3.1]

Trap Macro Name	Trap Word	Reference Section
_ShowPen	$A897	[I:5.2.3]
_ShowWindow	$A915	[II:3.3.1]
†_Shutdown	$A895	[IV:2.1.5–2.1.6]
_SizeControl	$A95C	[II:6.3.2]
_SizeRsrc	$A9A5	[I:6.4.3]
_SizeWindow	$A91D	[II:3.3.2]
†_SmallFract2Fix	$A82E (2)	[IV:2.4.1]
_SpaceExtra	$A88E	[I:8.3.2]
*_StackSpace	$A065	[I:3.3.4]
_Status	$A005	[III:3.2.3]
_StdArc	$A8BD	[III:2.1.4]
_StdBits	$A8EB	[III:2.1.2]
_StdComment	$A8F1	[III:2.1.7]
_StdGetPic	$A8EE	[III:2.1.6]
_StdLine	$A890	[III:2.1.3]
†_StdOpCodeProc	$ABF8	[IV:5.5.1]
_StdOval	$A8B6	[III:2.1.4]
_StdPoly	$A8C5	[III:2.1.4]
_StdPutPic	$A8F0	[III:2.1.6]
_StdRect	$A8A0	[III:2.1.4]
_StdRgn	$A8D1	[III:2.1.4]
_StdRRect	$A8AF	[III:2.1.4]
_StdText	$A882	[III:2.1.5]
_StdTxMeas	$A8ED	[III:2.1.5]
_StillDown	$A973	[II:2.4.2]
_StopAlert	$A986	[II:7.4.2]
_StringToNum	$A9EE (1)	[I:2.3.4]
_StringWidth	$A88C	[I:8.3.4]
†_StripAddress	$A055	[IV:2.1.3]
_StuffHex	$A866	[I:2.2.4]
_SubPt	$A87F	[I:4.4.1]
†_SwapMMUMode	$A05D	[IV:2.1.3]
_SysBeep	$A9C8	[II:2.8.1]
_SysEdit	$A9C2	[II:4.5.3, III:6.2.3]
†_SysEnvirons	$A090	[IV:2.1.1]
_SystemClick	$A9B3	[II:3.5.3, III:6.2.2]
_SystemEvent	$A9B2	[III:6.2.2]
_SystemMenu	$A9B5	[III:6.2.3]
_SystemTask	$A9B4	[II:2.7.2, III:6.2.4]

Trap Macro Name	Trap Word	Reference Section
_TEActivate	$A9D8	[II:5.4.3]
*_TEAutoView	$A813	[II:5.3.3]
_TECalText	$A9D0	[II:5.3.1]
_TEClick	$A9D4	[II:5.4.1]
†_TEContinuousStyle	$A83D (10)	[IV:7.3.3]
_TECopy	$A9D5	[II:5.5.2, IV:7.3.5]
_TECut	$A9D6	[II:5.5.2, IV:7.3.5]
_TEDeactivate	$A9D9	[II:5.4.3]
_TEDelete	$A9D7	[II:5.5.3]
†_TEDispatch	$A83D	[IV:7.3.1–7.3.6]
_TEDispose	$A9CD	[II:5.2.2]
†_TEGetHeight	$A83D (9)	[IV:7.3.2]
†_TEGetOffset	$A83C	[IV:7.3.2]
†_TEGetPoint	$A83D (8)	[IV:7.3.2]
†_TEGetStyle	$A83D (3)	[IV:7.3.3]
_TEGetText	$A9CB	[II:5.2.3]
_TEIdle	$A9DA	[II:5.4.3]
_TEInit	$A9CC	[II:5.2.1]
_TEInsert	$A9DE	[II:5.5.3]
_TEKey	$A9DC	[II:5.5.1]
_TENew	$A9D2	[II:5.2.2]
†_TENumStyles	$A83D (13)	[IV:7.3.3]
_TEPaste	$A9DB	[II:5.5.2, IV:7.3.5]
*_TEPinScroll	$A812	[II:5.3.3]
†_TEReplaceStyle	$A83D (2)	[IV:7.3.4]
_TEScroll	$A9DD	[II:5.3.3]
*_TESelView	$A811	[II:5.3.3]
_TESetJust	$A9DF	[II:5.3.1]
_TESetSelect	$A9D1	[II:5.4.2]
†_TESetStyle	$A83D (1)	[IV:7.3.4]
_TESetText	$A9CF	[II:5.2.3]
_TestControl	$A966	[II:6.4.1]
†_TestDeviceAttribute	$AA2C	[IV:4.3.5]
†_TEStyleNew	$A83E	[IV:7.3.1]
†_TEStylInsert	$A83D (7)	[IV:7.3.6]
†_TEStylPaste	$A83D (0)	[IV:7.3.5]
_TEUpdate	$A9D3	[II:5.3.2]
_TextBox	$A9CE	[II:5.3.2]
_TextFace	$A888	[I:8.3.2]

Trap Macro Name	Trap Word	Reference Section
_TextFont	$A887	[I:8.3.2]
_TextMode	$A889	[I:8.3.2]
_TextSize	$A88A	[I:8.3.2]
_TextWidth	$A886	[I:8.3.4]
_TickCount	$A975	[II:2.7.1]
*_TrackBox	$A83B	[II:3.5.4]
_TrackControl	$A968	[II:6.4.2]
_TrackGoAway	$A91E	[II:3.5.4]
†_Unimplemented	$A89F	[IV:2.1.2]
_UnionRect	$A8AB	[I:4.4.5]
_UnionRgn	$A8E5	[I:4.4.8]
_UniqueID	$A9C1	[I:6.5.3]
*_Unique1ID	$A810	[I:6.5.3]
_UnloadSeg	$A9F1	[I:7.1.2]
_UnlodeScrap	$A9FA	[I:7.4.4]
_UnmountVol	$A00E	[II:8.1.3]
_UpdateResFile	$A999	[I:6.5.4]
*_UpdtControls	$A953	[II:6.3.1]
*_UpdtDialog	$A978	[II:7.4.1]
_UprString	$A854	[I:2.1.2]
_UseResFile	$A998	[I:6.2.2]
_ValidRect	$A92A	[II:3.4.2]
_ValidRgn	$A929	[II:3.4.2]
_WaitMouseUp	$A977	[II:2.4.2]
†_WaitNextEvent	$A860	[IV:3.1.3]
_Write	$A003	[II:8.2.3, III:3.2.2]
_WriteResource	$A9B0	[I:6.5.4]
_XOrRgn	$A8E7	[I:4.4.8]
_ZeroScrap	$A9FC	[I:7.4.3]
*_ZoomWindow	$A83A	[II:3.3.2]

Trap Words

Here is the same list sorted numerically by trap number. Again, routine selectors are given in parentheses following the trap word for routines belonging to the standard packages or accessed via "universal" traps; routines marked with an asterisk (*) were introduced in the Macintosh Plus ROM; and those with a dagger (†) are new in the Macintosh SE and Macintosh II ROMs.

Trap Word	Trap Macro Name	Reference Section
$A000	_Open	[II:8.2.2, III:3.2.1]
$A001	_Close	[II:8.2.2, III:3.2.1]
$A002	_Read	[II:8.2.3, III:3.2.2]
$A003	_Write	[II:8.2.3, III:3.2.2]
$A004	_Control	[III:3.2.3]
$A005	_Status	[III:3.2.3]
$A006	_KillIO	[III:3.2.3]
$A007	_GetVolInfo	[II:8.1.1]
$A008	_Create	[II:8.2.1]
$A009	_Delete	[II:8.2.7]
$A00A	_OpenRF	[II:8.2.2]
$A00B	_Rename	[II:8.2.7]
$A00C	_GetFileInfo	[I:7.3.3]
$A00D	_SetFileInfo	[I:7.3.3]
$A00E	_UnmountVol	[II:8.1.3]
$A00F	_MountVol	[II:8.1.3]
$A010	_Allocate	[II:8.2.5]
$A011	_GetEOF	[II:8.2.5]
$A012	_SetEOF	[II:8.2.5]
$A013	_FlushVol	[II:8.1.3]
$A014	_GetVol	[II:8.1.2]
$A015	_SetVol	[II:8.1.2]
$A017	_Eject	[II:8.1.3]
$A018	_GetFPos	[II:8.2.4]
$A01C	_FreeMem	[I:3.3.1]
$A11D	_MaxMem	[I:3.3.1]
$A11E	_NewPtr	[I:3.2.1]
$A31E	_NewPtrClear	[IV:2.2.2]
$A51E	_NewPtrSys	[IV:2.2.2]

Trap Word	Trap Macro Name	Reference Section
$A71E	_NewPtrSysClear	[IV:2.2.2]
$A01F	_DisposPtr	[I:3.2.2]
$A020	_SetPtrSize	[I:3.2.3]
$A021	_GetPtrSize	[I:3.2.3]
$A122	_NewHandle	[I:3.2.1]
$A322	_NewHandleClear	[IV:2.2.2]
$A522	_NewHandleSys	[IV:2.2.2]
$A722	_NewHandleSysClear	[IV:2.2.2]
$A023	_DisposHandle	[I:3.2.2]
$A024	_SetHandleSize	[I:3.2.3]
$A025	_GetHandleSize	[I:3.2.3]
$A027	_ReallocHandle	[I:3.3.3]
$A128	_RecoverHandle	[I:3.2.1]
$A029	_HLock	[I:3.2.4]
$A02A	_HUnlock	[I:3.2.4]
$A02B	_EmptyHandle	[I:3.3.3]
$A02D	_SetApplLimit	[I:3.3.4]
$A02E	_BlockMove	[I:3.2.5]
$A02F	_PostEvent	[II:2.3.2]
$A032	_FlushEvents	[II:2.3.1]
$A035	_OffLine	[II:8.1.3]
$A036	_MoreMasters	[I:3.2.5]
$A03A	_SetDateTime	[I:2.4.1]
$A03B	_Delay	[II:2.7.1]
$A03C	_CmpString	[I:2.1.2]
$A040	_ResrvMem	[I:3.2.1]
$A041	_SetFilLock	[II:8.2.6]
$A042	_RstFilLock	[II:8.2.6]
$A044	_SetFPos	[II:8.2.4]
$A146	_GetTrapAddress	[IV:2.1.2]
$A047	_SetTrapAddress	[IV:2.1.2]
$A049	_HPurge	[I:3.2.4]
$A04A	_HNoPurge	[I:3.2.4]
$A04C	_CompactMem	[I:3.3.2]
$A04D	_PurgeMem	[I:3.3.3]
*$A050	_RelString	[I:2.1.2]
†$A055	_StripAddress	[IV:2.1.3]

Trap Word	Trap Macro Name	Reference Section
†$A05D	_SwapMMUMode	[IV:2.1.3]
†$A05E	_NMInstall	[IV:3.2.2]
†$A05F	_NMRemove	[IV:3.2.2]
*$A061	_MaxBlock	[I:3.3.1]
*$A162	_PurgeSpace	[I:3.3.1]
*$A063	_MaxApplZone	[I:3.3.4]
*$A064	_MoveHHi	[I:3.2.5]
*$A065	_StackSpace	[I:3.3.4]
*$A166	_NewEmptyHandle	[I:3.2.1]
*$A067	_HSetRBit	[I:3.2.4]
*$A068	_HClrRBit	[I:3.2.4]
*$A069	_HGetState	[I:3.2.4]
*$A06A	_HSetState	[I:3.2.4]
†$A090	_SysEnvirons	[IV:2.1.1]
†$A809	_GetCVariant	[IV:6.4.3]
†$A80A	_GetWVariant	[IV:6.3.5]
†$A80C	_RGetResource	[IV:2.3.2]
*$A80D	_Count1Resources	[I:6.3.3]
*$A80E	_Get1IxResource	[I:6.3.3]
*$A80F	_Get1IxType	[I:6.3.3]
*$A810	_Unique1ID	[I:6.5.3]
*$A811	_TESelView	[II:5.3.3]
*$A812	_TEPinScroll	[II:5.3.3]
*$A813	_TEAutoView	[II:5.3.3]
*$A816	_Pack8	[I:7.2.1]
*$A817	_CopyMask	[I:5.1.4, IV:5.4.4]
*$A818	_FixATan2	[I:2.3.6]
*$A81C	_Count1Types	[I:6.3.3]
*$A81F	_Get1Resource	[I:6.3.1]
*$A820	_Get1NamedResource	[I:6.3.1]
*$A821	_MaxSizeRsrc	[I:6.4.3]
*$A826	_InsMenuItem	[II:4.3.1]
*$A827	_HideDItem	[II:7.3.3]
*$A828	_ShowDItem	[II:7.3.3]
*$A82B	_Pack9	[I:7.2.1]
*$A82C	_Pack10	[I:7.2.1]
*$A82D	_Pack11	[I:7.2.1]

Trap Word	Trap Macro Name	Reference Section
*$A82E	_Pack12	[I:7.2.1]
†$A82E (1)	_Fix2SmallFract	[IV:2.4.1]
†$A82E (2)	_SmallFract2Fix	[IV:2.4.1]
†$A82E (3)	_CMY2RGB	[IV:4.2.2]
†$A82E (4)	_RGB2CMY	[IV:4.2.2]
†$A82E (5)	_HSL2RGB	[IV:4.2.2]
†$A82E (6)	_RGB2HSL	[IV:4.2.2]
†$A82E (7)	_HSV2RGB	[IV:4.2.2]
†$A82E (8)	_RGB2HSV	[IV:4.2.2]
†$A82E (9)	_GetColor	[IV:4.2.3]
*$A82F	_Pack13	[I:7.2.1]
*$A830	_Pack14	[I:7.2.1]
*$A831	_Pack15	[I:7.2.1]
*$A834	_SetFScaleDisable	[I:8.2.8]
*$A835	_FontMetrics	[I:8.2.6]
*$A837	_MeasureText	[I:8.3.4]
*$A838	_CalcMask	[I:5.1.6]
*$A839	_SeedFill	[I:5.1.6]
*$A83A	_ZoomWindow	[II:3.3.2]
*$A83B	_TrackBox	[II:3.5.4]
†$A83C	_TEGetOffset	[IV:7.3.2]
†$A83D	_TEDispatch	[IV:7.3.1–7.3.6]
†$A83D (0)	_TEStylPaste	[IV:7.3.5]
†$A83D (1)	_TESetStyle	[IV:7.3.4]
†$A83D (2)	_TEReplaceStyle	[IV:7.3.4]
†$A83D (3)	_TEGetStyle	[IV:7.3.3]
†$A83D (4)	_GetStylHandle	[IV:7.3.1]
†$A83D (5)	_SetStylHandle	[IV:7.3.1]
†$A83D (6)	_GetStylScrap	[IV:7.3.6]
†$A83D (7)	_TEStylInsert	[IV:7.3.6]
†$A83D (8)	_TEGetPoint	[IV:7.3.2]
†$A83D (9)	_TEGetHeight	[IV:7.3.2]
†$A83D (10)	_TEContinuousStyle	[IV:7.3.3]
†$A83D (11)	_SetStylScrap	[IV:7.3.6]
†$A83D (13)	_TENumStyles	[IV:7.3.3]
†$A83E	_TEStyleNew	[IV:7.3.1]
*$A83F	_Long2Fix	[I:2.3.1]
*$A840	_Fix2Long	[I:2.3.1]

Trap Word	Trap Macro Name	Reference Section
*$A841	_Fix2Frac	[I:2.3.3]
*$A842	_Frac2Fix	[I:2.3.3]
*$A847	_FracCos	[I:2.3.6]
*$A848	_FracSin	[I:2.3.6]
*$A849	_FracSqrt	[I:2.3.4]
*$A84A	_FracMul	[I:2.3.4]
*$A84B	_FracDiv	[I:2.3.4]
*$A84D	_FixDiv	[I:2.3.2]
$A850	_InitCursor	[II:2.5.2]
$A851	_SetCursor	[II:2.5.2]
$A852	_HideCursor	[II:2.5.3]
$A853	_ShowCursor	[II:2.5.3]
$A854	_UprString	[I:2.1.2]
$A855	_ShieldCursor	[II:2.5.4]
$A856	_ObscureCursor	[II:2.5.4]
$A858	_BitAnd	[I:2.2.2]
$A859	_BitXOr	[I:2.2.2]
$A85A	_BitNot	[I:2.2.2]
$A85B	_BitOr	[I:2.2.2]
$A85C	_BitShift	[I:2.2.2]
$A85D	_BitTst	[I:2.2.1]
$A85E	_BitSet	[I:2.2.1]
$A85F	_BitClr	[I:2.2.1]
†$A860	_WaitNextEvent	[IV:3.1.3]
$A861	_Random	[I:2.3.5]
$A862	_ForeColor	[IV:4.1.2]
$A863	_BackColor	[IV:4.1.2]
$A864	_ColorBit	[IV:4.1.3]
$A865	_GetPixel	[I:4.2.3]
$A866	_StuffHex	[I:2.2.4]
$A867	_LongMul	[I:2.3.3]
$A868	_FixMul	[I:2.3.2]
$A869	_FixRatio	[I:2.3.2]
$A86A	_HiWord	[I:2.2.3]
$A86B	_LoWord	[I:2.2.3]
$A86C	_FixRound	[I:2.3.1]
$A86D	_InitPort	[I:4.3.2]
$A86E	_InitGraf	[I:4.3.1]
$A86F	_OpenPort	[I:4.3.2]

Trap Word	Trap Macro Name	Reference Section
$A870	_LocalToGlobal	[I:4.4.2]
$A871	_GlobalToLocal	[I:4.4.2]
$A872	_GrafDevice	[I:8.3.2]
$A873	_SetPort	[I:4.3.3]
$A874	_GetPort	[I:4.3.3]
$A875	_SetPBits	[I:4.3.4]
$A876	_PortSize	[I:4.3.5]
$A877	_MovePortTo	[I:4.3.5]
$A878	_SetOrigin	[I:4.3.4]
$A879	_SetClip	[I:4.3.6]
$A87A	_GetClip	[I:4.3.6]
$A87B	_ClipRect	[I:4.3.6]
$A87C	_BackPat	[I:5.1.1]
$A87D	_ClosePort	[I:4.3.2]
$A87D	_CloseCPort	[IV:5.1.5]
$A87E	_AddPt	[I:4.4.1]
$A87F	_SubPt	[I:4.4.1]
$A880	_SetPt	[I:4.1.1]
$A881	_EqualPt	[I:4.4.1]
$A882	_StdText	[III:2.1.5]
$A883	_DrawChar	[I:8.3.3]
$A884	_DrawString	[I:8.3.3]
$A885	_DrawText	[I:8.3.3]
$A886	_TextWidth	[I:8.3.4]
$A887	_TextFont	[I:8.3.2]
$A888	_TextFace	[I:8.3.2]
$A889	_TextMode	[I:8.3.2]
$A88A	_TextSize	[I:8.3.2]
$A88B	_GetFontInfo	[I:8.2.6]
$A88C	_StringWidth	[I:8.3.4]
$A88D	_CharWidth	[I:8.3.4]
$A88E	_SpaceExtra	[I:8.3.2]
†$A88F	_OSDispatch	[IV:2.2.3–2.2.4]
†$A88F (21)	_MFMaxMem	[IV:2.2.4]
†$A88F (22)	_MFTopMem	[IV:2.2.4]
†$A88F (24)	_MFFreeMem	[IV:2.2.4]
†$A88F (29)	_MFTempNewHandle	[IV:2.2.3]
†$A88F (30)	_MFTempHLock	[IV:2.2.3]

Trap Word	Trap Macro Name	Reference Section
†$A88F (31)	_MFTempHUnlock	[IV:2.2.3]
†$A88F (32)	_MFTempDisposHandle	[IV:2.2.3]
$A890	_StdLine	[III:2.1.3]
$A891	_LineTo	[I:5.2.4]
$A892	_Line	[I:5.2.4]
$A893	_MoveTo	[I:5.2.4]
$A894	_Move	[I:5.2.4]
†$A895	_Shutdown	[IV:2.1.5–2.1.6]
†$A895 (1)	_SDPowerOff	[IV:2.1.5]
†$A895 (2)	_SDRestart	[IV:2.1.5]
†$A895 (3)	_SDInstall	[IV:2.1.6]
†$A895 (4)	_SDRemove	[IV:2.1.6]
$A896	_HidePen	[I:5.2.3]
$A897	_ShowPen	[I:5.2.3]
$A898	_GetPenState	[I:5.2.1]
$A899	_SetPenState	[I:5.2.1]
$A89A	_GetPen	[I:5.2.4]
$A89B	_PenSize	[I:5.2.2]
$A89C	_PenMode	[I:5.2.2]
$A89D	_PenPat	[I:5.2.2]
$A89E	_PenNormal	[I:5.2.2]
†$A89F	_Unimplemented	[IV:2.1.2]
$A8A0	_StdRect	[III:2.1.4]
$A8A1	_FrameRect	[I:5.3.2]
$A8A2	_PaintRect	[I:5.3.2]
$A8A3	_EraseRect	[I:5.3.2]
$A8A4	_InverRect	[I:5.3.2]
$A8A5	_FillRect	[I:5.3.2]
$A8A6	_EqualRect	[I:4.4.5]
$A8A7	_SetRect	[I:4.1.2]
$A8A8	_OffsetRect	[I:4.4.4]
$A8A9	_InsetRect	[I:4.4.4]
$A8AA	_SectRect	[I:4.4.5]
$A8AB	_UnionRect	[I:4.4.5]
$A8AC	_Pt2Rect	[I:4.1.2]
$A8AD	_PtInRect	[I:4.4.3]
$A8AE	_EmptyRect	[I:4.4.4]
$A8AF	_StdRRect	[III:2.1.4]

Trap Word	Trap Macro Name	Reference Section
$A8B0	_FrameRoundRect	[I:5.3.3]
$A8B1	_PaintRoundRect	[I:5.3.3]
$A8B2	_EraseRoundRect	[I:5.3.3]
$A8B3	_InverRoundRect	[I:5.3.3]
$A8B4	_FillRoundRect	[I:5.3.3]
$A8B6	_StdOval	[III:2.1.4]
$A8B7	_FrameOval	[I:5.3.4]
$A8B8	_PaintOval	[I:5.3.4]
$A8B9	_EraseOval	[I:5.3.4]
$A8BA	_InvertOval	[I:5.3.4]
$A8BB	_FillOval	[I:5.3.4]
$A8BD	_StdArc	[III:2.1.4]
$A8BE	_FrameArc	[I:5.3.5]
$A8BF	_PaintArc	[I:5.3.5]
$A8C0	_EraseArc	[I:5.3.5]
$A8C1	_InvertArc	[I:5.3.5]
$A8C2	_FillArc	[I:5.3.5]
$A8C3	_PtToAngle	[I:5.3.5]
$A8C5	_StdPoly	[III:2.1.4]
$A8C6	_FramePoly	[I:5.3.6]
$A8C7	_PaintPoly	[I:5.3.6]
$A8C8	_ErasePoly	[I:5.3.6]
$A8C9	_InvertPoly	[I:5.3.6]
$A8CA	_FillPoly	[I:5.3.6]
$A8CB	_OpenPoly	[I:4.1.4]
$A8CC	_ClosePgon	[I:4.1.4]
$A8CD	_KillPoly	[I:4.1.4]
$A8CE	_OffsetPoly	[I:4.4.6]
$A8D1	_StdRgn	[III:2.1.4]
$A8D2	_FrameRgn	[I:5.3.7]
$A8D3	_PaintRgn	[I:5.3.7]
$A8D4	_EraseRgn	[I:5.3.7]
$A8D5	_InverRgn	[I:5.3.7]
$A8D6	_FillRgn	[I:5.3.7]
$A8D8	_NewRgn	[I:4.1.6]
$A8D9	_DisposRgn	[I:4.1.6]
$A8DA	_OpenRgn	[I:4.1.6]
$A8DB	_CloseRgn	[I:4.1.6]

Trap Word	Trap Macro Name	Reference Section
$A8DC	_CopyRgn	[I:4.1.7]
$A8DD	_SetEmptyRgn	[I:4.1.7]
$A8DE	_SetRecRgn	[I:4.1.7]
$A8DF	_RectRgn	[I:4.1.7]
$A8E0	_OfsetRgn	[I:4.4.7]
$A8E1	_InsetRgn	[I:4.4.7]
$A8E2	_EmptyRgn	[I:4.4.7]
$A8E3	_EqualRgn	[I:4.4.8]
$A8E4	_SectRgn	[I:4.4.8]
$A8E5	_UnionRgn	[I:4.4.8]
$A8E6	_DiffRgn	[I:4.4.8]
$A8E7	_XOrRgn	[I:4.4.8]
$A8E8	_PtInRgn	[I:4.4.3]
$A8E9	_RectInRgn	[I:4.4.3]
$A8EA	_SetStdProcs	[III:2.1.1]
$A8EB	_StdBits	[III:2.1.2]
$A8EC	_CopyBits	[I:5.1.2, IV:5.4.4]
$A8ED	_StdTxMeas	[III:2.1.5]
$A8EE	_StdGetPic	[III:2.1.6]
$A8EF	_ScrollRect	[I:5.1.5]
$A8F0	_StdPutPic	[III:2.1.6]
$A8F1	_StdComment	[III:2.1.7]
$A8F2	_PicComment	[III:2.1.7]
$A8F3	_OpenPicture	[I:5.4.2]
$A8F4	_ClosePicture	[I:5.4.2]
$A8F5	_KillPicture	[I:5.4.2]
$A8F6	_DrawPicture	[I:5.4.3]
$A8F8	_ScalePt	[I:4.4.9]
$A8F9	_MapPt	[I:4.4.9]
$A8FA	_MapRect	[I:4.4.9]
$A8FB	_MapRgn	[I:4.4.9]
$A8FC	_MapPoly	[I:4.4.9]
*$A8FD	_PrGlue	[III:4.2–4.5]
*$A8FD ($04000C00)	_PrOpenDoc	[III:4.3.1]
*$A8FD ($08000484)	_PrClosDoc	[III:4.3.1]
*$A8FD ($10000808)	_PrOpenPage	[III:4.3.2]
*$A8FD ($1800040C)	_PrClosPage	[III:4.3.2]
*$A8FD ($20040480)	_PrintDefault	[III:4.2.2]

Trap Word	Trap Macro Name	Reference Section
*$A8FD ($2A040484)	_PrStlDialog	[III:4.2.3]
*$A8FD ($32040488)	_PrJobDialog	[III:4.2.3]
*$A8FD ($3C04040C)	_PrStlInit	[III:4.5.1]
*$A8FD ($44040410)	_PrJobInit	[III:4.5.1]
*$A8FD ($4A040894)	_PrDlgMain	[III:4.5.1]
*$A8FD ($52040498)	_PrValidate	[III:4.2.2]
*$A8FD ($5804089C)	_PrJobMerge	[III:4.2.3]
*$A8FD ($60051480)	_PrPicFile	[III:4.3.3]
*$A8FD ($80000000)	_PrDrvrOpen	[III:4.4.1]
*$A8FD ($88000000)	_PrDrvrClose	[III:4.4.1]
*$A8FD ($94000000)	_PrDrvrDCE	[III:4.4.2]
*$A8FD ($9A000000)	_PrDrvrVers	[III:4.4.2]
*$A8FD ($A0000E00)	_PrCtlCall	[III:4.4.3]
*$A8FD ($A8000000)	_PrPurge	[III:4.4.2]
*$A8FD ($B0000000)	_PrNoPurge	[III:4.4.2]
*$A8FD ($BA000000)	_PrError	[III:4.2.4]
*$A8FD ($C0000200)	_PrSetError	[III:4.2.4]
*$A8FD ($C8000000)	_PrOpen	[III:4.2.1]
*$A8FD ($D0000000)	_PrClose	[III:4.2.1]
$A8FE	_InitFonts	[I:8.2.4]
$A8FF	_GetFName	[I:8.2.5]
$A900	_GetFNum	[I:8.2.5]
$A902	_RealFont	[I:8.2.5]
$A903	_SetFontLock	[I:8.2.7]
$A904	_DrawGrowIcon	[II:3.3.4]
$A906	_NewString	[I:8.1.2]
$A907	_SetString	[I:8.1.2]
$A908	_ShowHide	[II:3.3.1]
$A910	_GetWMgrPort	[II:3.6.1]
$A912	_InitWindows	[II:3.2.1]
$A913	_NewWindow	[II:3.2.2]
$A914	_DisposWindow	[II:3.2.3]
$A915	_ShowWindow	[II:3.3.1]
$A916	_HideWindow	[II:3.3.1]
$A917	_GetWRefCon	[II:3.2.4]
$A918	_SetWRefCon	[II:3.2.4]
$A919	_GetWTitle	[II:3.2.4]
$A91A	_SetWTitle	[II:3.2.4]
$A91B	_MoveWindow	[II:3.3.2]

Trap Word	Trap Macro Name	Reference Section
$A91C	_HiliteWindow	[II:3.3.4]
$A91D	_SizeWindow	[II:3.3.2]
$A91E	_TrackGoAway	[II:3.5.4]
$A91F	_SelectWindow	[II:3.5.2]
$A920	_BringToFront	[II:3.3.3]
$A921	_SendBehind	[II:3.3.3]
$A922	_BeginUpdate	[II:3.4.1]
$A923	_EndUpdate	[II:3.4.1]
$A924	_FrontWindow	[II:3.3.3]
$A925	_DragWindow	[II:3.5.4]
$A927	_InvalRgn	[II:3.4.2]
$A928	_InvalRect	[II:3.4.2]
$A929	_ValidRgn	[II:3.4.2]
$A92A	_ValidRect	[II:3.4.2]
$A92B	_GrowWindow	[II:3.5.4]
$A92C	_FindWindow	[II:3.5.1]
$A92D	_CloseWindow	[II:3.2.3]
$A92E	_SetWindowPic	[II:3.4.3]
$A92F	_GetWindowPic	[II:3.4.3]
$A930	_InitMenus	[II:4.2.1]
$A931	_NewMenu	[II:4.2.2]
$A932	_DisposMenu	[II:4.2.3]
$A933	_AppendMenu	[II:4.3.1]
$A934	_ClearMenuBar	[II:4.4.1]
$A935	_InsertMenu	[II:4.4.1]
$A936	_DeleteMenu	[II:4.4.1]
$A937	_DrawMenuBar	[II:4.4.3]
$A938	_HiliteMenu	[II:4.5.4]
$A939	_EnableItem	[II:4.6.2]
$A93A	_DisableItem	[II:4.6.2]
$A93B	_GetMenuBar	[II:4.4.4]
$A93C	_SetMenuBar	[II:4.4.4]
$A93D	_MenuSelect	[II:4.5.1]
$A93E	_MenuKey	[II:4.5.1]
$A93F	_GetItmIcon	[II:4.6.5]
$A940	_SetItmIcon	[II:4.6.5]
$A941	_GetItmStyle	[II:4.6.3]
$A942	_SetItmStyle	[II:4.6.3]

Trap Word	Trap Macro Name	Reference Section
$A943	_GetItmMark	[II:4.6.4]
$A944	_SetItmMark	[II:4.6.4]
$A945	_CheckItem	[II:4.6.4]
$A946	_GetItem	[II:4.6.1]
$A947	_SetItem	[II:4.6.1]
$A948	_CalcMenuSize	[II:4.7.1]
$A949	_GetMHandle	[II:4.4.5]
$A94A	_SetMFlash	[II:4.7.2]
$A94C	_FlashMenuBar	[II:4.7.2]
$A94D	_AddResMenu	[II:4.3.3]
$A94E	_PinRect	[I:4.4.3]
$A94F	_DeltaPoint	[I:4.4.1]
$A950	_CountMItems	[II:4.3.4]
$A951	_InsertResMenu	[II:4.3.3]
*$A952	_DelMenuItem	[II:4.3.4]
*$A953	_UpdtControls	[II:6.3.1]
$A954	_NewControl	[II:6.2.1]
$A955	_DisposControl	[II:6.2.2]
$A956	_KillControls	[II:6.2.2]
$A957	_ShowControl	[II:6.3.1]
$A958	_HideControl	[II:6.3.1]
$A959	_MoveControl	[II:6.3.2]
$A95A	_GetCRefCon	[II:6.2.3]
$A95B	_SetCRefCon	[II:6.2.3]
$A95C	_SizeControl	[II:6.3.2]
$A95D	_HiliteControl	[II:6.3.3]
$A95E	_GetCTitle	[II:6.2.3]
$A95F	_SetCTitle	[II:6.2.3]
$A960	_GetCtlValue	[II:6.2.4]
$A961	_GetMinCtl	[II:6.2.4]
$A962	_GetMaxCtl	[II:6.2.4]
$A963	_SetCtlValue	[II:6.2.4]
$A964	_SetMinCtl	[II:6.2.4]
$A965	_SetMaxCtl	[II:6.2.4]
$A966	_TestControl	[II:6.4.1]
$A967	_DragControl	[II:6.4.3]
$A968	_TrackControl	[II:6.4.2]
$A969	_DrawControls	[II:6.3.1]
$A96A	_GetCtlAction	[II:6.4.2]

Trap Word	Trap Macro Name	Reference Section
$A96B	_SetCtlAction	[II:6.4.2]
$A96C	_FindControl	[II:6.4.1]
$A96E	_Dequeue	[III:3.1.7]
$A96F	_Enqueue	[III:3.1.7]
$A970	_GetNextEvent	[II:2.2.1]
$A971	_EventAvail	[II:2.2.1]
$A972	_GetMouse	[II:2.4.1]
$A973	_StillDown	[II:2.4.2]
$A974	_Button	[II:2.4.2]
$A975	_TickCount	[II:2.7.1]
$A976	_GetKeys	[II:2.6.1]
$A977	_WaitMouseUp	[II:2.4.2]
*$A978	_UpdtDialog	[II:7.4.1]
$A979	_CouldDialog	[II:7.5.3]
$A97A	_FreeDialog	[II:7.5.3]
$A97B	_InitDialogs	[II:7.2.1]
$A97C	_GetNewDialog	[II:7.2.2]
$A97D	_NewDialog	[II:7.2.2]
$A97E	_SelIText	[II:7.3.2]
$A97F	_IsDialogEvent	[II:7.4.4]
$A980	_DialogSelect	[II:7.4.4]
$A981	_DrawDialog	[II:7.4.1]
$A982	_CloseDialog	[II:7.2.3]
$A983	_DisposDialog	[II:7.2.3]
*$A984	_FindDItem	[II:7.3.4]
$A985	_Alert	[II:7.4.2]
$A986	_StopAlert	[II:7.4.2]
$A987	_NoteAlert	[II:7.4.2]
$A988	_CautionAlert	[II:7.4.2]
$A989	_CouldAlert	[II:7.5.3]
$A98A	_FreeAlert	[II:7.5.3]
$A98B	_ParamText	[II:7.4.6]
$A98C	_ErrorSound	[II:7.5.1]
$A98D	_GetDItem	[II:7.3.1]
$A98E	_SetDItem	[II:7.3.1]
$A98F	_SetIText	[II:7.3.2]
$A990	_GetIText	[II:7.3.2]

Trap Word	Trap Macro Name	Reference Section
$A991	_ModalDialog	[II:7.4.3]
$A992	_DetachResource	[I:6.3.2]
$A993	_SetResPurge	[I:6.5.5]
$A994	_CurResFile	[I:6.2.2]
$A997	_OpenResFile	[I:6.2.1]
$A998	_UseResFile	[I:6.2.2]
$A999	_UpdateResFile	[I:6.5.4]
$A99A	_CloseResFile	[I:6.2.1]
$A99C	_CountResources	[I:6.3.3]
$A99D	_GetIndResource	[I:6.3.3]
$A99E	_CountTypes	[I:6.3.3]
$A99F	_GetIndType	[I:6.3.3]
$A9A0	_GetResource	[I:6.3.1]
$A9A1	_GetNamedResource	[I:6.3.1]
$A9A3	_ReleaseResource	[I:6.3.2]
$A9A4	_HomeResFile	[I:6.4.3]
$A9A5	_SizeRsrc	[I:6.4.3]
$A9A6	_GetResAttrs	[I:6.4.2]
$A9A7	_SetResAttrs	[I:6.4.2]
$A9A8	_GetResInfo	[I:6.4.1]
$A9A9	_SetResInfo	[I:6.4.1]
$A9AA	_ChangedResource	[I:6.5.2]
$A9AB	_AddResource	[I:6.5.3]
$A9AD	_RmveResource	[I:6.5.3]
$A9AF	_ResError	[I:6.6.1]
$A9B0	_WriteResource	[I:6.5.4]
$A9B1	_CreateResFile	[I:6.5.1]
$A9B2	_SystemEvent	[III:6.2.2]
$A9B3	_SystemClick	[II:3.5.3, III:6.2.2]
$A9B4	_SystemTask	[II:2.7.2, III:6.2.4]
$A9B5	_SystemMenu	[III:6.2.3]
$A9B6	_OpenDeskAcc	[II:4.5.2, III:6.2.1]
$A9B7	_CloseDeskAcc	[II:4.5.2, III:6.2.1]
$A9B8	_GetPattern	[I:5.1.1]
$A9B9	_GetCursor	[II:2.5.2]
$A9BA	_GetString	[I:8.1.2]
$A9BC	_GetPicture	[I:5.4.2]
$A9BD	_GetNewWindow	[II:3.2.2]
$A9BE	_GetNewControl	[II:6.2.1]

Trap Word	Trap Macro Name	Reference Section
$A9BF	_GetRMenu	[II:4.2.2]
$A9C0	_GetNewMBar	[II:4.4.2]
$A9C1	_UniqueID	[I:6.5.3]
$A9C2	_SysEdit	[II:4.5.3, III:6.2.3]
$A9C6	_Secs2Date	[I:2.4.3]
$A9C7	_Date2Secs	[I:2.4.3]
$A9C8	_SysBeep	[II:2.8.1]
$A9CB	_TEGetText	[II:5.2.3]
$A9CC	_TEInit	[II:5.2.1]
$A9CD	_TEDispose	[II:5.2.2]
$A9CE	_TextBox	[II:5.3.2]
$A9CF	_TESetText	[II:5.2.3]
$A9D0	_TECalText	[II:5.3.1]
$A9D1	_TESetSelect	[II:5.4.2]
$A9D2	_TENew	[II:5.2.2]
$A9D3	_TEUpdate	[II:5.3.2]
$A9D4	_TEClick	[II:5.4.1]
$A9D5	_TECopy	[II:5.5.2, IV:7.3.5]
$A9D6	_TECut	[II:5.5.2, IV:7.3.5]
$A9D7	_TEDelete	[II:5.5.3]
$A9D8	_TEActivate	[II:5.4.3]
$A9D9	_TEDeactivate	[II:5.4.3]
$A9DA	_TEIdle	[II:5.4.3]
$A9DB	_TEPaste	[II:5.5.2, IV:7.3.5]
$A9DC	_TEKey	[II:5.5.1]
$A9DD	_TEScroll	[II:5.3.3]
$A9DE	_TEInsert	[II:5.5.3]
$A9DF	_TESetJust	[II:5.3.1]
$A9E0	_Munger	[II:5.5.6]
$A9E1	_HandToHand	[I:3.2.5]
$A9E2	_PtrToXHand	[I:3.2.5]
$A9E3	_PtrToHand	[I:3.2.5]
$A9E4	_HandAndHand	[I:3.2.6]
$A9E5	_InitPack	[I:7.2.2]
$A9E6	_InitAllPacks	[I:7.2.2]
$A9E7	_Pack0	[I:7.2.1]
$A9E8	_Pack1	[I:7.2.1]
$A9E9	_Pack2	[I:7.2.1]

Trap Word	Trap Macro Name	Reference Section
$A9E9 (0)	_DIBadMount	[II:8.4.1]
$A9E9 (2)	_DILoad	[II:8.4.3]
$A9E9 (4)	_DIUnload	[II:8.4.3]
$A9E9 (6)	_DIFormat	[II:8.4.2]
$A9E9 (8)	_DIVerify	[II:8.4.2]
$A9E9 (10)	_DIZero	[II:8.4.2]
$A9EA	_Pack3	[I:7.2.1]
$A9EA (1)	_SFPutFile	[II:8.3.3]
$A9EA (2)	_SFGetFile	[II:8.3.2]
$A9EB	_Pack4	[I:7.2.1]
$A9EC	_Pack5	[I:7.2.1]
$A9ED	_Pack6	[I:7.2.1]
$A9ED (0)	_IUDateString	[I:2.4.4]
$A9ED (2)	_IUTimeString	[I:2.4.4]
$A9EE	_Pack7	[I:7.2.1]
$A9EE (0)	_NumToString	[I:2.3.4]
$A9EE (1)	_StringToNum	[I:2.3.4]
$A9EF	_PtrAndHand	[I:3.2.6]
$A9F0	_LoadSeg	[I:7.1.2]
$A9F1	_UnloadSeg	[I:7.1.2]
$A9F2	_Launch	[I:7.1.1]
$A9F3	_Chain	[I:7.1.1]
$A9F4	_ExitToShell	[I:7.1.3]
$A9F5	_GetAppParms	[I:7.3.4]
$A9F6	_GetResFileAttrs	[I:6.6.2]
$A9F7	_SetResFileAttrs	[I:6.6.2]
$A9F9	_InfoScrap	[I:7.4.2]
$A9FA	_UnlodeScrap	[I:7.4.4]
$A9FB	_LodeScrap	[I:7.4.4]
$A9FC	_ZeroScrap	[I:7.4.3]
$A9FD	_GetScrap	[I:7.4.3]
$A9FE	_PutScrap	[I:7.4.3]
†$AA00	_OpenCPort	[IV:5.1.5]
†$AA01	_InitCPort	[IV:5.1.5]
†$AA03	_NewPixMap	[IV:5.1.2]
†$AA04	_DisposPixMap	[IV:5.1.2]
†$AA05	_CopyPixMap	[IV:5.1.2]
†$AA06	_SetPortPix	[IV:5.1.2]

Trap Word	Trap Macro Name	Reference Section
†$AA07	_NewPixPat	[IV:5.2.2]
†$AA08	_DisposPixPat	[IV:5.2.2]
†$AA09	_CopyPixPat	[IV:5.2.3]
†$AA0A	_PenPixPat	[IV:5.2.4]
†$AA0B	_BackPixPat	[IV:5.2.4]
†$AA0C	_GetPixPat	[IV:5.2.2]
†$AA0D	_MakeRGBPat	[IV:5.2.3]
†$AA0E	_FillCRect	[IV:5.4.2]
†$AA0F	_FillCOval	[IV:5.4.2]
†$AA10	_FillCRoundRect	[IV:5.4.2]
†$AA11	_FillCArc	[IV:5.4.2]
†$AA12	_FillCRgn	[IV:5.4.2]
†$AA13	_FillCPoly	[IV:5.4.2]
†$AA14	_RGBForeColor	[IV:5.4.1]
†$AA15	_RGBBackColor	[IV:5.4.1]
†$AA16	_SetCPixel	[IV:5.1.6]
†$AA17	_GetCPixel	[IV:5.1.6]
†$AA18	_GetCTable	[IV:4.4.3]
†$AA19	_GetForeColor	[IV:5.4.1]
†$AA1A	_GetBackColor	[IV:5.4.1]
†$AA1B	_GetCCursor	[IV:6.2.2]
†$AA1C	_SetCCursor	[IV:6.2.2]
†$AA1E	_GetCIcon	[IV:6.1.2]
†$AA1F	_PlotCIcon	[IV:6.1.2]
†$AA21	_OpColor	[IV:5.3.2]
†$AA22	_HiliteColor	[IV:5.3.4]
†$AA23	_CharExtra	[IV:7.3.2]
†$AA24	_DisposCTable	[IV:4.4.3]
†$AA25	_DisposCIcon	[IV:6.1.2]
†$AA26	_DisposCCursor	[IV:6.2.2]
†$AA27	_GetMaxDevice	[IV:4.3.4]
†$AA28	_GetCTSeed	[IV:4.4.3]
†$AA29	_GetDeviceList	[IV:4.3.3]
†$AA2A	_GetMainDevice	[IV:4.3.4]
†$AA2B	_GetNextDevice	[IV:4.3.3]
†$AA2C	_TestDeviceAttribute	[IV:4.3.5]
†$AA2D	_SetDeviceAttribute	[IV:4.3.5]
†$AA2E	_InitGDevice	[IV:4.3.2]
†$AA2F	_NewGDevice	[IV:4.3.2]

Trap Word	Trap Macro Name	Reference Section
†$AA30	_DisposGDevice	[IV:4.3.2]
†$AA31	_SetGDevice	[IV:4.3.4]
†$AA32	_GetGDevice	[IV:4.3.4]
†$AA33	_Color2Index	[IV:4.4.4]
†$AA34	_Index2Color	[IV:4.4.4]
†$AA35	_InvertColor	[IV:4.4.4]
†$AA36	_RealColor	[IV:4.4.4]
†$AA37	_GetSubtable	[IV:4.4.4]
†$AA39	_MakeITable	[IV:4.4.2]
†$AA3A	_AddSearch	[IV:4.6.2]
†$AA3B	_AddComp	[IV:4.6.2]
†$AA3C	_SetClientID	[IV:4.6.2]
†$AA3D	_ProtectEntry	[IV:4.4.6]
†$AA3E	_ReserveEntry	[IV:4.4.6]
†$AA3F	_SetEntries	[IV:4.4.5]
†$AA40	_QDError	[IV:5.1.7]
†$AA41	_SetWinColor	[IV:6.3.5]
†$AA42	_GetAuxWin	[IV:6.3.5]
†$AA43	_SetCtlColor	[IV:6.4.3]
†$AA44	_GetAuxCtl	[IV:6.4.3]
†$AA45	_NewCWindow	[IV:6.3.4]
†$AA46	_GetNewCWindow	[IV:6.3.4]
†$AA47	_SetDeskCPat	[IV:5.2.4]
†$AA48	_GetCWMgrPort	[IV:6.3.7]
†$AA49	_SaveEntries	[IV:4.4.5]
†$AA4A	_RestoreEntries	[IV:4.4.5]
†$AA4B	_NewCDialog	[IV:6.5.1]
†$AA4C	_DelSearch	[IV:4.6.2]
†$AA4D	_DelComp	[IV:4.6.2]
†$AA4E	_SetStdCProcs	[IV:5.5.1]
†$AA4F	_CalcCMask	[IV:5.4.5]
†$AA50	_SeedCFill	[IV:5.4.5]
†$AA60	_DelMCEntries	[IV:6.6.3]
†$AA61	_GetMCInfo	[IV:6.6.2]
†$AA62	_SetMCInfo	[IV:6.6.2]
†$AA63	_DispMCInfo	[IV:6.6.2]
†$AA64	_GetMCEntry	[IV:6.6.3]
†$AA65	_SetMCEntries	[IV:6.6.3]

Trap Word	Trap Macro Name	Reference Section
†$AA90	_InitPalettes	[IV:4.5.2]
†$AA91	_NewPalette	[IV:4.5.3]
†$AA92	_GetNewPalette	[IV:4.5.3]
†$AA93	_DisposePalette	[IV:4.5.3]
†$AA94	_ActivatePalette	[IV:6.3.6]
†$AA95	_SetPalette	[IV:6.3.6]
†$AA96	_GetPalette	[IV:6.3.6]
†$AA97	_PMForeColor	[IV:5.4.1]
†$AA98	_PMBackColor	[IV:5.4.1]
†$AA99	_AnimateEntry	[IV:5.4.3]
†$AA9A	_AnimatePalette	[IV:5.4.3]
†$AA9B	_GetEntryColor	[IV:4.5.4]
†$AA9C	_SetEntryColor	[IV:4.5.4]
†$AA9D	_GetEntryUsage	[IV:4.5.4]
†$AA9E	_SetEntryUsage	[IV:4.5.4]
†$AA9F	_CTab2Palette	[IV:4.5.5]
†$AAA0	_Palette2CTab	[IV:4.5.5]
†$AAA1	_CopyPalette	[IV:4.5.5]
†$ABF8	_StdOpCodeProc	[IV:5.5.1]

APPENDIX

Summary of Assembly-Language Variables

System Globals

Listed below are all assembly-language global variables covered in the four volumes of this book, together with their hexadecimal addresses. *Warning:* The addresses given may be subject to change in future versions of the Toolbox; always refer to these variables by name instead of using the addresses directly. Variables marked with an asterisk (*) were introduced in the 128K Macintosh Plus ROM (version $75); those with a dagger (†) are new in the 256K ROMs for the Macintosh SE (version $76) or Macintosh II (version $78).

Variable Name	Address	Reference Section	Meaning
ACount	$A9A	[II:7.5.2]	Stage of last alert minus 1
ANumber	$A98	[II:7.5.2]	Resource ID of last alert
ApFontID	$984	[I:8.2.1]	True font number of current application font
ApplLimit	$130	[I:3.3.4]	Application heap limit

467

Variable Name	Address	Reference Section	Meaning
ApplZone	$2AA	[I:3.1.3]	Pointer to start of application heap
AppParmHandle	$AEC	[I:7.3.4]	Handle to Finder startup information
†AuxCtlHead	$CD4	[IV:6.4.1]	Handle to first record in auxiliary control list
†AuxWinHead	$CD0	[IV:6.3.2]	Pointer to first record in auxiliary window list
BufPtr	$10C	[I:3.1.3]	Pointer to end of application global space
CaretTime	$2F4	[II:5.4.3]	Current blink interval in ticks
CurActivate	$A64	[II:3.4.3]	Pointer to window awaiting activate event
CurApName	$910	[I:7.3.4]	Name of current application (maximum 31 characters)
CurApRefNum	$900	[I:6.2.2, I:7.3.4]	Reference number of application resource file
CurDeactivate	$A68	[II:3.4.3]	Pointer to window awaiting deactivate event
CurMap	$A5A	[I:6.2.2]	Reference number of current resource file
CurPageOption	$936	[I:7.1.1]	Integer specifying screen and sound buffers
CurPitch	$280	[III:5.1.2]	Count value for current square-wave tone
CurrentA5	$904	[I:3.1.3, IV:2.1.4]	Base pointer for application globals
CurStackBase	$908	[I:3.1.3]	Pointer to base of stack
DABeeper	$A9C	[II:7.5.1]	Pointer to current sound procedure
DAStrings	$AA0	[II:7.4.6]	Handles to four text substitution strings
DeskPattern	$A3C	[I:5.1.2]	Screen background pattern

Variable Name	Address	Reference Section	Meaning
†DeviceList	$8A8	[IV:4.3.3]	Handle to first graphics device in device list
DlgFont	$AFA	[II:7.5.1]	Current font number for dialogs and alerts
DoubleTime	$2F0	[II:5.4.1]	Current double-click interval in ticks
FinderName	$2E0	[I:7.1.3]	Name of program to exit to (maximum 15 characters)
*FractEnable	$BF4	[I:8.2.8]	Use fractional character widths? (1 byte)
FScaleDisable	$A63	[I:8.2.8]	Turn off font scaling? (1 byte)
GrayRgn	$9EE	[II:3.6.1, IV:6.3.7]	Handle to desktop region
HeapEnd	$114	[I:3.1.3]	Pointer to end of application heap
†HiliteMode	$938	[IV:5.3.4]	Highlighting flag
†HiliteRGB	$DA0	[IV:5.3.4]	Initial highlighting color
Key1Trans	$29E	[I:8.4.4]	Pointer to keyboard configuration routine
Key2Trans	$2A2	[I:8.4.4]	Pointer to keypad configuration routine
KeyMap	$174	[II:2.6.1]	System keyboard map
KeypadMap	$17C	[II:2.6.1]	System keypad map
Lo3Bytes	$31A	[I:3.2.4]	Mask for extracting address from a master pointer
†MainDevice	$8A4	[IV:4.3.4]	Handle to main screen device
*MBarHeight	$BAA	[II:4.4.3]	Height of menu bar in pixels
MBState	$172	[II:2.4.2]	State of mouse button
MemTop	$108	[I:3.1.3]	Pointer to end of physical memory
†MenuCInfo	$D50	[IV:6.6.1]	Handle to current menu color information table
MenuFlash	$A24	[II:4.7.2]	Current flash count for menu items

Variable Name	Address	Reference Section	Meaning
MenuList	$A1C	[II:4.4.4]	Handle to current menu bar
†MMU32Bit	$CB2	[IV:2.1.3]	Current address mode (1 byte)
PrintErr	$944	[III:4.2.4]	Result code from last printing operation
†QDColors	$8B0	[IV:4.2.2]	Handle to table of primary color values
ResErr	$A60	[I:6.6.1]	Result code from last resource-related call
ResLoad	$A5E	[I:6.3.4]	Load resources auto-matically?
ResumeProc	$A8C	[II:7.2.1]	Pointer to restart procedure
ROMBase	$2AE	[I:3.1.3]	Pointer to start of ROM
ROMFont0	$980	[I:8.2.1]	Handle to system font
*ROMMapInsert	$B9E	[I:6.6.3]	Include ROM-based resources in search? (1 byte)
ScrapCount	$968	[I:7.4.2]	Current scrap count
ScrapHandle	$964	[I:7.4.2]	Handle to contents of desk scrap
ScrapName	$96C	[I:7.4.2]	Pointer to scrap file name
ScrapSize	$960	[I:7.4.2]	Current size of desk scrap
ScrapState	$96A	[I:7.4.2]	Current state of desk scrap
ScrDmpEnb	$2F8	[III:6.3.1]	Intercept Command-Shift keystrokes? (1 byte)
ScrnBase	$824	[I:3.1.3]	Pointer to start of screen buffer
SdEnable	$261	[III:5.1.1]	Sound generator cur-rently enabled? (1 byte)
SdVolume	$260	[III:5.2.2]	Current speaker volume (1 byte)
SEvtEnb	$15C	[III:6.2.2]	Intercept system events? (1 byte)
SoundActive	$27E	[III:5.1.1]	Sound generator cur-rently active? (1 byte)

Variable Name	Address	Reference Section	Meaning
SoundBase	$266	[I:3.1.3, III:5.1.1]	Pointer to start of sound buffer
SoundDCE	$27A	[III:5.1.1]	Pointer to sound driver's device control entry [3.1.4]
SoundPtr	$262	[III:5.1.3]	Pointer to current four-tone sound record
SPFont	$204	[I:8.2.1]	True font number of default application font
†SynListHandle	$D32	[IV:7.1.2]	Handle to first font in synthetic font list
SysEvtMask	$144	[II:2.3.2]	System event mask
SysMap	$A58	[I:6.2.2]	True reference number (not 0) of system resource file
SysMapHndl	$A54	[I:6.2.2]	Handle to resource map of system resource file
SysResName	$AD8	[I:6.2.2]	Name of system resource file (string, maximum 19 characters)
SysZone	$2A6	[I:3.1.3]	Pointer to start of system heap
TEScrpHandle	$AB4	[II:5.5.4]	Handle to text scrap
TEScrpLength	$AB0	[II:5.5.4]	Length of text scrap in characters
TEWdBreak	$AF6	[II:5.6.2]	Pointer to built-in word-break routine
TheCrsr	$844	[II:2.5.2]	Current cursor record
†TheGDevice	$CC8	[IV:4.3.4]	Handle to current graphics device
TheMenu	$A26	[II:4.5.4]	Menu ID of currently highlighted menu
Ticks	$16A	[II:2.7.1]	System clock
Time	$20C	[I:2.4.1]	Current date and time in "raw" seconds
*TmpResLoad	$B9F	[I:6.6.3]	Load resources automatically just this once? (1 byte)

Variable Name	Address	Reference Section	Meaning
TopMapHndl	$A50	[I:6.2.2]	Handle to resource map of most recently opened (not necessarily current) resource file
UnitNtryCnt	$1D2	[III:3.1.3]	Number of entries in unit table
UTableBase	$11C	[III:3.1.3]	Pointer to start of unit table
*WidthTabHandle	$B2A	[I:8.2.6]	Handle to global width table for current font
WindowList	$9D6	[II:3.1.1]	Pointer to first window in window list
WMgrPort	$9DE	[II:3.6.1]	Pointer to Window Manager port

QuickDraw Globals

The QuickDraw global variables listed below are located at the given offsets relative to the QuickDraw globals pointer, which in turn is pointed to by address register A5.

Variable Name	Offset in Bytes	Reference Section	Meaning
ThePort	0	[I:4.3.3]	Current graphics port
White	-8	[I:5.1.2]	Standard white pattern
Black	-16	[I:5.1.2]	Standard black pattern
Gray	-24	[I:5.1.2]	Standard gray pattern
LtGray	-32	[I:5.1.2]	Standard light gray pattern
DkGray	-40	[I:5.1.2]	Standard dark gray pattern
Arrow	-108	[II:2.5.2]	Standard arrow cursor
ScreenBits	-122	[I:4.2.1]	Screen bit map
RandSeed	-126	[I:2.3.8]	"Seed" for random number generation

Glossary

The following is a glossary of technical terms used in this volume. *Note:* Terms shown in *italic* are defined elsewhere in this glossary.

A5 world: Another name for a program's *application global space,* located by means of a *base address* kept in processor register A5.

accept-suspend/resume bit: A flag bit in a program's *size resource* that tells whether the program is prepared to accept *suspend* and *resume events* from *MultiFinder.*

accessory window: A *window* with rounded corners, used for displaying a *desk accessory* on the screen.

activate event: A *window event* generated by the Toolbox to signal that a given window has become the *active window.*

active window: The frontmost *window* on the screen, to which the user's mouse and keyboard actions are directed.

ADB: See *Apple Desktop Bus.*

additive color: The mixing of colors in a luminescent or transparent medium, such as a video screen, which adds together *primary colors* to produce the range of colors perceived by the eye; compare *subtractive color.*

additive primary colors: The three *primary colors* (red, green, and blue) that combine in a luminescent or transparent medium, such as a video screen, to produce the range of colors perceived by the eye; see *additive color.*

address bus: The set of transmission lines used by the *processor* to specify a memory address to be read or written; compare *data bus.*

address mode: A state of the Macintosh system that determines the number of bits constituting a memory address; see *24-bit mode, 32-bit mode.*

address space: The total range of memory addresses available in a given system.

alert: Short for *alert box.*

alert box: A form of *dialog box* that prevents the user from interacting with any other window for as long as the alert remains on the screen, and in which the only meaningful action is to *dismiss* the alert by clicking a *pushbutton;* compare *modal dialog box, modeless dialog box.*

allocate: To set aside a *block* of memory from the *heap* for a particular use.

allocation block: The unit in which space is allocated on a given storage device, such as a disk *volume.*

amplitude: The maximum *magnitude* attained at the peak of a sound or light wave, which determines the volume (loudness) of the sound or the intensity (brightness) of the light.

and: A bit-level operation in which each bit of the result is a 1 if both operands have 1s at the corresponding bit position, or 0 if either or both have 0s.

animating color: An entry in a *palette* that *reserves* an entry in the *current color table* for use in *color table animation,* making that entry unavailable for use by other programs; compare *tolerant color, courteous color, explicit color, dithered color.*

anti-aliasing: (1) A police technique for apprehending criminals operating under assumed names. (2) A *font* definition technique in which the "jaggies" on the edges of characters are smoothed out with suitably weighted gray pixels instead of plain black and white.

APDA: The Apple Programmers and Developers Association, a membership organization sponsored by Apple that provides services and publications for professional and advanced amateur programmers working on Apple equipment.

Apple Desktop Bus: A connector on the back of recent Macintosh models for connecting low-speed, user-operated input devices such as the keyboard, mouse, trackball, or graphics tablet.

Apple Extended Keyboard: The huge, 105-key keyboard available on some Macintosh models for compatibility with brand-X computers and their clones.

Apple mark: A special character (*character code* $14) that appears on the Macintosh screen as a small Apple symbol; used for the title of the *Apple menu.*

Apple menu: A *menu* listing the available *desk accessories*, conventionally placed first in the *menu bar* with the *Apple mark* as its title.

Apple Sound Chip: The custom-designed chip used in recent models of Macintosh to control the digital stereo *sound generator.*

AppleTalk: A network to which the Macintosh can be connected for communication with other computers.

AppleTalk drivers: The standard *device drivers* used for communicating with other computers over the *AppleTalk* network.

application: A particular use or purpose to which the Macintosh (or any computer) can be applied, such as word processing, graphics, or telecommunications.

application event: Any of the four *event types* originally reserved for the running application program to use in any way it wished. One of these, type App4Evt (15), is now redefined to stand for *MultiFinder events* instead.

application file: The *file* containing the executable code of an *application program*, with a *file type* of 'APPL' and the program's own signature as its *creator signature.*

application global space: The area of memory containing a program's *application globals, application parameters*, and *jump table;* located by means of a *base address* kept in processor register A5.

application globals: Global variables belonging to the running application program, which reside in the *application global space* and are located at negative offsets from the *base address* in register A5.

application globals pointer: The *base address* kept in processor register A5 and used to locate the contents of a program's *application global space.*

application heap: The portion of the *heap* available for use by the running application program; compare *system heap.*

application parameters: Descriptive information about the running program, located in the *application global space* at positive offsets from the *base address* in register A5. The application parameters are a vestige of the *Lisa* software environment, and most are unused on the Macintosh; the only ones still in use are the *QuickDraw globals pointer* and the *startup handle.*

application program: A stand-alone program for the Macintosh that the user can start up from the *Finder* by double-clicking the *icon* of its *application file.*

application resource file: The *resource fork* of a program's *application file,* containing *resources* belonging to the program itself.

application window: A *window* used by the running program itself; compare *system window.*

arc: A part of an *oval,* defined by a given *starting angle* and *arc angle.*

arc angle: The angle defining the extent of an *arc* or *wedge;* compare *starting angle.*

arrow cursor: The standard, general-purpose *cursor,* an arrow pointing upward at an angle of "eleven o'clock."

ASC: See *Apple Sound Chip.*

ascent: (1) For a text character, the height of the character above the *baseline,* in *dots* or *pixels.* (2) For a *font,* the maximum ascent of any character in the font.

ascent line: The line marking a font's maximum *ascent* above the *baseline.*

ASCII: American Standard Code for Information Interchange, the industry-standard 7-bit character set on which the Macintosh's 8-bit *character codes* are based, commonly pronounced "asky."

asynchronous: Describes an input/output operation that is queued for later execution, returning control immediately to the calling program without waiting for the operation to be carried out. The calling program may supply an optional *completion routine* to be executed on completion of the operation. Compare *synchronous.*

autograph: A *Finder resource* whose *resource type* is the same as a program's *signature*, and which serves as the program's representative in the *desktop file*; also called a *version data* resource.

auto-key event: An *event* reporting that the user held down a key on the keyboard or keypad, causing it to repeat automatically.

A/UX: The version of the *Unix* operating system developed by Apple for use on the Macintosh.

auxiliary control list: A linked list of all *auxiliary control records* belonging to a given program, chained together through a field in the records.

auxiliary control record: A data structure containing information about a control's color-related properties, supplementing the more general information in the main *control record*.

auxiliary port record: A data structure associated with a *color graphics port*, containing additional information relating to color drawing operations in the port.

auxiliary window list: A linked list of all *auxiliary window records* belonging to a given program, chained together through a field in the records.

auxiliary window record: A data structure containing information about a window's color-related properties, supplementing the more general information in the main *window record*.

background: (1) Under *MultiFinder*, the state in which a program is not in active control of the system, while some other program displays its *windows* frontmost on the screen and receives and responds to the user's actions with the mouse and keyboard. (2) In *monochrome* drawing, the portion of a graphical image represented by bits with a value of 0, drawn in the *background color* of its *graphics port*. Compare *foreground*.

background color: The color in which the *background* portion of a graphical image is to be drawn in a given *graphics port;* compare *foreground color*.

background-only bit: A flag bit in a program's *size resource* that indicates that the program wishes to run exclusively in the *background* under *MultiFinder* and never interact directly with the user.

background pattern: The *pattern* used for *erasing* shapes in a given *graphics port*.

background processing: Useful work performed by a program while running in the *background* under *MultiFinder*.

base address: In general, any memory address used as a reference point from which to locate desired data in memory. Specifically, (1) the address of the *bit image* or *pixel image* belonging to a given *bit map* or *pixel map*; (2) the address of a program's *application parameters*, kept in processor register A5 and used to locate the contents of the program's *application global space*.

base of stack: The end of the *stack* that remains fixed in memory and is not affected when items are added and removed; compare *top of stack*.

baseline: The reference line used for defining the *character images* in a *font*, and along which the *graphics pen* travels as text is drawn.

Binary/Decimal Conversion Package: A standard *package*, provided in the *system resource file* (or in ROM on some models), that converts numbers between their internal binary format and their external representation as strings of decimal digits.

binary point: The binary equivalent of a decimal point, separating the integer and fractional parts of a *fixed-point number*.

bit image: An array of bits in memory representing the *pixels* of a monochrome graphical image.

bit map: A data structure containing the information needed to interpret and display a given *bit image* in memory.

bit-mapped display: A video display screen on which each *pixel* can be individually controlled.

bit pattern: A *pattern* composed of single bits representing the *foreground* and *background colors* of the *current port*, for use in *monochrome* drawing operations; compare *pixel pattern*.

bit resolution: A property of an *inverse table* that measures its ability to discriminate among closely differing colors. When looking up a *color value* in the table, the bit resolution tells how many high-order bits of each *color component* to use in constructing the corresponding table index.

block: An area of contiguous memory within the *heap*, either *allocated* or *free*.

block map: A table containing information needed by the *file system* about the usage of all *allocation blocks* on a given *volume*.

bottleneck record: A data structure containing pointers to the *bottleneck routines* associated with a given *graphics port.*

bottleneck routine: A specialized routine for performing a low-level drawing operation in a given *graphics port,* used for *customizing* QuickDraw operations.

boundary rectangle: (1) For a *bit map* or *pixel map,* the *rectangle* that defines the bit map's extent and determines its system of coordinates. (2) For a *graphics port,* the boundary rectangle of the port's bit map or pixel map.

bounding box: The smallest *rectangle* completely enclosing a *polygon* or *region* on the coordinate grid.

brightness: See *value.*

bundle: A *Finder resource* that identifies all of a program's other Finder resources, so that they can be installed in the *desktop file* when the program's *application file* is copied to a new *volume.*

bus: A set of transmission lines used to transfer many bits of information in parallel from one component of a computer system to another.

button: A *control* with two possible *settings,* on (1) and off (0); compare *dial.*

byte: An independently addressable group of 8 bits in the computer's memory.

can-background bit: A flag bit in a program's *size resource* that tells whether the program is prepared to do useful work while running in the *background* behind another program under *MultiFinder.*

Caps Lock key: A *modifier key* on the Macintosh keyboard, used to convert lowercase letters to uppercase while leaving all nonalphabetic keys unaffected.

centered: A method of text *justification* in which each line of text is positioned midway between the left and right margins; compare *flush left, flush right, full justification.*

central processing unit: The main *processor* of a computer system, which carries out the operations specified by the instructions of the running program.

character code: An integer code representing a text character; compare *key code.*

character image: A graphical image that defines the appearance of a text character in a given *typeface* and *type size.*

character key: A key on the keyboard or keypad that produces a character when pressed; compare *modifier key*.

character position: An integer marking a point between characters in a *file* or other collection of text, from 0 (the very beginning of the text, before the first character) to the length of the text (the very end, after the last character).

character style: See *type style*.

character width: The distance in pixels by which the *graphics pen* advances after drawing a character.

character-width table: An optional table in a *font record*, containing *fractional character widths* for the characters in the font.

checkbox: A *button* that retains an independent on/off setting to control the way some future action will occur; compare *pushbutton, radio buttons*.

choose: To designate a *menu item* by pointing with the mouse.

chrominance: The portion of a *composite video* signal used only by color receivers, defining the *hue* and *saturation* of the color picture; compare *luminance*.

chunky: A *storage format* for *pixel images* in which each pixel is represented in memory by a contiguous "chunk" of bits specifying the color of that pixel, usually in the form of a *color index* into a *color lookup table*; compare *planar, chunky/planar*.

chunky/planar: A *storage format* for *pixel images* in which the full-color image is resolved into separate *color planes*, each of which is in turn a *chunky* pixel image with a *pixel depth* greater than 1, representing the intensity level of a single constituent color; not supported by the current version of *Color QuickDraw*. Compare *chunky, planar*.

classic Macintosh: Any of the early, first-generation models of *Macintosh*, including the *Macintosh 128K* ("Skinny Mac"), *Macintosh 512K* ("Fat Mac"), *Macintosh 512K enhanced*, and *Macintosh Plus*.

classic QuickDraw: The original version of the *QuickDraw* graphics routines, found in the *classic Macintosh*; compare *Color QuickDraw*.

client ID: An identifying number that allows a program's color-matching requests to be recognized by its own custom *matching routines*.

clip: To confine a drawing operation within a specified boundary, suppressing any drawing that falls outside the boundary.

Clipboard: The term used in Macintosh user's manuals to refer to the *scrap.*

clipping boundaries: The boundaries to which all drawing in a given *graphics port* is confined, consisting of the port's *boundary rectangle, port rectangle, clipping region,* and *visible region.*

clipping rectangle: See *view rectangle.*

clipping region: A general-purpose *clipping boundary* associated with a *graphics port,* provided for the application program's use.

close box: The small box near the left end of the *title bar,* by which a *document window* can be closed with the mouse.

close region: The area of a *window* by which it can be closed with the mouse; also called the "go-away region." In a *document window,* the close region is the *close box.*

CLUT: See *color lookup table.*

CMY: A method of color representation that characterizes colors according to the relative intensities of the three *subtractive primary colors* (*cyan, magenta,* and *yellow*); compare *RGB, HSV, HSL.*

code segment: A *resource* containing all or part of a program's executable machine code.

color bit: A field of the *graphics port* record that designates the *color plane* of its *pixel image* into which the port is currently drawing.

color box: Either of the two rectangular areas near the top-left corner of the *Color Picker dialog* box displaying the currently selected color and the one initially proposed by the application program.

color component: Any of the three constituent values that characterize a color in *RGB, CMY, HSV,* or *HSL* representation.

color constant: An integer value representing one of the eight standard colors in the *planar* model of color representation used by *classic QuickDraw.*

color cursor handle: A *handle* to a *color cursor record.*

color cursor record: A data structure defining the appearance of a *cursor* based on a color *pixel image* instead of a monochrome *bit image.*

color dialog record: A *dialog record* based on a *color window* *record,* containing descriptive information about a color *alert* or *dialog box.*

color environment: Those global settings and system attributes that determine the effects of color drawing operations, such as the *current graphics device,* its current *pixel depth,* and the contents of its *color lookup table.*

color font: A *font* whose *font image* is a full-color *pixel image* rather than a monochrome *bit image.*

color graphics port: A complete drawing environment containing all the information needed for *Color QuickDraw* drawing operations.

color icon handle: A *handle* to a *color icon record.*

color icon record: A data structure defining the appearance of an *icon* based on a color *pixel image* instead of a monochrome *bit image.*

color index: An integer identifying a color by its position in a *color lookup table.*

color lookup table: A table containing the *color values* currently available for display on a *mapped device.*

Color Picker dialog: The standard *dialog box* displayed by the *Color Picker Package,* allowing the user to supply a *color value* for a Toolbox operation.

Color Picker Package: A standard *package,* provided in the *system resource file,* that provides a convenient, standard way for the user to supply *color values* for Toolbox operations.

color plane: A component of a *pixel image* in *planar* or *chunky/ planar* format, representing one of the constituent colors making up the image. In planar format, each color plane is a *bit image* 1 bit deep; in chunky/planar format, it is a pixel image with a *pixel depth* greater than 1.

color port: See *color graphics port.*

Color QuickDraw: The full-color version of the *QuickDraw* graphics routines, found in the *Macintosh II;* compare *classic QuickDraw.*

color record: A data structure defining a *color value* to be used by the Toolbox.

color specification: The association between a *color index* and its corresponding *color value.*

color table: A table of *color specifications* mapping *color indices* to their corresponding *color values;* commonly (but not exclusively) used for the *color lookup table* of a *mapped device.*

color table animation: A technique for producing animation in a *pixel image* by manipulating the *color values* of the pixels in its *color table,* rather than changing the *pixel values* in the image itself.

color value: An exact color to be used by the Toolbox, specified in a form (such as *RGB*) that is independent of any particular *graphics device* or *color environment.*

color wheel: The target-shaped image displayed in the *Color Picker dialog* box for setting the *hue* and *saturation* of the desired color.

color window: A *window* that supports color drawing using the full capabilities of *Color QuickDraw.*

Color Window Manager port: The *color graphics port* in which the Toolbox draws all *window frames.*

color window pointer: A pointer to a *color window record.*

color window record: A *window record* based on a *color graphics port,* containing descriptive information about a given *color window.*

Command key: A *modifier key* on the Macintosh keyboard, used in combination with *character keys* to type *keyboard aliases* for *menu items.*

comment data: The information a *picture comment* contains.

comment type: An integer code that identifies the kind of information a *picture comment* contains.

compaction: The process of moving together all *relocatable blocks* in the *heap,* in order to coalesce the available free space.

complement: (1) A bit-level operation that reverses the bits of its operand, changing each 0 to a 1 and vice versa. (2) The color opposite to a given color, which combines with it to yield pure white in an *additive* display medium or pure black in a *subtractive* medium.

complement procedure: A procedure for finding the closest approximation to the *complement* of a requested color on a given *graphics device.*

completion routine: A routine supplied in conjunction with an *asynchronous* input/output request, to be executed on completion of the requested operation.

composite video: A form of *video* transmission used in broadcast television receivers, in which separate *luminance* and *chrominance* signals are combined to form a single broadcast signal.

content: The information displayed in a *window*.

content region: The area of a *window* in which information is displayed, and which a program must draw for itself; compare *window frame*.

continuous property: A *style attribute* or *style variation* that is possessed by every character within a given range of text.

control: An object on the Macintosh screen that the user can manipulate with the mouse in order to operate on the contents of a *window* or control the way they're presented.

control color table: A data structure specifying the colors to be used in drawing a *control*.

control definition function: A routine, stored as a *resource*, that defines the appearance and behavior of a particular type of *control*.

control definition ID: A coded integer representing a *control type*, which includes the *resource ID* of the *control definition function* along with a *variation code* giving additional modifying information.

control handle: A handle to a *control record*.

control list: A linked list of all the *controls* belonging to a given *window*, beginning in a field of the *window record* and chained together through a field of their *control records*.

Control Panel: A standard *desk accessory* with which the user can set optional operating characteristics of the Macintosh system, such as the speaker volume and keyboard repeat rate.

control record: A data structure containing descriptive information about a given *control*.

control template: A *resource* containing all the information needed to create a *control*.

control title: The string of text characters displayed on the screen as part of a *control*.

control type: A category of *control*, identified by a *control definition ID*, whose appearance and behavior are determined by a *control definition function*.

coprocessor: An auxiliary *processor* included in a computer system in addition to the *central processing unit* to perform specialized processing tasks such as *floating-point* arithmetic or *virtual memory* management.

courteous color: An entry in a *palette* that will always match the closest *color value* available in the *current color table*, no matter how much it may differ from the requested color; compare *tolerant color, animating color, explicit color, dithered color.*

covered: Describes a *window, control,* or other object that is obscured from view by other overlapping objects. A covered object is never displayed on the screen, even if *visible;* compare *exposed.*

CPU: See *central processing unit.*

CPU code: An integer code in the *system environment record* identifying the type of *central processing unit* on which a program is currently running.

creator signature: A four-character string identifying the application program to which a given *file* belongs, and which should be started up when the user opens the file in the *Finder.*

current color table: The *color table* belonging to the *current graphics device.*

current device: See *current graphics device.*

current graphics device: The *graphics device* whose *color table* and other attributes establish the *color environment* for all color drawing operations.

current port: The *graphics port* in use at any given time, to which most *QuickDraw* operations implicitly apply.

current resource file: The *resource file* that will be searched first in looking for a requested *resource*, and to which certain resource-related operations implicitly apply.

current volume: The *volume* or *directory* under consideration at any given time, to which many *file system* operations implicitly apply.

cursor: A small (16-by-16-pixel) graphical image whose movements can be controlled with the *mouse* to designate positions on the Macintosh screen.

cursor record: A data structure defining the form and appearance of a *cursor* on the screen.

customize: To redefine an aspect of the Toolbox's operation to meet the specialized needs of a particular program.

cut and paste: The standard method of editing used on the Macintosh, in which text, graphics, or other information is transferred from one place to another by way of an intermediate *scrap* or *Clipboard.*

cyan: One of the three *subtractive primary colors,* complementary to red and formed, in an *additive* medium, by mixing blue and green.

cycle: A single repetition of a regularly recurring wave, such as a sound or light wave.

dangling pointer: An invalid pointer to an object that no longer exists at the designated address.

data bus: The set of transmission lines used by the *processor* to transfer information to or from memory; compare *address bus.*

data fork: The *fork* of a *file* that contains the file's data, such as the text of a document; compare *resource fork.*

deactivate event: A *window event* generated by the Toolbox to signal that a given window is no longer the *active window.*

deallocate: To free a *block* of memory that is no longer needed, allowing the space to be reused for another purpose.

declaration ROM: A collection of information stored in *read-only memory* on an *expansion card,* consisting of *slot resources* describing the characteristics of the card or of the device it controls.

default button: The *pushbutton* displayed with a heavy black double border in an *alert* or *dialog box;* pressing the Return or Enter key is considered equivalent to clicking the default button with the mouse.

definition routine: See *control definition function, window definition function, menu definition procedure, menu bar definition function, list definition procedure.*

dereference: (1) In general, to convert any pointer to the value it points to. (2) Specifically, to convert a *handle* to the corresponding *master pointer.*

descender: A portion of a text character that extends below the *baseline,* as in the lowercase letters g, j, p, q, and y.

descent: (1) For a text character, the distance the character extends below the *baseline,* in *dots* or *pixels.* (2) For a *font,* the maximum descent of any character in the font.

descent line: The line marking a font's maximum *descent* below the *baseline.*

desk accessory: A type of *device driver* that operates as a "mini-application," which can coexist on the screen with any other program.

desk scrap: The *scrap* maintained by the Toolbox to hold information being *cut and pasted* from one application program or *desk accessory* to another; compare *Toolbox scrap.*

desktop: (1) The gray background area of the Macintosh screen, outside of any window. (2) The arrangement of *windows, icons,* and other objects on the screen, particularly in the *Finder.*

desktop file: A file containing *Finder*-related information about the files on a *volume,* including their *file types, creator signatures,* and locations on the Finder *desktop.*

desktop region: A *region* defining the size and shape of the total area in which drawing can take place on the screens of all available *graphics devices* combined.

destination rectangle: The boundary to which text is *wrapped* in an *edit record,* determining the placement of the *line breaks;* also called the "wrapping rectangle."

device: See *peripheral device.*

device attributes: A set of flags describing the characteristics of a given *graphics device,* kept in a field of its *device record.*

device code: An integer identifying the output device a *graphics port* draws on, used in selecting the appropriate *fonts* for drawing text.

device driver: A specialized piece of software that enables the Macintosh to control and communicate with a particular *peripheral device.* An important special category of device drivers are *desk accessories.*

device list: A linked list of all *graphics devices* currently available in the system, chained together through a field of their *device records.*

device record: A data structure containing descriptive information about a given *graphics device.*

device type: An integer code identifying the general method of color specification used by a *graphics device;* see *direct device, mapped device, fixed device, variable CLUT device.*

dial: A *control* that can take on any of a range of possible *settings*, depending on the position of a moving *indicator* that can be manipulated with the mouse; compare *button*.

dialog: Short for *dialog box*.

dialog box: A *window* used for requesting information or instructions from the user.

dialog item: A single element displayed in an *alert* or *dialog box*, such as a piece of text, an *icon*, a *control*, or a *text box*.

dialog pointer: A pointer to a *dialog record*.

dialog record: A data structure containing descriptive information about a given *alert* or *dialog box*.

dialog template: A *resource* containing all the information needed to create a *dialog box*.

dialog window: See *dialog box*.

diameters of curvature: The width and height of the *ovals* forming the corners of a *rounded rectangle*.

dimmed: Describes an object, such as a *menu item* or a *file icon*, that is displayed in gray instead of black to show that it is not currently available or active.

direct device: A color *graphics device* that accepts colors in explicit *RGB* format and reproduces them directly on the screen; not supported by the current version of *Color QuickDraw*. Compare *mapped device*.

directory: A table containing information about the *files* on a *volume*. Under the *Hierarchical File System*, directories may in turn contain other directories (*subdirectories*) and correspond to *folders* displayed on the *desktop* by the *Finder*.

directory name: Under the *Hierarchical File System*, a string of text characters identifying a particular *directory*.

directory reference number: An identifying number assigned by the *Hierarchical File System* to stand for a given *directory*.

disk driver: The *device driver* built into ROM for communicating with the Macintosh's built-in Sony disk drive.

Disk Initialization Package: A standard *package*, provided in the *system resource file*, that takes corrective action when an unreadable disk is inserted into the disk drive, usually by initializing the disk.

disk-inserted event: An *event* reporting that the user inserted a disk into a disk drive.

dismiss: To remove an *alert* or *dialog box* from the screen, typically by clicking a *pushbutton.*

dispatch table: A table in memory containing the *trap address* associated with each *trap number,* used by the *Trap Dispatcher* to locate Toolbox routines in ROM.

display: (1) To present information in a dynamically changing graphical form. (2) An arrangement of information presented in such a form. (3) A *peripheral device* capable of presenting information in such a form, such as the screen of a video picture tube.

display mode: A state of a *graphics device* that determines the way it presents an image on the screen; typically corresponds to a particular *pixel depth,* but may also affect other aspects of the device's operation, such as the use of gray scale instead of full color.

dithered color: An entry in a *palette* that constructs a *dithered pattern* to approximate the requested color if it is not directly available in the *current color table;* not supported by the current version of *Color QuickDraw.* Compare *tolerant color, courteous color, animating color, explicit color.*

dithered pattern: A *pixel pattern* constructed to approximate the appearance of a desired color by *dithering* two or more other colors.

dithering: A technique of combining two or more colors in a pattern of dots that blend visually to approximate the appearance of another color.

document: A coherent unit or collection of information to be operated on by a particular *application program.*

document file: A file containing a *document.*

document window: The standard type of *window* used by application programs to display information on the Macintosh screen.

dot: A single spot forming part of a graphical image when printed on paper; compare *pixel.*

double click: Two presses of the *mouse* button in quick succession, considered as a single action by the user.

down arrow: The arrow at the bottom or right end of a *scroll bar,* which causes it to scroll down or to the right a line at a time when clicked with the mouse.

drag: (1) To roll the *mouse* while holding down the button. (2) To move a *window, icon,* or other object to a new location on the screen by dragging with the mouse.

drag region: The area of a *window* by which it can be *dragged* to a new location with the mouse. In a *document window,* the drag region consists of the *title bar* minus the *close box* and *zoom box,* if any.

driver: See *device driver.*

driver event: See *I/O driver event.*

driver reference number: An identifying number designating a particular *device driver.*

edge color: The pixel color defining the border of the region to be selected by the *lasso* drawing tool.

edit record: A complete text editing environment containing all the information needed for *TextEdit* operations.

eject: To remove a disk *volume* physically from a disk drive, placing the volume *off-line.*

electronic mail: A type of computer application that enables users to send and receive messages over a network or other communication line.

empty handle: A *handle* that points to a NIL *master pointer,* indicating that the underlying block has been *purged* from the heap.

empty rectangle: A *rectangle* that encloses no pixels on the coordinate grid.

empty region: A *region* that encloses no pixels on the coordinate grid.

emulator trap: A form of *trap* that occurs when the *M68000*-series processors attempt to execute an *unimplemented instruction;* used to "emulate" the effects of such an instruction in software instead of hardware.

enclosing rectangle: (1) The *rectangle* within which an *oval* is inscribed. (2) The rectangle that defines the location and extent of a *control* within its *owning window.*

end-of-file: The *character position* following the last byte of meaningful information included in a *file* (the *logical end-of-file*) or the last byte of physical storage space allocated to it (the *physical end-of-file*).

environment record: See *system environment record.*

EOF: See *end-of-file.*

erase: To fill a *shape* with the *background pattern* of the *current port.*

error code: A nonzero *result code*, reporting an error of some kind detected by a Toolbox routine.

error sound: A sound emitted from the Macintosh speaker by an *alert.*

event: An occurrence reported by the Toolbox for a program to respond to, such as the user's pressing the mouse button or typing on the keyboard.

event-driven: Describes a program that is structured to respond to *events* reported by the Toolbox.

event loop: See *main event loop.*

event mask: A coded integer specifying the *event types* to which a given operation applies.

event message: A field of the *event record* containing information that varies depending on the *event type.*

event modifiers: A field of the *event record* containing flags that describe conditions pertaining to the event, such as the state of the mouse button and of the *modifier keys* on the keyboard.

event queue: The data structure in which *events* are recorded for later processing.

event record: A data structure containing descriptive information about a given *event.*

event type: An integer code identifying the kind of occurrence reported by an *event.*

exception: See *trap.*

exclusive or: A bit-level operation in which each bit of the result is a 1 if the corresponding bits of the two operands are different, or 0 if they are the same.

expansion card: An integrated-circuit card that can be plugged into one of the Macintosh's *expansion slots* to extend or enhance the capabilities of the system.

expansion slot: An internal connector in some models of Macintosh, in which an *expansion card* can be installed.

explicit color: An entry in a *palette* that refers directly to a given *color index* in the *current color table*, without reference to the *color value* specified in the palette entry itself; compare *tolerant color, courteous color, animating color, dithered color.*

exposed: Describes a *window, control,* or other object that is not obscured from view by other overlapping objects. An exposed object is displayed on the screen if *visible;* compare *covered.*

external disk drive: A disk drive physically separate from the Macintosh itself and connected to it via a connector on the back of the machine.

Fat Mac: See *Macintosh 512K.*

field: One of the components of a Pascal record.

FIFO: First in, first out; the order in which items are added to and removed from a queue such as the *event queue.* Compare *LIFO, LIOF.*

file: A collection of information stored as a named unit on a disk or other mass storage device.

file directory: A table containing information needed by the *file system* about the *files* on a given *volume.*

file icon: The *icon* used by the *Finder* to represent a *file* on the screen.

file name: A string of text characters identifying a particular *file.*

file reference: A *Finder resource* that establishes the connection between a *file type* and its *file icon.*

file reference number: An identifying number assigned by the *file system* to stand for a given *file.*

file system: The part of the *Macintosh Operating System* that deals with *files* on a disk or other mass storage device.

file type: A four-character string that characterizes the kind of information a *file* contains, assigned by the program that created the file.

fill: To color a *shape* with a specified *pattern.*

fill pattern: A *pattern* associated with a *graphics port,* used privately by *QuickDraw* for *filling* shapes.

Finder: The Macintosh application program with which the user can manipulate files and start up applications; normally the first program to be run when the Macintosh is turned on.

Finder resources: The *resources* associated with a program that tell the *Finder* how to represent the program's *files* on the screen. Finder resources include *autographs, icon lists, file references,* and *bundles.*

Finder startup handle: See *startup handle.*

Finder startup information: See *startup information.*

fixed device: A *mapped device* in which the selection of colors available in the *color lookup table* is predefined by the device itself and cannot be changed; compare *variable CLUT device.*

fixed-point number: A binary number with a fixed number of bits before and after the *binary point;* specifically, a value of the Toolbox data type `Fixed` [I:2.3.1], consisting of a 16-bit integer part and a 16-bit fractional part.

fixed-width font: A *font* in which all *character widths* are equal.

flat file system: A *file system* in which all *files* on a *volume* reside in a single *directory,* with no *subdirectories.*

Floating-Point Arithmetic Package: A standard *package,* provided in the *system resource file* (or in ROM on some models), that performs arithmetic on *floating-point numbers* in accordance with the *IEEE standard,* using the *Standard Apple Numeric Environment* (SANE).

floating-point coprocessor: An auxiliary *processor* included in some models of Macintosh for performing high-speed *floating-point* computations.

floating-point number: A binary number in which the *binary point* can "float" to any required position; the number's internal representation includes a binary exponent, or order of magnitude, that determines the position of the point.

flush left: A method of text *justification* in which the left margin is straight and the right margin is "ragged"; compare *flush right, centered, full justification.*

flush right: A method of text *justification* in which the right margin is straight and the left margin is "ragged"; compare *flush right, centered, full justification.*

folder: An object in the *desktop file* of a disk or other *volume,* represented on the screen by an *icon* or *window,* that can contain *files* or other folders; used for organizing the files on the volume. Under the *Hierarchical File System,* folders correspond to *directories.*

font: (1) A *resource* containing all of the *character images* and other information needed to draw text characters in a given *typeface* and *type size.* (2) Sometimes used loosely (and incorrectly) as a synonym for *typeface,* as in the terms *font number* and *text font.*

font color table: A *color table* defining the *color values* for the pixels in the *font image* of a *color font*.

font depth: The *pixel depth* of a *font image*, stored in a portion of the *font type* field in the *font record*.

font family: A term used in recent Apple publications for what we, in these books, have called a *typeface*.

font height: The overall height of a font, from *ascent line* to *descent line*.

font image: A *bit image* or *pixel image* consisting of all the individual *character images* in a given *font*, arranged consecutively in a single horizontal row; also called a *strike* of the font.

font number: An integer denoting a particular *typeface*.

font record: A data structure containing descriptive information about a given *font*.

font type: A field of the *font record* containing flags and other descriptive information about the properties of a *font* (including, in particular, the *font depth*).

foreground: (1) Under *MultiFinder*, the state in which a program is in active control of the system, displaying its *windows* frontmost on the screen and receiving and responding to the user's actions with the mouse and keyboard. (2) In *monochrome* drawing, the portion of a graphical image represented by bits with a value of 1, drawn in the *foreground color* of its *graphics port*. Compare *background*.

foreground color: The color in which the *foreground* portion of a graphical image is to be drawn in a given *graphics port;* compare *background color*.

fork: One of the two parts of which every *file* is composed: the *data fork* or the *resource fork*.

fraction: A *fixed-point* value of the Toolbox data type `Fract` [I:2.3.3], consisting of a 2-bit integer part and a 30-bit fractional part.

fractional character widths: A feature included in recent versions of the Toolbox that allows the *character widths* for a *font* to be expressed as fractional, rather than integral, numbers of *points*. The resulting character positions are then rounded to the available resolution of whatever device they're drawn on (such as a printer or the screen of a *graphics device*).

frame: (1) To draw the outline of a *shape*, using the *pen size, pen pattern*, and *pen mode* of the *current port*. (2) See *window frame*.

(3) A single painting of the Macintosh screen by the display tube's electron beam, from the top-left corner to the bottom-right.

free block: A contiguous *block* of space available for allocation within the *heap*.

frequency: The speed with which a regularly recurring wave (such as a sound or light wave) is repeated, which determines the pitch of the sound or the color of the light; measured in *hertz* (cycles per second).

full justification: A method of text *justification* (not supported by *TextEdit*) in which both the left and right margins are straight, with the spaces between words adjusted accordingly; compare *flush left, centered, flush right*.

gamma table: A table of the correction values needed to compensate for the nonlinear color response of the screen phosphors on a given *graphics device*.

get-front-clicks bit: A flag bit in a program's *size resource* that indicates that the program wishes to receive *mouse-down events* reporting the mouse clicks with which the user switches the program from the *background* to the *foreground* under *MultiFinder*.

gigabyte: A unit of memory capacity equal to 2^{30} (1,073,741,824) bytes.

global coordinate system: The coordinate system associated with a given *bit image* or *pixel image*, in which the top-left corner of the image has coordinates $(0, 0)$. The global coordinate system is independent of the *boundary rectangle* of any *bit map, pixel map*, or *graphics port* based on the image.

glue routine: See *interface routine*.

go-away region: See *close region*.

good-bye kiss: A special call to a *device driver* or *desk accessory*, warning it that the *application heap* is about to be reinitialized and allowing it to take any special action it may require.

graphics device: A *peripheral device* that presents information in graphical form, such as a video *display* screen.

graphics pen: The imaginary drawing tool used for drawing lines and text characters in a *graphics port*.

graphics port: A complete drawing environment containing all the information needed for *QuickDraw* drawing operations.

grow icon: The visual representation of a window's *size region* on the screen; for a standard *document window*, a pair of small overlapping squares in the bottom-right corner of the window.

grow region: See *size region.*

handle: A pointer to a *master pointer*, used to refer to a *relocatable block.*

hardcopy: A copy of a *document* printed physically on paper.

heap: The area of memory in which space is allocated and deallocated at the explicit request of a running program; compare *stack.*

hertz: A unit of *frequency*, equivalent to *cycles* (or any other regularly recurring event) per second; abbreviated *Hz.*

HFS: See *Hierarchical File System.*

hide: To make a window, control, or other object *invisible.*

Hierarchical File System: The *file system* built into recent models of Macintosh in ROM, designed for use with double-sided and high-density disks, hard disks, and other large-capacity storage devices; also available for older models in RAM-based form.   Compare *Macintosh File System.*

highlight: To display a *window, control, menu item,* or other object in some distinctive way as a visual signal to the user, often (but not necessarily) by *inverting* white and black pixels when displayed in monochrome, or by exchanging the *background color* with a specified *highlighting color.*

highlighting color: The color to be exchanged with the *background color* when *highlighting* text or other material in a *color graphics port.*

host program: The application program with which a *desk accessory* shares the system.

hot spot: The point in a *cursor* that coincides with the mouse position on the screen.

HSL: A method of color representation that characterizes colors according to their *hue, saturation,* and *lightness;* compare *HSV, RGB, CMY.*

HSV: A method of color representation that characterizes colors according to their *hue, saturation,* and *value* or *brightness;* also called the *Munsell color system.*   Compare *HSL, RGB, CMY.*

hue: The property of a color determined by the *frequency* of its light wave, and corresponding to the subjective quality referred to by names such as green, orange, yellow, or blue; compare *saturation, value, lightness.*

hypertext: A type of computer application, typified by Apple's HyperCard, in which text, graphics, and other information are linked together into a free-form, interconnected information base that the user can traverse in arbitrary order.

Hz: See *hertz.*

I-beam cursor: A standard *cursor* included in the *system resource file* (or in ROM on some models) for use in text selection.

icon: A small graphical image (typically 32 pixels by 32) used on the Macintosh screen to represent an object such as a disk or file.

icon list: A *resource* containing any number of *icons;* commonly used to hold a *file icon* and its mask for use by the *Finder.*

icon number: An integer used to identify an *icon* to be displayed on a *menu,* equal to the icon's *resource ID* plus 256.

identifying information: The properties of a *resource* that uniquely identify it: its *resource type, resource ID,* and (optional) *resource name.*

IEEE standard: A set of standards and conventions for *floating-point* arithmetic, published by the Institute of Electrical and Electronic Engineers.

image-height table: An optional table in a *font record,* containing information on the heights of the *character images* in the font.

ImageWriter: A dot-matrix impact printer originally developed by C. Itoh & Company and marketed by Apple Computer, with a maximum resolution of 144 dots per inch vertically by 160 horizontally and a maximum printing speed of 120 characters per second.

ImageWriter LQ: An upgraded model of the *ImageWriter* printer, with a maximum resolution of 216 dots per inch and improved paper handling capabilities.

ImageWriter II: An enhanced version of the original *ImageWriter* printer with a maximum printing speed of 250 characters per second, finer dot placement for better print quality, improved paper handling including an optional automatic sheet feeder for non-continuous, separately cut sheets, a limited color capability using a special four-color ribbon, and an optional *AppleTalk* network connection for sharing the printer among two or more users.

indicator: The moving part of a *dial* that can be manipulated with the mouse to control the dial's setting.

insertion point: An empty *selection* in a text document, denoted by a *selection range* that begins and ends at the same *character position*.

Inside Macintosh: The comprehensive manual on the Macintosh *Toolbox*, produced by Apple Computer, Inc., and published by Addison-Wesley Publishing Company, Inc.

Integrated Wozniak Machine: The custom-designed chip used to control the Macintosh floppy-disk drive, based on an original design by Apple cofounder Steve Wozniak.

interactive item: A *dialog item*, such as a *control* or *text box*, that accepts information from the user via the mouse and keyboard; compare *static item*.

intercepted event: An *event* that is handled automatically by the Toolbox before being reported to the running program.

interface: A set of rules and conventions by which one part of an organized system communicates with another.

interface routine: A routine that mediates between the *stack-based* parameter-passing conventions of a Pascal calling program and those of a *register-based* Toolbox routine; also called a "glue routine."

internal disk drive: The 3½-inch single- or double-sided Sony disk drive built into the Macintosh.

International Utilities Package: A standard *package*, provided in the *system resource file*, that helps programs conform to the prevailing conventions of different countries in such matters as formatting of numbers, dates, times, and currency; use of metric units; and alphabetization of foreign-language accents, diacriticals, and ligatures.

interrupt: A *trap* triggered by a signal to the Macintosh processor from a peripheral device or other outside source.

interrupt-driven: Describes a piece of software that is designed to be executed in response to an *interrupt*.

interrupt handler: The *trap handler* for responding to an *interrupt*.

invalid region: An area of a window's *content region* whose contents are not accurately displayed on the screen, and which must therefore be *updated;* compare *valid region.*

inverse table: A data structure that maps *color values* to their most closely matching *color indices* relative to a given *color table.*

invert: (1) Generally, to reverse the colors of *pixels* in a monochrome graphical image, changing white to black and vice versa. (2) Specifically, to reverse the colors of all pixels inside the boundary of a given *shape.*

invisible: Describes a *window, control,* or other object that is logically hidden from view. An invisible object is never displayed on the screen, even if *exposed;* compare *visible.*

I/O driver event: A type of *event* used internally by the Toolbox to handle communication with *peripheral devices.*

item color list: A data structure specifying the colors to be used in drawing the *dialog items* in a color *alert* or *dialog box.*

item color table: See *item color list.*

item data: The descriptive information about a given *dialog item* in an *item color list.*

item handle: A handle to a *dialog item,* kept in its dialog's *item list.*

item header: A word of descriptive information about a *dialog item* in an *item color list,* whose exact format and meaning vary depending on the *item type.*

item list: A data structure defining all of the *dialog items* associated with an *alert* or *dialog box,* located via a handle in the *dialog record.*

item number: The sequential position of a *menu item* within its menu, or of a *dialog item* within its dialog's *item list;* used as an identifying number to refer to the item.

item offset: An integer giving the location of the *item data* for a given *dialog item* in an *item color list,* expressed in bytes relative to the start of the list.

item type: An integer code denoting a kind of *dialog item.*

IWM: See *Integrated Wozniak Machine.*

Juggler: An early internal code name for *MultiFinder.*

jump table: A table used to direct external references between *code segments* to the proper addresses in memory; located in the *application global space*, at positive offsets from the *base address* kept in register A5.

justification: The way in which text in an *edit record* is aligned to the left and right edges of the *destination rectangle*; see *flush left, centered, flush right, full justification.*

K: See *kilobyte.*

key code: An integer code representing a physical key on the Macintosh keyboard or keypad; compare *character code.*

key-down event: An *event* reporting that the user pressed a key on the keyboard or keypad.

key-up event: An *event* reporting that the user released a key on the keyboard or keypad.

keyboard: A set of keys for typing text characters into the computer.

keyboard alias: A character that can be typed in combination with the *Command key* to stand for a particular *menu item.*

keyboard code: An integer code in the *system environment record* identifying the type of *keyboard* connected to the system on which a program is currently running.

keyboard configuration: The correspondence between keys on the Macintosh *keyboard* or *keypad* and the characters they produce when pressed.

keyboard driver: The low-level part of the Toolbox that communicates directly with the keyboard and keypad.

keyboard event: An *event* reporting an action by the user with the keyboard or keypad; see *key-down event, key-up event, autokey event.*

keyboard routine: A routine to be executed directly by the *keyboard driver* when the user types a number key while holding down the *Command* and *Shift keys*; stored as a *resource* of type `'FKEY'`.

keypad: See *numeric keypad.*

kHz: See *kilohertz.*

kilobyte: A unit of memory capacity equal to 2^{10} (1024) bytes.

kilohertz: A unit of *frequency* equal to 1000 *hertz*; abbreviated *kHz.*

LaserWriter: A high-resolution laser printer manufactured and marketed by Apple Computer, with a resolution of 300 dots per inch, an *MC68000* processor, 512K of ROM containing a

PostScript interpreter and 11 built-in fonts, and a RAM capacity of 1.5 megabytes for page imaging and additional font storage.

LaserWriter Plus: An upgraded version of the original *LaserWriter* printer with an expanded ROM capacity and 35 built-in fonts.

LaserWriter II-NT: An upgraded model of the *LaserWriter* printer with a faster version of the *PostScript* interpreter, 35 built-in fonts, and an expanded RAM capacity of 2 megabytes.

LaserWriter II-NTX: An upgraded model of the *LaserWriter* printer with an *MC68020* processor, an *MC68881* floating-point coprocessor, a faster version of the *PostScript* interpreter, 35 built-in fonts, an expandable RAM capacity of up to 12 megabytes, and an optional hard disk connection.

LaserWriter II-SC: An inexpensive model of the *LaserWriter* printer with no *PostScript* interpreter or built-in fonts, driven directly with *QuickDraw* operations in the same way as an *ImageWriter*.

lasso: A drawing tool included in many graphics-editing programs, which selects the largest closed shape enclosed within a specified boundary in a graphical image.

launch: To start up a new program after reinitializing the *stack*, *application global space*, and *application heap*.

leading: (Rhymes with "heading," not "heeding.") The amount of extra vertical space between lines of text, measured in *dots* or *pixels* from the *descent line* of one to the *ascent line* of the next.

length byte: The first byte of a *Pascal-format string*, which gives the number of characters in the string, from 0 to 255.

LIFO: Last in, first out; the order in which items are added to and removed from the *stack*. Compare *FIFO, LIOF*.

lightness: The quality of a color captured by monochrome video or photographic film, which expresses its shade as an equivalent gray level between pure black and pure white; compare *hue, saturation, value*.

line ascent: The vertical distance, in *dots* or *pixels*, from the *ascent line* to the *baseline* of a line of text in a *styled edit record*.

line breaks: The *character positions* marking the beginning of each new line when text is *wrapped* to a boundary.

line drawing: Drawing in a *graphics port* by moving the *graphics pen*, using the QuickDraw routines `Move`, `MoveTo`, `Line`, and `LineTo`.

line height: The vertical distance, in *dots* or *pixels*, between the *baseline* of a line of text and that of the previous line in a *styled edit record*.

line-height table: A data structure defining the *line height* and *line ascent* for each line of text in a *styled edit record*.

LIOF: "Last in, OK, fine"; describes the allocation and deallocation of items in the *heap*, which can occur in any order at all. Compare *FIFO*, *LIFO*.

Lisa: A personal computer manufactured and marketed by Apple Computer, Inc.; the first reasonably priced personal computer to feature a high-resolution bit-mapped display and a hand-held mouse pointing device. Later called *Macintosh XL*.

list definition procedure: A routine, stored as a *resource*, that defines the appearance and behavior of a particular type of scrollable list to be displayed by the *List Manager Package*.

List Manager Package: A standard *package*, provided in the *system resource file*, that displays scrollable lists of items from which the user can choose with the mouse (like the one used in selecting files to be read from the disk).

load: To read an object, such as a *resource* or the *desk scrap*, into memory from a file.

local coordinate system: The coordinate system associated with a given *graphics port*, determined by the *boundary rectangle* of the port's *bit map* or *pixel map*.

lock: To temporarily prevent a *relocatable block* from being *purged* or moved within the heap during *compaction*.

lock bit: A flag associated with a *relocatable block* that marks the block as *locked*.

logical address: The address by which a memory location is referred to at the software level; compare *physical address*.

logical end-of-file: The *character position* following the last byte of meaningful information included in a *file*.

logical shift: A bit-level operation that shifts the bits of a given operand left or right by a specified number of positions, with bits shifted out at one end being lost and 0s shifted in at the other end.

long integer: A data type provided by most Pascal compilers, consisting of double-length integers: 32 bits including sign, covering the range ±2147483647.

long word: A group of 32 bits (2 *words*, or 4 *bytes*) beginning at a *word boundary* in memory.

luminance: The portion of a *composite video* signal used by both monochrome and color receivers, defining the *lightness* of the color picture; compare *chrominance*.

machine code: (1) The representation of a program in a form that can be executed directly by the *processor* of a particular computer. (2) An integer code in the *system environment record* identifying the model of Macintosh on which a program is currently running.

Macintosh: A personal computer manufactured and marketed by Apple Computer, Inc., featuring a high-resolution bit-mapped display and a hand-held mouse pointing device.

Macintosh 128K: The original model of *Macintosh*, with an *MC68000* processor clocked at 7.8336 MHz, a RAM capacity of 128K, 64K of ROM, a 400K single-sided disk drive, and two *RS–232/RS–422* serial ports; also known as the "Skinny Mac."

Macintosh 512K: A model of *Macintosh* with an *MC68000* processor clocked at 7.8336 MHz, a RAM capacity of 512K, 64K of ROM, a 400K single-sided disk drive, and two *RS–232/ RS–422* serial ports; also known as the "Fat Mac."

Macintosh 512K enhanced: An upgraded version of the *Macintosh 512K* including the 128K *Macintosh Plus* ROM and an 800K double-sided disk drive.

Macintosh 512Ke: See *Macintosh 512K enhanced*.

Macintosh Family Hardware Reference: A technical reference manual describing the hardware characteristics of the Macintosh computers, produced by Apple Computer, Inc., and published by Addison-Wesley Publishing Company, Inc.

Macintosh File System: The *flat file system* built into the original Macintosh Toolbox; superseded in recent models by the *Hierarchical File System*.

Macintosh Operating System: The body of machine code built into the Macintosh *ROM* to handle low-level tasks such as memory management, disk input/output, and serial communications.

Macintosh Plus: A model of *Macintosh* with an *MC68000* processor clocked at 7.8336 MHz, a RAM capacity of 1 megabyte (expandable to 4 megabytes), 128K of ROM containing an updated and expanded version of the *Toolbox*, an 800K double-sided disk drive, a redesigned keyboard, two *RS–232/RS–422* serial ports, and a *SCSI* parallel port.

Macintosh Programmer's Workshop: A software development system produced and marketed by Apple Computer, including a Pascal compiler, C compiler, M68000-series assembler, and other development tools; commonly called MPW for short.

Macintosh SE: A model of *Macintosh* with an *MC68000* processor clocked at 7.8336 MHz, a RAM capacity of 1 megabyte (expandable to 4 megabytes), 256K of ROM containing an updated and expanded version of the *Toolbox*, an 800K double-sided disk drive with optional second drive or 20- or 40-megabyte internal hard disk, two *RS–232/RS–422* serial ports, a *SCSI* parallel port, two *Apple Desktop Bus* ports, and one custom expansion slot.

Macintosh SE/30: A model of *Macintosh* with an *MC68030* processor clocked at 15.6672 MHz, an *MC68882* floating-point coprocessor, a RAM capacity of 1 megabyte (expandable to 8 megabytes) with built-in *paged memory management unit*, 256K of ROM containing an updated and expanded version of the *Toolbox*, a 1.44-megabyte high-density disk drive with optional 40- or 80-megabyte internal hard disk, two *RS–232/RS–422* serial ports, a *SCSI* parallel port, two *Apple Desktop Bus* ports, one custom expansion slot, and digital stereo sound.

Macintosh Technical Notes: An ongoing series of documents on Macintosh programming, providing useful hints, tips, techniques, and up-to-the-minute technical information; published several times a year by Apple and widely available through Macintosh user groups, bulletin boards, and the Apple Programmers and Developers Association (*APDA*).

Macintosh II: A model of *Macintosh* with an *MC68020* processor clocked at 15.6672 MHz, an *MC68881* floating-point coprocessor, a RAM capacity of 1 megabyte (expandable to 8 megabytes) with optional *paged memory management unit*, 256K of ROM containing an updated and expanded version of the *Toolbox* with full color support, an 800K double-sided disk drive with optional second 800K or 1.44-megabyte high-density disk drive, a 40-, 80-, or 160-megabyte internal hard disk, two *RS–232/RS–422* serial ports, a *SCSI* parallel port, two *Apple Desktop Bus* ports, six *NuBus* expansion slots, and digital stereo sound.

Macintosh IIci: A model of *Macintosh* with an *MC68030* processor clocked at 25 MHz, an *MC68882* floating-point co-processor, a RAM capacity of 1 megabyte (expandable to 8 megabytes) with built-in *paged memory management unit* and optional high-speed RAM cache, 512K of ROM containing an updated and expanded version of the *Toolbox* with full color support and *32-bit-clean* addressing, redesigned video circuitry with built-in 8-bit color video controller, a 1.44-megabyte high-density disk drive with optional 40- or 80-megabyte internal hard disk, two *RS–232/RS–422* serial ports, a *SCSI* parallel port, two *Apple Desktop Bus* ports, three *NuBus* expansion slots, and digital stereo sound.

Macintosh IIcx: A model of *Macintosh* with an *MC68030* processor clocked at 15.6672 MHz, an *MC68882* floating-point coprocessor, a RAM capacity of 1 megabyte (expandable to 8 megabytes) with built-in *paged memory management unit*, 256K of ROM containing an updated and expanded version of the *Toolbox* with full color support, a 1.44-megabyte high-density disk drive with optional 40- or 80-megabyte internal hard disk, two *RS–232/RS–422* serial ports, a *SCSI* parallel port, two *Apple Desktop Bus* ports, three *NuBus* expansion slots, and digital stereo sound.

Macintosh IIx: A model of *Macintosh* with an *MC68030* processor clocked at 15.6672 MHz, an *MC68882* floating-point coprocessor, a RAM capacity of 1 megabyte (expandable to 8 megabytes) with built-in *paged memory management unit*, 256K of ROM containing an updated and expanded version of the *Toolbox* with full color support, a 1.44-megabyte high-density disk drive with optional second drive, a 40-, 80-, or 160-megabyte internal hard disk, two *RS–232/RS–422* serial ports, a *SCSI* parallel port, two *Apple Desktop Bus* ports, six *NuBus* expansion slots, and digital stereo sound.

Macintosh XL: A *Lisa* computer running Macintosh software under the *MacWorks* emulator.

MacWorks: The software emulator program that enables a *Lisa* computer to run Macintosh software without modification.

magenta: One of the three *subtractive primary colors*, complementary to green and formed, in an *additive* medium, by mixing red and blue.

magnitude: The intensity of a sound or light at any point in time, measured by the height of the curve defining its *waveform*.

main device: See *main graphics device.*

main entry point: The point in a program's code where execution begins when the program is first started up.

main event loop: The central control structure of an *event-driven* program, which requests *events* one at a time from the Toolbox and responds to them as appropriate.

main graphics device: The *graphics device* on which the *menu bar* is displayed, and whose *boundary rectangle* establishes the *global coordinate system* in which those of all other devices (if any) are expressed.

main screen: See *main graphics device.*

mapped device: A color *graphics device* that accepts *color indices* and uses a *color lookup table* to map them into the actual *color values* they stand for; compare *direct device, fixed device, variable CLUT device.*

master pointer: A pointer to a *relocatable block*, kept at a known, fixed location in the *heap* and updated automatically by the Toolbox whenever the underlying block is moved during *compaction.* A pointer to the master pointer is called a *handle* to the block.

match record: A data structure specifying an *edge color* for use by the *lasso* drawing tool or a *seed color* for the *paint bucket* tool.

matching routine: A routine for approximating colors or their *complements* on a given *graphics device;* see *search function, complement procedure.*

MC68000: The *microprocessor* used in the *Macintosh 128K, 512K, 512K enhanced, Plus,* and *SE,* manufactured by Motorola, Inc.; usually called "68000" for short.

MC68020: The *microprocessor* used in the *Macintosh II,* manufactured by Motorola, Inc.; usually called "68020" or just "020" for short.

MC68030: The *microprocessor* used in the *Macintosh SE/30, IIx, IIcx,* and *IIci,* manufactured by Motorola, Inc.; usually called "68030" or just "030" for short.

MC68881: The *floating-point coprocessor* used in the *Macintosh II,* manufactured by Motorola, Inc.; usually called "68881" or just "881" for short.

MC68882: The *floating-point coprocessor* used in the *Macintosh SE/30, IIx, IIcx,* and *IIci,* manufactured by Motorola, Inc.; usually called "68882" or just "882" for short.

megabyte: A unit of memory capacity equal to 2^{20} (1,048,576) bytes.

megahertz: A unit of *frequency* equal to 1,000,000 *hertz;* abbreviated *MHz.*

memory management unit: A component in some models of Macintosh that controls the transfer of information between the processor and memory.

memory-mapped I/O: The use of specified memory addresses for communication with *peripheral devices* rather than for data storage.

memory partition: The segment of memory reserved for a given program to operate in under *MultiFinder.*

menu: A list of choices or options from which the user can *choose* with the mouse.

menu bar: The horizontal strip across the top of the screen from which *menus* can be "pulled down" with the mouse.

menu bar definition function: A routine, stored as a *resource,* that defines the appearance and behavior of a program's *menu bar.*

menu color information table: A data structure specifying the colors to be used in drawing a *menu.*

menu color table: See *menu color information table.*

menu definition procedure: A routine, stored as a *resource,* that defines the appearance and behavior of a particular type of *menu.*

menu handle: A *handle* to a *menu record.*

menu ID: An identifying integer designating a particular *menu;* commonly the *resource ID* under which the menu is stored in a resource file.

menu item: One of the choices or options listed on a *menu.*

menu list: A data structure maintained by the Toolbox, containing handles to all of a program's currently active *menus.*

menu record: A data structure containing descriptive information about a given *menu.*

menu type: A category of *menu* whose appearance and behavior are determined by a *menu definition procedure.*

MFS: See *Macintosh File System.*

MHz: See *megahertz.*

microprocessor: A computer *processor* constructed in the form of a single silicon microchip.

`MiniEdit`: The extensive example application program originally developed in Volume Two of this series and further expanded in subsequent volumes.

minimum memory size: The size of the smallest *memory partition* in which a program can successfully operate, specified in its *size resource*; compare *preferred memory size*.

MMU: See *memory management unit*.

MMU mode: See *address mode*.

modal dialog box: A form of *dialog box* that prevents the user from interacting with any other window for as long as the dialog remains on the screen, but which allows actions beyond merely *dismissing* the dialog by clicking a *pushbutton*; compare *alert box, modeless dialog box*.

mode: A state of the system that determines its response to the user's actions with the mouse and keyboard.

modeless dialog box: A form of *dialog box* that allows the user to interact with other windows while the dialog remains on the screen; compare *alert box, modal dialog box*.

modifier key: A key on the Macintosh keyboard that doesn't generate a character of its own, but may affect the meaning of any *character key* pressed at the same time; see *Shift key, Caps Lock key, Option key, Command key*.

monochrome: Describes a graphical image with a *pixel depth* of 1 bit per pixel, drawn in the *foreground* and *background colors* of its *graphics port* (typically, but not necessarily, black and white).

mouse: A hand-held pointing device that controls the movements of the *cursor* to designate positions on the Macintosh screen.

mouse-down event: An *event* reporting that the user pressed the mouse button.

mouse event: An *event* reporting an action by the user with the mouse; see *mouse-down event, mouse-up event*. Note that *mouse-moved events* are considered *MultiFinder events* and *not* mouse events.

mouse-moved event: A *MultiFinder event* notifying a program that the mouse has been moved into a different region of the screen and that the appearance of the *cursor* must be adjusted accordingly.

mouse-up event: An *event* reporting that the user released the mouse button.

MPW: See *Macintosh Programmer's Workshop.*

M68000: The family of Motorola *microprocessors* used in the Macintosh, including the *MC68000*, MC68008, MC68010, *MC68020*, and *MC68030.*

MultiFinder: A software environment that allows the user to switch freely among two or more *application programs*, all of which may be resident in memory at the same time.

MultiFinder-aware bit: A flag bit in a program's *size resource* that tells whether the program is prepared to take full advantage of *MultiFinder's* features and capabilities.

MultiFinder event: An *event* reported to a running program by *MultiFinder*, using the *application event* type App4Evt; see *suspend event, resume event, mouse-moved event.*

Munsell color system: The most widely used method of color classification, which characterizes colors according to their *hue, saturation,* and *value* or *brightness;* also called *HSV* representation.

network event: A type of *event* used internally by the Toolbox to handle communication with other computers over a network.

nonrelocatable block: A *block* that cannot be moved within the heap during *compaction,* referred to by single indirection with a simple pointer; compare *relocatable block.*

notification: A facility provided by *MultiFinder* for communicating error messages, program status, or other important information to the user while running in the *background.*

notification queue: A list of pending *notifications* maintained by the Toolbox.

notification record: A data structure defining the content and behavior of a *notification.*

NTSC: (1) National Television Standards Committee, an industry group that established the standard format for *composite video* signals used by broadcast television receivers in the United States. (2) The video format defined by this group.

NuBus: An industry-standard interface for *expansion cards,* developed by Texas Instruments, Inc., and used in the Macintosh II's *expansion slots.*

null event: An *event* generated by the Toolbox when a program requests an event and there are none to report.

null style: The *style attributes* to be applied to text entered at an *insertion point* in a *styled edit record* .

null-style record: The data structure defining the *null style* for a *styled edit record.*

numeric keypad: A set of keys for typing numbers into the computer. On recent Macintosh models, the keypad is physically built into the keyboard unit; on earlier models, it's an optional separate unit that connects to the *keyboard* with a cable.

off-line: Describes a *volume* (such as a disk that has been *ejected* from a disk drive) for which only a minimal amount of the descriptive information needed by the *file system* is immediately available in memory; compare *on-line.*

offset/width table: A table in the *font record* containing information on the width and spacing of each character in a given *font.*

old-style graphics port: A *graphics port* of the kind used by *classic QuickDraw,* supporting *monochrome* drawing and limited *planar* color.

on-line: Describes a *volume* (such as a disk currently in a disk drive) for which all of the descriptive information needed by the *file system* is immediately available in memory; compare *off-line.*

Operating System: See *Macintosh Operating System.*

Operating System trap: A form of *trap word* denoting a low-level, typically *register-based,* system management operation such as memory allocation or disk input/output.

Option key: A *modifier key* on the Macintosh keyboard, used for typing special characters such as foreign letters and accents.

or: A bit-level operation in which each bit of the result is a 1 if either or both operands have 1s at the corresponding bit position, or 0 if both have 0s.

origin: (1) The top-left corner of a *rectangle.* (2) For a *bit map, pixel map,* or *graphics port,* the top-left corner of the *boundary rectangle,* whose coordinates determine the *local coordinate system.*

OS: Short for "operating system"; see *Macintosh Operating System.*

OS trap: See *Operating System trap.*

oval: A graphical figure, circular or elliptical in shape; defined by an *enclosing rectangle.*

owning window: The *window* with which a given *control* is associated.

package: A *resource*, usually residing in the *system resource file* (or in *ROM* on some models), containing a collection of general-purpose routines that can be loaded into memory when needed; used to supplement the *Toolbox* with additional facilities.

package number: The *resource ID* of a *package;* must be between 0 and 15 (or 0 and 7 on earlier Macintosh models).

package trap: A Toolbox *trap* used at the machine-language level to call a routine belonging to a *package*. In the original Toolbox there are eight package traps, named _Pack0 to _Pack7; on more recent models there are sixteen, named _Pack0 to _Pack15.

page-down region: The area of a scroll bar's *shaft* below or to the right of the *scroll box*, which causes it to scroll down or to the right a windowful ("page") at a time when clicked with the mouse.

page-up region: The area of a scroll bar's *shaft* above or to the left of the *scroll box*, which causes it to scroll up or to the left a windowful ("page") at a time when clicked with the mouse.

paged memory management unit: An auxiliary *processor* included in some models of Macintosh that maintains a system of *virtual memory*, in which portions ("pages") of a program's logical memory space are kept on a hard disk or other mass storage device and transferred in and out of physical memory as needed.

paint: To fill a *shape* with the *pen pattern* of the *current port.*

paint bucket: A drawing tool included in many graphics-editing programs, which fills a contiguous region in a graphical image with a specified *pattern.*

palette: A predefined selection of colors requested by a program for use in its drawing operations.

palette index: An integer identifying a color by its position within a *palette.*

palette record: A data structure specifying the contents of a *palette.*

palette template: A *resource* defining the contents of a *palette.*

parallel port: A connector on the back of the Macintosh for communicating with *peripheral devices* via the *SCSI* parallel interface.

parameter RAM: A small amount (256 bytes) of *read/write memory* that is stored on the Macintosh's real-time *clock chip* and powered independently by a battery even when the machine's main power is turned off; used to store operating characteristics of the system that must be retained from one working session to the next, such as those set by the user via the *Control Panel* desk accessory.

part code: An integer denoting the part of the screen, or of a *window* or *control*, in which the mouse was pressed; compare *part identifier*.

part identifier: An integer denoting the part of a *window* or *control* to which an entry in its *window* or *control color table* applies; compare *part code*.

partition: See *memory partition*.

Pascal-format string: A sequence of text characters represented in the internal format typically used by Pascal compilers, consisting of a *length byte* followed by from 0 to 255 bytes of *character codes*.

patch: To replace a standard Toolbox routine with a *customized* version of your own by changing its *trap address* in the *dispatch table*.

pattern: A small graphical image that can be repeated indefinitely to fill an area, like identical floor tiles laid end to end.

pattern list: A *resource* consisting of any number of patterns.

pattern transfer modes: A set of *transfer modes* used in *classic QuickDraw* for drawing lines or shapes or filling areas with a *pattern*; compare *source transfer modes*.

pen: See *graphics pen*.

pen level: An integer associated with a *graphics port* that determines the visibility of the port's *graphics pen*. The pen is visible if the pen level is zero or positive, hidden if it's negative.

pen location: The coordinates of the *graphics pen* in a given *graphics port*.

pen mode: The *transfer mode* with which a *graphics port* draws lines and frames or paints shapes; should be one of the *pattern transfer modes*.

pen pattern: The *pattern* in which a *graphics port* draws lines and frames or paints shapes.

pen size: The width and height of the *graphics pen* belonging to a *graphics port*.

pen state: The characteristics of the *graphics pen* belonging to a *graphics port*, including its *pen location, pen size, pen mode,* and *pen pattern*.

period: The duration in time of one *cycle* of a regularly recurring wave, such as a sound or light wave.

periodic task: An operation that a *device driver* or *desk accessory* must perform at regular intervals in order to function properly.

peripheral device: An article of input/output or other equipment that is separate from the Macintosh and connected to it with a cable, such as a disk drive, printer, or modem.

physical address: The address at which a memory location is actually found at the hardware level; compare *logical address*.

physical end-of-file: The *character position* following the last byte of physical storage space allocated to a *file*.

picture: A recorded sequence of *QuickDraw* operations that can be repeated on demand to reproduce a graphical image.

picture comment: A special command embedded in a *picture* to convey additional information unused by *QuickDraw* but meaningful to some other application program. The general nature of the information is identified by an integer *comment type*; the information itself constitutes the *comment data*.

picture frame: The reference *rectangle* within which a *picture* is defined, and which can be mapped to coincide with any other specified rectangle when the picture is drawn.

pixel: A single spot forming part of a graphical image when displayed on the screen; short for "picture element." Compare *dot*.

pixel depth: The number of bits representing each *pixel* in a *pixel image*, which determines the number of distinct colors the image can contain.

pixel image: An array of values in memory representing the *pixels* of a color graphical image.

pixel map: A data structure containing the information needed to interpret and display a given *pixel image* in memory.

pixel pattern: A *pattern* composed of *pixel values* representing multiple colors, for use in color drawing operations; compare *bit pattern*.

pixel value: The combination of bits representing a *pixel* of a particular color in a *pixel image*.

plain text: Text set in plain *type style*, with no *style variations* such as bold or italic.

planar: A *storage format* for *pixel images* in which the full-color image is resolved into separate *color planes*, each of which is a *bit image* 1 bit deep representing the presence or absence of a single constituent color; compare *chunky, chunky/planar*.

plane: (1) A *window's* front-to-back position relative to other windows on the screen. (2) See *color plane*.

plane offset: The number of bytes in each *plane* of a *pixel image* in *planar* or *chunky/planar* format.

PMMU: See *paged memory management unit*.

point: (1) A position on the *QuickDraw* coordinate grid, specified by a pair of horizontal and vertical coordinates. (2) A unit used by printers to measure type sizes, equal to approximately 1/72 of an inch.

point size: See *type size*.

polygon: A graphical figure defined by any closed series of connected straight lines.

pop: To remove a data item from the top of a *stack*.

port: (1) A connector on the back of the Macintosh for communication with a peripheral device, such as a printer or modem. (2) See *graphics port*.

port rectangle: The rectangle defining the portion of a *bit map* or *pixel map* that a *graphics port* can draw into.

post: To record an *event* in the *event queue* for later processing.

PostScript: A device-independent page description language, developed by Adobe Systems Incorporated and licensed by Apple for use in the *LaserWriter* printer.

preferred memory size: The ideal size of a program's *memory partition*, specified in its *size resource*; compare *minimum memory size*.

primary colors: A set of three colors that can be combined in varying proportions to produce the full range of colors perceived by the eye; see *additive primary colors, subtractive primary colors*.

printer driver: The *device driver* for communicating with a printer through one of the Macintosh's built-in *ports*.

processor: The component of a computer that carries out the operations specified by a program.

prompting string: A string of text characters supplied by the application program for display in the *Standard File* or *Color Picker dialog*, prompting the user to select a file name or color value.

protect: To lock the contents of an entry in a *color table*, preventing other programs from changing its *color value*; compare *release*.

pseudo-random numbers: Numbers that seem to be random but can be reproduced in exactly the same sequence if desired.

pull down: To display a *menu* on the screen by pressing the mouse inside its title in the *menu bar*.

purge: To remove a *relocatable block* from the heap to make room for other blocks. The purged block's *master pointer* remains allocated, but is set to NIL to show that the block no longer exists in the heap; all existing *handles* to the block become *empty handles*.

purge bit: A flag associated with a *relocatable block* that marks the block as *purgeable*.

purgeable block: A *relocatable block* that can be *purged* from the heap to make room for other blocks.

push: To add a data item to the top of a *stack*.

pushbutton: A *button* that causes some immediate action to occur, either instantaneously when clicked with the mouse or continuously for as long as the mouse button is held down; compare *checkbox, radio buttons*.

pushdown stack: See *stack*.

QuickDraw: The extensive collection of graphics routines built into the Macintosh in ROM.

QuickDraw globals pointer: A pointer to the global variables used by *QuickDraw*, kept at address 0(A5) in the *application global space*.

radio buttons: A group of two or more related *buttons*, exactly one of which can be on at any given time; turning on any button in the group turns off all the others. Compare *pushbutton, checkbox*.

RAM: See *random-access memory*.

random-access memory: A common but misleading term for *read/write memory*.

raw key code: A device-dependent *key code* generated directly by the hardware of a *keyboard*, *keypad*, or other text-entry device; compare *virtual key code*.

read-only memory: Memory that can be read but not written; usually called *ROM*. The Macintosh ROM contains the built-in machine code of the *Macintosh Operating System*, *QuickDraw*, and the *User Interface Toolbox*; on larger models it also includes some *packages*, *device drivers*, and other frequently used *resources*. Compare *read/write memory*.

read/write memory: Memory that can be both read and written; commonly known by the misleading term *random-access memory*, or *RAM*. Compare *read-only memory*.

reallocate: To allocate fresh space for a *relocatable block* that has been *purged*, updating the block's *master pointer* to point to its new location. Only the space is reallocated; the block's former contents are not restored.

recalibrate: To recalculate the *line breaks* in an *edit record* after any change in its text, *text characteristics*, or *destination rectangle*.

rectangle: A four-sided graphical figure defined by two *points* specifying its top-left and bottom-right corners, or by four integers specifying its top, left, bottom, and right edges.

reference constant: A 4-byte field included in a Toolbox data structure (such as a *window record* or *control record*) for the application program to use in any way it wishes.

region: A graphical figure that can be of any arbitrary shape. It can have curved as well as straight edges, and can even have holes or consist of two or more separate pieces.

register-based: Describes a Toolbox routine that accepts its parameters and returns its results directly in the processor's registers; compare *stack-based*.

regular slot space: In *32-bit mode*, a 16-megabyte area of *address space* allotted for use by a given *expansion slot*; compare *super slot space*.

release: (1) To unlock the contents of an entry in a *color table*, again allowing other programs to change its *color value*; compare *protect*. (2) See *deallocate*.

relinquish: To give up exclusive possession of an entry in a *color table*, making it again available to other programs for drawing operations; compare *reserve*.

relocatable block: A *block* that can be moved within the heap during *compaction*, referred to by double indirection with a *handle*; compare *nonrelocatable block*.

request list: A list of table indices specifying which entries of a *color table* to save or restore.

reserve: To claim exclusive possession of an entry in a *color table*, making it unavailable to other programs for drawing operations; compare *relinquish*.

resource: A unit or collection of information kept in a *resource file* on a disk or other mass storage device and loaded into memory when needed. (On recent Macintosh models, frequently-used system resources are permanently available in ROM and needn't be loaded for use.)

resource data: The information a *resource* contains.

resource file: A collection of *resources* stored together as a unit on a disk or other mass storage device; technically not a *file* as such, but merely the *resource fork* of a particular file.

resource fork: The *fork* of a *file* that contains the file's *resources*; usually called a *resource file*. Compare *data fork*.

resource ID: An integer that identifies a particular *resource* within its *resource type*.

resource name: An optional string of text characters that identifies a particular *resource* within its *resource type*, and by which the resource can be listed on a *menu*.

resource specification: The combination of a *resource type* and *resource ID*, or a *resource type* and *resource name*, which uniquely identifies a particular resource.

resource type: A four-character string that identifies the kind of information a *resource* contains.

response procedure: (1) A procedure that defines the action to be taken when the mouse is clicked in a *dialog item* of a printing-related *dialog*. (2) A procedure supplied by a program to be executed when posting a *notification* to the user.

result code: An integer code returned by a *Toolbox* routine to signal successful completion or report an error.

resume: Under *MultiFinder*, to move a program from the *background* to the *foreground*; compare *suspend*.

resume event: A *MultiFinder event* notifying a program that it has just been moved from the *background* to the *foreground*; compare *suspend event*.

return link: The address of the instruction following a routine call, to which control is to return on completion of the routine.

RGB: (1) A method of color representation that characterizes colors according to the relative intensities of the three *additive primary colors* (red, green, and blue); compare *CMY, HSV, HSL*. (2) A form of *video* transmission used in closed-circuit studio monitors and computer displays, in which the relative intensities of the additive primary colors are represented by three independent signals.

ROM: See *read-only memory*.

ROM-based resource: A system *resource* that resides in *read-only memory* for rapid access, rather than in a *resource file* on a disk or other mass storage device.

rounded rectangle: A graphical figure consisting of a *rectangle* with rounded corners; defined by the rectangle itself and the dimensions of the *ovals* forming the corners.

routine selector: An integer used at the machine-language level to identify a specific routine that is called via a more general Toolbox *trap*, such as a *package trap* or a "universal" trap like `_OSDispatch` or `_TEDispatch`.

row width: The number of bytes in each row of a *bit image* or *pixel image*.

RS–232: An industry-standard interface convention for serial communication with *peripheral devices*, supported by the *serial ports* built into all models of Macintosh.

RS–422: An industry-standard interface convention for serial communication with *peripheral devices*, supported by the *serial ports* built into all models of Macintosh.

run: See *style run*.

run list: A list of *style runs* contained in a *style record*, defining the *style attributes* of the text characters in the corresponding *styled edit record*.

SANE: See *Standard Apple Numeric Environment*.

saturation: The property of a color determined by the "signal-to-noise ratio" of its light wave, and corresponding to the subjective purity or vividness of the color (distinguishing, for example, fire-engine red from rose pink); compare *hue, value, lightness.*

SCC: See *Serial Communications Controller.*

scrap: The vehicle by which information is *cut and pasted* from one place to another.

scrap count: An integer maintained by the Toolbox that tells when the contents of the *desk scrap* have been changed by a *desk accessory.*

scrap file: A *file* holding the contents of the *desk scrap.*

scrap handle: A *handle* to the contents of the *desk scrap,* kept by the Toolbox in a *system global.*

scrap information record: A data structure summarizing the contents and status of the *desk scrap.*

scrap style element: A single entry in a *scrap style table,* defining the location and *style attributes* of a single *style run* within the text being *cut and pasted* via the *desk scrap.*

scrap style table: A table in a *style-scrap record* defining the *style runs* within the text being *cut and pasted* via the *desk scrap,* along with their associated *style attributes.*

scrapless editing: The insertion or deletion of text in an *edit record* without reference to the contents of the *desk scrap* or *Toolbox scrap.*

scrapless styling: The application of *style attributes* to text in a *styled edit record* without reference to the contents of the *style scrap.*

screen buffer: The area of memory reserved to hold a *screen image.*

screen configuration: A *resource* kept in the *system resource file* defining the *display modes* and spatial arrangement of all *graphics devices* in the system.

screen depth: The *pixel depth* of the *screen image* on a given *graphics device.*

screen image: The *bit image* or *pixel image* that defines what is displayed on the screen of a *graphics device.*

screen map: The *bit map* or *pixel map* representing the screen of a *graphics device,* kept in the QuickDraw global variable `ScreenBits` [I:4.2.1] (under *classic QuickDraw*) or located via a handle in the `gdPMap` field of the *device record* [4.3.1] (under *color QuickDraw*). Its *bit image* or *pixel image* is the *screen image;* its *boundary rectangle* has the same dimensions as the screen, with the *origin* at coordinates (0, 0).

scroll: To move the contents of a *window* with respect to the window itself, changing the portion of a document or other information that's visible within the window.

scroll bar: A *control* associated with a *window* that allows the user to *scroll* the window's contents.

scroll box: The *indicator* of a *scroll bar*, a small white box that can be *dragged* to any desired position within the scroll bar's *shaft;* also called the "thumb."

SCSI: Small Computer Standard Interface, a parallel interface built into some Macintosh models for communicating with *peripheral devices;* commonly pronounced "scuzzy" (or "sexy," according to personal temperament).

search function: A function for finding the closest approximation to a requested color on a given *graphics device.*

seed: (1) The starting value used in generating a sequence of *pseudo-random numbers.* (2) A numerical value used for coordinating the contents of a *color table* and its corresponding *inverse table.* (3) The *point* within a graphical image that designates the region to be filled by the *paint bucket* drawing tool.

seed color: The color of the *pixel* at the *seed* location in a graphical image, which defines the extent of the region to be filled by the *paint bucket* drawing tool.

selection: An object or part of a *document* designated by the user to be acted on by subsequent commands or operations.

selection range: A pair of *character positions* defining the beginning and end of the *selection* in an *edit record.*

Serial Communications Controller: A special-purpose controller chip, the Zilog Z8530, used in the Macintosh to control communication with *peripheral devices* via the *serial port.*

serial driver: The *device driver* built into ROM for communicating with *peripheral devices* through the Macintosh's built-in *serial ports.*

serial port: A connector on the back of the Macintosh for communicating with *peripheral devices* such as a hard disk, printer, or modem.

setting: An integer specifying the current state or value of a *control.*

shaft: The vertical or horizontal body of a *scroll bar*, within which the *scroll box* slides.

shape: Any of the figures that can be drawn with QuickDraw *shape-drawing* operations, including *rectangles, rounded rectangles, ovals, arcs* and *wedges, polygons,* and *regions.*

shape drawing: Drawing *shapes* in a *graphics port*, using the operations *frame, paint, fill, erase,* and *invert.*

Shift key: A *modifier key* on the Macintosh keyboard, used to convert lowercase letters to uppercase or to produce the upper character on a nonalphabetic key.

show: To make a window, control, or other object *visible.*

shutdown procedure: A special procedure provided by a program to perform last-minute housekeeping before the system is shut down or restarted.

signature: A four-character string that identifies a particular *application program*, used as a *creator signature* on files belonging to the program and as the *resource type* of the program's *autograph* resource.

sine wave: A *waveform* whose shape is defined by the trigonometric sine function.

6522: See *SY6522.*

68000: See *M68000, MC68000.*

68020: See *MC68020.*

68030: See *MC68030.*

68881: See *MC68881.*

68882: See *MC68882.*

size box: The small box at the bottom-right corner of a *document window*, with which it can be resized by dragging with the mouse.

size region: The area of a *window* with which it can be resized by dragging with the mouse; also called the "grow region." In a *document window*, the size region is the *size box.*

size resource: A *resource* defining a program's *preferred memory size, minimum memory size,* and other *MultiFinder*-related properties.

Skinny Mac: See *Macintosh 128K.*

slot: See *expansion slot.*

slot card: See *expansion card.*

slot number: The identifying number designating a particular *expansion slot*, consisting of a single hexadecimal digit between $9 and $E.

slot resource: An item of information (not a true *resource* in the usual sense) stored in *declaration ROM* on an *expansion card*, describing the characteristics of the card or of the device it controls.

slot space: The portion of *address space* reserved for use by an *expansion card* plugged into a given *expansion slot*. In *24-bit mode*, each slot is allotted 1 megabyte of slot space; in *32-bit mode*, each slot has 16 megabytes of *regular slot space* and 256 megabytes of *super slot space*.

small fraction: A value of the Toolbox data type `SmallFract` [2.4.1], representing a 16-bit fractional value between 0 and 1 with a binary point preceding the first bit; equivalent to the low-order (fractional) half of a *fixed-point number* of type `Fixed` [I:2.3.1].

small icon: A graphical image half the size of a standard *icon* (16 pixels by 16), used on the Macintosh screen to represent an object such as a disk or file.

sound chip: The special-purpose chip that controls the Macintosh *sound generator*. The sound chip in the *classic Macintosh* and *Macintosh SE* is manufactured by Sony Corporation; the *Macintosh II* uses a custom *Apple Sound Chip*.

sound driver: The *device driver* built into ROM for controlling the sounds emitted by the Macintosh's built-in speaker.

sound number: An integer identifying the *error sound* to be emitted by an *alert*.

sound generator: The electronic circuitry that produces sounds through the Macintosh's built-in speaker.

sound procedure: A procedure that defines the *error sounds* to be emitted by *alerts*.

source transfer modes: A set of *transfer modes* used in *classic QuickDraw* for transferring pixels from one *bit map* or *pixel map* to another or for drawing text characters into a bit or pixel map; compare *pattern transfer modes*.

stack: (1) Generally, a data structure in which items can be added (*pushed*) and removed (*popped*) in *LIFO* order: the last item added is always the first to be removed. (2) Specifically, the area of Macintosh *RAM* that holds parameters, local variables, return addresses, and other temporary storage associated with a program's procedures and functions; compare *heap.*

stack-based: Describes a Toolbox routine that accepts its parameters and returns its results on the *stack,* according to Pascal conventions; compare *register-based.*

stack pointer: The address of the current *top of the stack,* kept in processor register A7.

Standard Apple Numeric Environment: A set of routines for performing arithmetic on *floating-point numbers* in accordance with the *IEEE standard;* available on the Macintosh through the *Floating-Point Arithmetic Package.* Commonly called by the acronym *SANE.*

Standard File dialog: The *dialog box* displayed by the *Standard File Package,* allowing the user to supply a file name for an input/output operation.

Standard File Package: A standard *package,* provided in the *system resource file,* that provides a convenient, standard way for the user to supply file names for input/output operations.

standard fill tones: A set of five *bit patterns* representing a range of homogeneous tones from solid white to solid black, provided as global variables by the *QuickDraw* graphics routines.

starting angle: The angle defining the beginning of an *arc* or *wedge;* compare *arc angle.*

startup handle: A *handle* to a program's *startup information,* passed to the program by the Finder as an *application parameter.*

startup information: A list of *document files* selected by the user to be opened or printed on starting up an application program.

static item: A *dialog item,* such as a piece of text, an *icon,* or a *picture,* that conveys information to the user without accepting any in return; compare *interactive item.*

storage format: The form in which color values are represented in memory as part of a *pixel image;* see *chunky, planar, chunky/planar.*

strike: See *font image.*

structure region: The total area occupied by a *window,* including both its *window frame* and *content region.*

style: See *text style.*

style attribute: Any of the individual properties composing a *text style*, including *typeface, type size, type style,* and *text color;* compare *style variation.*

style element: A single entry in a *style table,* defining the *style attributes* for one or more *style runs* in the *run list* of the associated *style record.*

style handle: A handle to the *style record* associated with a *styled edit record.*

style record: A data structure defining the *style attributes* for the text of a *styled edit record.*

style run: A sequence of consecutive characters in the text of a *styled edit record* that all share the same *style attributes.*

style scrap: An item written to the *desk scrap* to define the *style attributes* of text being *cut and pasted* via the scrap.

style-scrap record: The data structure constituting the *style scrap.*

style table: A data structure containing the specific *style attributes* for the *style runs* defined in the *run list* of a *style record.*

style variation: Any of the individual variations composing a *type style,* such as bold, italic, underline, outline, or shadow; compare *style attribute.*

styled edit record: A modified form of *edit record* used by the *styled TextEdit* routines for working with *styled text.*

styled text: Text whose *style attributes* are not uniform, but can vary from character to character.

styled TextEdit: The version of the *TextEdit* editing routines that supports *styled text.*

subdirectory: Under the *Hierarchical File System,* a *directory* contained within another directory.

subtractive color: The mixing of colors in an opaque medium, such as paint or ink on paper, which subtracts *primary colors* from reflected light to produce the range of colors perceived by the eye; compare *additive color.*

subtractive primary colors: The three *primary colors (cyan, magenta,* and yellow) that combine in an opaque medium, such as paint or ink on paper, to produce the range of colors perceived by the eye; see *subtractive color.*

super slot space: In *32-bit mode,* a 256-megabyte area of *address space* allotted for use by a given *expansion slot;* compare *regular slot space.*

suspend: Under *MultiFinder*, to move a program from the *foreground* to the *background*; compare *resume*.

suspend event: A *MultiFinder event* notifying a program that it is about to be moved from the *foreground* to the *background*; compare *resume event*.

Switcher: An early precursor of *MultiFinder*, developed privately by the renowned Macintosh programmer Andy Hertzfeld.

SY6522:   The *Versatile Interface Adapter* chip used in the Macintosh, manufactured by Synertek Incorporated; usually called "6522" for short.

synchronous: Describes an input/output operation that is performed to completion, returning control to the calling program only after the operation has been carried out in its entirety; compare *asynchronous*.

synthetic font: A temporary version of a *font* converted to the current *screen depth* of the *graphics device* on which it is to be used, created automatically by the Toolbox for more efficient text display.

synthetic-font list: A data structure listing all *synthetic fonts* currently in existence.

system clock: The clock that records the elapsed time in *ticks* since the system was last started up.

system environment record: A data structure containing descriptive information about the configuration of the Macintosh system on which a program is currently running.

system event mask: A global *event mask* maintained by the Toolbox that controls which types of *event* can be *posted* into the *event queue*.

`System` **file:**   See *system resource file*.

system font: The *typeface* (normally `Chicago`) used by the Toolbox for displaying its own text on the screen, such as *window titles* and *menu items*.

system global: A fixed memory location reserved for use by the Toolbox.

system heap: The portion of the *heap* reserved for the private use of the Macintosh Operating System and Toolbox; compare *application heap*.

system resource file: The *resource fork* of the file `System`, containing shared *resources* that are available to all programs.

system window: A window in which a *desk accessory* is displayed on the screen; compare *application window*.

temporary memory allocation: A form of memory allocation available under *MultiFinder*, in which blocks of memory are allocated on a short-term basis from the portion of memory not currently in use by any program.

text box: A *dialog item* consisting of a box into which the user can type text from the keyboard.

text characteristics: The properties of a *graphics port* or *edit record* that determine the way it draws text characters, including its *text face*, *text size*, *text style*, and *text mode*.

text color: The color in which a *graphics port* draws text characters.

text face: The *typeface* in which a *graphics port* draws text characters.

text file: A file of file type `'TEXT'`, containing pure text characters with no additional formatting or other information.

text font: A term sometimes used loosely (and incorrectly) as a synonym for *text face*.

text handle: A *handle* to a sequence of text characters in memory.

text menu: The standard *menu type* used by the Toolbox, consisting of a vertical list of item titles.

text mode: The *transfer mode* with which a *graphics port* draws text characters.

text scrap: See *Toolbox scrap*.

text size: The *type size* in which a *graphics port* draws text characters.

text style: (1) A set of *style attributes* defining the visual appearance of text characters, including *typeface, type size, type style*, and *text color*; compare *type style*. (2) The *type style* in which a *graphics port* draws text characters.

text style record: A data structure defining the *style attributes* of a particular *text style*.

TextEdit: The collection of text-editing routines included in the *User Interface Toolbox*.

32-bit-clean: Describes software in which no extraneous information is stored in the high-order byte of any memory address, allowing unimpeded operation in full *32-bit mode*.

32-bit mode: A state of the Macintosh system in which memory addresses can be a full *long word* (32 bits) in length.

thumb: See *scroll box.*

tick: The basic unit of time on the *system clock;* the interval between successive occurrences of the *vertical retrace interrupt,* equal to approximately one sixtieth of a second.

title bar: The area at the top of a *document window* that displays the window's title, and by which the window can be *dragged* to a new location on the screen.

tolerance: The degree of difference that is acceptable in matching a *tolerant color* from a *palette* against the colors available in the *current color table.*

tolerant color: An entry in a *palette* that will match the closest *color value* available in the *current color table,* provided that it differs from the requested color by less than a specified *tolerance;* if no such color exists, the color table will be modified to make the exact requested color available. Compare *courteous color, animating color, explicit color, dithered color.*

Toolbox: (1) The *User Interface Toolbox.* (2) Loosely, the entire contents of the Macintosh *ROM,* including the *Macintosh Operating System* and *QuickDraw* in addition to the *User Interface Toolbox* proper.

Toolbox scrap: The private *scrap* maintained internally by the *TextEdit* routines to hold text being *cut and pasted* from one place to another within an application program; compare *desk scrap.*

Toolbox trap: A form of *trap word* denoting a higher-level, typically *stack-based,* user-interface operation, such as window or menu management.

top of stack: The end of the *stack* at which items are added and removed; compare *base of stack.*

track: To follow the movements of the *mouse* while the user *drags* it, taking some continuous action (such as providing visual feedback on the screen) until the button is released.

Transcendental Functions Package: A standard *package,* provided in the *system resource file* (or in ROM on some models), that calculates various transcendental functions on *floating-point numbers,* such as logarithms, exponentials, trigonometric functions, compound interest, and discounted value.

transfer mode: A method of combining *pixels* being transferred to a *bit map* or *pixel map* with those already there.

translate: To move a *point* or graphical figure a given distance horizontally and vertically.

trap: An error or abnormal condition that causes the *M68000*-series processor to suspend normal program execution temporarily and execute a *trap handler* routine to respond to the problem; also called an *exception.*

trap address: The memory address of the Toolbox routine associated with a given *trap number.*

Trap Dispatcher: The *trap handler* routine for responding to the *emulator trap,* which examines the contents of the *trap word* and jumps to the corresponding Toolbox routine in ROM.

trap handler: The routine executed by the *central processing unit* to respond to a particular type of *trap.*

trap macro: A macroinstruction used to call a Toolbox routine from an assembly-language program; when assembled, it produces the appropriate *trap word* for the desired routine. Trap macros are defined in the assembly-language interface to the Toolbox and always begin with an underscore character (_).

trap number: The last 8 or 9 bits of a *trap word,* which identify the particular Toolbox routine to be executed; used as an index into the *dispatch table* to find the address of the routine in ROM.

trap type: The internal format of a *trap word,* which determines the kind of operation it represents; see *OS trap, Toolbox trap.*

trap vector: The address of the *trap handler* routine for a particular type of *trap,* kept in the *vector table* in memory.

trap word: An *unimplemented instruction* used to stand for a particular Toolbox operation in a machine-language program. The trap word includes a *trap number* identifying the Toolbox operation to be performed; when executed, it causes an *emulator trap* that will execute the corresponding Toolbox routine in ROM.

24-bit mode: A state of the Macintosh system in which all memory addresses are limited to 24 bits in length.

type size: The size in which text characters are drawn, measured in printer's *points* and sometimes referred to as a "point size."

type style: A set of *style variations* modifying the basic form in which text characters are drawn, such as bold, italic, underline, outline, or shadow; compare *text style.*

typecasting: A feature of some Pascal compilers that allows data items to be converted from one data type to another with the same underlying representation (for example, from one pointer type to another).

typeface: The overall form or design in which text characters are drawn, independent of size or style. Macintosh typefaces are conventionally named after world cities, such as New York, Geneva, or Athens.

unimplemented instruction: A machine-language instruction whose effects are not defined by the *M68000*-series processors. Attempting to execute such an instruction causes an *emulator trap* to occur, allowing the effects of the instruction to be "emulated" in software instead of hardware.

unimplemented trap: A special *trap number* that is guaranteed by Apple to remain forever unassigned to any Toolbox routine; used for comparison with the *trap addresses* of other Toolbox routines to find whether they are available in a given version of the Macintosh system.

Unix: A popular operating system available on many computers, developed at the Bell Laboratories of AT&T and implemented for the Macintosh as *A/UX*.

unload: To remove an object, such as a *resource* or the *desk scrap*, from memory, often (though not necessarily) by writing it out to a *file*.

unlock: To undo the effects of *locking* a *relocatable block*, again allowing it to be moved within the heap during *compaction*.

unmount: To make a *volume* unknown to the file system by releasing the memory space occupied by its *file directory* and *block map*.

unpurgeable block: A *relocatable block* that cannot be *purged* from the heap to make room for other blocks.

unstyled edit record: An *edit record* of the kind used by the original version of *TextEdit*, which cannot support the use of *styled text*.

up arrow: The arrow at the top or left end of a *scroll bar*, which causes it to scroll up or to the left a line at a time when clicked with the mouse.

update: To redraw all or part of a window's *content region* on the screen, usually because it has become *exposed* as a result of the user's manipulations with the mouse.

update event: A *window event* generated by the Toolbox to signal that all or part of a given window has become *exposed* and must be *updated* (redrawn).

update rectangle: The rectangle within which text is to be redrawn when an *edit record* is *updated.*

update region: The *region* defining the portion of a *window* that must be redrawn when *updating* the window.

usage level: An integer code associated with a color requested in a *palette,* specifying the way in which the color is to be matched against those available in the *current color table;* see *tolerant color, courteous color, animating color, explicit color, dithered color.*

user: The human operator of a computer.

user event: An *event* reporting an action by the user; see *mouse event, keyboard event, disk-inserted event.*

user interface: The set of rules and conventions by which a human *user* communicates with a computer system or program.

User Interface Guidelines: An Apple document (part of the *Inside Macintosh* manual) that defines the standard *user interface* conventions to be followed by all Macintosh application programs.

User Interface Toolbox: The body of machine code built into the Macintosh *ROM* to implement the features of the standard *user interface.*

valid region: An area of a window's *content region* whose contents are already accurately displayed on the screen, and which therefore need not be *updated;* compare *invalid region.*

value: The property of a color determined by the *amplitude* of its light wave, and corresponding to the subjective strength or intensity of the color; also called *brightness.* Compare *hue, saturation, lightness.*

variable CLUT device: A *mapped device* in which the selection of colors available in the *color lookup table* can be changed as needed by the running program; compare *fixed device.*

variation code: An integer code, part of a *window* or *control definition ID,* that carries modifying information or distinguishes among different types of window or control implemented by the same *definition function.*

VBL interrupt: Short for "vertical blanking interrupt"; see *vertical retrace interrupt.*

VBL interval: Short for "vertical blanking interval"; see *vertical retrace interval.*

VBL task: Short for "vertical blanking task"; see *vertical retrace task.*

vector table: A table of *trap vectors* kept in the first kilobyte of RAM, used by the *M68000*-series processors to locate the *trap handler* routine to execute when a *trap* occurs.

Versatile Interface Adapter: A special-purpose controller chip, the Synertek *SY6522*, used in the Macintosh to control a variety of input/output devices such as the mouse, keyboard, disk motor, sound generator, and real-time clock.

version data: Another name for a program's *autograph* resource, so called because its *resource data* typically holds a string identifying the version and date of the program.

vertical blanking interrupt: See *vertical retrace interrupt.*

vertical blanking interval: See *vertical retrace interval.*

vertical blanking task: See *vertical retrace task.*

vertical retrace interrupt: An *interrupt* generated by the Macintosh's video display circuitry when the display tube's electron beam reaches the bottom of the screen and returns to the top to begin the next *frame.* This interrupt, recurring regularly at intervals of one *tick* (approximately sixty times per second) forms the "heartbeat" of the Macintosh system.

vertical retrace interval: The interval between successive occurrences of the *vertical retrace interrupt*, equal to one *tick* or approximately one sixtieth of a second.

vertical retrace task: A routine supplied by a program for periodic execution during the *vertical retrace interrupt.*

VIA: See *Versatile Interface Adapter.*

video: An electronic *display* medium in which images are drawn by a dynamically varying beam of electrons sweeping across the screen of a cathode-ray tube.

video card: An *expansion card* that controls the operation of a video-based *graphics device.*

view rectangle: The boundary to which text is *clipped* when displayed in an *edit record;* also called the "clipping rectangle."

virtual key code: A device-independent *key code* reported by the Macintosh *keyboard driver* in place of the *raw key code* received directly from the device.

virtual memory: A form of memory management in which portions ("pages") of a program's logical memory space are kept on a hard disk or other mass storage device and transferred in and out of physical memory as needed.

visible: Describes a *window, control,* or other object that is logically in view on the screen.   A visible object is actually displayed only if *exposed;* compare *invisible.*

visible region: A *clipping boundary* that defines, for a *graphics port* associated with a *window,* the portion of the *port rectangle* that's *exposed* to view on the screen.

volume: A collection of *files* grouped together as a logical unit on a disk or other storage device.

volume name: A string of text characters identifying a particular *volume.*

volume reference number: An identifying number assigned by the *file system* to stand for a given *volume.*

waveform: A curve describing the variations over time in the *magnitude* of a wave, such as a sound or light wave.

wavelength: The spatial distance a wave (such as a sound or light wave) propagates during one complete *cycle.*

wedge: A graphical figure bounded by a given *arc* and the radii joining its endpoints to the center of its *oval.*

wide-open region: A rectangular *region* extending from coordinates (-32768, -32768) to (+32767, +32767), encompassing the entire QuickDraw coordinate plane.

window: An area of the Macintosh screen in which information is displayed, and which can overlap and hide or be hidden by other windows.

window class: An integer code that identifies the origin and general purpose of a *window,* as opposed to its appearance and behavior; compare *window type.*

window color table: A data structure specifying the colors to be used in drawing a window's *frame.*

window definition function: A routine, stored as a *resource,* that defines the appearance and behavior of a particular type of *window.*

window definition ID: A coded integer representing a *window type,* which includes the *resource ID* of the *window definition function* along with a *variation code* giving additional modifying information.

window event: An *event* generated by the Toolbox to coordinate the display of *windows* on the screen; see *activate event, deactivate event, update event.*

window frame: The part of a *window* that is independent of the information it displays, and which is drawn automatically by the Toolbox; compare *content region.*

window list: A linked list of all *windows* belonging to a given program, chained together through a field of their *window records.*

Window Manager port: The *graphics port* in which the Toolbox draws all *window frames.*

window palette: A *palette* associated with a *color window,* defining the colors to be made available for drawing in the window's *content region.*

window pointer: A pointer to a *window record.*

window record: A data structure containing descriptive information about a given *window.*

window template: A *resource* containing all the information needed to create a *window.*

window title: The string of text characters displayed in the *title bar* of a *window.*

window type: A category of *window,* identified by a *window definition ID,* whose appearance and behavior are determined by a *window definition function;* compare *window class.*

word: A group of 16 bits (2 *bytes*) beginning at a *word boundary* in memory.

word boundary: Any even-numbered memory address. Every *word* or *long word* in memory must begin at a word boundary.

word break: A *character position* marking the beginning or end of a word.

word-break routine: A function associated with an *edit record* that determines the locations of the *word breaks* in the record's text.

word wrap: A method of *wrapping* text in which an entire word is carried forward when beginning a new line, so that no word is ever broken between lines.

wrap: To format text or other information against a boundary by beginning a new line whenever the edge of the boundary is reached.

wrapping rectangle: See *destination rectangle.*

wristwatch cursor: A standard *cursor* included in the *system resource file* (or in ROM on some models) for use in signaling processing delays.

Z8530: The *Serial Communications Controller* chip used in the Macintosh, manufactured by Zilog, Inc.

zoom: To alternate a *window* between a smaller and a larger size by clicking with the mouse in its *zoom region.*

zoom box: The small box near the right end of the *title bar*, by which a *document window* can be *zoomed* with the mouse.

zoom in: To *zoom* a *window* from its larger to its smaller size.

zoom-in rectangle: A *rectangle* defining the screen location of a *window* when *zoomed in* to its smaller size.

zoom out: To *zoom* a *window* from its smaller to its larger size.

zoom-out rectangle: A *rectangle* defining the screen location of a *window* when *zoomed out* to its larger size.

zoom region: The area of a *window* by which it can be *zoomed* with the mouse. In a *document window*, the zoom region is the *zoom box.*

Index